INSTRUCTOR'S MANUAL AND TEST BANK

to accompany

INTERNATIONAL BUSINESS
Competing In The Global Marketplace

Second Edition

Charles W. L. Hill
University of Washington

Duane Helleloid
University of Washington
and
Stockholm School of Economics

IRWIN

Chicago • Bogotá • Boston • Buenos Aires • Caracas
London • Madrid • Mexico City • Sydney • Toronto

Irwin's COMPUTEST Testing Software and Teletest Information

This Manual of Tests/Test Bank can be used to select questions from Irwin's COMPUTEST Testing Software data disks for computerized test generation. It also serves as the source for questions available on the Teletest service.

You will receive a separate Irwin's COMPUTEST Testing Software package from Irwin that will include the program/question disk, and the documentation. COMPUTEST is available for DOS, Windows, and Macintosh computers. Simply follow the documentation and you will be able to add questions, delete questions, and edit existing questions on the data disks, as well as create your own test masters and answer keys.

If you do not have access to a microcomputer, you may want to use the Teletest service. Simply select the questions for the test from those available in the computerized test bank, or define the parameters of the test by chapter range, type of question, level of difficulty, other optional criteria, and the number of questions. Then call (800) 242-7468. You may request as many as three versions of the same test. We will create the masters within twenty-four hours and mail them to you First Class Mail. Please allow sufficient mail time. Of course, you may use copies of the enclosed order form and mail us your Teletest request if time permits.

Irwin's COMPUTEST Testing Software Features

Irwin's COMPUTEST Testing Software has an easy to use menu system which allows quick access to all the powerful features available. The Keyword Search option lets you browse through the question bank for problems containing a specific word or phrase. Irwin's COMPUTEST Testing Software allows you to build a library of tests that you have designed. You can load in these saved tests and modify them to your current needs at any time. Password protection is available for saved tests or the entire database. You can add your own questions, modify existing questions, and delete questions. Online help is available from any point in Irwin's COMPUTEST Testing Software.

For technical assistance with Irwin's COMPUTEST Testing Software contact:

Chariot Software Group
123 Camino De La Reina
San Diego, CA 92108
(800) 242-7468
(800) CHARIOT

Teletest INFORMATION SHEET

RICHARD D. IRWIN
c/o Chariot Software Group
123 Camino De La Reina
San Diego, CA 92108

Teletest is a testing service designed to provide adopters of selected **Irwin** titles a testing alternative.

Teletest emphasizes convenience and flexibility. Customized exam preparation is available with only a toll-free phone call.

WHY USE Teletest?

Teletest is provided at **no charge** as an option for professors who want assistance with exam preparation and:
- Do not have the time to design each test.
- Do not have access to a computerized testing system.
- Do not have the time or the desire to use the computer in their testing process.

HOW DOES Teletest WORK?

When one of the selected titles is adopted, your local Irwin representative can provide you with a question bank and **order forms** for the title. This question bank is the **only** source to be consulted when utilizing the service. After consulting the question bank and choosing the questions and desired method of question selection, you may order your test by either:

    1) Calling 1-800-242-7468 and reading us your order.
    2) Mailing your **order form** to **Teletest**

                Richard D. Irwin
                c/o Chariot Software Group
                123 Camino De La Reina
                San Diego, CA 92108

Within 24 hours of receiving your phone call or order form, we will mail your exam and answer key by First Class Mail. Remember to allow ample time for the Postal Service to deliver your **Teletest** masters.

WHAT ARE THE CONVENIENT, FLEXIBLE FEATURES OF Teletest?

Teletest is based on printed question banks and allows you to:

- Preface the exam with any instruction or identifying information you desire, e.g.:

  Professor John Doe
  Economics 101
  Fall, 1990, Exam 1
  120 Minutes
  Good Luck!

- Select from a large, diverse question pool. Most **Teletest** banks contain over 1,500 questions, some in excess of 4,500 items. They provide the user with years of testing alternatives.

- Choose **Random** question selection, **Specific** question selection, or a **Combination** of both. If you wish to mail us your **order form**, remember to attach additional sheets with all the necessary information.

- Choose from 1 to 3 versions of each test. Each version contains the same questions printed in a different order accompanied by its own answer key.

- Customize **Teletest** by selecting your questions according to:

FORM	LEVEL	OPTIONAL CRITERIA
1. TRUE/FALSE	1. EASY	(Determined by Authors)
2. MULTIPLE CHOICE	2. MEDIUM	
3. ESSAY	3. DIFFICULT	

Each question in every **Teletest** question bank is classified by **FORM** and **LEVEL**, and this classification scheme forms the basis of the Random question selection method. The **FORM** and **LEVEL** are listed in the question bank along with the question number and the answer. Consult this listing before making your question selection to be certain enough questions exist in the category you request.

These features provide the **Teletest** user with a highly flexible, convenient system that emphasizes ease of use and the ability to customize each **Teletest**.

IS THERE A CHARGE FOR Teletest?

Again, **Teletest** is provided free to adopters of the selected titles. We have many Irwin titles available with **Teletest**. Call your local representative for further details.

Teletest ORDER FORM

RICHARD D. IRWIN
c/o Chariot Software Group
123 Camino De La Reina
San Diego, CA 92108

Available for selected Irwin titles
Call TOLL-FREE 1-800-242-7468 Ask for **Teletest**

FOR OFFICE USE ONLY
RECEIVED
SHIPPED

Business Hours: 9:00 a.m. - 5:00 p.m. PST
Monday through Friday

SHIPPING ADDRESS OTHER THAN SCHOOL

Needed By: (Date) _____

Name _____

Department _____

School _____

Address _____

City _____ State _____ Zip _____

Title of Text _____

Author _____ ____/Edition

How Many Versions of Test? (up to 3) _____ Telephone No. _____

FORMAT
We will send you one copy of each version of the test for duplication purposes. Each version is accompanied by its own answer key.

IDENTIFYING INFORMATION OR INSTRUCTIONS
Use this space to indicate what information you wish to include at the beginning of the test.

_____

_____

_____

_____

_____

RANDOM SELECTION

Chapter(s) _____   Total Number of Questions _____

            Number of Questions   Level of Difficulty

                                                  (Easy, medium, difficult, easy and medium, medium and difficult, any difficulty)

True-False _____   _____

Multiple Choice _____   _____

Essay _____   _____

(Example: Chapter 1-3, 60 Total, 25 T/F any, 25 M/C medium, 10 essay difficult)

SPECIFIC QUESTION SELECTION

CHAPTER NUMBER	QUESTION NUMBER	QUESTION NUMBER	QUESTION NUMBER	QUESTION NUMBER	QUESTION NUMBER	QUESTION NUMBER	QUESTION NUMBER	QUESTION NUMBER	QUESTION NUMBER	QUESTION NUMBER
___	___	___	___	___	___	___	___	___	___	___
___	___	___	___	___	___	___	___	___	___	___
___	___	___	___	___	___	___	___	___	___	___
___	___	___	___	___	___	___	___	___	___	___
___	___	___	___	___	___	___	___	___	___	___
___	___	___	___	___	___	___	___	___	___	___
___	___	___	___	___	___	___	___	___	___	___
___	___	___	___	___	___	___	___	___	___	___
___	___	___	___	___	___	___	___	___	___	___
___	___	___	___	___	___	___	___	___	___	___
___	___	___	___	___	___	___	___	___	___	___
___	___	___	___	___	___	___	___	___	___	___

                                                   TOTAL QUESTIONS _____

Attach additional sheets if necessary.

For additional information on **TELETEST,** contact your local Irwin representative or call our Toll-Free number.

IRWIN   4/95

Contents

I. Introduction

This Instructor's manual is designed to present you with a complete teaching package to accompany International Business: Competing in the Global Marketplace, Second Edition. International Business, Second Edition contains 20 chapters and 14 short case studies. In addition to this manual, the supplements include 6 video segments, a collection of color transparencies, and a series of slides in electronic format. The manual also provides information on other sources of material you may find useful in your teaching.

The Instructor's Manual is composed of 4 remaining parts. Part II has several suggested course outlines for quarter and semester long courses in international business. In addition to proposing ways to utilize the text chapters and short cases, suggestions for the use of more extensive cases related to the material in the book are included. While each instructor will design a course that best fits their interests, these suggested outlines should assist you in getting the most out of the text and cases.

A chapter overview with teaching suggestions and material is included in Part III. This includes for each chapter: 1) a chapter outline; 2) a list of teaching objectives; 3) a detailed lecture outline; 4) suggested answers to the critical discussion questions in the text; 5) ideas for student exercises and projects; 6) suggestions for additional reading and teaching material; 7) transparency masters based on the lecture outline and figures from the text. It is possible to lecture directly from these outlines and the transparency masters. The critical discussion questions are intended to both draw upon the material presented in the text and extend it for further discussion. These can be used either to focus in class discussions or as written assignments. At times we have assigned one of these questions to a study group at the end of one class session, and asked them to make a brief oral presentation on the question at the start of the next class. The ideas for student exercises and projects are drawn from a variety of sources as well as our own teaching experiences. While some give explicit ideas and reference well tested activities, others sketch a more general framework that you can adapt for use given your own interests and those of your students. The suggestions for additional reading and teaching material reference both some of the classic material on the topic as well as books related to the text. You may want to use these for your own reading, use material from these sources to supplement the text in class, or use them as a basis for assigned book reports. The transparency masters include many of the figures, tables, and maps from the text, but in a format for use on an overhead projector.

In Part IV you will find teaching notes to accompany the 14 short cases contained in International Business. These cases were selected with great care to ensure that they serve the purpose of illustrating the material contained in the text. Each teaching note contains a brief synopsis of the case, a list of teaching objectives for the case, and a series of discussion questions and answers. The discussion questions can be used either for leading an in-class discussion or guiding students in writing a case analysis. Part V contains similar material for the videos available for use with the text.

Part VI contains the test bank. Here you will find a comprehensive test bank that contains 50 multiple choice questions per chapter, 10-15 short answer essay questions, and the suggested answers to all of these. They are comprehensive in covering the material in the chapters, and range in difficulty from easy to hard.

In addition to the material in the text and this Instructor's Manual, we have set up a world wide web page where we place the most current information related to International Business. You can access this directly yourself, and/or suggest that your students look to the page for late breaking updates and examples of international business decisions taking place during the course. The address of the web page is http://weber.u.washington.edu/~chill. We are confident you will find the teaching material available with International Business, Second Edition comprehensive and valuable in your teaching.

PART II

COURSE OUTLINES

II. Course Outlines

The following course outlines suggest some reasonable groupings of chapters for a quarter (10 week) or semester (14 week) length course. Depending on an instructor's use of cases or videos, the school's schedule (classes meeting 1, 2, or 3 days per week), preferences regarding quizzes or and mid-term exams, and an instructor's own preferences regarding favorite topics, we have seen considerable variations when looking at course syllabi. These, however, represent what we have found to be fairly common across a number of schools and pedagogical styles. The case notes in section V suggest one or more chapters with which the cases in the text may be paired. On the following page is a suggested outline for a semester course that makes use of longer case studies available from other sources. We have also provided brief introductions to two different simulation exercises that you may want to incorporate into your course schedule.

Quarter Length Course:

Week 1:	Chapters 1, 2, 3
Week 2:	Chapters 4, 5
Week 3:	Chapters 6, 7
Week 4:	Chapter 8, extended discussion of EU or NAFTA
Week 5:	Chapters 9, 10, 11
Week 6:	Chapters 12, 13
Week 7:	Chapters 14, 15
Week 8:	Chapters 16, 17
Week 9:	Chapter 18
Week 10:	Chapters 19, 20

This outline allows for coverage of an average of 2 chapters per week, but grouped such that a week's topics are fairly closely related. Thus most topics related to international finance are covered in weeks 5 and 10. Instructors who prefer greater emphasis on these topics may want to extend the time allowed, as would an instructor who wants to cover cross-cultural management or international logistics in detail. This schedule allows for all topics to be covered in brief, but none in detail.

Semester Length Course:

Week 1:	Chapters 1, 2
Week 2:	Chapter 3
Week 3:	Chapters 4, 5
Week 4:	Chapters 6, 7
Week 5:	Chapter 8
Week 6:	Chapters 9, 10
Week 7:	Chapter 11
Week 8:	Chapters 12, 13
Week 9:	Chapters 14, 15
Week 10:	Chapter 16
Week 11:	Chapter 17
Week 12:	Chapter 18
Week 13:	Chapter 19
Week 14:	Chapter 20

This schedule allows for a little longer coverage of several topics. As outlined above, most of the stretch is the latter chapters on the various functional areas of a firm (e.g. HRM, Marketing). While this necessarily requires rather quick coverage of some of the material in the earlier chapters, users of this schedule will often go back and look again in more detail at some of the material in the earlier chapters as it relates to specific cases and issues in the functional areas.

Semester Length Case Intensive Course:

Week	Book	Case	
Week 1:	Chapters 1, 2	Schweizerische Maschinenfabrik Zug. A.G.	HBS#9-795-026
		Gallo Rice	HBS#9-593-018
Week 2:	Chapter 3	ITT Automotive: Global Manufacturing	HBS#9-695-002
Week 3:	Chapters 4, 5	A Note on the Malaysian Pewter Industry	WBS#994-M014
		B-W Footwear	HBS#9-387-022
Week 4:	Chapters 6, 7	French Telecommunications (A)	HBS#9-388-160
		French Telecommunications (B)	HBS#9-389-037
Week 5:	Chapter 8	Canadian Packers and the FTA	HBS#9-391-177
Week 6:	Chapters 9, 10	International Foodstuffs	HBS#9-181-049
Week 7:	Chapter 11	Dell Computer Corp.	HBS#9-294-051
Week 8:	Chapters 12, 13	Asea Brown Boveri	HBS#9-192-139
		Asea Brown Boveri: The ABACUS System	HBS#9-192-140
		ABB: Accountability Times Two (A)	HBS#9-192-141
		ABB: Accountability Times Two (B)	HBS#9-192-142
		ABB's Relays Business: Global Matrix	HBS#9-394-016
Week 9:	Chapters 14, 15	The European Retail Alliance	HBS#9-392-096
		Xerox and Fuji Xerox	HBS#9-391-156
		Bajaj Auto Ltd.	HBS#9-593-097
Week 10:	Chapter 16	Nokia Telecommunications	HBS#9-996-006
		ITT Automotive: Global Manufacturing	HBS#9-695-002
Week 11:	Chapter 17	Becton Dickenson: Blood Collection	HBS#9-395-021
		Proctor & Gamble: Vizir Launch	HBS#9-384-139
Week 12:	Chapter 18	Colgate-Palmolive: Managing Intl Careers	HBS#9-394-184
		Kentucky Fried Chicken (Japan) Ltd.	HBS#9-387-043
Week 13:	Chapter 19	AB Astra	HBS#9-192-091
		AB Astra: Growth with Quality	HBS#9-194-003
Week 14:	Chapter 20	Ciba-Geigy AG: Inflation & Currency	HBS#9-389-176
		Alco Holdings Ltd.	HBS#9-294-131

The above listed cases starting with HBS are available through Harvard Business School Publishing. The case starting with WBS is available through the Western Business School at the University of Western Ontario. These are just a very small sample of the overall tremendous number of cases available from various sources for use with International Business. The ones listed above were chosen based on our familiarity with the cases, and our own teaching styles and preferences. We recommend that you purchase and carefully read an evaluation copy of each case (and when available, the teaching note) before adopting it for use in your class. We know of some cases that one instructor is able to use with ease and eloquence, and that another instructor simply has a terrible time using. Also different cases can be used to bring out slightly different points, and depending upon the class and your own interests you may find some cases uninteresting.

There are several good simulation exercises that can be used during a course in International Business. These typically run over several weeks, and involve a significant amount of time for students outside the regular class hours. If you interested in using a simulation, we find it generally preferable to start it near the beginning of a course. The simulations can help initiate group activity, and students generally seem to have more slack time at the beginning of a semester. Two that we are most familiar with are INTOPIA and FINS.

- FINS has been developed by Prof. Richard Moxon, and is a negotiation exercise where groups of students take the roles of multinational firms from different countries, potential partner firms in emerging countries, and host governments. Considerable background material on the industry, countries, and companies is provided, making the setting seem very realistic. The goal is for each group to assure that whatever investment decisions are made serve their best interests. Thus the somewhat conflicting goals of the parties affect the negotiation strategies of all. No computers or other equipment is required, as the simulation is based off of a set of printed instructions. The cost is $10 per participant for the instructional material. Sample copies and full materials can be obtained through Richard Moxon, 8215 NE 8th St, Medina, WA 98039. Phone 1-206-543-4587. Fax 1-206-685-9392. email moxon@u.washington.edu.

- Intopia has been developed by Prof. Hans Thorelli, and is a computer based simulation where groups of students make international strategy and investment decisions for firms over a series of quarters or years. There are a large number of variables that can be manipulated by the instructor or the students to simulate real operations and strategic decisions in international businesses. The cost for the software and instructions is around $1250 for unlimited usage at a school. More information is available on his home page at Indiana University (http://ezinfo.ucs.indiana.edu/~thorelli).

PART III

CHAPTER OVERVIEWS AND TEACHING SUGGESTIONS

CHAPTER 1: OVERVIEW AND TEACHING SUGGESTIONS

OUTLINE OF CHAPTER 1

OPENING CASE: DEUTSCHE TELEKOM POSITIONS ITSELF FOR
        GLOBAL COMPETITION
INTRODUCTION
THE GLOBALIZATION OF THE WORLD ECONOMY
        Management Focus: Harry Ramsden's Plans
        Declining Trade and Investment Barriers
        The Role of Technological Change
        Implications for Management
THE CHANGING NATURE OF INTERNATIONAL BUSINESS
        The Changing World Output and World Trade Picture
        The Changing Foreign Direct Investment Picture
        The Changing Nature of the Multinational Enterprise
        Country Focus: South Korea's New Multinationals
        The Changing World Order
HOW INTERNATIONAL BUSINESS IS DIFFERENT
ORGANIZATION OF THIS BOOK
        The Environmental Context
        The Firm
        Business Operations
SUMMARY OF CHAPTER
CRITICAL DISCUSSION QUESTIONS
CLOSING CASE: KODAK VERSUS FUJI IN 1995

OBJECTIVES OF CHAPTER 1

1.   Introduce the student to the contemporary issues in international business that illustrate the
        unique challenges of international business.

2.   Point out the macro-economic and political changes that have taken place in the last 30 years,
        and suggest the implications of these changes for international business

3.   Illustrate the importance of technological changes in driving the globalization of products and
        markets.

4.   Explain how international business is different from purely domestic business.

5.   Outline the remainder of the text and how the chapters and topics will be integrated.

LECTURE OUTLINE FOR CHAPTER 1

A.   Introduction

1   Starting off the study of international business with a few interesting and provocative questions can stimulate discussion at the start of a course.

One type of question can revolve around the students' clothing. Is anyone wearing shoes that say Made in USA? While Nike is an American brand, most all of its shoes are made by contract manufacturers in Southeast Asia. Where was your watch made? If you had to take off all your clothes that were not made in North America (or any particular country), do you think you'd be wearing very much?

Another is about the types of cars they of their families' own. What is the nationality of the brand? Where was it made? What is its "domestic content"? Is Saab a Swedish car? (Saab is partially owned by General Motors of the USA with many mechanical parts imported from GM in Germany and assembled in Sweden.) Is a BMW assembled in South Carolina more "American" than a Pontiac assembled in Korea?

These questions (or others like them) illustrate how international business affects and impacts everyone's every day life. An example of a local firm's involvement in international business also suggests how local jobs depend upon open international markets. How would Seattle's economy be different if Boeing and Microsoft had no international sales? Would Atlanta have been in a position to host the 1996 Summer Olympics if it did not have major international firms like Coca-Cola and Turner Television (Cable News Network, etc.). How different would Silicon Valley (and San Jose and San Francisco) be today if Intel, National Semi-conductor, and Hewlett-Packard had not been able to sell internationally in their early days? How much less successful would any of these companies be without international sales, and would they likely still be in business if they had not been able to develop export markets?

2.   Whether a business student is studying marketing, finance, accounting, strategy, human relations, or operations management, the differences between countries in which a firm does business will affect decisions which must be made.

3.   The opening case on Deutsche Telekom illustrates the difficult challenges faced by firms that thought they had an nice easy protected national market. It also illustrates the increasing importance of global strategic alliances. Discussion of the case, even if it involves handing out copies in class and giving students a few minutes to read, provides a natural lead-in to the next topic - the globalization of the world economy.

B.   The globalization of the world economy

1.   There is a movement towards a globalization of markets, as the tastes and preferences of consumers in different nations are beginning to converge upon some global norm. The global acceptance of Coca-Cola, Levi's jeans, Sony Walkmans, and McDonald's hamburgers are all examples. Yet there are still significant differences - German's still lead in per capita beer consumption, French in wine consumption, and Italians in pasta eaten, and these differences are unlikely to be eliminated any time soon. Hence often there is still a need for marketing strategies and product features be customized to local conditions.

2.   There is a movement towards a globalization of production, as firms disperse parts of their production processes to different locations around the globe to take advantage of national differences in the cost and quality of factors of production. The example of the Pontiac Le Mans

illustrates how at a broad level the production is dispersed, and one could surmise that individual component parts down to the level of bolts and bearings come from many countries.

3.   Two key factors seem to underlie the trend towards the increasing globalization of markets and production: The decline of barriers to trade and increased technological capabilities.

4.   After WWII, the industrialized countries of the West started a process of removing barriers to the free flow of goods, services, and capital between nations. Under GATT, over 100 nations negotiated even further decreases in tariffs and made significant progress on a number of non-tariff issues (e.g. intellectual property, trade in services).

5.   This removal of barriers to trade has taken place in conjunction with increased trade, world output, foreign direct investment. Figure 1.1

6.   While lowering trade barriers has made the globalization of markets and production a possibility, technological changes have made it a reality.

7.   Improved information processing and communication allow firms to have better information about distant markets and coordinate activities worldwide. The explosive growth of the World Wide Web and the Internet provide a means to rapid communication of information and the ability of firms and individuals to find out about what is going on worldwide for a fraction of the cost and hassle as was required only a couple of years ago. Here I have illustrated to students information that I was able to find out via the world wide web (copies of course syllabi of professors who also use this text in other countries), products I have purchased based on searches on the Web (a turtleneck sweater for my wife), and acquaintances I have made via web pages (I own a couple of rather unusual cars, and have been able to find other collectors who have unique parts for sale).

8.   Improvements in transportation technology, including jet transport, temperature controlled containerized shipping, and coordinated ship-rail-truck systems have made firms better able to respond to international customer demands. The change in rate at which people and mail now travel is well illustrated in Figure 1.2.

9.   As a consequence of these trends, a manager in today's firm operates in an environment that offers more opportunities, but is also more complex and competitive than that faced a generation ago. People now work with individuals and companies from many countries, and while communications technology the universality of English as the language of business has decreased the absolute level of cultural difficulties individuals face, the frequency with which they face inter-cultural and international challenges has increased.

C.   The changing nature of international business.

1.   The US share of world output has declined dramatically in the past 30 years (See Table 1.2), and a much more balanced picture is now developing among industrialized countries. Looking ahead into the next century, the share of world output of what are now referred to as "developing countries" is expected to greatly surpass that of the current "industrialized countries." (See Figure 1.3)

2.   The source and destinations of FDI has also dramatically changed over recent years, with the US and industrialized countries becoming less important (although still dominant) as developing countries are becoming increasingly considered as an attractive and stable location for investment (See Figure 1.5)

3.   A number of large multinationals are now non-US based, and many are recognizable brand names in the worldwide (e.g. Sony, Philips, Toshiba, Honda, BMW). Not only are the new large multinationals originating in other developed countries, but there are an increasing number of multinationals based in developing countries. The country focus on Korea's new multinationals clearly illustrates this point.

4.   An increasing number of small firms are becoming global leaders in their field, giving rise to the mini-multinational. The management focus segment on Harry Ramsden's illustrates the opportunities available to small firms.

5.   The fall of communism and the development of free markets in Eastern Europe and the former Soviet Union create profound opportunities, challenges, potential threats for firms.

6.   The economic development of China presents huge opportunities and risks, in spite of its continued Communist control.

7.   For North American firms, the growth and market reforms in Mexico and Latin America also present tremendous new opportunities both as markets and sources of materials and production.

D.   Why international business is different.

1.   Different countries in which a firm operates have different cultures, political systems, economic systems, legal systems, and are at different levels of economic development. Each of these differences has profound effects on how a firm and its employees conduct business and represent themselves to customers, suppliers, competitors, and authorities.

2.   The complexity of managing in international business is much greater than that of a domestic business.

3.   International firms must find ways to work with different governments and the within the limits imposed by international trade and investment systems.

4.   International business requires dealing in different currencies, converting between currencies, and managing the risks of currency exchange rate changes.

E.   A plan of the book (and the remainder of the course).
        Figure 1.6 can be used as an overview, while writing in the various "areas" the topics of the chapters.

1.   The Environmental Context of international business:

        Chapter 2 looks at the foundations of national differences in political and economic systems. We will discuss the different political, economic and legal systems found in the world and outline the implications of these differences for an international business.

        Chapter 3 looks at the foundations of national differences in culture. We will identify the various factors of a society that go to make up its culture (e.g. social structure, religion, language, education), identify how these differ from country to country and draw out the implications of these differences for the practice of international business.

        Chapter 4 reviews the economic theories of international trade. These theories form the basis of the intellectual case for free trade.

Chapter 5 moves from trade theory to trade practice with a close look at the political economy of international trade. While the theory of international trade advocates unrestricted free trade, in practice, to varying degrees, all countries use trade policies to restrict foreign imports and protect producers in certain sectors of their economy.

Chapter 6 discusses the economic theories of foreign direct investment (FDI). These theories outline the conditions under which it makes sense for a firm to establish operations in a foreign country, as opposed to exporting goods and services from its home country or licensing a foreign firm to produce its output.

Chapter 7 takes a look at the political economy of foreign direct investment. Governments around the world have adopted a variety of postures towards foreign direct investment, ranging from, at one extreme, a free market view that adopts a laissez fair attitude towards FDI to, at the other extreme, a radical view that prohibits FDI under all circumstances.

Chapter 8 focuses on regional economic integration - the emergence of regional trade blocks. The ultimate purpose of regional economic integration is to remove all barriers to the free flow of goods, services and factors of production between countries within a regional grouping, thereby enabling member countries to realize the gains from trade that we discuss in detail in chapter 4.

Chapter 9 explains how money can be converted from one currency to another by using the medium of the foreign exchange market. The chapter also outlines the economic theories that explain how exchange rates are determined.

Chapter 10 builds upon chapter 9 by taking a close look at the international monetary system, of which the foreign exchange market is just one part. The international monetary system plays a key role in determining the way in which the foreign exchange market works.

Chapter 11 reviews the reasons for the growth of the global capital market and discusses the attractions of the market to international businesses. We also look at various components of the market including, most importantly, the eurocurrency market, the international bond market and the international equity market.

2.   The Firm

Chapter 12 focuses upon the strategy of international business. The pros and cons of the various strategies that international businesses pursue are reviewed.

Chapter 13 builds upon chapter 12 by looking at the structure of international businesses. A central theme is that the structure of the firm must be matched to its strategy if it is to survive.

Chapter 14 focuses upon the different entry modes that firms can chose to enter a foreign market - exporting, licensing, franchising, entering into a joint venture with a local firm, and setting up a wholly owned subsidiary. It compares and contrasts these different entry modes, highlighting the advantages and disadvantages of each mode, and identifying the factors that help determine which is the appropriate mode in any given situation.

3.   Business Operations

The remaining six chapters of the book focus upon business operations. Throughout these chapters a deliberate attempt is made to link the material back to that covered in the earlier chapters on the environment, and on the strategy and the structure of international business.

Chapter 15 looks at exporting, importing and countertrade. It is a "nuts and bolts chapter".

Chapter 16 looks at manufacturing and materials management, including a discussion of the various factors that determine the optimal global location for manufacturing facilities, the issue of make or buy decisions, and coordinating a globally dispersed manufacturing and supply system.

Chapter 17 looks at marketing and R&D in an international business. It reviews the debate on the globalization of markets, variation in the four elements of the marketing mix, and new product development in an international business (including the implications that this has for the organization of the R&D function within the firm).

Chapter 18 looks at the human resource management (HRM) function within an international business. In an international business the execution of staffing, management development, performance evaluation and compensation activities is complicated by the profound differences that exist between countries in labor markets, culture, legal systems, economic systems, and the like.

Chapter 19 focuses upon accounting within the multinational firm. It emphasizes how and why accounting standards differ from country to country, and at the efforts now underway to harmonize accounting practices across countries.

The final chapter in the book, chapter 20, is concerned with financial management in an international business. The focus is on how investment decisions, financing decisions, and money management decisions in an international business are complicated by the fact that different countries have different currencies, different tax regimes, different levels of political and economic risk.

F.   The closing case on Kodak and Fuji briefly touches on the complexity of international business strategies for firms over time, and the "political economy" influences that profoundly affect strategy and the success of firms.

ANSWERS TO CRITICAL DISCUSSION QUESTIONS FOR CHAPTER 1

QUESTION 1: Describe the shifts in the world economy over the last 30 years. What are the implications of these shifts for international businesses based in Britain, North America, and Hong Kong?

ANSWER 1: There has been a significant shift away from the USA and Western European countries as being dominators of world business. While the role of these countries is still large, developing countries and Asian countries are becoming increasingly active and aggressive in international trade and investment. Significant implications for British firms involve their need to look beyond Europe America for investment and opportunities. They also face the opportunity (and threat) of attracting Asian firms interested in Britain as a launchpad for the European market. For North American firms the same holds true, although the importance of the increasing prosperity in Latin America suggests a potentially huge market in "their backyard". Hong Kong, while losing its "independence", is perceived as the gateway to the immense market of mainland China. While the free market freedoms Hong Kong firms have enjoyed are now under question, the access to China is improving along with the move towards a market economy within China.

QUESTION 2: "The study of international business is fine if you are going to work in a large multinational enterprise, but it has no relevance for individuals who are going to work in small firms." Critically evaluate this statement.

ANSWER 2: Persons who believe in this view, and the firms that they work for, may find that they do not achieve their full potential (at best) and may ultimately fail because of their myopia. As barriers to trade decrease and state of the art technological developments take place throughout the world, new opportunities and threats exist on a worldwide basis. The rise of the mini-multinationals suggests there are global opportunities for even small firms. But staying attuned to international markets isn't only important from the perspective of seeking profitable opportunities for small firms, it can also be critical for long term competitive survival. Firms from other countries may be developing products that, if sold internationally, may wipe out small domestic competitors. Scanning international markets for the best suppliers is also important for small firms, for if a domestic competitor is able to tap into a superior supplier from a foreign country, it may be able to seriously erode a small firm's competitive position before the small firm understands the source of its competitor's competitive advantage and can take appropriate counter actions.

QUESTION 3: How have changes in technology contributed towards the globalization of markets and of production? Would the globalization of products and markets have been possible without these technological changes?

ANSWER 3: Technological changes have significantly contributed to the globalization of products and markets, and accelerated the creation of a global village. While increasing globalization of markets has been taking place since before either Marco Polo or Christopher Columbus traveled across the globe in search of trade, recent technological developments have brought the world closer together more quickly than at any time in the past. Developments in information processing and communication have decreased the costs of managing a global production system, and improvements in transportation have made the shipment of goods more timely and less costly than at any time in the past. International firms can locate facilities wherever it is most advantageous, coordinate the activities between facilities, and ship products to customers worldwide more cost effectively than at any time in the past.

QUESTION 4: How might the Internet and the associated World Wide Web affect international business activity and the globalization of the world economy?

ANSWER 4: The ability of firms and individuals to both market their products or services, and find out about interesting new products or services worldwide, is greatly enhanced by the World Wide Web. Using this as an initial point of contact, we can imagine how this could then initiate new flows of trade and investment. The example on page 11 helps illustrate this point.

QUESTION 5: If current trends continue, China may emerge as the world's largest economy by 2020. Discuss the possible implications for such a development for the world trading system, the world monetary system, the business strategy of today's European and US-based global corporations.

ANSWER 5: The world trading system would clearly be affected by such a development. Currently China enjoys a somewhat privileged status within the World Trade Organization as a "developing" country. Such a rise to eminence, however, would clearly force it to become a full and equal member, with all the rights and responsibilities. China would also be in a position to actively affect the terms of trade between many countries. On the monetary front, one would expect that China would have to have fully convertible and trading currency, and it could become one of the "benchmark" currencies of the world. From the perspective of Western global firms, China would represent both a huge market, and potentially the home base of some very capable competitors.

QUESTION 6: "Ultimately, the study of international business is no different from the study of domestic business. Thus, there is no point in having a separate course on international business." Critically evaluate this statement.

ANSWER 6: While the fundamentals of business may not be any different domestically or internationally - developing products that customers want at prices the permit profitable operation - achieving success internationally requires different skills and understanding than necessary for strictly domestic business. In the first instance, countries are different, with different cultures, political systems, economic systems, legal systems, and levels of economic development. These differences make it necessary for international firms to vary practices on a country by country basis. Both because of the differences, and the dispersion of operations internationally, managing an international business is much more complex than simply managing a domestic firm. It also requires dealing with different governments, differing government regulations, and multiple currencies. A separate course on international business can provide an understanding of these differences, and how conducting international business requires consideration of issues not typically covered in other courses.

STUDENT EXERCISES AND PROJECTS FOR CHAPTER 1

- Suggest to students that over the next week they search the World Wide Web for some product available in another country that they would like to buy. Suggest that it be something in which they have genuine interest, but they probably would not have found out about without using the web. (I was able to find the description of a particular Scotch Whiskey that I had never had nor seen, and then subsequently bought a bottle to try.)
- Students could be asked to scan the pages of local or regional papers to identify small firms that were active in international sales, or had recently signed a large international purchase or sales agreement.
- Ask students to keep track of all purchases over the next week, and attempt to determine the "country of origin" for each product. Encourage students to attempt to clearly define the country of origin for each product so that you can get an accurate picture of the worldwide consumption habits of this group of students. At the next class meeting, or perhaps a couple weeks later, either randomly sample students for their consumption patterns, or build a tally that includes the entire class. While these results will be interesting, you can also probe them on the accuracy of their classifications. How do they know, for example, that the case of cheap beer they bought on Friday was purely "domestic". Where did the hops come from, or the aluminum can (while the water may be domestic, domestic content should be considered on the basis of value and not just volume)? My experience is that some students will become very intrigued with the "origin" of components of some particular product (e.g. a computer game), and will make a point of saying how complicated it is to know and how stupid (impossible) an assignment this was. My response is that they have in fact perfectly illustrated how "international" business is, and how unaware they and most of us are about the extent of the global nature of the products we buy and the world economy.

SUGGESTED READINGS FOR CHAPTER 1

The footnotes suggest some appropriate additional readings. The following may be of particular interest:

Dicken, Peter 1992. Global shift. New York: Guilford Press.

Economist. The Economist magazine frequently publishes special reports ("surveys" in their terminology) that I have used through out courses. These can help bring material in the text "up to the current time" as well as provide more extensive background. Copies of reprints are available through the magazine for distribution in class You can peruse through recent editions to find the most current reports. On my shelf right now are the following:
- 1 October 1994: "The global economy", 46 pages including advertisements
- 24 June 1995: "A survey of multinationals", 24 pages including advertisements
- 7 October 1995: "A survey of the world economy", 44 pages including advertisements

Naisbitt, John 1994. Global Paradox: The bigger the world economy, the more powerful its smallest players. New York: William Morrow and Company.

Ohmae, Kenichi 1990. The borderless world: Power and strategy in the interlinked economy. New York: Harper-Collins.

Vernon, Raymond and Louis T. Wells, Jr. 1986. The economic environment of international business. Englewood Cliffs, NJ: Prentice Hall.

TRANSPARENCY MASTERS FOR CHAPTER 1 FOLLOW

The Growth of World Trade and World Output

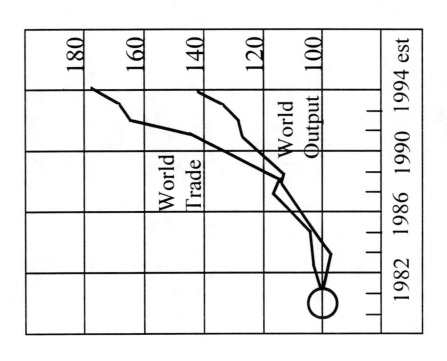

Source: F. Williams, "World Trade in Goods Jumps 9%. Financial Times, April 4, 1995, p. 22.

Figure 1.1

The Shrinking Globe

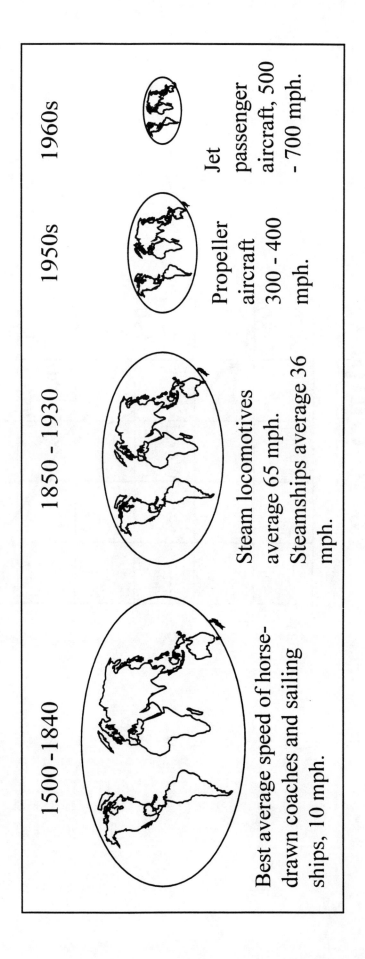

1500 -1840

Best average speed of horse-drawn coaches and sailing ships, 10 mph.

1850 - 1930

Steam locomotives average 65 mph. Steamships average 36 mph.

1950s

Propeller aircraft 300 - 400 mph.

1960s

Jet passenger aircraft, 500 - 700 mph.

Source: P. Dicken, Global Shift (New York: Guillford Press, 1992) p. 104.

Figure 1.2

The Changing Pattern of World Output and Trade

Country	Share of World Output 1963	Share of World Output 19993	Share of World Exports 1993
United States	40.3%	25.6%	11.8%
Japan	5.5	15.9	9.5
Germany	9.7	7.8	12.0
France	6.3	5.7	6.5
Great Britain	6.5	3.9	5.3
Italy	3.4	5.3	5.0
Canada	3	2.1	3.7

*1963 figure for Germany refers to the former West Germany.
Source: World Bank, World Development Report (New York: Oxford University Press, various issues).

Table 1.2

The Changing Nature of Global Output

Shares of World Output

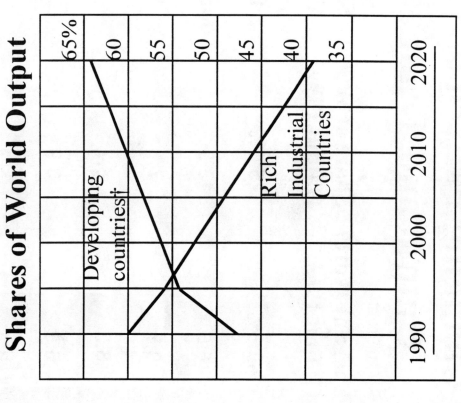

Source: World Bank data

Figure 1.3

Changes in the Annual Inflows of Foreign Direct Investment

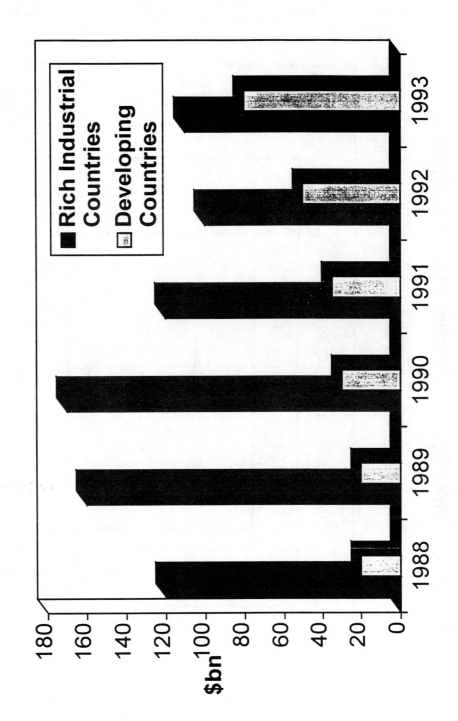

Source: United Nations, World Investment Report, 1994.

Figure 1.5

The Structure of the Book

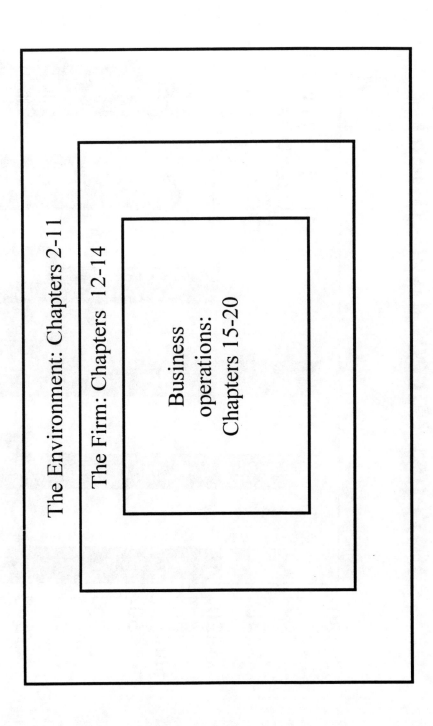

The Environment: Chapters 2-11

The Firm: Chapters 12-14

Business operations: Chapters 15-20

IRWIN © Times Mirror Higher Education Group Inc., Company 1997

Figure 1.6

CHAPTER 2: OVERVIEW AND TEACHING SUGGESTIONS

OUTLINE OF CHAPTER 2

OPENING CASE: GENERAL ELECTRIC STUMBLES IN HUNGARY
INTRODUCTION
POLITICAL SYSTEMS
      Collectivism and Individualism
      Democracy and Totalitarianism
      The Complexions of Government
ECONOMIC SYSTEMS
      Market Economy
      Command Economy
      Mixed Economy
LEGAL SYSTEMS
      Property Rights
      The Protection of Intellectual Property
      Product Safety and Product Liability
      Contract Law
THE DETERMINANTS OF ECONOMIC DEVELOPMENT
      Differences in Economic Development
      Political Economy and Economic Progress
STATES IN TRANSITION
      Eastern Europe and the Former Soviet Union
      Western Europe
      Asia
      Latin America
      Africa
      Implications
IMPLICATIONS FOR BUSINESS
      Attractiveness
      Ethical Issues
SUMMARY OF CHAPTER
CRITICAL DISCUSSION QUESTIONS
CLOSING CASE: TRINITY MOTORS STRUGGLES IN RUSSIA

OBJECTIVES OF CHAPTER 2

1. Describe how the political systems of countries vary along 'collectivist vs. individualist' and 'democratic vs. totalitarian' dimensions. This can be best visualized by looking at the degree of economic and political freedom enjoyed by a country's citizens.

2. Explain the differences in economic systems between countries, by looking specifically at market economies, command economies, and mixed economies.

3. Look at differences in the economic development of different countries. Economic development measures like GDP, purchasing power, and human development indices are presented and described.

4. Suggest that the potential for future economic growth and the growth rate may be as or more important than static measures of economic development when considering international expansion.

5. Explain how differences in the legal systems of countries can dramatically affect the attractiveness and ease of doing business in different countries. Differences in protections of intellectual property (patents, copyrights, and trademarks), product safety and liability, and contract law are highlighted to suggest how legal systems affect the conduct of international business.

6. Show how changes in the world order in the 1980s and 1990s affected countries in Europe, Asia, Latin America, and Africa, and how these changes present both great new opportunities and risks for international business.

7. Summarize issues that affect the attractiveness of doing business in different countries, including the benefits, costs, and risks determined by the political economy of nations.

8. Present some ethical concerns of doing business in countries that have different standards, political ideologies, economic systems, and patterns of acceptable and expected behavior (i.e. bribes).

LECTURE OUTLINE FOR CHAPTER 2

A.   Introduction

1.   Differences between countries have a profound affect on how managers and firms work and act internationally. In this chapter we look at the political, economic, and legal infrastructures of different countries, while in the next chapter we will consider differences in culture, religion, and education.

2.   With the emergence of a new world order (or perhaps disorder), firms have significant new opportunities for doing business as well as huge risks. Discussing a international trouble spot currently in the news, and the implications for businesses, can get the discussion going. A few years ago I liked to talk about the Elan ski company in Slovenia. This company made some of the highest performing downhill snow skis, and was an innovator in technology. But as Yugoslavia was falling apart, there were significant difficulties, and retailers worldwide that had been expecting to receive their fall shipments were left scrambling to find alternative suppliers. Elan, and their retailers, were fortunate, as Slovenia's route to independence was relatively smooth compared to that of firms from Serbia, Bosnia, and Croatia.

3.   The opening case regarding General Electric in Hungary highlights the problems in dealing with organizations and people in the former communist countries. The time and effort required to turn around a business is difficult to estimate, particularly when knowledge of the "system" is limited.

B.   Political Systems

1.   Political systems can be assessed according to two related dimensions: collectivism vs. individualism and democracy vs. totalitarianism.

2.   The modern day roots of collectivism can be traced to Marx, yet the foundations can be found in Plato's *Republic*. The general premise of collectivism is that the state must manage enterprises if they are to benefit society as a whole rather than individual capitalists. Communists generally believed that this could only be achieved though revolution and totalitarian dictatorship, while Social Democrats worked to achieve the same goals by democratic means. Examples of communism include the Soviet Union, most Eastern European nations from 1950 to 1989, Cuba, and China. Social Democratic nations include Sweden, Germany, France, and Norway, although Social Democratic parties have not always held power in these nations.

3.   While state owned firms may have been intended to promote the public interest, experience suggests that this isn't always the case. In many countries the performance of state owned companies has been poor. Protected from significant competition by their monopoly position, and guaranteed governmental financial assistance, many state owned enterprises have become increasingly inefficient. Thus both in former communist and Western European countries, previously state owned enterprises are being privatized.

4.   Individualism, while advocated by Aristotle, in modern days was encouraged by David Hume, Adam Smith, John Stuart Mill, and most recently, Hayek and Milton Friedman. Individualism focuses on i) guaranteeing individual freedom and self expression, and ii) letting people pursue their own self-interest in order to achieve the best overall good for society. The US Declaration of Independence and the Bill of Rights embody the spirit of individualism.

5.   While collectivism asserts the primacy of the collective over the individual, individualism asserts the opposite. This ideological difference shapes much of recent history and the Cold War.

[An interesting digression one can take here (at the risk of getting side-tracked) is to discuss another hot topic, environmentalism, in the context of collectivism vs. individualism. While one might expect that countries with a collectivist approach would have much higher environmental standards "for the common good" than individualist countries where "anyone can do what they want on their own land", the record is less clear. While the Social Democratic countries of Norway and Sweden have some of the best overall environmental records, the pollution problems in many of the former communist states are horrendous. And the US has a environmental record similar to many other social democratic countries in Western Europe. In fact as we will see in later discussions on GATT and NAFTA, different countries environmental standards are becoming an increasingly important issue in international trade negotiations.]

6. Democracy and totalitarianism are at different ends of a political dimension. The democratic vs. totalitarian dimension is not independent of the collectivism vs. individualism dimension. Democracy and individualism go hand in hand, as do the communist version of collectivism and totalitarianism. However, gray areas also exist; it is possible to have a democratic state where collective values predominate, and it is possible to have a totalitarian state that is hostile to collectivism and in which some degree of individualism - particularly in the economic sphere - is encouraged.

7. Democracy in its pure state, with each individual voting on every issue, has generally been replaced by representative democracy, where elected representatives vote on behalf of constituents. Yet in Switzerland many issues are decided by referendum, and in many US states referendums decided directly by voters on election day are becoming increasingly common. (A recent example in your state can help illustrate this point. If it is something that directly affects businesses, then an analogy can be drawn to how referendums in different countries could affect business operations and decisions.)

8. Under totalitarianism, a single political party, individual, or group of individuals monopolize the political power and do not permit opposition. There are four major forms of totalitarianism: communist, theocratic, tribal, right wing (often military). There has been a general trend away from communist and right wing totalitarianism and towards democracy in the 1980s and 1990s. Issues relating to theocratic and tribal totalitarianism are presently at the root of some unrest in Asia and Africa.

9. A good way to discuss countries' relative political and economic freedom is to draw a diagram with political freedom on one dimension and economic freedom on the other (similar to that on figure 2.4). You can then ask students to relatively position different countries on the dimensions of economic and political freedom. Map 2.1 can be used to help highlight differences in the political freedom of different countries and help place countries on the political freedom.

10. The political environment of a country matters because i) when economic freedoms are restricted, so may be the ability of an international business to operate in the most efficient manner and ii) when political freedoms are restricted there are both ethical and risks concerns that have to be considered.

C. Economic Systems

1. There are three broad types of economic systems: market, command, and mixed. In reality almost all are mixed to some extent, for even the most market oriented have some governmental controls on business and even the most command based either explicitly allow some free markets to exist or have black markets for some goods and services. Yet all countries can be considered to be at some point on a continuum between pure market and pure command.

2.   In a pure market economy the goods and services that a country produces, and the quantity in which they are produced, is not planned by anyone. Rather price and quantity are determined by supply and demand. For a market economy to work, there must be no restrictions on either supply or demand - no monopolistic sellers or buyers.

3.   In a pure command economy the goods and services that a country produces, the quantity in which they are produced, and the price at which they are sold are all planned by the government. Resources are allocated "for the good of society". Most, if not all, businesses are owned by the government.

4.   A mixed economy includes some elements of each. In Canada, for example, while most business is privately owned and operated under market principles, health care, electrical power, and liquor distribution are run by state owned enterprises in most provinces.

D.   Legal Systems

1.   The legal environment of a country is of immense importance to international business. A country's laws regulate business practice, define the manner in which business transactions are to be executed, and set down the rights and obligations of those involved in business transactions. Differences in the structure of law can have an important impact upon the attractiveness of a country as an investment site and/or market.

2.   Control over property rights are very important for the functioning of business. Property rights refer to the bundle of legal rights over the use to which a resource is put and over the use made of any income that may be derived from that source. Property rights can be violated by either private action (theft, piracy, blackmail, Mafia) or public action (governmental bribery and corruption, nationalization). Lack of confidence in a country's fair treatment of property rights significantly increases the costs and risks of doing business.

3.   Intellectual property rights (patents, copyrights, and trademarks) are important for businesses if they are to capitalize on what they have developed. Firms like Microsoft, Levis, Coca-Cola, or McDonalds would have little reason to invest overseas if other firms in other countries were able to use the same name and copy their products without permission. The management focus article on Microsoft in China illustrates the issue well.

3.   Different countries have different product safety and liability laws. In some cases US businesses must customize products to adhere to local standards if they are to do business in a country, whether these standards are higher or just different.

4.   When product standards are lower in other countries, firms face an important ethical dilemma. Should they produce products only of the highest standards even if this puts them at a competitive disadvantage relative other producers and results in not maximizing value to shareholders? Or should they produce products that respond to local differences, even if that means that consumers may not be assured of the same levels of safety in different countries?

5.   Differences in contract law force firms to use different approaches when negotiating contracts. In countries with common law traditions, contracts tend to be much more detail oriented and need to specify what will happen under a variety of contingencies. Under civil law systems, contracts tend to be much shorter and less specific since many of the issues relating to contracts are covered in the civil code of the country.

E.   The Determinants of Economic Development

1.   Different countries have dramatically different levels of development, as shown in Map 2.2. GDP/capita is a good yardstick of economic activity, as it measures average value of the goods and services produced by an individual.

2.   But GDP/capita does not consider the differences in costs of living. The UN's PPP index as shown in Figure 2.1 shows the differences in the standards of living of people in different countries.

3.   A problem with both GDP/capita and PPP is that they are static in nature. From an international business perspective it is good to look at the rate of growth in the economy as well as the status of its people. Figure 2.2 shows that some of the fastest growing countries economically are those have been slower to develop.

4.   A broader approach to assessing the overall quality of life in different countries is the Human Development Index. This is based on life expectancy, literacy rates, and whether (based on PPP indices) incomes are sufficient to meet the basic needs of individuals. Figure 2.3 lists the Human Development index for several countries. It is disturbing to notice that some of the worst off countries are heavily populated and have rapidly expanding populations.

5.   What is the relationship between political economy and economic progress? This is a difficult issue. One thing that is generally accepted is that innovation is the engine of long-run economic growth. Another thing that we have come to generally accept in recent years is that a market economy is better at stimulating innovation than a command economy that does not have the same types of incentives for individual initiative.

6.   Innovation also depends on a strong protection of property rights, as innovators and entrepreneurs need some level of assurance that they will be able to reap the benefits of their initiative.

7.   While it is possible to have innovation and economic growth in a totalitarian state, many believe that economic growth and a free market system will eventually lead a country to becoming more democratic.

F.   States in Transition

1.   Since the late 1980s there have been two major changes in the political economy of many of the worlds nations. First, a wave of democratic revolutions swept the world, and many of the previous totalitarian regimes collapsed. Secondly, there has been a more away from centrally planned and mixed economies towards free markets. Figure 2.4 helps illustrate this point.

2.   The revolutions in the USSR and Eastern Europe have (in general) moved these countries towards democracy (away from totalitarianism), towards individualism (away from collectivism), and towards mixed economies (away from command). The transitions have been difficult, however, and economic progress has not been easy as illustrated in figure 2.5. Recent elections have brought "reformed" communists back into power in some countries, and the economic problems facing the people are significant.

3.   In western Europe there has been a general trend towards privatization of state owned companies and deregulation of industry. Any recent edition of the Financial Times or the Economist will likely discuss the problems facing some previously protected and overstaffed industry.

4.   In Asia there has been a movement towards free or freer market economies in a number of countries, most notably China and Vietnam. There has been less opening of the political systems, however.

5.   During the 1980s most Latin American countries changed from being run by dictatorship to democratically elected governments. While most countries previously had erected high barriers to imports and investment (to keep multinationals from "dominating" their economies), they now mostly are encouraging investment, lowering barriers, and privatizing state owned enterprises.

6   In Africa, while economic development is still progressing slowly, recent political reforms are encouraging. Yet while socialism is in retreat, legal systems are often poorly developed and poorly paid public officials encourage corrupt practices.

7.   These transitions are creating huge opportunities for international business, as well as creating huge risks. It is not clear what direction future changes will take, and if these will be entirely favorable for business.

G.   Implications for Business

1.   The political, economic, and legal environment of a country clearly influence the attractiveness of a country. A country's attractiveness can be best evaluated by looking at the benefits, costs, and risks of doing business in that country.

2.   The long run monetary benefits of doing business in a country are a function of the size of the market, the present wealth (purchasing power) of consumers, and the likely future wealth of consumers. By identifying and investing early in a potential future economic star, firms may be able to gain first mover advantages and establish loyalty and experience in a country. Two factors that are reasonably good predictors of a country's future economic prospects are its economic system and property rights regime.

3.   The costs of doing business in a country are determined by a number of political, economic, and legal factors. Political costs can involve the cost of paying bribes or lobbying for favorable or fair treatment. Economic costs relate primarily to the sophistication of the economic system, including the infrastructure and supporting businesses. Regarding legal factors, it can be more costly to do business in countries with dramatically different product, workplace, and pollution standards, or where there is poor legal protection for property rights.

4.   Political risk is the likelihood that political forces will cause drastic changes in a country's business environment that adversely affects the profits or other goals of the business. Economic risk is the likelihood the economic mismanagement will likewise affect a business. Legal risk is the likelihood that a trading partner may opportunistically break a contract or expropriate intellectual property rights.

5.   As a general point, it should be noted that the costs and risks associated with doing business in a foreign country are typically lower in economically advanced and politically stable democratic nations, whereas they are greater in less developed and politically unstable nations. The calculus is complicated, however, by the fact that the potential long-run benefits bear little relationship to a nation's current stage of economic development or political stability. Rather, they are dependent upon likely future economic growth rates. In turn, among other things, economic growth appears to be a function of a free market system and a country's capacity for growth (which may be greater in less developed nations). This leads one to the conclusion that, other things being equal, the benefit, cost, risk tradeoff is likely to be most favorable in the case of politically stable developing nations that have free market systems. It is likely to be least

favorable in the case of politically unstable developing nations that operate with a mixed or command economy.

6.   One ethical concern regards whether firms should invest in countries where the government represses its citizens in political and/or economic freedom. While some argue that investing in these countries is implicitly supporting the repression, others argue that the best way to encourage change is from within, and that increasing economic development of the country will lead to greater political and economic freedoms.

7.   A second ethical concern regards whether an international firm should adopt consistent and high levels of product safety, worker safety, and environmental protection worldwide, or whether they should focus only on meeting local regulations. If they adopt high standards, and subsequently lose business to other competitors with lower standards, was this an ethically correct position for it to take in light its requirements to act in the best interest of shareholders and provide advancement opportunities for its personnel?

8.   Another ethical concern regards whether firms should pay bribes to governmental officials or business partners in exchange for business access. Should paying bribes be completely avoided, or are bribes just another cost of doing business that "grease the wheels" and lead to benefits for both the firm and consumers. If bribes are an integral part of business transactions in a country, is a firm being culturally insensitive and elitist if it finds bribes repulsive and refuses to pay them?

9.   The closing case illustrates clearly the risks of doing business in Russia given the influence of the Mafia and minimal legal infrastructure.

ANSWERS TO CRITICAL DISCUSSION QUESTIONS IN CHAPTER 2

QUESTION 1: Free market economies stimulate greater economic growth, whereas command economies stifle growth! Discuss.

ANSWER 1: Over the past 30 years, the countries that have achieved the highest levels of GNP per capita or GDP per capita with PPP are clearly free market economies. Making crude comparisons with individual countries over this same period (i.e. North Korea vs. South Korea, USSR vs. USA, Germany vs. Poland) leads to the same conclusion - free market economies stimulate greater economic growth. But when looking at growth rates over just the 1980s, the fact that countries like India and China have some of the highest growth rates needs to be explained in light of the economic management of these countries. While neither of these countries can be considered to be free market economy, their recent high growth may be explained by two factors. Firstly, like the other high growth countries of South Korea and Thailand, they began with a very low base level and hence had a high capacity for growth. Secondly, in both cases there were free market reforms that coincided with the growth. Thus there would appear to be a basis for saying that free (or at least freer) market economies stimulate growth.

QUESTION 2: "A democratic political system is an essential condition for sustained economic progress." Discuss.

ANSWER 2: There are a number of situations that can be cited where economic growth has been rapid under totalitarian regimes. It is rare, however, to have sustained (decades) of strong economic growth without democratic principles at work. Thus it is perhaps most accurate to say that we in the west believe that democratic regimes are far more conducive to long term economic growth than a dictatorship, even a benevolent one.

QUESTION 3: During the late 1980s and early 1990s China was routinely cited by various international organizations such as Amnesty International and Freedom Watch for major human rights violations, including torture, beatings, imprisonment and executions of political dissidents. Despite this, in 1991 China was the recipient of record levels of foreign direct investment, principally from firms based in democratic societies such as the United States, Japan, and Germany. Evaluate this trend from an ethical perspective. If you were the CEO of a firm that had the option of making a potentially very profitable investment in China, what would you do?

ANSWER 3: While there are those who argue that investing in totalitarian countries provides comfort to dictators and can help prop-up repressive regimes, in the case of China these arguments appear to have been ineffective. Western firms have continued to invest in spite of these concerns, either out of opportunism or a belief in a different ethical perspective. The alternate ethical perspective suggests that investment by a Western firm, by raising the level of economic development of a totalitarian country, can help change it from within. Since economic well being and political freedoms often go hand in hand, and investment can create jobs and provide needed goods for individuals, an investment may be good for the people both in the short and the long run. Perhaps it was based on this rationale that the Bush administration claimed that US. firms should continue to be allowed to invest in mainland China even after the 1989 crackdown on the democracy movement. As the CEO of a firm that had the option of making a potentially very profitable investment in China, not only should this ethical tradeoff be considered, but so should the importance of the opportunity and the ethical responsibility one has to shareholders. If there are opportunities in China, passing these up may simply be allowing a competitor to gain a first mover advantage that will be difficult to overcome. Unless all potential competitors from all countries have the same ethical principles, it is likely that some firm will decide to undertake the investment in spite of the ethical concerns. (Investment withholding, like any other form of collusion or sanction adherence, requires compliance by all parties if it is to be effective.) Hence the CEO must consider the ethical responsibility to shareholders to maximize the value of the firm. In the end the decision must rest on both ethical concerns about doing business in China and ethical concerns about what is in the best interest of shareholders. There is no right or wrong decision, as each involves different tradeoffs.

QUESTION 4: You are the CEO of a company that has to chose between making a $100 million investment in either Russia or the Czech Republic. Both investments promise the same long run return, so your choice of which investment to make is driven by risk considerations. Assess the various risks of doing business in each of these nations. Which investment would you favor and why?

ANSWER 4: When assessing the risks of investment, one should consider the political, economic, and legal risks of doing business in either Russia or the Czech Republic. At this time (Spring 1996), the political risk in Russia is high as it is undergoing constitutional crises, a presidential election, great social unrest, and significant divisions in the country both ideologically and ethnically. Relatively, the Czech Republic is more stable. On the economic front, both countries have inflation and high economic turmoil as unproductive factories are still struggling. From the legal perspective, the Czech Republic is making clear progress, while the situation in Russia is in flux. Thus at this time, the risk in Russia would clearly be higher. Depending upon when you are using the book, this situation could be different. (You also may want to substitute other countries into this question depending on current events and the countries with which you feel your students will be most familiar.)

STUDENT EXERCISES AND PROJECTS FOR CHAPTER 2

This chapter provides a good opportunity to help students realize how little they know about many of the countries of the world. One exercise I have done is to assign groups of students (3-5) a country and give them 10 minutes to write down on a overhead transparency or flip chart page all they know about the country and present their findings to the rest of the class. I suggested that the class might be interested in knowing the location, political system, economic system, capital, head of state, main trading partner, etc. Some were pretty embarrassed by how little they knew about "prominent" countries (e.g. France), and some were not able to state one piece of useful information about Liberia, Liechtenstein, or Latvia. I suggested that for next week they do a little homework on these topics, as well as on the culture, and be prepared to tell the whole class something interesting about the country.

SUGGESTED READINGS FOR CHAPTER 2

The footnotes suggest some appropriate additional readings. The following may be of particular interest:

Friedman, Milton and Rose Friedman 1980. Free to choose. London: Penguin.

Hayak, F.A. 1989. The fatal conceit: Errors of socialism. Chicago: University of Chicago Press.

North, Douglass 1991. Institutions, institutional change, and economic performance. Cambridge, UK: Cambridge University Press

North, Douglass 1981. Structure and change in economic history. New York: Norton.

TRANSPARENCY MASTERS FOR CHAPTER 2 FOLLOW

Political Freedom in 1994

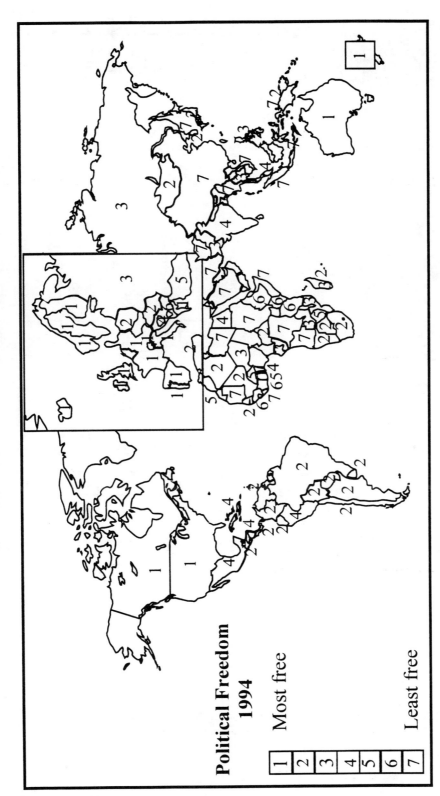

Political Freedom 1994

Most free

1
2
3
4
5
6
7

Least free

Source: Map data from Freedom Review 23, *no.1 (Jan - Feb 1992)* pp. 17-19

Map 2.1a

Political Freedom in 1994 *CONTINUED*

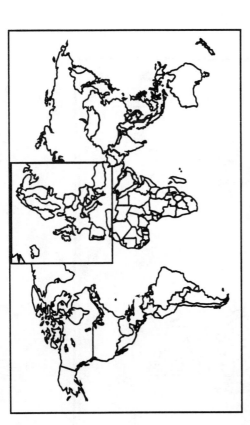

Political Freedom 1994

Most free

| 1 |
| 2 |
| 3 |
| 4 |
| 5 |
| 6 |
| 7 |

Least free

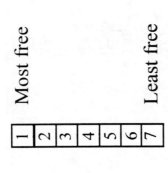

Am. Samoa	[1]
Andorra	[4]
Antigua & Barbuda	[2]
Bahamas	[4]
Bahrain	[1]
Barbados	[6]
Bermuda	[1]
Cape Verde Islands	[1]

Cayman Islands	[5]
Comoros Islands	[1]
Dominica	[1]
Fiji	[6]
French Polynesia	[1]
Grenada	[1]
Guadeloupe	[1]
Guam	[1]

Hong Kong	[5]
Kiribati	[1]
Liechtenstein	[1]
Macao	[6]
Maldives	[6]
Malta	[1]
Martinique	[1]
Mauritius	[1]

Monaco	[3]
Nauru	[1]
Netherlands Antilles	[1]
New Cadedonia	[2]
Reunion	[2]
St. Kitts and Nevis	[2]
St. Lucia	[1]
St. Vincent	[2]

San Marino	[1]
Sao Tome & Principe	[1]
Seychelles	[3]
Singapore	[5]
Solomon Islands	[1]
Tonga	[6]
Trinidad and Tobago	[1]
Tuvalu	[1]

UK Virgin Islands	[1]
US Virgin Islands	[1]
Vanuatu	[1]
Western Samoa	[2]

Source: Map data from Freedom Review 23, *no.1 (Jan - Feb 1992)* pp. 17-19

Map 2.1b

1993 GNP Per Capita

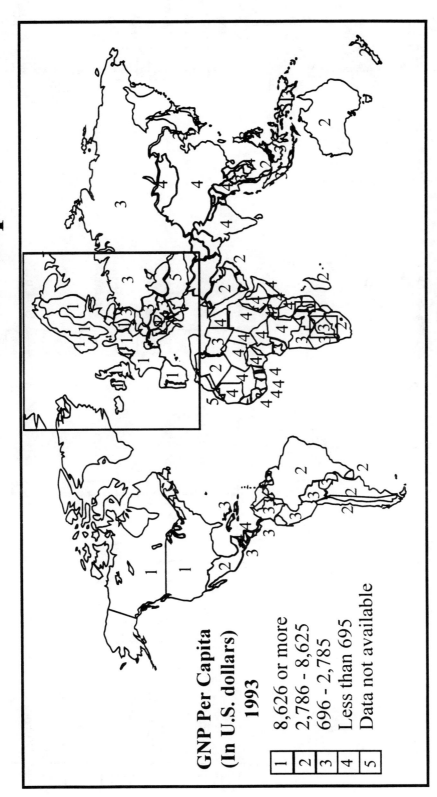

**GNP Per Capita
(In U.S. dollars)
1993**

1	8,626 or more
2	2,786 - 8,625
3	696 - 2,785
4	Less than 695
5	Data not available

Source: Map data from World Bank, World Development Report, 1994.

Map 2.2a

1993 GNP Per Capita *CONTINUED*

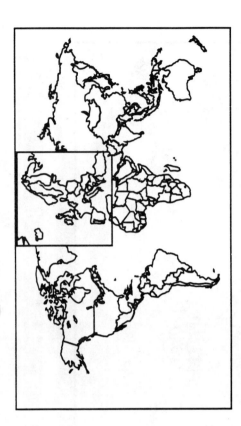

GNP Per Capita
(In U.S. dollars)
1993

1	8,626 or more
2	2,786 - 8,625
3	696 - 2,785
4	Less than 695
5	Data not available

2	Am. Samoa	1	Cayman Islands	5	Monaco
1	Andorra	4	Comoros Islands	5	Nauru
2	Antigua & Barbuda	3	Dominica	2	Netherlands Antilles
1	Bahamas	3	Fiji	2	New Cadedonia
2	Bahrain	1	French Polynesia	2	Reunion
2	Barbados	3	Grenada	4	St. Kitts and Nevis
2	Bermuda	2	Guadeloupe	4	St. Lucia
3	Cape Verde Islands	2	Guam	4	St. Vincent

1	Hong Kong	5	San Marino	5	UK Virgin Islands
3	Kiribati	4	Sao Tome & Principe	1	US Virgin Islands
5	Liechtenstein	2	Seychelles	3	Vanuatu
2	Macao	1	Singapore	3	Western Samoa
3	Maldives	3	Solomon Islands		
2	Malta	3	Tonga		
2	Martinique	2	Trinidad and Tobago		
2	Mauritius	5	Tuvalu		

Source: Map data from World Bank, World Development Report, 1994.

Map 2.2b

Index for Selected Countries

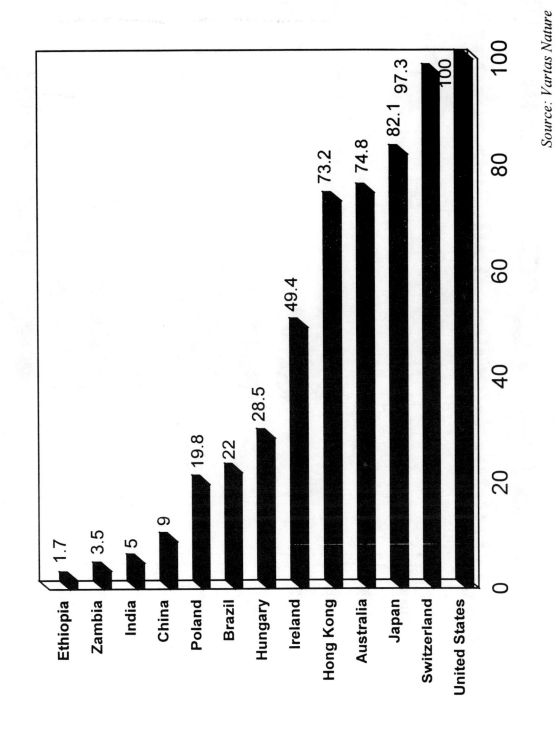

Source: Vartas Nature

Figure 2.1

Average Annual Percentage Change in Real GDP for Select Countries, 1985–93

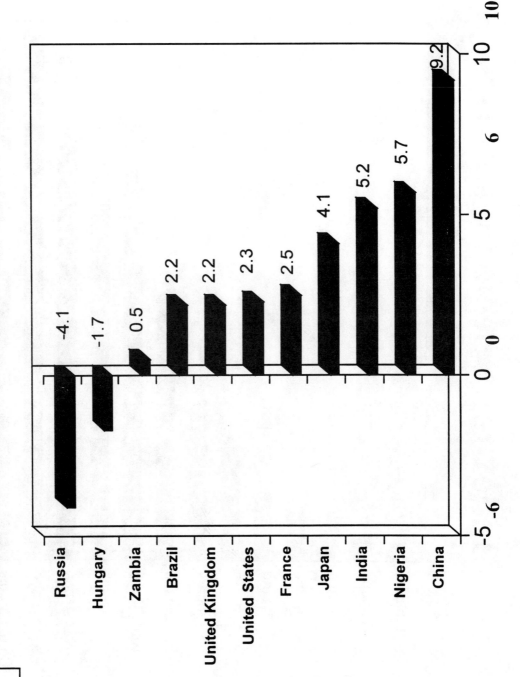

Source: Vartas Nature

Figure 2.2

Real Percentage GDP Growth, 1990–94, for Five Post-Communist States

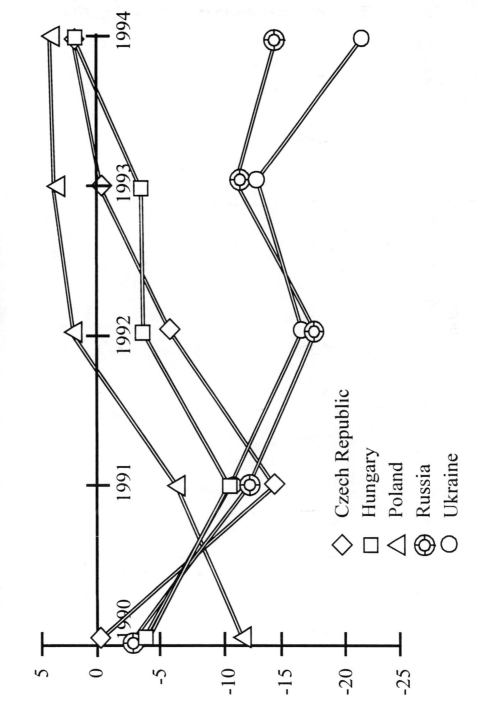

Source: M. Wolf and C. Freeland, "The Long Day's Journey to Market," Financial Times, March 7, 1995, p. 15.

Figure 2.5

CHAPTER 3: OVERVIEW AND TEACHING SUGGESTIONS

<u>OUTLINE OF CHAPTER 3</u>

OPENING CASE: "BUT WHERE ARE ALL THE FRENCH" - THE TRIALS AND
      TRIBULATIONS OF EURODISNEY
INTRODUCTION
WHAT IS CULTURE?
      Values and Norms
      Culture, Society, and the Nation-State
      The Determinants of Culture
SOCIAL STRUCTURE
      Individuals and Groups
      Social Stratification
RELIGION
      Christianity
      Islam
      Hinduism
      Buddhism
      Confucianism
LANGUAGE
      Spoken Language
      Unspoken Language
EDUCATION
CULTURE AND THE WORKPLACE
      Hofstede's Model
      Evaluating Hofstede's Model
CULTURAL CHANGE
IMPLICATIONS FOR BUSINESS
      Cross-Cultural Literacy
      Culture and Competitive Advantage
SUMMARY OF CHAPTER
CRITICAL DISCUSSION QUESTIONS
CLOSING CASE: TRANSFORMING CULTURAL DIFFERENCES INTO A SOURCE
      STRENGTH AT ABB

OBJECTIVES OF CHAPTER 3

1. Provide a basis for understanding what culture is -what are the norms and values of a society, and how these affect interpersonal dealings.

2. Describes differences in the social structures of people and businesses in different countries.

3. Describe the heritage and key philosophies underlying the major religions of world, and discuss the economic implications of these religious beliefs both for a nation's economy and for the practice of business in countries with different religions.

4. Introduce how a country's language and education are intertwined with its culture.

5. Show that culture is not a constant, but evolves over time.

6. The key reason to describe aspects of culture, social structure, religion, language, and education is to provide a basis for understanding i) the importance of cross-cultural literacy and ii) how competitive advantage can be affected.

7. The connection between culture and competitive advantage has important implications for deciding where a firm may want to locate facilities and expand its presence in the market.

LECTURE OUTLINE FOR CHAPTER 3

A.   Introduction

1   The focus of this chapter is on culture, and what some of the underlying characteristics of a
      country are that help define the values and norms of a society. Figure 3.1 pictorially describes
      this, as well as the relationship with economic and political philosophy described in Chapter 2.

2.   Two themes run through the chapter: 1) cross-cultural literacy is critical to success in a foreign
      country and 2) the culture of a country can directly and indirectly affect the costs of doing
      business in country.

3.   The opening case helps to highlight a number of cultural blunders that have affected the success
      of EuroDisney.

B.   What is Culture

1.   Culture has been defined a number of different ways. In this course we will view culture *as a
      system of values and norms that are shared among a group of people and that when taken
      together constitute a design for living.*

2.   While culture is a characteristic of society as a whole, it shapes individual behavior by identifying
      appropriate and inappropriate forms of human interaction.

3.   The fundamental building blocks of culture are values and norms.

4.   Values are abstract ideas about what a society believes to be good, right, and desirable. As was
      discussed in chapter 2, values affect political and economic systems as well as culture. Values
      include attitudes towards concepts like freedom, honesty, loyalty, justice, responsibility, and
      personal relations including marriage.

5.   Norms are social rules and guidelines that prescribe the appropriate behavior in particular
      situations. Norms shape the actions of people towards one another. Norms can be divided into
      folkways and mores:
              Folkways are the routines conventions of everyday life, but generally have little moral
      significance. Examples would be dress, eating habits, and social graces. Foreigners may be
      easily excused for making a few *faux pas*. Timeliness is a good example, and you can discuss
      when timeliness is critical (test days) as well as when one may be expected to be "fashionably
      late". If students come from different parts of the country or world, you can ask for opinions on
      when they should arrive for a party if the invitation said 8pm.
              Mores are more serious standards of behavior, the breaking of which may be illegal or
      very inappropriate. Examples would be theft, adultery, murder, or use of mind altering
      substances (including alcohol, caffeine, and marijuana). Mores can vary greatly between
      countries: what in one country may be viewed as an innocent flirt may constitute a serious affront
      to someone's dignity or harassment in another's.

6.   Norms and values are an evolutionary product of a number of factors that are at work in a society,
      including political and economic philosophy, social structure, religion, language, and education.
      Culture both affects these factors, and is affected by them.

7.   The nation-state is only a rough approximation of a culture. Within a nation-state multiple
      cultures can easily exist (as we can only too painfully see in the former Yugoslavia), and cultures
      can also cut across national borders. This can often be easily illustrated by describing how

different people are within a country. It is quite easy to get a class of students in the Western US to agree that the people in New York are really different and generally rude, while Eastern students will comment on Californians or Southerners, etc. Likewise, students in Stockholm will have clear opinions about how different Swedes are from the far North or far South. In virtually any country or state students will easily be able to describe the differences between city-folks and country-folks, and some students will "defend" their culture while making disparaging remarks about the other.

C.   Social Structure

1.   The social structure of a country can be described along two major dimensions: <u>individualism vs. group</u> and <u>degree of stratification into classes or castes</u>.

2.   A focus on the individual, and individual achievement, is common in many Western societies. In Chapter 2 the implications of this for political and economic systems was discussed. An emphasis on individual achievement has positive and negative implications. On the positive side, the dynamism of the US economy owes much to people like Sam Walton, Steve Jobs, and Ross Perot - people who took chances, tried new things, succeeded, and encouraged others to do likewise. On the other hand, individualism can lead to a lack of company loyalty and failure to gain company specific knowledge, competition between individuals in a company rather than team building, and limit people's ability to develop a strong network of contacts within a firm.

3.   In sharp contrast to the Western emphasis on the individual, in many Asian societies the group is the primary unit of social organization. While in earlier times the group was usually the family or the village, today the group may be a work team or business organization. When meeting someone they may say they work for Sony rather than say they are an engineer that designs disk drives. The worth of an individual is more linked to the success of the group than individual achievement. This emphasis on the group may discourage job switching between firms, encourage lifetime employment systems, and lead to cooperation in solving business problems. On the other hand, individual creativity and initiative is suppressed.

4.   All societies have some sort of stratification, where individuals in higher strata or castes are likely to have a better education, standard of living, and work opportunities. What matters is less what these strata are, but rather the <u>mobility between strata</u> and the <u>significance of strata levels</u> for business.

5.   The mobility permitted by culture affects whether individuals can move up (or down) in strata, and can limit the types of jobs and education available. In the US individuals are very mobile ("anyone can become president"), in Britain there is less mobility, and the caste system in India severely limits mobility.

6.   The significance of the social strata can have important implications for the management and organization of businesses. In cultures where there is a great deal of consciousness over the class of others, the way individuals from different classes work together (i.e. management and labor) may be very prescribed and strained in some cultures (i.e. Britain), or have almost no significance in others (i.e. Japan). The class of a person may be very important in some hiring and promotion decisions, particularly in sales organizations where the person will be dealing with customers that may also come from a particular class.

D.   Religion

1.   Religion can be defined *as a system of shared beliefs and rituals that are concerned with the realm of the sacred.* While there are literally thousands of religions worldwide, five that have the largest following will be discussed: Christianity, Islam, Hinduism, Buddhism, and Confucianism. Figure 3.2 shows the numbers and relative proportion of adherents.

2.   Christianity is the largest religion and is common throughout Europe, the Americas, and other countries settled by Europeans. Within Christianity there are three major branches: Protestant, Roman Catholic, and Eastern Orthodox. At the turn of the century Weber suggested that is was the "Protestant work ethic" that was the driving force of capitalism. This focus on hard work, wealth creation, and frugality encouraged capitalism while the Catholic promise of salvation in the next world did not foster the same kind of work ethic. The Protestant emphasis on individual religious freedom, in contrast to the hierarchical Catholic church, was also consistent with the individualist economic and political philosophy discussed in Chapter 2.

3.   Islam has the same underlying roots of Christianity (Christ is viewed as a prophet), and suggests many of the same underlying societal mores. Islam, however, extends this to more of an all-embracing way of life that governs one's being. It also prescribes many more "laws" on how people should act and live that are entirely counter the US "separation of church and state." In Islam people do not own property, but only act as stewards for God and thus must take care of that which they have been entrusted with. They must use property in a righteous, socially beneficial, and prudent manner; not exploit others for their own benefit; and have obligations to help the disadvantaged. Thus while Islam is supportive of business, the way business is practiced is prescribed.

4.   Hinduism, practiced primarily on the Indian sub-continent, focuses on the importance of achieving spiritual growth and development, which may require material and physical self-denial. Since Hindus are valued by their spiritual rather than material achievements, there is not the same work ethic or focus on entrepreneurship found in some other religions. Likewise, promotion and adding new responsibilities may not be the goal of an employee, or may be infeasible due to the employee's caste.

5.   Buddhists also stress spiritual growth and the afterlife, rather than achievement while in this world. Buddhism, practiced mainly in South East Asia, does not support the caste system, however, so individuals do have some mobility not found in Hinduism and can work with individuals from different classes.

6.   Confucianism, practiced mainly in China, teaches the importance of attaining personal salvation through right action. The need for high moral and ethical conduct and loyalty to others are central in Confucianism. Three key teachings of Confucianism - loyalty, reciprocal obligations, and honesty - may all lead to a lowering of the cost of doing business in Confucian societies. The close ties between Japanese auto companies and their suppliers, which has been an important ingredient in the Japanese success in the auto industry, are facilitated by loyalty, reciprocal obligations, and honesty. In countries where these relationships are more adversarial and not bound by these same values, the costs of doing business are probably higher.

E.   Language

1.   The language of a society not only allows it to communicate, but directs the attention of people towards certain features of the world and human interactions. A good example is how the Inuit have 24 words for snow, but no word for the overall concept. Language helps describe how different people see the world.

2.   Figure 3.4 shows the most common mother tongues is the world. While English is clearly the language of international business, knowing at least some of the local language can greatly help when working in another country. In some situations knowing the local language can be critical for business success.

3.   Unspoken language can be just as important for communication. Using a few facial expressions and hand gestures to the class can illustrate the point. The fact that these can have different interpretations in different cultures, and that many of these actions may be automatic or reflexive, obviously complicates international communication. Not only may the person you are dealing with be unintentionally sending non-verbal signals that you are not understanding or mis-understanding, you may be unconsciously sending your own signals. One example I have used in class is to show different perceptions of "personal space" in communications. I have an conversation with one student (about sports or the weather) with us standing "a long distance apart" and a similar conversation with another student with our faces only a few inches apart. Most of the class finds both of these extreme, although a few reserved midwesterners will find the long distance quite acceptable. Students from different countries will also comment on their perceptions, and how distance also varies with familiarity with the person.

F.   Education

1.   Schools, as a part of the social structure of a society, and one that students are exposed to in their formative years, convey many cultural values and norms.

2.   The knowledge base, training, and educational opportunities available to a country's citizens can also give it a competitive advantage in the market and make it a more or less attractive place for expanding business. In nations that have a ready trained workforce for particular types of jobs, it is easier to start operations than in nations where an investor will also have to undertake time-consuming and costly training.

3.   Map 3.1 shows the percentage of a country's GNP that was devoted to education in 1991. Map 3.2 shows the literacy rates. Although there is not a perfect correspondence between educational spending and literacy rates, a relation does exist, and spending on education does give an indication of a country's commitment to education.

G.   Culture and the Workplace

1.   For an international business with operations in different countries, it is important to understand how a society's culture impacts on the values found in the workplace. The EuroDisney example provides several instances of culture affecting the workplace.

2.   Hofstede made a study of IBM employees worldwide, and identified four dimensions that summarize different cultures: power distance, individualism vs. collectivism, uncertainty avoidance, and masculinity vs. femininity. Figures 3.5 and 3.6 plot some of the findings of his study and can be used to discuss sets of countries, outliers, and differences between the primary country of the students and other countries. While critics have concerns about Hofstede's methodology and it perhaps is important to caution students from taking it all too seriously, the study does suggest what individuals should consider when doing business from individuals from another country.

H.   Cultural Change

1.   Culture is not a constant, but does evolve over time. What was acceptable behavior in the US in the 1960s is now considered "insensitive" or even harassment. Changes are taking place all the time, as the Management Focus on Japan suggests.

2.   As countries become economically stronger and increase in the globalization of products bought and sold, cultural change is particularly common.

I.   Implications for Business

1.   Individuals and firms must develop cross-cultural literacy. International businesses that are ill-informed about the practices of another culture are unlikely to succeed in that culture. One way to develop cross-cultural literacy is to regularly rotate and transfer people internationally.

2.   One must also beware of ethnocentric behavior, or a belief in the superiority of one's own culture. Perhaps in our presentation of this material we are guilty of this, and have been unable to find some of the obvious weaknesses in US culture and strengths of other cultures.

3.   Cultural values can influence the costs of doing business in different countries, and ultimately the competitive advantage of the country. The text suggests some positive and negative aspects of US and Japanese culture than may have contributed to the economic success of these countries. Understanding what countries may have a competitive advantage has implications both for looking for potential competitors in world markets and deciding where to undertake international expansion.

ANSWERS TO CRITICAL DISCUSSION QUESTIONS FOR CHAPTER 3

QUESTION 1: Outline why the culture of a country influences the costs of doing business in that country. Illustrate your answer with examples.

ANSWER 1: (Since in a sense the entire chapter is about this question, there can be numerous reasons and examples of how culture influences the costs of doing business. Several are highlighted in the following sentences, but there could be numerous others.) When there are simply different norms between how individuals from different countries interact, the costs of doing business rise as people grapple with unfamiliar ways of doing business. For example, while in the US we may get down to business first, and then get to know each other socially later, in many South American countries it is important develop a good social relationship before trying to discuss business issues. Different class structures and social mobility also raise the costs of doing business, for if there are inhibitions against working with people from different classes, then the efficiency with which information can flow may be limited and the cost of running a business increased. A country's religion can also affect the costs of business, as religious values can affect attitudes towards work, entrepreneurship, honesty, fairness, and social responsibility. In Hindu societies where the pursuit of material well being can be viewed as making spiritual well being less likely, worker productivity may be lower than in nations with other religious beliefs. Finally, a country's education system can have important implications for the costs of business. In countries where workers receive excellent training and are highly literate, the need for specific worker training programs are decreased and the hiring of additional employees is facilitated.

QUESTION 2: How do you think business practices in an Islamic country are likely to differ from business practices in the United States?

ANSWER 2: A number of aspects of the cultural differences between an Islamic country and the US will cause business practices to differ. The role women can take, appropriate etiquette (including simple things like not passing papers with the left hand), holidays, and wining and dining all differ from in the US But beyond these, the underlying philosophy and role of business differs from in the US Since Muslims are stewards of property for God, rather than owners, they are more likely to use their resources carefully and may be less likely to give up or sell something to a person who may not practice the same stewardship. The importance of fairness to all parties in relations means that over-aggressiveness in self interest may not be well received, and breaking an agreement, even if technically/legally permissible, may be viewed as very inappropriate. Finally, the prohibitions on interest payments in some Islamic countries means that the wording of the terms of an agreement must be done carefully so that "fair profits" are not construed as being "interest payments."

QUESTION 3: What are the implications for international business of the dominant religion of a country?

ANSWER 3: Differences in the dominant religion of a country affect relationships, attitudes toward business, and overall economic development. Firstly, differences in religion require inter-cultural sensitivity. This sensitivity requires things like simply knowing the religious holidays, accepting that some unexpected things may happen "because of Allah's will," or understanding how interpersonal relationships may be different between "believers" and "non-believers." (Hence non-believers may be treated differently.) Secondly, religious beliefs can significantly affect a countries attitude toward business, work, and entrepreneurship. In one country successfully beating a competitor may be considered a great achievement while in another it may be thought of as showing a lack of compassion and disruptive to the society and persons involved, both attitudes that may be derived from underlying religious beliefs. Likewise, hard work may be either rewarded positively or viewed as something of secondary importance to spiritual peace and harmony. Thirdly, different dominant religions may affect the overall competitiveness and potential for economic growth of a nation, and hence attractiveness of a country for international business.

QUESTION 4: Choose two countries that appear to be culturally diverse. Compare the culture of those countries and then indicate how cultural differences influence (a) the costs of doing business in each country, (b) the likely future economic development of that country, and (c) business practices.

ANSWER 4: The answers will obviously vary based on the countries chosen by the students, and their knowledge of the countries. Hopefully the student can present some information on along the dimensions of values, norms, social structure, religion, language, and education of the countries and also describe the key differences and similarities of the countries along these dimensions. Relating the differences between the countries along these dimensions to differences in the costs of doing business, the potential for economic development, and business practices would fully answer the question. (While it may be more difficult for students to come up with really good examples relative to business practices, the costs and prospects for economic development should be quite feasible.)

STUDENT EXERCISES AND PROJECTS FOR CHAPTER 3

If there is significant cultural diversity in the class, there is a great deal one can do. If the class is fairly homogenous, these become more difficult. Here are a couple of things I have done.

- Have the students assemble into relatively homogeneous groups, and then assign them a question like "Describe what would be a wonderful romantic evening for a young couple dating". I had them write down a paragraph long description on a piece of paper and hand it in. Then I took two that were quite different and read them to the class. (I may have embellished a few points and ad libbed a little to make it more humorous.) The point was well made that people from these two different cultures might have a very awkward evening.

- A more conservative question could involve "a perfect dinner" or a "perfect weekend away". In an older class when I did the weekend away exercise some went camping with the kids, while others sent the kids off to the grandparents and stayed home alone. While this was all done in one "culture", the fact that different people had very different preferences transitioned nicely into a discussion of how cultural differences and preferences affect how people act and interact.

This is also a good time in the course to introduce a simulation or exercise that can take several weeks. Several popular and frequently used simulation exercises are outlined in Part II of this manual following the suggested course outlines.

SUGGESTED READINGS FOR CHAPTER 3

The footnotes suggest some appropriate additional readings. The following may be of particular interest:

Hampden-Turner, Charles and Fons Trompenaars 1993. The seven cultures of capitalism. New York: Doubleday.

Hofstede, Geert 1980. Culture's consequences. Newbury Park, CA, USA: Sage Publications

Lane, Henry, Joseph DiStefano, and Martha Mavnezski 1996. International management behavior. Cambridge, MA: Blackwell.

Mavnezski, Martha, and Joseph DiStefano 1995. Measuring culture in international management: The cultural perspectives questionnaire. Western Business School Working Paper. This is a modern and theory based approach to measuring cultural perspectives that corrects many of the problems in Hofstede's approach. The general ideas are contained in the following book, which may be more accessible for some people.

Mead, R. 1994. International management: Cross cultural dimensions. Cambridge, MA: Blackwell.

Namerwirth, J.Z. and R.P. Weber 1987. Dynamics of culture. Boston: Allen and Unwin.

Ricks, David A. 1993. Blunders in international business. Cambridge, MA: Blackwell. An excellent little book full of anecdotes, some cultural.

Rosenzweig, Philip M. 1994. National culture and management. Harvard Business School Publishing, Publication #9-394-177.

Sjögren, Annick and Lena Janson 1994. Culture and management in a changing Europe. Stockholm: Institute of International Business.

TRANSPARENCY MASTERS FOR CHAPTER 3 FOLLOW

The Determinants of Culture

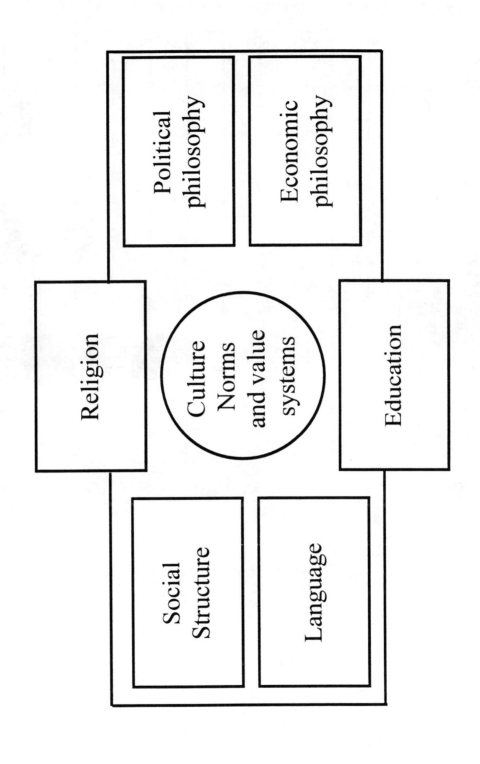

IRWIN © Times Mirror Higher Education Group Inc., Company 1997

Figure 3.1

World's Major Religions (Millions of Adherents)

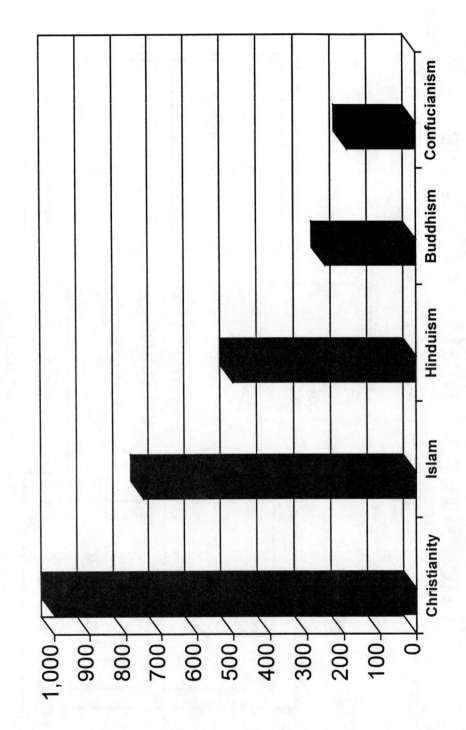

Figure 3.2

Percentage of Gross National Product (GNP) Spent on Education

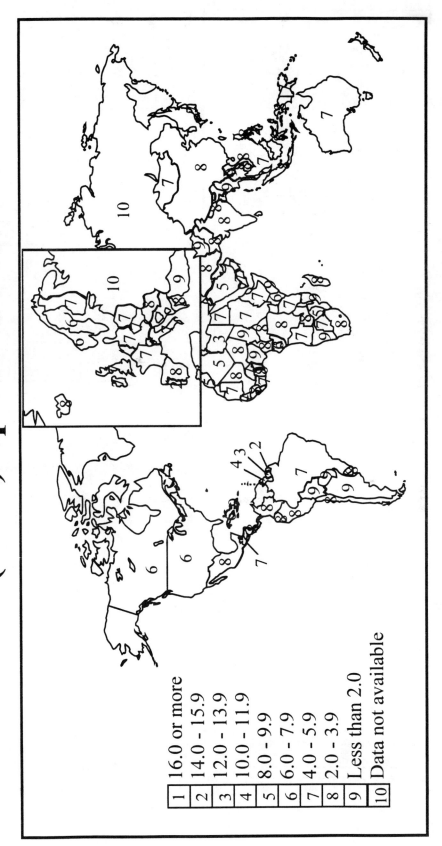

1	16.0 or more
2	14.0 - 15.9
3	12.0 - 13.9
4	10.0 - 11.9
5	8.0 - 9.9
6	6.0 - 7.9
7	4.0 - 5.9
8	2.0 - 3.9
9	Less than 2.0
10	Data not available

Map 3.1a

Percent of Gross National Product (GNP) Spent on Education CONTINUED

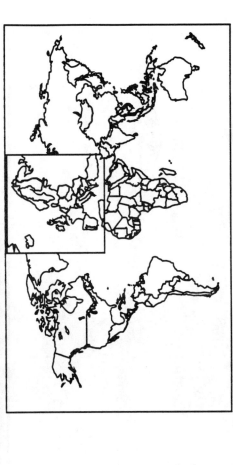
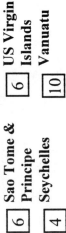

1	16.0 or more
2	14.0 - 15.9
3	12.0 - 13.9
4	10.0 - 11.9
5	8.0 - 9.9
6	6.0 - 7.9
7	4.0 - 5.9
8	2.0 - 3.9
9	Less than 2.0
10	Data not available

Am. Samoa	5
Andorra	10
Antigua & Barbuda	8
Bahamas	7
Bahrain	7
Barbados	6
Bermuda	8
Cape Verde Islands	8

Cayman Islands	10
Comoros Islands	5
Dominica	10
Fiji	6
French Polynesia	4
Grenada	7
Guadeloupe	1
Guam	5

Hong Kong	8
Kiribati	5
Liechtenstein	10
Macao	10
Maldives	9
Malta	8
Martinique	2
Mauritius	9

Monaco	10
Nauru	10
Netherlands Antilles	4
New Cadedonia	2
Reunion	1
St. Kitts and Nevis	7
St. Lucia	6
St. Vincent	6

San Marino	10
Sao Tome & Principe	6
Seychelles	4
Singapore	8
Solomon Islands	7
Tonga	7
Trinidad and Tobago	7
Tuvalu	10

UK Virgin Islands	7
US Virgin Islands	6
Vanuatu	10
Western Samoa	7

Source: Map data copyright © 1992 PC Globe, Inc., Tempe, Arizona, USA. All Rights Reserved Worldwide.

Map 3.1b

Percentage World Literacy Rates

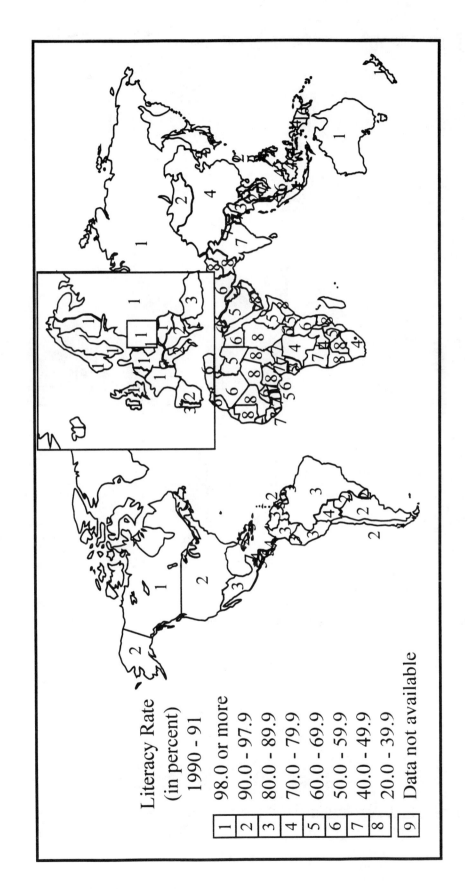

Literacy Rate
(in percent)
1990 - 91

1	98.0 or more
2	90.0 - 97.9
3	80.0 - 89.9
4	70.0 - 79.9
5	60.0 - 69.9
6	50.0 - 59.9
7	40.0 - 49.9
8	20.0 - 39.9
9	Data not available

Source: Map data copyright © 1992 PC Globe, Inc., Tempe, Arizona, USA. All Rights Reserved Worldwide.

Map 3.2a

Percentage World Literacy Rates

CONTINUED

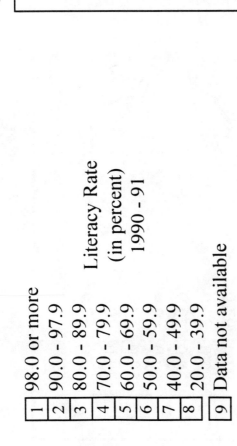

Literacy Rate (in percent) 1990 - 91

1	98.0 or more
2	90.0 - 97.9
3	80.0 - 89.9
4	70.0 - 79.9
5	60.0 - 69.9
6	50.0 - 59.9
7	40.0 - 49.9
8	20.0 - 39.9
9	Data not available

Am. Samoa	2	Cayman Islands	1	Hong Kong	2	Monaco	1	San Marino	2
Andorra	1	Comoros Islands	6	Kiribati	2	Nauru	1	Sao Tome & Principe	5
Antigua & Barbuda	3	Dominica	2	Liechtenstein	1	Netherlands Antilles	2	Seychelles	5
Bahamas	1	Fiji	3	Macao	2	New Cadedonia	2	Singapore	3
Bahrain	4	French Polynesia	1	Maldives	2	Reunion	5	Solomon Islands	5
Barbados	1	Grenada	1	Malta	3	St. Kitts and Nevis	1	Tonga	1
Bermuda	1	Guadeloupe	2	Martinique	2	St. Lucia	5	Trinidad and Tobago	2
Cape Verde Islands	5	Guam	2	Mauritius	5	St. Vincent	2	Tuvalu	2
								UK Virgin Islands	1
								US Virgin Islands	2
								Vanuatu	5
								Western Samoa	2

Map 3.2b

Key to Countries and Regions in Hofstede's Graphs

ARA	Arab countries (Egypt, Lebanon, Lybia, Kuwait, Iraq, Saudi-Arabia, U.A.E.)	FIN	Finland
ARG	Argentina	FRA	France
AUL	Australia	GBR	Great Britain
AUT	Austria	GER	Germany
BRA	Brazil	GRE	Greece
BEL	Belgium	GUA	Guatemala
CAN	Canada	HOK	Hong Kong
CHL	Chile	IDO	Indonesia
COL	Colombia	IND	India
COS	Costa Rica	IRA	Iran
DEN	Denmark	IRE	Ireland
EAF	East Africa (Kenya, Ethiopia, Zambia)	ISR	Israel
EOA	Equador	ITA	Italy

Source: G. Hofstede, "The Cultural Relativity of Organizational Practices and Theories," Journal of International Business Studies 14 (Fall 1983), pp. 75-89.

Figure 3-4a

Key to Countries and Regions in Hofstede's Graphs *CONTINUED*

JAM	Jamaica		SAL	Salvador
JPN	Japan		SIN	Singapore
KOR	South Korea		SPA	Spain
MAL	Malaysia		SWE	Sweden
MEX	Mexico		SWI	Switzerland
NET	Netherlands		TAI	Taiwan
NOR	Norway		THA	Thailand
NZL	New Zealand		TUR	Turkey
PAK	Pakistan		URU	Uruguay
PAN	Panama		USA	United States
PER	Peru		VEN	Venezuela
PHI	Philippines		WAF	West Africa (Nigeria, Ghana, Sierra Leone)
POR	Portugal		YUG	Yugoslavia
SAF	South Africa			

Source: G. Hofstede, "The Cultural Relativity of Organizational Practices and Theories," *Journal of International Business Studies 14 (Fall 1983), pp. 75-89.*

Figure 3-4b

Individualism and Power Distance

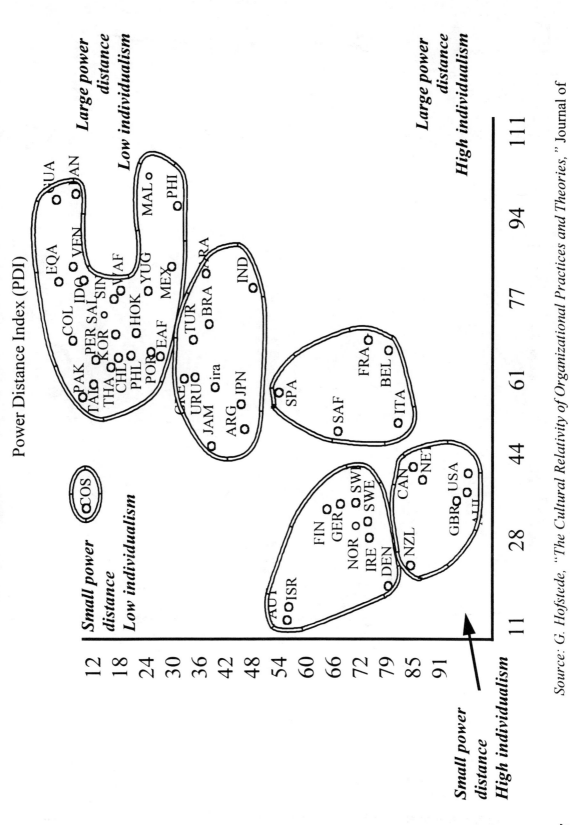

Power Distance Index (PDI)

Figure 3-5

Source: G. Hofstede, "The Cultural Relativity of Organizational Practices and Theories," Journal of International Business Studies 14 (Fall 1983), pp. 75-89.

Uncertainty Avoidance and Masculinity

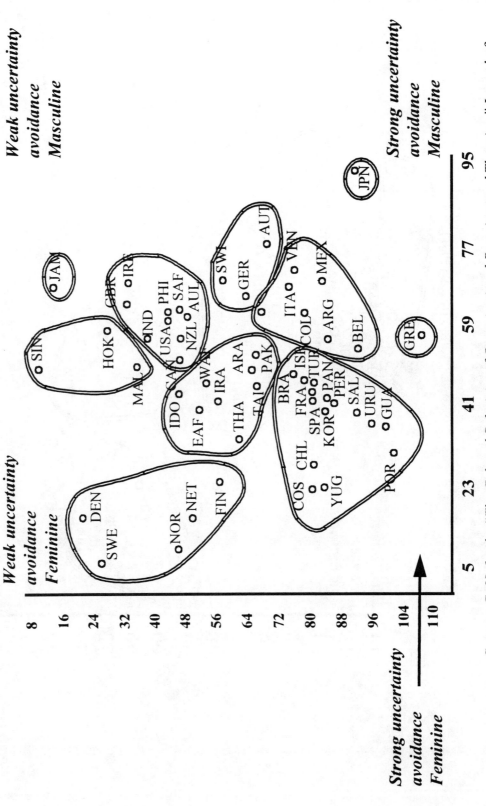

Weak uncertainty avoidance Masculine

Strong uncertainty avoidance Masculine

Weak uncertainty avoidance Feminine

Strong uncertainty avoidance Feminine

Masculinity Index (MAS)

Source: G. Hofstede, "The Cultural Relativity of Organizational Practices and Theories," Journal of International Business Studies 14 (Fall 1983), pp. 75-89.

Figure 3-6

CHAPTER 4: OVERVIEW AND TEACHING SUGGESTIONS

OUTLINE OF CHAPTER 4

OBJECTIVES OF CHAPTER 4

1.   Outline and critically evaluate the major theories that attempt to explain i) why nations should engage in international trade and ii) the patterns of international trade.

2.   Show, via simple examples, the case for free trade and how all countries can benefit from free trade.

3.   Suggest the conditions under which governments should consider adopting policies that can influence an industry's competitiveness and/or the flow of trade.

4.   Describe how each of the theories presented certainly has some validity and seems logical, how in many ways the theories build on each other, and how taken together they explain a great deal of the world trade picture. Yet there is still a great deal more to understand.

LECTURE OUTLINE FOR CHAPTER 4

A.   Introduction and Overview of Trade Theory

1.   The opening case comparing Ghana and South Korea illustrates how South Korea's policy of encouraging trade fueled its economic growth, while Ghana's policies resulted in a reallocation of resources away from their most productive uses.

2.   This chapter reviews a number of different theories of international trade to show why it is beneficial for a country to engage in trade and what patterns of international trade might be expected.

3.   Having completely free trade is certain to hurt some domestic industries that are not competitive on a worldwide basis. This will be looked at in more detail in Chapter 5.

4.   Some patterns of trade are fairly easy to explain - it is obvious why Saudi Arabia exports oil, the US exports agricultural products, and Mexico exports labor intensive goods. Yet others are not so obvious or easily explained.

5.   I have often used in the introduction to this and/or the next chapter some recent examples regarding trade issues in the news. There always seem to be election campaigns with rhetoric on "protecting jobs" or industries, some current dispute between the US and Japan, or some posturing going on in the EU regarding its Eastern neighbors or former colonies over trade. I suggest that the class keep whatever this issue is in mind as we look at the trade theories to follow.

B.   Mercantilism

1.   Since gold and silver were viewed as valuable and a sign of wealth, mercantilism suggested that countries should design policies that led to an increase in their holdings of gold and silver.

2.   Countries should run a balance of trade surplus, and have exports of greater value than imports. Thus imports were limited by tariffs and quotas, while exports were subsidized.

3.   Hume pointed out how a persistent trade surplus would begin to affect money supplies, and in the long run close the trade surplus.

4.   The key problem with the mercantilist view is that it views trade as a zero sum game, where if one country benefits the other must lose.

5.   As an economic philosophy, mercantilism is flawed and not valid. Yet many political views today have the goal of boosting exports while limiting imports by seeking only selective liberalization of trade.

C.   Absolute Advantage

1.   Adam Smith argued that countries differed in their ability to produce goods efficiently, and should specialize in the production of the goods they can produce the most efficiently.

2.   If Britain were to specialize in textile production, and France in wine production, Smith argued that both Britain and France could consume more textiles and wine than if each only produced for their own consumption. Thus trade is a positive sum game.

3. These gains from trade can be showed graphically by looking again at Ghana and South Korea. Figure 4.1 shows both countries' production possibilities frontiers.

4. Table 4.1 can be used to show how consumers in both countries can be better off with specialization of production and trade.

5. When each country has an absolute advantage in one of the products, it is clear that trade is beneficial. But what if one country has an absolute advantage in both products.

D. Comparative advantage

1. Ricardo showed how it makes sense for a country to specialize in the production of goods in which it simply has a comparative advantage, even if it can produce both more efficiently than the other country.

2. Figure 4.2 shows the production possibilities frontiers for Ghana and South Korea when Ghana has an absolute advantage in both cocoa and rice. Points A & B illustrate possible levels of consumption and production without trade.

3. Ghana has a comparative advantage in the production of cocoa since it can produce 4 times as much cocoa as South Korea, but only 1.5 times as much rice. Ghana is comparatively more efficient at producing cocoa than rice.

4. Points C and K' in Figure 4.2 show a possible new production point for each country. Table 4.2 shows how, with trade, both Ghana and South Korea can increase consumption of both products.

5. This simple example makes a number of assumptions: only two countries and two goods; zero transportation costs; similar prices and values; resources are mobile between goods within countries, but not across countries; constant returns to scale; fixed stocks of resources; and no effects on income distribution within countries. While these are all unrealistic, the general proposition that countries will produce and export those goods which they are the most efficient at producing has been shown to be quite valid.

6. Diminishing returns to specialization simply suggest that after some point, the more of a good that a country produces, the greater will be the units of resources required to produce each additional item. If crops are grown on increasingly less fertile land, mining is done on less productive ore, or less skilled personnel need to be hired to perform high skilled jobs, production per unit of input will decrease. Diminishing returns implies a PPF which is convex (as shown in Figure 4.3). In reality countries do not specialize entirely, but produce a range of goods. It is worthwhile to specialize up until that point where the resulting gains from trade are offset by diminishing returns.

7. Opening an economy to trade is likely to generate dynamic gains of two types. First, trade might increase a country's stock of resources as increased supplies become available from abroad. Secondly, free trade might increase the efficiency of resource utilization, and free up resources for other uses. Figure 4.4 shows how dynamic gains can shift a country's PPF outwards.

E. Hecksher-Ohlin Theory

1. The Hecksher-Ohlin theory predicts that countries will export those goods that make intensive use of factors of production which are locally abundant, while importing goods that make

intensive use of factors that are locally scarce. Thus it focuses on differences in relative factor endowments rather than differences in relative productivity.

2.   When we look at US agricultural exports, Icelandic and Norwegian fish exports, Canadian lumber exports, Saudi oil exports, and South African gold exports, the Hecksher-Ohlin theory seems to make sense.

3.   Using the Hecksher-Ohlin theory, Leontief postulated that the US should be an exporter of capital intensive goods and an importer of labor intensive goods. To his surprise, however, he found that US imports were less capital intensive than US exports. Hence, while we can see some support for Hecksher-Ohlin, other evidence contradicts it.

F.   The Product Life Cycle Theory

1.   Vernon suggested that as products mature, both the location of sales and the optimal production location will change, affecting the direction and flow of imports and exports. This effects of this theory are illustrated in Figure 4.5.

2.   While the product life cycle theory accurately explains what has happened for products like photocopiers and a number of other high technology products developed in the US in the 1960s and 1970s, the increasing globalization and integration of the world economy has made this theory less valid in today's world.

G.   The New Trade Theory

1.   New trade theory suggests that because of economies of scale and increasing returns to specialization, in some industries there are likely to be only a few profitable firms. Thus firms with first mover advantages will develop economies of scale and create barriers to entry for other firms. The commercial aircraft industry is an excellent example.

2.   Productive efficiency may not be the result of factor endowments or specific national characteristics, but instead be a result a firm's first mover advantages.

3.   New trade theory does not contradict the theory of comparative advantage, but instead identifies a source of comparative advantage.

4.   An obvious and controversial extension of new trade theory is the implication that governments should consider strategic trade policies. Strategic trade policies would suggest that governments should nurture and protect firms and industries where first mover advantages and economies of scale are likely to be important, as doing so can make it more likely that a firm will build economies of scale and eventually end up a winner in the global competitive race.

H.   National Competitive Advantage: Porter's Diamond

1.   Porter's study tried to explain why a nation achieves international success in a particular industry. This study found 4 broad attributes that promote or impede the creation of competitive advantage. These are shown in Figure 4.6.

2.   Factor Endowments: A nation's position in factors of production such as skilled labor or infrastructure necessary to compete in a given industry can be critical. These factors can be either basic (natural resources, climate, location) or advanced (skilled labor, infrastructure,

technological know-how). While either can be important, advanced factors are more likely to lead to competitive advantage

3.   Demand Conditions: The nature of home demand for the industries product or service influences the development of capabilities. Sophisticated and demanding customers pressure firms to be competitive.

4.   Relating and Supporting Industries: The presence in a nation of supplier industries and related industries that are internationally competitive can spill over and contribute to other industries. Successful industries tend to be grouped in clusters in countries - having world class manufacturers of semi-conductor processing equipment can lead to (and be a result of having) a competitive semi-conductor industry.

5.   Firm Strategy, Structure, and Rivalry: The conditions in the nation governing how companies are created, organized, and managed, and the nature of domestic rivalry impacts firms' competitiveness. Firms that face strong domestic competition will be better able to face competitors from other firms.

6.   In addition to these four main attributes, government policies and chance can impact any of the four. Government policy can affect demand through product standards, influence rivalry through regulation and antitrust laws, and impact the availability of highly educated workers and advanced transportation infrastructure.

7.   The four attributes of the diamond, government policy, and chance work as a reinforcing system, complementing each other and in combination creating the conditions appropriate for competitive advantage. The Management Focus on Nokia, provides a good example of how this Finnish firm built its competitive advantage as a result of factors in Porter's diamond.

I.   Implications for Business

1.   Most of the theories discussed have implications for the location of production activities. Firms will attempt to locate different activities in the location that is optimal for the production of that good, component, or service.

2.   Being a first mover can have important competitive implications, especially if there are economies of scale and the global industry will only support a few competitors. Firms need to be prepared to undertake huge investments and suffer losses for several years in order to reap the eventual rewards.

3.   Governmental policies with respect to free trade or protecting domestic industries can significantly impact global competitiveness. The opening case showed how Ghana's policies negatively impacted the global success of its cocoa business. While new trade theory may suggest that governments subsidize specific industries, Porter's theory focuses how policies can influence the attributes of the diamond.

ANSWERS TO CRITICAL DISCUSSION QUESTIONS FOR CHAPTER 4

QUESTION 1: "Mercantilism is a bankrupt theory that has no place in the modern world." Discuss.

ANSWER 1: As a economically viable and rational theory, mercantilism is bankrupt. It is clear that free trade is not a zero sum game, and that the overall benefits from trade are positive, even if some sectors of a country's economy are likely to be hurt by imports. It is because of this that mercantilism is still viable as a political theory. Many countries do try to liberalize trade in industries where their comparative advantage is the strongest, and resist liberalization in industries where they are less competitive.

QUESTION 2: The "Country Focus" contained in this chapter reviews the arguments of those who suggest that Japan is a neo-merchantilist nation. Do you agree with this assessment? Can you think of cases in which your country has taken a neo-merchantilist stance to foreign competitors?

ANSWER 2: Based on only the information in the country focus, it is hard to not agree with this assessment. The answer to the second part of the question obviously depends upon the student's nationality. Virtually every country supports some protectionist measures for some industries.

QUESTION 3: Using the theory of comparative advantage to support your arguments, outline the case for free trade.

ANSWER 3: If each country specializes in the production of goods in which it has a comparative advantage relative to its trading partners, and then trades these goods for those produced by trading partners that have a comparative advantage in other goods, all countries can end up increasing their utility and consuming higher quantities (or at least the same) of all goods than if they only consumed what they produced.

QUESTION 4: Using the new trade theory and Porter's theory of national competitive advantage, outline the case for government policies designed to build a national competitive advantage in a particular industry. What kind of policies would you recommend the government adopt? Are these policies at variance with the basic free trade philosophy?

ANSWER 4: The new trade theory suggests that government can have a role in helping industries "get a head start" and obtain first mover advantages in international markets, especially if it is an industry where there are likely to be economies of scale, increasing returns to specialization, and barriers to entry. Porter's theory suggests that government policy can either assist or detract from a country's ability to develop a "diamond" that can lead to a competitive advantage in an industry or industries. While new trade theories may suggest direct government support and subsidization of specific industries, Porter's theory would imply that more underlying factors like education, a transportation infrastructure, or competitive domestic markets should be supported by a government in order to promote the creation of competitive industries. These sorts of investments in factors that underlie basic competitiveness are not at variance with a basic free trade philosophy, while subsidization of specific industries is at odds with free trade, especially if these industries are or become major exporters.

QUESTION 5: You are the CEO of a textile firm that designs and manufactures clothing products for a mass market in the United States. Your manufacturing process is labor intensive and does not require highly skilled employees. Currently you have design facilities in Paris and New York, and manufacturing facilities in North Carolina. Drawing upon the theory of international trade, assess whether these are the optimal locations to undertake these particular activities.

ANSWER 5: Having design facilities in Paris and New York, where the top design talent lives and most demanding buyers shop, make sense since these cities have a comparative advantage in design. Since manufacturing is a more labor intensive, having manufacturing in a North Carolina location with lower cost labor also seems appropriate. Yet it is certainly possible that, if the manufacturing is very labor intensive and cannot use more automated machinery, a even lower cost labor country would be more appropriate. Since many Asian countries like Thailand and Bangladesh have significant clothing industries, these and other countries should be considered for manufacturing.

QUESTION 6: "In general, policies designed to limit competition from low-cost foreign competitors do not help a country to achieve greater economic growth." Discuss this statement.

ANSWER 6: Overall, this appears to be true. Protecting industries that are not competitive in world markets tends to insulate them from competitive pressures, and make them even less able to compete for global customers. In addition, these industries take resources from the economy that could be used in industries where the country has a competitive advantage and could be exporting goods worldwide.

STUDENT EXERCISES AND PROJECTS FOR CHAPTER 4

- This chapter is a good one for students to look at contemporary trade issues and trade disputes. You can suggest that students look in recent business journals, or just do some searching on a database like ABI/Inform. At any point in time there is almost always some trade dispute between the US and Canada (forest products, agriculture, or fishing are most common), between various countries and the EU (particularly Japan, but more frequently from Eastern Europe in recent years), between the US and Japan (electronics and autos always seem to be in turmoil), and between everyone and China. For this chapter they can be asked to look at the issue from the standpoint of trade theory. For the next chapter this can be expanded to consider in more detail the political dimensions.

- You can also set up a very simple simulation regarding the gains from trade. Organize students into some small groups, and provide each of them with some quantity of some particular good. Then within their group they are allowed to trade amongst each other at whatever price they want. I have done it with soda, small bags of chips, candy bars, etc. Before long each group will establish some prices (i.e. a can of soda is worth .5 bags of chips or 25 M&Ms). The people with the chips are the first to realize that all these chips are really not all that good without some soda to drink. A necessary rule is that all the goods must either be consumed during the class, or they will be returned to me. It can be interesting to see how prices differ across different groups, and one can extend the exercise to allow cross group trading after some point in time. When teaching in executive education the same sort of exercise can be used at the end of the day with more adult beverages. (Not many people just want tonic without gin, etc., and some real hard core types think they have the most important good and try to drive very hard bargains.)

SUGGESTED READINGS FOR CHAPTER 4

The footnotes suggest some appropriate additional readings. The following may be of particular interest:

Cline, William R. 1983. Trade policy in the 1980s. Washington, DC: Institute of International Economics. While a bit dated in some respects, gives a good overview of trade policy history and debates.

Hecksher, Eli F. and Bertil Ohlin 1991. Heckscher-Ohlin trade theory. Cambridge, MA: MIT Press.

Helpman, Elhanan and Paul R. Krugman 1989. Trade policy and market structure. Cambridge, MA: MIT Press.

Krugman, Paul R. 1990. Rethinking international trade. Cambridge, MA: MIT Press.

Porter, Michael E. 1990. The competitive advantage of nations. New York: Free Press.

TRANSPARENCY MASTERS FOR CHAPTER 4 FOLLOW

The Theory of Absolute Advantage

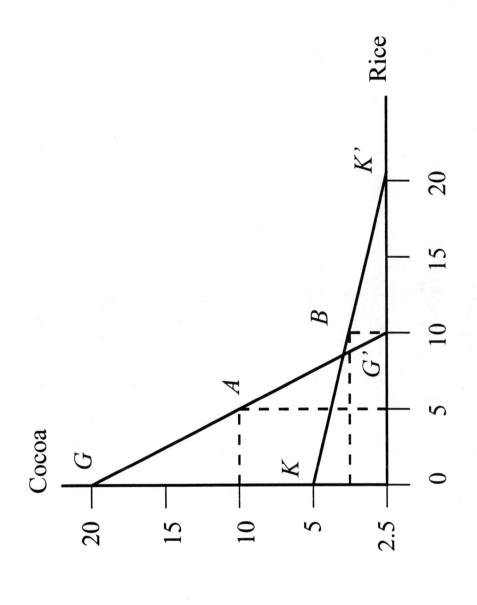

IRWIN © Times Mirror Higher Education Group Inc., Company 1997

Figure 4.1

Absolute Advantage and the Gains from Trade

Resources Required to Produce 1 Ton of Cocoa and Rice

	Cocoa	Rice
Ghana	10	20
South Korea	40	10

Production and Consumption without Trade

	Cocoa	Rice
Ghana	10.0	5.0
South Korea	2.5	10.0
Total production	12.5	15.0

Production with Specialization

	Cocoa	Rice
Ghana	20.0	0.0
South Korea	0.0	20.0
Total production	20.0	20.0

IRWIN © Times Mirror Higher Education Group Inc., Company 1997

Table 4.1a

Absolute Advantage and the Gains from Trade *CONTINUED*

Consumption after Ghana Trades 6 Tons of Cocoa for 6 Tons of South Korean Rice

	Cocoa	Rice
Ghana	14.0	6.0
South Korea	6.0	14.0

Increase in Consumption as a Result of Specialization and Trade

Ghana	4.0	1.0
South Korea	3.5	4.0

IRWIN © Times Mirror Higher Education Group Inc., Company 1997

Table 4.1b

The Theory of Comparative Advantage

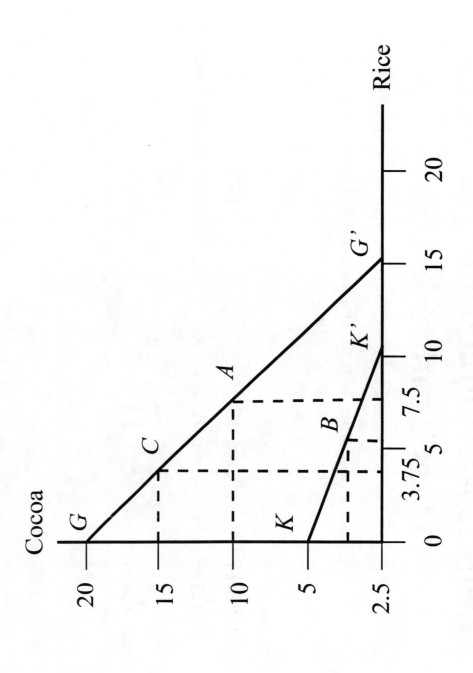

Figure 4.2

Comparative Advantage and the Gains from Trade

Resources Required to Produce 1 Ton of Cocoa and Rice

	Cocoa	Rice
Ghana	10	13.33
South Korea	40	20

Production and Consumption without Trade

	Cocoa	Rice
Ghana	10.0	7.5
South Korea	2.5	5.0
Total production	12.5	12.5

Production with Specialization

	Cocoa	Rice
Ghana	15.0	3.75
South Korea	0.0	10.0
Total production	15.0	13.75

IRWIN © Times Mirror Higher Education Group Inc., Company 1997

Table 4.2a

Comparative Advantage and the Gains from Trade *CONTINUED*

Consumption after Ghana Trades 4 Tons of Cocoa for 4 Tons of South Korean Rice

	Cocoa	Rice
Ghana	11.0	7.75
South Korea	4.0	6.0

Increase in Consumption as a Result of Specialization and Trade

	Cocoa	Rice
Ghana	1.0	0.25
South Korea	1.5	1.0

IRWIN © Times Mirror Higher Education Group Inc., Company 1997

Table 4.2b

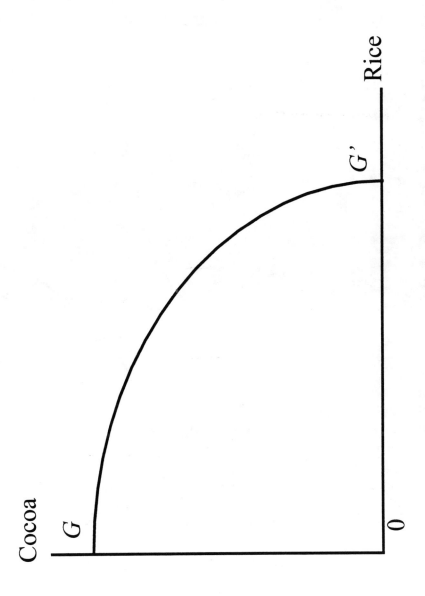

Ghana's PPF under Diminishing Returns

Cocoa

G

G'

0

Rice

IRWIN © Times Mirror Higher Education Group Inc., Company 1997

Figure 4.3

The Influence of Free Trade on the PPF

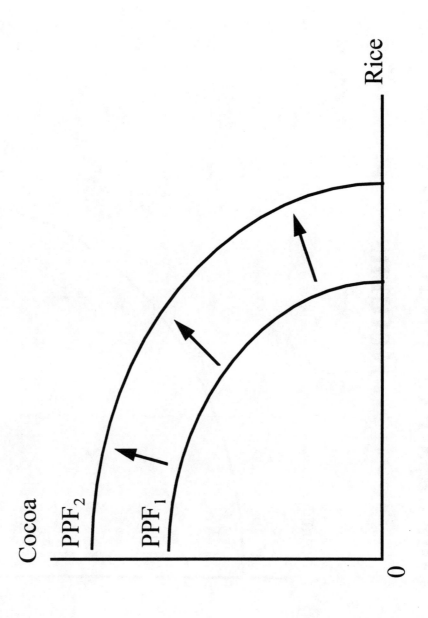

IRWIN © Times Mirror Higher Education Group Inc., Company 1997

Figure 4.4

The Product Life-Cycle Theory

a. United States

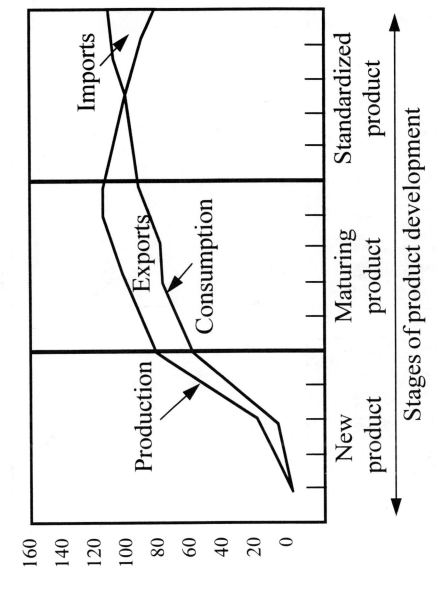

Source: Adapted from R. Vernon and L.T. Wells, The Economic Environment of International Business, *4th Ed.* (Englewood Cliffs, NJ: Prentice Hall, 1986)

Figure 4.5a

The Product Life–Cycle Theory

b. Other Advanced Countries

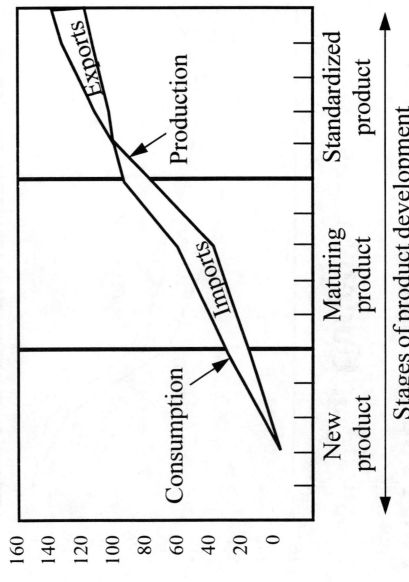

Source: Adapted from R. Vernon and L.T. Wells, The Economic Environment of International Business, 4th Ed. (Englewood Cliffs, NJ: Prentice Hall, 1986)

Figure 4.5b

The Product Life–Cycle Theory

c. Developing Countries

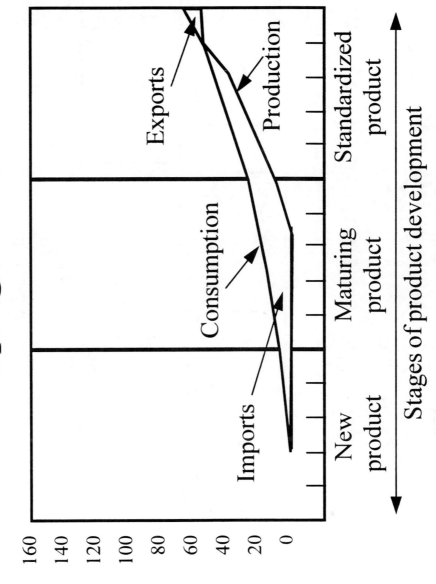

Source: Adapted from R. Vernon and L.T. Wells, The Economic Environment of International Business, 4th Ed. (Englewood Cliffs, NJ: Prentice Hall, 1986)

Figure 4.5c

Determinants of National Competitive Advantage: Porter's Diamond

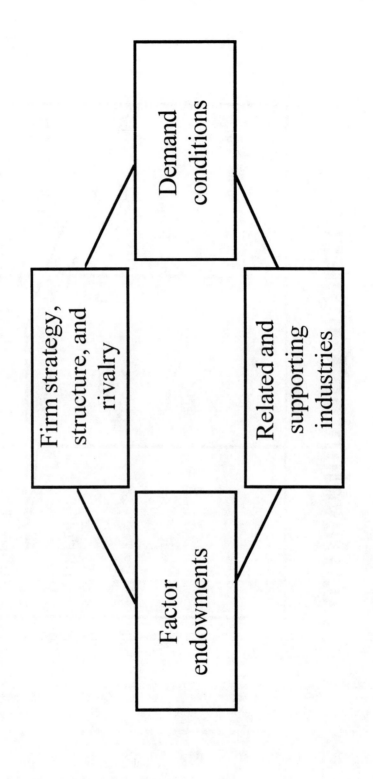

Source: Adapted from M.E. Porter, "The Competitive Advantage of Nations," Harvard Business Review. March - April 1990. p. 77.

Figure 4.6

CHAPTER 5: OVERVIEW AND TEACHING SUGGESTIONS

<u>OUTLINE OF CHAPTER 5</u>

OPENING CASE: ANATOMY OF A TRADE DISPUTE - THE US PRIES OPEN JAPAN'S
        CELLULAR TELEPHONE MARKET
INTRODUCTION
THE INSTRUMENTS OF TRADE POLICY
        Tariffs
        Subsidies
        Import Quotas and Voluntary Export Restraints
        Local Content Requirements
        Administrative Policies
THE CASE FOR GOVERNMENT INTERVENTION
        Political Arguments for Intervention
        Economic Arguments for Intervention
THE REVISED CASE FOR FREE TRADE
        Retaliation and Trade War
        Domestic Politics
THE DEVELOPMENT OF THE WORLD TRADING SYSTEM
        From Smith to the Great Depression
        1947-1979: GATT, Trade Liberalization, and Economic Growth
        1980-1993: Disturbing Trends
        The Uruguay Round and the World Trade Organization
        The Future: Unresolved Issues
IMPLICATIONS FOR BUSINESS
        Trade Barriers and Firm Strategy
        Policy Implications
SUMMARY OF CHAPTER
CLOSING CASE: MALAYSIA AND BRITAIN ENTER INTO A TRADE DISPUTE

<u>OBJECTIVES OF CHAPTER 5</u>

1.   While Chapter 4 discussed the economic theories of international trade and outlined the case for free trade, it was mostly silent on the political aspects of trade policy. This chapter focuses on the political systems and tools of trade policy. The major objective of this chapter is to describe how political realities have shaped, and continue to shape, the international trading system.

2.   Provide a history of the development of the current world trading system, leading to an understanding of the current international trade framework.

3.   Outline the primary trade policy instruments available to governments: tariffs, subsidies, quotas, voluntary export restraints, local content requirements, and administrative policies.

4.   Present the political and economic arguments for governmental intervention in trade, as well as the counter arguments that suggest that intervention is rarely successful in the long run.

5.   Discuss the implications of trade barriers for business.

LECTURE OUTLINE FOR CHAPTER 5

A.   Introduction

1   While Chapter 4 discussed the economic theories of international trade and outlined the case for
       free trade, it was mostly silent on the political aspects of trade policy. This chapter focuses on the
       political systems and tools of trade policy.

2.   The major objective of this chapter is to describe how political realities have shaped, and
       continue to shape, the international trading system.

3.   While in theory many countries adhere to the free trade ideal outlined in Chapter 4, in practice
       most have been reluctant to engage in unrestricted free trade. The US continues to restrict trade
       in textiles, sugar, and other basic products in response to domestic political pressures, in addition
       to more technological and militarily sensitive products.

4.   The opening case describes some of the issues relating to the ongoing US-Japan trade dispute,
       and in particular discusses issues related to the Japanese cellular phone market.

B.   Instruments of Trade Policy

1.   Tariffs are one of the oldest, easiest to recognize and regulate, and simplest forms of trade policy.
       Specific tariffs specify an amount that will be levied on each unit of imported good. ($10/ton of
       tea.) Ad valorem tariffs are based on a percentage of the value of the imported good (5% of the
       import value). Tariffs raise the cost of foreign goods relative to domestic goods.

2.   Tariffs benefit the government due to the revenue raised, benefit domestic producers since they
       can charge higher prices, and hurt domestic consumers. Tariffs are unambiguously pro-producer
       and anti-consumer. They reduce the overall efficiency of the world economy - a protective tariff
       encourages domestic firms to produce products at home that in theory, could be produced more
       efficiently abroad.

3.   A subsidy is a government payment to a domestic producer. Subsidies take many forms
       including cash grants, low interest rate loans, tax breaks, and government equity participation in
       domestic firms. Subsidies help domestic producers in two ways. 1) Subsidies help domestic
       producers compete against low cost foreign imports, and 2) Subsidies help domestic producers
       gain export markets.

4.   Subsidies clearly benefit domestic producers, and damage foreign producers. Subsidies must be
       paid for by domestic consumers, however, usually through taxes. When subsidies are in the form
       of price supports (i.e. often in agriculture), domestic consumers may also pay directly.

5.   An import quota is a direct restriction on the quantity of some good that can be imported into a
       country. Import quotas are usually regulated by issuing import licenses for the import of some
       specific quantity of goods.

6.   A voluntary export restraint (VER) may have the same effect as a quota. In a VER, another
       country or countries agree to not export more than a certain quantity to another country or
       countries. VERs are usually only enacted when it is feared that a more restrictive tariff or quota
       will be levied unless exports are "voluntarily" reduced.

7.   Import quotas and VERs benefit domestic producers and harm domestic consumers. They can also even help foreign producers, as foreign producers can raise the price they charge for the limited supply they can sell, and take the difference as additional profit.

8.   Local content requirements specify that some portion of a good must be produced domestically. The purpose of a local content requirement is usually to aid the formation of domestic industries, to keep manufacturers from switching to foreign suppliers, or to keep foreign firms from setting up "screwdriver plants", where imported manufactured components undergo simple assembly in order to avoid some other trade restriction on the importation of the fully assembled product. Domestic suppliers benefit, and domestic consumers must bear the costs.

9.   A wide range of administrative barriers can be enacted. Taking so much time to inspect goods that they spoil or setting down specific regulations on "product standards" that are very expensive to meet.

C.   The Case for Government Intervention

1.   The most common political reason for trade restrictions is "protecting jobs and industries." Usually this results from political pressures by groups or industries that are "threatened" by more efficient foreign producers, and have more political clout than the consumers that will eventually pay the costs.

2.   Keeping industries "vital for national security" viable is an oft used argument for trade restrictions. While this is reasonable for industries like aerospace and electronics, in the US the shoe industry has regularly lobbied that soldiers need boots, and thus the US needs to have a viable shoe industry in order to be able to provide shoes during a time of war.

3.   Government intervention in trade can be used as part of a "get tough" policy to open foreign markets. By taking, or threatening to take, specific actions, other countries may remove trade barriers. But when threatened governments don't back down, an tensions can escalate and new trade barriers may be enacted.

4.   The "infant industry" argument suggests that an industry should be protected until it can develop and be viable and competitive internationally. A problem with this is determining when an industry "grows up." Some industries that are just plain inefficient and uncompetitive have argued they are still infants after 50 years. The other problem is that given the existence of global capital markets, if the country has the potential to develop a viable competitive position its firms should be capable of raising the necessary funds without additional support from the government.

5.   Strategic trade policy suggests that in cases where there may be important first mover advantages, governments can help firms from their countries attain these advantages.

6.   Strategic trade policy also suggests that governments can help firms overcome barriers to entry into industries where foreign firms have an initial advantage.

D.   The Revised Case for Free Trade

1.   While strategic trade policy identifies conditions where restrictions on trade may provide economic benefits, there are two problems that may make restrictions inappropriate: retaliation and politics.

2.   Intervening to aid domestic firms will only be successful if other countries do not take similar actions that offset the effects.

3.   While it could be very difficult to identify situations where strategic intervention in trade is economically appropriate, various interest groups will be certain to lobby that particular firms should be aided. Given the ease with which special interest groups seem to be able to capture the attention of the government, it is more likely that consumers will be harmed needlessly than producers fairly chosen. It is unreasonable to expect the government to be completely fair and objective in "targeting" industries, when different industries, lobbies, and politicians all have there own objectives for "getting their paws in the honey pot" of governmental funds.

E.   The Development of the World Trading System

1.   Up until the Great Depression of the 1930s, most countries had some degree of protectionism. Great Britain, as a major trading nation, was one of the strongest supporters of free trade.

2.   Although the world was already in a depression, in 1930 the US enacted the Smoot-Hawley tariff, which created significant import tariffs on foreign goods. As other nations took similar steps and the depression deepened, world trade fell further.

3.   After WWII, the US and other nations realized the value of freer trade, and established the General Agreement on Tariffs and Trade (GATT). [Referred to sometimes as the General Agreement to Talk and Talk.]

4.   The approach of GATT is to gradually eliminate barriers to trade. Over 100 countries are members of GATT, and work together to further liberalize trade. Figure 5.1 shows the different rounds of GATT negotiations and the resulting reductions in tariffs.

5.   During the 1980s and early 1990s the world trading system as "managed" by GATT underwent strains. First, Japan's economic strength and huge trade surplus stressed what had been more equal trading patterns, and Japan's perceived protectionist (neo-merchantilist) policies created intense political pressures in other countries. Second, the persistent trade deficits by the US, the world's largest economy, caused significant economic problems for some industries and political problems for the government. Thirdly, many countries found that although limited by GATT from utilizing tariffs, there were many other more subtle forms of intervention that had the same effects and did not technically violate GATT (e.g. VERs).

6.   Against the background of rising protectionist pressures, in 1986 GATT members embarked on their eighth round of negotiations to reduce tariffs (called the Uruguay Round). This was the most ambitious round to date, as the goal was to expand beyond the regulation of manufactured goods and address trade issues related to intellectual property, agriculture, services, and enforcement mechanism. Table 5.1 illustrates the main features of the agreement that was finally reached in 1993.

7.   The agreement, however, left several important matters unaddressed: financial services, broadcast entertainment, environmental matters, worker's rights, and foreign direct investment. These are left to further negotiations under the auspices of the World Trade Organization.

F.   Implications for Business

1.   Trade barriers clearly negatively impact the ability of firms to locate activities in the economically optimal location or source materials from the best producers. Trade barriers can change the underlying costs and benefits of different locations, and force firms to undertake operations in specific locations rather than import or export.

2.   Even if specific quotas, tariffs, local content, etc. regulations do not specifically require that certain actions be taken, a firm may choose to locate facilities or buy from certain suppliers in order to reduce the threat of mandatory and more punitive governmental intervention.

3.   Certain trade barriers may even make some operations no longer viable, and force a firm to give up particular markets or production sites.

4.   In general international firms have an incentive to lobby for free trade, and keep protectionist pressures from causing them to have to change strategies. While there may be short term benefits to having governmental protection in some situations, in the long run these can back fire and other governments can retaliate

ANSWERS TO CRITICAL DISCUSSION QUESTIONS FOR CHAPTER 5

QUESTION 1: Do you think the US government is correct to use a "get tough" approach in its trade negotiations with Japan (see opening case)? What are the risks of such an approach?

ANSWER 1: This is a question that can lead to good discussion, but for which there is no "correct" answer. Advocates of the "get tough" approach believe that this is the only thing that seems to work with negotiations with Japan, and that things have to be brought to the brink before they are resolved. Others will suggest that this is not the way to resolve matters, especially with countries that are not generally thought to be confrontational in nature. The clear danger is that the get tough approach could result in an escalation of tensions and lead to further problems, rather than resolving the current problem.

QUESTION 2: Whose interests should be the paramount concern of government trade policy - the interests of producers (businesses and their employees) or the interests of consumers?

ANSWER 2: The long run interests of consumers should be the primary concern of governments. Unfortunately consumers, each of whom may be negatively impacted by only a few dollars, are less motivated and effective lobbyists than a few producers that have a great deal at stake. While in some instances it could be argued that domestic consumers will be better off if world-class domestic producers are nurtured and allowed to gain first mover advantages in international markets, it is doubtful that the government will be better than international capital markets at "picking winners", and will more likely pick the firms with the greatest political clout. While employees may well lose jobs if there are more efficient foreign competitors, some would argue that this is just the nature of competition, and that the role of government should be to help these employees get jobs where they can be efficiently employed rather than to protect them from reality in inefficient firms.

QUESTION 3: Given the arguments relating to the new trade theory and strategic trade policy, what kind of trade policy should business be pressuring government to adopt?

ANSWER 3: Most economists would probably argue that the best interests of international business are served by a free trade stance, but not a *laissez fair* stance. Put differently, it is probably in the best long run interests of the business community to encourage the government to aggressively promote greater free trade by, for example, strengthening the GATT and WTO. In general, business has probably much more to gain from government efforts to open up protected markets to imports and foreign direct investment, than from government efforts to support certain domestic industries in a manner consistent with the recommendations of strategic trade policy.

QUESTION 4: You are an employees of an US firm that produces personal computers in Thailand and then exports them to the US and other countries for sale. The personal computers were originally produced in Thailand to take advantage of relatively low labor costs and a skilled workforce. Other possible locations considered at that time were Malaysia and Hong Kong. The US government imposes punitive 100% ad valorem tariffs on imports of computers from Thailand to punish the country for administrative trade barriers that restrict US exports to Thailand. How should your firm respond? What does this tell you about the use of targeted trade barriers?

ANSWER 4: As long as the manufacturing requirements haven't changed significantly, looking at Malaysia or Hong Kong again for production would appear obvious. By the US government introducing a specific ad valorem tariff on Thai computer imports, it would be easy to get around these by looking at other locations. Hence such targeted trade barriers can often be easily circumvented without having to locate production facilities in an expensive country like the US

STUDENT EXERCISES AND PROJECTS FOR CHAPTER 5

- This chapter is a good one for students to look at contemporary trade issues and trade disputes. You an either extend the exercise suggested in chapter 4, or extend it. The rest of this paragraph is just copied from chapter 4's suggested exercise. "You can suggest that students look in recent business journals, or just do some searching on a database like ABI/Inform. At any point in time there is almost always some trade dispute between the US and Canada (forest products, agriculture, or fishing are most common), between various countries and the EU (particularly Japan, but more frequently from Eastern Europe in recent years), between the US and Japan (electronics and autos always seem to be in turmoil), and between everyone and China." For the last chapter they can be asked to look at the issue from the standpoint of trade theory. For this chapter this can be expanded to consider in more detail the political dimensions.
- This is also a very good chapter where you can ask students to "write a law". When I have done this I have taken some recent and actual trade dispute, or created a fictional one, and asked students to write a law or regulation to deal with the situation. For example, "assume that the clothes pin manufacturers are seeking relief from what they claim to be unfair practices by foreign competitors. In particular, South East Asian firms are manufacturing clothes pins using wood that is considered rare (i.e. they're chopping down the rain forests), using child labor in assembly, and having the harvesters of the trees do the cutting without providing adequate safety equipment. As a result, they are able to sell clothes pins on the local market for 30% the domestic producers manufacturing costs. The domestic producers want relief from what they perceive as unfair competition." Students can then be asked to consider what sort of regulations would be appropriate in this situation. A variation on this would be to assign different student groups to represent different interests (e.g. the producers, consumers, domestic exporters of other products to these countries who fear possible retaliation and subsequent loss of domestic jobs, free trade economists, environmentalists, etc.). Then after giving the groups some time to prepare their positions, each must lobby before a panel of politicians who will ultimately decide what law should, or shouldn't be enacted.

SUGGESTED READINGS FOR CHAPTER 5

The footnotes suggest some appropriate additional readings. The following may be of particular interest:

Bhagwati, Jagdish 1988. Protectionism. Cambridge, MA: MIT Press.

Helpman, Elhanan and Paul R. Krugman 1985. Market structure and foreign trade: Increasing returns, imperfect competition, and the international economy. Cambridge, MA: MIT Press.

Krugman, Paul 1986. Strategic trade theory and the new international economics. Cambridge, MA: MIT Press

Krugman, Paul and M. Obstfeld 1994. International Economics: Theory and Policy. New York: Harper Collins.

Vousden, Neil 1990. The economics of trade protection. Cambridge, UK: Cambridge University Press.

Yoffie, David B. and Benjamin Gomes-Casseres 1994. International trade and competition: Cases and notes in strategy and management. New York: McGraw-Hill.

TRANSPARENCY MASTERS FOR CHAPTER 5 FOLLOW

Average Reductions in U.S. Tariffs Rates, 1947 - 85

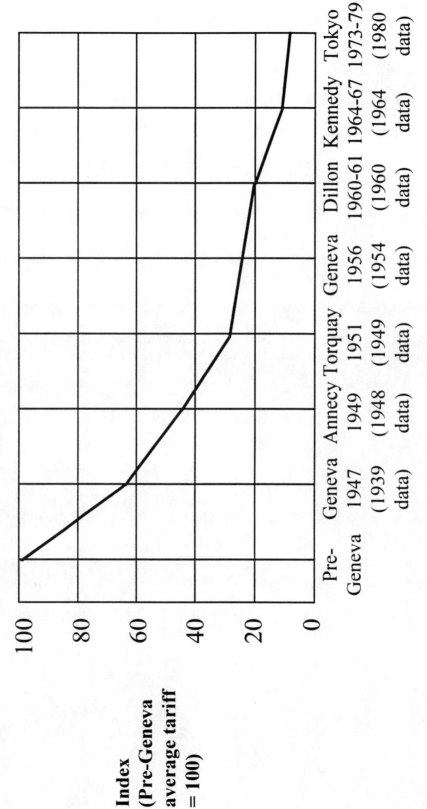

Index
(Pre-Geneva
average tariff
= 100)

| | Pre-Geneva | Geneva 1947 (1939 data) | Annecy 1949 (1948 data) | Torquay 1951 (1949 data) | Geneva 1956 (1954 data) | Dillon 1960-61 (1960 data) | Kennedy 1964-67 (1964 data) | Tokyo 1973-79 (1980 data) |

GATT Negotiation Rounds

Note: Indexes are calculated from percentage reductions in average weighted tariff rates given in Finger, 1979 (Table 1. p. 425), World Bank 1987 (Table 8.1, p. 136), and World Bank World Development Report, Oxford University Press, 1994. Weighted average U.S. tariff rate after Tokyo Round was 4.6 percent (World Bank, 1987).

Figure 5.1

CHAPTER 6: OVERVIEW AND TEACHING SUGGESTIONS

OUTLINE OF CHAPTER 6

OPENING CASE: ELECTROLUX INVESTS IN ASIA AND EASTERN EUROPE
INTRODUCTION
FOREIGN DIRECT INVESTMENT IN THE WORLD ECONOMY
    The Growth of FDI
    Changes in the Source of FDI
    Changes in the Recipients of FDI
    FDI by Medium Sized and Small Firms.
HORIZONTAL FOREIGN DIRECT INVESTMENT
    Transportation Costs
    Market Imperfections (Internalization Theory)
    Following Competitors
    The Product Life Cycle
    Location-Specific Advantages
VERTICAL FOREIGN DIRECT INVESTMENT
    Market Power
    Market Imperfections
IMPLICATIONS FOR BUSINESS
SUMMARY OF CHAPTER
CRITICAL DISCUSSION QUESTIONS
CLOSING CASE: HONDA IN NORTH AMERICA

OBJECTIVES OF CHAPTER 6

1. Describe the importance of foreign direct investment (FDI) in the world economy, and the changing patterns of FDI over time.

2. Present a number of different theories that attempt to explain *horizontal* FDI, and suggest the conditions under which each may be most applicable.

3. Present a number of different theories that attempt to explain *vertical* FDI, and suggest the conditions under which each may be most applicable.

4. Explain carefully the importance of market imperfections in understanding FDI, specifically as it pertains to the transfer of know-how and technological information.

5. Suggest the implications of these theories of FDI for the process of international expansion for business firms, particularly comparing licensing to FDI. A more detailed discussion of modes of entry is contained in Chapter 14.

LECTURE OUTLINE FOR CHAPTER 6

A.   Introduction

1   The focus of this chapter is foreign direct investment (FDI). FDI can take the form of a foreign
        firm buying a firm in a different country, or deciding to invest in a different country and build
        operations there.

2.   With FDI, a firm has a significant ownership in a foreign operation and the potential to affect
        managerial decisions of the operation.

3.   The goal of our coverage of FDI is to understand the pattern of FDI that occurs between
        countries, and why firms undertake FDI and become multinational in their operations.

4.   The opening case describes Electrolux's investments outside Sweden, and the closing case
        described Honda's FDI in the US Besides the suggestions illustrated in the cases (e.g. growth
        opportunities, trade barriers, access to markets, localization), this chapter will describe some of
        the basic theories of FDI, and why firms undertake FDI rather than simply exporting products or
        licensing their know-how.

B.   Foreign Direct Investment in the World Economy

1.   When discussing foreign direct investment it is important to distinguish between the **flow of FDI**
        and the **stock of FDI**. The flow of FDI refers to the amount of FDI undertaken over a given time
        period (normally one year). The stock of FDI refers to the total accumulated value of foreign
        owned assets at a given point in time.

2.   Figure 6.1 illustrates how FDI flows have increased relative to world output and trade. Figure
        6.2 illustrates the great increase in the flows of FDI between 1981-93. It also shows how the
        portion of FDI from various countries changes over time. The significant growth in FDI has both
        to do with the political economy of trade as outlined in the previous chapter and the political and
        economic changes that have been taking place in developing countries.

3.   The opening case on Electrolux helps illustrate one very important trend in FDI - the
        globalization of the world economy is causing firms to invest world wide in order to assure their
        presence in every region of the world.

4.   Another important trend is has been the rise of inflows into the US. Table 6.2 shows how the
        stock of US FDI abroad and the stock of foreign FDI in the US changed from 1970-1994. Over
        this time not only did the total stock both inward and outward FDI increase substantially, but the
        stock of foreign FDI in the US increased more rapidly than US FDI abroad.

5.   A wide spread perception is that the majority of FDI inflows into the US during the 1980s and
        early 1990s were undertaken by Japanese corporations intent on buying up America's industrial
        base. In reality the British and the Dutch were actually the major investors.

6.   The rapid increase in FDI growth into the US may be due to the attractiveness of the US market,
        the falling value of the dollar, and a belief by some foreign corporations that they could manage
        US assets and workers more efficiently than their American managers.

7.   It is difficult to say whether the increase in the FDI into the US is good for the country or not. To the extent that foreigners are making more productive use of US assets and workers, it is probably good for the country.

8.   FDI is not just undertaken by large firms. The globalization of world markets has been accompanied by the rapid growth of FDI by small and medium sized firms.

C.   Horizontal Foreign Direct Investment

1.   Horizontal FDI is FDI in the same industry abroad as a firm operates in at home. FDI would seem to be more expensive and risky than exporting or licensing, so there must be some other good reasons for firms to undertake FDI.

2.   Transportation costs can make export infeasible, especially for products that have a low value/weight ratio (i.e. cement, soft drinks), or would require refrigeration or similar controlled environments. For items like electronics, software, medical equipment, transportation costs may not be an impediment to exporting.

3.   The most accepted reason for horizontal FDI relates to market imperfections. By imposing quotas, tariffs, or impediments, governments can make FDI and licensing more attractive than exporting.

4.   Technological or managerial know-how can be difficult and dangerous to license, however, making it an infeasible alternative. A firm can lose control of critical competitive know-how, may not be able to optimize the flow and configuration of operations between countries, or simply may be unable to codify its knowledge in a way that would make licensing a practical option. Figure 6.4 illustrates the impediments to the sale of know-how.

5.   Firms may choose to undertake FDI simply to follow the lead of a competitor so as not be left behind or locked out of an opportunity.

6.   FDI may be most likely to occur in certain stages of a products lifecycle - when other countries have a large enough market to justify local production or when there is a need to locate production in a low cost location.

7.   A firm may choose to undertake FDI in a particular country or region due to location specific advantages. An obvious example occurs with respect to natural resources, but it also applies to the ability to tap into a particular expertise (e.g. silicon valley) or be located near customers or suppliers with unique characteristics. Porter's diamond, as discussed in chapter 4, provides a partial explanation why firms in certain industries may find it attractive to invest in a particular country.

D.   Vertical Foreign Direct Investment

1.   Backward vertical FDI involves investment into an industry that provides inputs for a firm's domestic production processes. Forward vertical FDI involves investment in an industry that utilizes the outputs of a firm's domestic production processes.

2.   The market power explanation for vertical FDI suggests that firms try to either create new entry barriers or erode competitors entry barriers. While there certainly are some examples where the market power explanation seems to apply, the market imperfections explanation seems to present a more complete explanation.

3.   Market imperfections can result from impediments to the sale of know-how and the need to invest in specialized assets.

4.   Because specialized know-how can be difficult to sell or license, a firm may have to vertically integrate to be successful. The establishment of sales and services centers in high technology industries, or the investment in knowledge intensive extractive processes are two examples.

5.   When specialized assets must be invested in (i.e. the aluminum smelter), securing a supply of the needed inputs may be required to assure that these assets can be used efficiently.

E.   Implications for Business

1.   The market imperfections theory suggests that exporting should be preferred to licensing and horizontal FDI as long as transport costs are minor and tariff barriers are trivial. If this is not the case, then licensing and FDI must be considered.

2.   FDI is more costly than licensing, but may be the most reasonable option. Figure 6.5 presents a decision tree suggesting when licensing, FDI, and exporting are most appropriate.

3.   Licensing tends not to be a good option in high technology industries where protecting firm specific know-how is critical, in industries where a firm must carefully coordinate and orchestrate its worldwide activities, or where there are intense cost pressures.

ANSWERS TO CRITICAL DISCUSSION QUESTIONS FOR CHAPTER 6

QUESTION 1: In recent years Japanese FDI in the United States has grown far more rapidly than US FDI in Japan. Why do you think this is the case? What are the implications of this trend?

ANSWER 1: There are two primary explanations for the inequity in the growth of FDI between the US and Japan. Firstly, there has been a significant decrease in the US dollar relative to the Japanese Yen. This makes investment in the US more attractive to Japanese investors, and Japanese investments less attractive to US investors. Secondly, the nature of business in Japan, where long term business relationships are important and investments can take a significant period of time to pay off, makes Japan a less attractive place to invest than the more open US economy. To the extent that the trend is simply a result of exchange rate changes, the trend will follow changes in exchange rates, and could reverse if the exchange rate change reverses direction. The implication of this is simply that the value of international investing between the US and Japan will be determined by the relative value of the currencies. To the extent that the trend is a result of structural differences in the economies of the US and Japan, it suggests that there will continue to be a disparity in the flows of FDI between the US and Japan. Hence Japanese companies will find it easier to compete in the US market against US competitors than US companies will be able to compete in Japan against Japanese competitors.

QUESTION 2: Compare these explanations of horizontal FDI; the market imperfections approach, Vernon's product life cycle theory, and Knickerbocker's theory of FDI? Which theory do you think offers the best explanation of the historical pattern of horizontal FDI? Why?

ANSWER 2: Knickerbocker's theory suggests that firms imitate other firms in oligopolistic industries, and will "follow the leader" in undertaking FDI in certain countries. This theory does not explain why the first firm undertakes FDI, and why it chooses to do this rather than export or license. The product life cycle theory suggests that firms invest in foreign countries when demand in that country will support local production or when cost pressures make it necessary to locate production in low cost locations. While this theory does explain why some FDI takes place, it also does not explain why FDI is preferred over licensing or exporting. The market imperfections approach more directly confronts these issues, and explains why FDI may be preferable to other alternatives for expanding business activities. It identifies the importance and difficulty of transferring know-how and describes some of the impediments to exporting. By explaining better exactly why a firm may undertake, the market imperfections model is probably the best explanation of the historical pattern of horizontal FDI.

QUESTION 3: Compare these explanations of vertical FDI: the market power approach and the market imperfections approach? Which theory do you think offers the best explanation of the historical pattern of vertical FDI? Why?

ANSWER 3: The market power explanation suggests that a firm undertakes FDI to either create barriers to entry or to overcome the entry barriers protecting other firms. Hence it focuses on concerns that are external to the firm, and that the firm wants to take into its control. The market imperfections looks more at factors internal to a firm - know-how and specialized assets - and the difficulties firms have in utilizing their capabilities most efficiently. Although there certainly are some cases where the market power explanation makes sense, a great deal of the modern day FDI appears to involve industries where there is a great deal of know-how and investment in specialized assets. Even firms that have had a great deal of market power (i.e. IBM and Xerox), have also had a significant levels of know-how that would be difficult to fully profit from without FDI.

QUESTION 4: You are the international manager of a US business that has just invented a revolutionary new personal computer that can perform the same functions as IBM and Apple computers and their clones, but costs only half as much to manufacture. Your CEO has asked you to decide how to expand into the Western European market. Your options are (i) export from the US, (ii) license a European firm to manufacture and market the computer in Europe, and (iii) set up a wholly owned subsidiary in Europe. Evaluate the pros and cons of each alternative and suggest a course of action to your CEO.

ANSWER 4: In considering expansion into Western Europe, three options will be considered: FDI, licensing, and export. With export, assuming there are no trade barriers, the key considerations would likely be transport costs and localization. While transport costs may be quite low for a relatively light and high value product like a computer, localization can present some difficulties. Power requirements, keyboards, and preferences in model all vary from country to country. It may be difficult to fully address these localization issues from the US, but not entirely infeasible. Since there are many computer manufacturers and distributors in Europe, there are likely to be a number of potential licensees. But by signing up licensees, valuable technological information may have to be disclosed, and the competitive advantage lost if the licensees use or disseminate this information. FDI (setting up a wholly owned subsidiary) is clearly the most costly and time consuming approach, but the one that best guarantees that critical knowledge will not be disseminated and that localization can be done effectively. Given the fast pace of change in the personal computer industry, it is difficult to say how long this revolutionary new computer will retain its competitive advantage. If the firm can protect its advantage for a period of time, FDI may pay off and help assure that no technological know-how is lost. If, however, other firms can copy or develop even superior products relatively easily, than licensing, while speeding up knowledge dissemination, may also allow the firm to get the quickest large scale entry into Europe and make as much as it can before the advantage is lost.

STUDENT EXERCISES AND PROJECTS FOR CHAPTER 6

- One exercise that works well with this chapter is to ask students to investigate a recent significant example of FDI. The decision by a European auto firm to set up assembly operations in the US (e.g. BMW), the acquisition of a major "local" firm by a foreign-based multinational, or the decision by a "local" multinational to purchase a firm in another country or build a new factory are all things that make headlines in the business pages. Students can be asked to find several published stories about an example of FDI. I typically prefer that they choose the example by whatever means they choose, and then find how different business publications have reported the story. Often there is a formal press release that states the official rationale, but journalists and investment analysts may often cite additional reasons for the investment. Ask the students to list all the reasons cited, and then compare these with the reasons listed in the text before giving their assessment of the important reasons for the FDI. This analysis can also be extended for chapter 7 by considering in more detail the political reasons for FDI.
- An interesting variant on the above is to ask students to investigate the ownership of a particular "local" firm that is really owned by a foreign firm. Examples include Burger King in the US (owned by Grand Metropolitan of the UK), Jaguar in the UK (owned by Ford of the US), Pripps in Sweden (owned by Orkla of Norway), etc. In many cases the foreign ownership may have taken control many years ago, yet the firm or firms are viewed as local by most residents. Ask students to explain the rationale for the original FDI and evaluate if the reasons would still be valid today if the firm were to consider making the decision now.

SUGGESTED READINGS FOR CHAPTER 6

The footnotes suggest some appropriate additional readings. The following may be of particular interest:

Caves, Richard E. 1982. Multinational enterprise and economic analysis. Cambridge, UK: Cambridge University Press.

Chandler, Alfred 1990. Scale and scope: The dynamics of industrial capitalism. Boston, MA: Belknap Press.

Dunning, John 1988. Explaining international production. London: Unwin Hyman

Dunning, John 1993. Multinational enterprises and the global economy. Wokingham, UK: Addison Wesley

TRANSPARENCY MASTERS FOR CHAPTER 6 FOLLOW

Inflows and Outflows of FDI, 1981–94
(Billions of Dollars)

Inward FDI

	1981–85 Annual Average	1986–90 Annual Average	1990	1991	1992	1993	1994
Developed countries	37	130	176	121	102	109	117
Developing countries	13	25	31	39	51	80	80

Outward FDI

	1981–85 Annual Average	1986–90 Annual Average	1990	1991	1992	1993	1994
Developed countries	47	163	222	185	174	181	192
Developing countries	1	6	10	7	10	12	12

1994 figures are estimates.
Sources: 1981–93 data from United Nations, World Investment Report, 1994; 1994 data from G. de Jonquieres, Rocky Road to Liberalization, "Financial Times, April 10, 1995, p. 15.

Table 6.1

The Growth of FDI, World Trade and World Output

World indices rebased

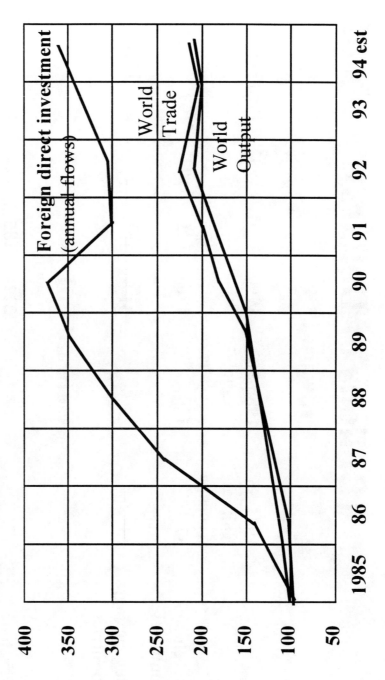

Source: Unctad.

Figure 6.1

Outflows of FDI from the Five Major Source Countries, 1981–93 (Billions of Dollars)

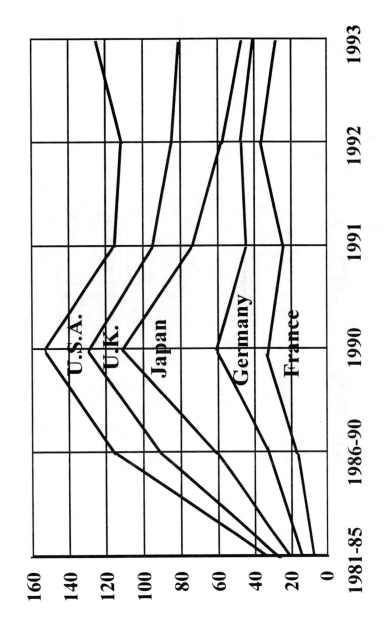

1981-85 and 1986-90 figures are annual averages.
Source: United Nations, World Investment Report, 1994

Figure 6.2

Impediments to the Sale of Know-how

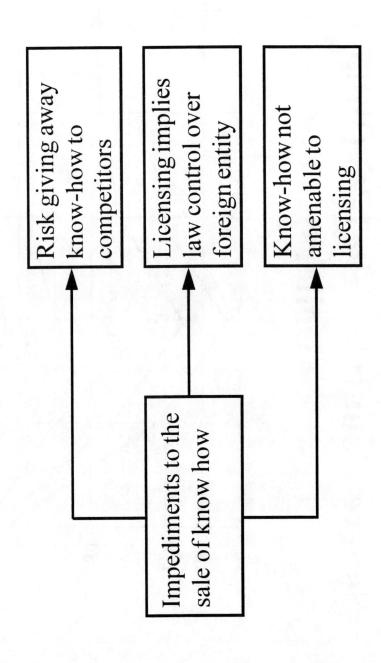

IRWIN © Times Mirror Higher Education Group Inc., Company 1997

Figure 6.4

A Decision Framework

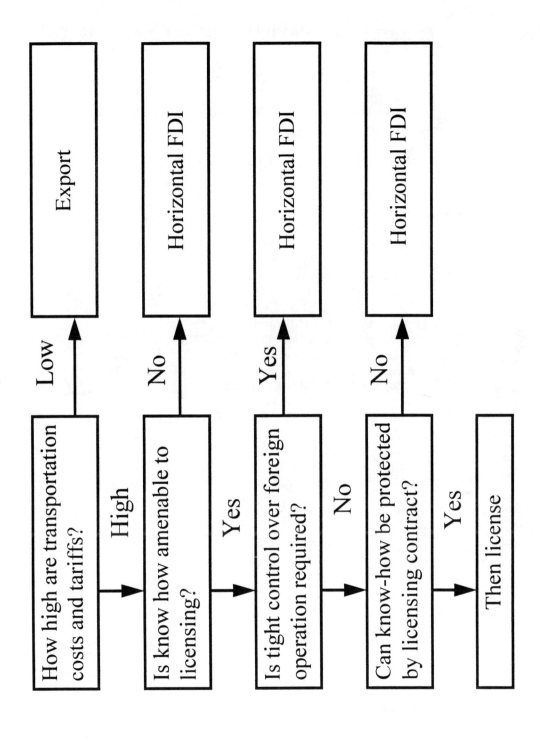

How high are transportation costs and tariffs? — Low → **Export**

High ↓

Is know how amenable to licensing? — No → **Horizontal FDI**

Yes ↓

Is tight control over foreign operation required? — Yes → **Horizontal FDI**

No ↓

Can know-how be protected by licensing contract? — No → **Horizontal FDI**

Yes ↓

Then license

Figure 6.5

CHAPTER 7: OVERVIEW AND TEACHING SUGGESTIONS

OBJECTIVES OF CHAPTER 7

1. Present the role governments play in restricting and encouraging flows of FDI.

2. Show how political philosophy affects the attitude of a government towards FDI.

3. Explain the sources of costs and benefits of FDI to host and home countries.

4. Describe the policy instruments available to governments interested in affecting FDI flows.

5. Discuss the negotiation and bargaining processes firms undertake with host governments.

LECTURE OUTLINE FOR CHAPTER 7

A.   Introduction

1   While the previous chapter focused on the economic rationale for FDI, the role of government was restricted to describing how trade barriers create market imperfections and decrease the feasibility of export. In this chapter we will look more directly at how host governments can encourage and restrict the flow of FDI.

2.   The opening case shows how the British and Japanese governments influenced Nissan's investment in Britain, and impacted the economics as well as the politics of FDI.

3.   Home country governments can also affect ability of firms to take resources out of the country for investment elsewhere.

4.   In addition to understanding the explicit rules laid out by home and host country governments, firms must evaluate their bargaining position and appropriate negotiating stances when the wish to alter established rules for FDI.

B.   Political Ideology and FDI

1.   The Radical/Marxist view of FDI suggested that FDI by MNEs from advanced capitalist nations keeps the less developed countries of the world relatively backward and dependent upon advanced capitalist nations for investment, jobs, and technology. According to this view, FDI is an instrument of economic domination - not economic development.

2.   The radical view was popular from WWII into the 1980s, and practiced in Eastern Europe, India, China, and many socialist third world countries.

3.   By the end of the 1980s the radical position was generally disregarded, due to the collapse of communism, the abysmal economic performance of most of the countries that practiced the radical approach, and the contrasting strong economic performance of those developing countries that had embraced a freer market approach (i.e. Singapore, Hong Kong, South Korea).

4.   The free market view sees the MNE as an instrument for dispersing the production and flow of goods and services in their most efficient manner. It is built on the philosophy of Smith and Ricardo, and supported by the market imperfections explanation of FDI.

5.   While the free market view is embraced by most advanced and developing nations, most all countries impose some restrictions on FDI.

6.   Most countries have adopted a policy of "pragmatic nationalism," which lies somewhere between the radical and free market views. (As depicted in Figure 7.1)

7.   The pragmatic approach suggests that governments should pursue policies designed to maximize the national benefits and minimize the national costs of FDI.

8.   Table 7.1 presents the key characteristics of the three major views and implications of these views for host government policies. The book presents examples of pragmatic policies in Japan and the EC.

C.   The Benefits of FDI to Host Countries

1.   From a free market view, the best policy would be for all countries to forebear from intervening in the investment decisions of MNEs. In their view the benefits are generally so much greater than the costs that pragmatic nationalism will likely end up creating many barriers in all countries, with the end result that all countries are worse off than they would be under a free market approach.

2.   Due to MNEs large size and access to international capital markets, they may have resources available to them that smaller nationally based firms do not, and be able to bring resources into a country that would not be brought in otherwise.

3.   Technology is critical to economic growth, and MNEs may bring product and process technology into a country. Hence not only the technology be valuable in itself, but it may spur economic growth and the development of new technological capabilities.

4.   FDI may bring in managerial skills, increase the productive use of a country's resources, and spill over into improving the management talent in other firms that come into contact with the MNE.

5.   FDI can lead to increased employment and the creation of new jobs. Critics point out, however, that the reported number of jobs created do not often take into account the loss of jobs that may have occurred in other firms or regions of a country.

6.   FDI can have a beneficial effect on a country's balance of payments by (i) the initial capital investment, (ii) substituting for imports that contribute to a current account deficit, and (iii) the current account surplus that results from exporting the products produced from a facility built with the initial FDI.

D.   The Costs of FDI to Host Countries

1.   MNEs operating in a particular country may have greater economic strength than domestic competitors, and may subsidize operations in a country in order to drive out domestic competitors.

2.   Countries may want to restrict FDI in industries they wish to protect until their own "infant" firms have the strength to compete against established MNEs.

3.   When MNEs repatriate profits from FDI, these outflows show up as debits to a capital account.

4.   If MNEs import a great deal of components for assembly into the products produced in a host country, it will have an unfavorable impact the trade or current account balance.

5.   Some countries may feel that their national sovereignty is threatened by foreign MNEs that make decisions that affect the country from distant locations.

E.   The Benefits and Costs of FDI to Home Countries

1.   The benefits of FDI to the home country include an improvement in the balance of payments as a result of the inward flow of foreign earnings, positive employment effects when the foreign subsidiary creates demands for home country exports, and benefits from a reverse resource transfer effect.

2.   The costs of FDI to the home country include adverse balance of payments effects that arise from the initial capital outflow, export substitution effects on the current account, and the potential loss of jobs to foreign operations. There is much political rhetoric in the US regarding lost jobs to Mexico by US firms that moved some assembly operations south of the border.

3.   Even when there are negative short term employment effects, in the long term these jobs would likely be lost in any case to foreign competitors. Moving production offshore can free up resources and people for other jobs where their value added is greater, and may prove a net benefit to consumers that now have access to less expensive products.

F.   Government Policy Instruments and FDI

1.   Home countries can encourage FDI by offering insurance, making funds available, pressuring host governments to remove barriers, and initiating tax incentives.

2.   Home countries can restrict FDI via explicit capital flow controls, punitive tax rules, or specific prohibitions for political concerns.

3.   Host countries are increasingly encouraging FDI by offering tax incentives, low interest rate loans, or outright grants and subsidies. Countries, and regions of countries, compete with each other for new plants and facilities.

4.   Host countries can restrict FDI by (i) imposing restraints on the ownership of domestic firms and assets and (ii) setting specific performance requirements relating to local content, export requirements, technology transfer, or local management participation.

G.   Implications for Business

1.   A host government's attitude to FDI is a critical issue when considering whether to invest in a particular country.

2.   There is both an art and a science to negotiating. Figure 7.2 identifies the four C's to be considered when negotiating.

3.   A number of the issues discussed in the chapter relate to the bargaining power of both the host government and the investing firm. Issues like the potential for technology transfer, effects on the balance of payments, and possibility of job creation (among others) all can change the relative bargaining power of both parties. Figure 7.3 summarizes some of the key determinates of a firm's bargaining position.

ANSWERS TO CRITICAL DISCUSSION QUESTIONS FOR CHAPTER 7

QUESTION 1: Explain how political ideology of a host government might influence the process of negotiating access between the host government and a foreign MNE.

ANSWER 1: If a host country subscribes to pure free market principles, then there is little to negotiate about. It may be possible, however, to negotiate with different regions of the country to obtain more favorable tax treatment or access to local resources. If a host country subscribes to pure radical views, there is also little to negotiate about since the government will likely prohibit any FDI. As a general rule, as the general nature of the ideology of a country moves from the left (radical) to the right (free market), the foreign MNE will need to spend less time negotiating matters relating to access and control and more time on matters relating to incentives and most favorable locations.

QUESTION 2: Under what circumstances is a MNE in a powerful negotiating position vis-à-vis a host government? What kind of concessions is a firm likely to win in such situations?

ANSWER 2: A MNE is in powerful negotiating position vis-à-vis a host government when it has a long time horizon, it has comparable alternatives, and when the value placed on its investment by the host government is high. A firm is likely to win concessions on future taxes, loan rates, profit repatriation, control of operations, and perhaps even the infrastructure surrounding a facility.

QUESTION 3: Under what circumstances is a MNE in a weak negotiating position vis-à-vis a host government? What kind of concessions is a host government likely to win in such situations?

ANSWER 3: A MNE is in a weak negotiating position vis-à-vis a host government when it has a short time horizon, has few comparable alternatives, and when the value placed on its investment by the host government is low. Host governments may be able to require relatively high levels of investment, technology transfer, local employment, future exports, and local management and ownership.

QUESTION 4: "Inward FDI is bad for the US economy and should be subjected to stricter controls." Discuss.

ANSWER 4: Advocates of this perspective generally believe that inward FDI can have adverse effects on competition, existing jobs, balance of payments, and/or national sovereignty. They believe that in many cases inward FDI is injurious to the interests of the US and should be carefully scrutinized and restricted. This perspective ignores, or at least finds unappealing, the view that FDI can supply the US economy with new jobs, technology, managerial resources, and improve the balance of payments. Proponents of the view quoted would have a tough time arguing how FDI in the auto industry in the US has overall been injurious to US consumers, the US auto industry as a whole (including suppliers), and the US economy overall.

QUESTION 5: "US firms should not be investing abroad when there is a need for investment to create jobs at home." Discuss.

ANSWER 5: While there may be a need for investment and job creation in the US, investors need to have the capability to adequately manage their investments. Hence some US firm may be much more able to exploit their technological advantages and invest internationally than they would be able benefit from domestic investment. If firm's primary goal is to maximize their shareholder's value, then they and probably the economy are better off if they invest where they can earn the best return. If firms from other countries have capabilities for which US workers and assets are most appropriate, then it is better that they make the investments in the US and use these resources to their best use rather than having US firms use these resource sub-optimally.

STUDENT EXERCISES AND PROJECTS FOR CHAPTER 7

- Students can be asked to extend the exercise outlined in the previous chapter and investigate the role incentives offered or restrictions imposed by governments impacted a recent significant example of FDI. Please refer to the exercise as outlined in the previous chapter for more details.
- Students could alternatively be asked to look in more detail at the bidding war that may have gone on when different countries, or regions of a country, sought to attract a particular investor. In many big FDI cases (e.g. auto assembly plants, semiconductor fabrication plants), firms simultaneously negotiate with different locations to try and strike the best deal. Since these deals require local governmental approval, the terms offered are frequently made public in the business press. Students can be asked to evaluate the different proposals, and try to understand not only why the firm selected a particular location (say France over Germany in the case of EuroDisney), but why other locations chose not to make their proposal more attractive (i.e. what political constraints exist on governments regarding levels of incentives).

SUGGESTED READINGS FOR CHAPTER 7

The footnotes suggest some appropriate additional readings. The following may be of particular interest:

Behrman, J. and R.E. Grosse 1990. International business and government: Issues and institutions. Columbia, SC: University of South Carolina Press.

Fayerweather, J. and A Kapoor 1976. Strategy and negotiation for the international corporation. Cambridge, MA: Ballinger.

Hood, Stephen and Neil Hood 1979. The economics of the multinational enterprise. London: Longman.

Krugman, Paul 1990. The age of diminished expectations. Cambridge, MA: MIT Press.

Reich, Robert B. 1991. The work of nations. New York: Alfred Knopf.

TRANSPARENCY MASTERS FOR CHAPTER 7 FOLLOW

The Spectrum of Political Ideology Toward FDI

Radical view	Pragmatic nationalism	Free market

Figure 7.1

Political Ideology Towards FDI

Ideology	Characteristics	Host-Government Policy Implications
Radical	Marxist roots Views the MNE as an instrument of imperialist domination	Prohibit FDI Nationalize subsidiaries of foreign-owned MNEs
Free market	Classical economic roots (Smith) Views the MNE as an instrument for allocating production to most efficient locations	No restrictions on FDI
Pragmatic nationalism	Views FDI as having both benefits and costs	Restrict FDI where costs outweigh benefits Bargain for greater benefits and fewer costs Aggressively court beneficial FDI by offering incentives

IRWIN © Times Mirror Higher Education Group Inc., Company 1997

Table 7.1

The Context of Negotiation —
The Four Cs

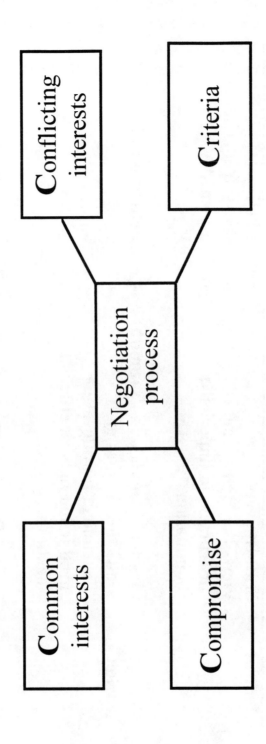

IRWIN © Times Mirror Higher Education Group Inc., Company 1997

Figure 7.2

CHAPTER 8: OVERVIEW AND TEACHING SUGGESTIONS

OUTLINE OF CHAPTER 8

OBJECTIVES OF CHAPTER 8

1. Explore the economic and political debate surrounding regional economic integration.

2. Review the progress towards regional integration in Europe, the Americas, and elsewhere.

3. Describe the implications of regional integration for businesses.

LECTURE OUTLINE FOR CHAPTER 8

A.   Introduction

1   The previous chapters presented the case for the free movement of goods and capital. While there have been decreases in the global barriers to trade and investment, the greatest progress had been made on a regional basis.

2.   An example from the current popular press on the EU (or NAFTA) and the effects the EU (or NAFTA) has had on a particular business or industry would help illustrate the point. The closing case on Martin's textiles is one example. The Martin's case shows the issue from the perspective of one manufacturer and his employees, but as consumers of a product used every day (underwear), most Americans will probably welcome the lower prices that NAFTA may bring.

3.   Perhaps the best example of the benefits of economic integration and political union is the USA. Before the current constitution was written, the 13 colonies had erected significant barriers to trade between each other and had separate currencies. Seeing that this was not working well, and wanting a better system for their citizens, the founding fathers agreed to combine their separate states into a "United States".

4.   The notion of regional economic integration is becoming increasingly important as countries strive to work together better and become more productive. While this takes place at a much broader level under the WTO, local regions with fewer countries to argue amongst have the ability to make much greater strides.

5.   Integration creates both winners and losers, however, as the opening case illustrates. An important challenge facing many firms and governments is what should be done to minimize the costs of transition to freer markets regionally as well as internationally.

B.   Levels of Economic Integration

1.   Free Trade Area: All barriers to trade among members are removed, but each member can determine its own trade policies with non-members.

2.   Customs Union: All barriers to trade among members are removed and a common external trade policy is adopted.

3.   Common Market: All barriers to trade among members are removed, a common external trade policy is adopted, and factors of production are allowed mobility between countries.

4.   Economic Union: All barriers to trade among members are removed, a common external trade policy is adopted, factors of production are allowed mobility between countries, a common currency is established, tax rates are harmonized, and a common monetary and fiscal policy is established.

5.   Political Union: Separate nations are essentially combined to form a single nation.

6.   Figure 8.1 diagrams the increasing levels of integration.

C.   The Case for Regional Integration

1.   The economic case for integration has been largely presented in the previous chapters. Free trade and movement of goods, services, capital, and factors of production allows for the most efficient use of resources. This is positive sum game, as all countries can benefit.

2.   Regional economic integration is an attempt to go beyond the limitations of GATT. While it is hard for 100 countries to agree on something, only a few countries with close proximity and common interests are much more likely to be able to agree to even fewer restrictions on the flows between their countries.

3.   The political case for integration has two main points: (i) by linking countries together, making them more dependent on each other, and forming a structure where they regularly have to interact, the likelihood of violent conflict and war will decrease. (ii) by linking countries together, they have greater clout and are politically much stronger in dealing with other nations.

4.   In the case of the EU, both a desire to decrease the likelihood of another world war and an interest in being strong enough to stand up to the US and USSR were factors in its creation.

5.   There are two main impediments to integration: (i) there are always painful adjustments, and groups that are likely to be directly hurt by integration will lobby hard to prevent losses, (ii) concerns about loss of sovereignty and control over domestic interests. Canada has always been concerned about being dominated by its southern neighbor, and Britain is very hesitant to give much control to European bureaucrats.

D.   The Case Against Regional Integration

1.   The case for integration is not accepted by many groups within a country, especially those that are likely to be hurt or those that feel that sovereignty and individual discretion will be reduced. Thus it is not surprising that most attempts to achieve integration have progressed slowly, and with hesitation.

2.   Whether regional integration is in the economic interests of the participants depends upon the extent of **trade creation** as opposed to **trade diversion**. Trade creation occurs when high cost domestic producers are replaced by low cost producers within the free trade area. Trade diversion occurs when lower cost external suppliers are replaced by higher cost suppliers within the free trade area. A regional free trade agreement will only make the world better off if the amount of trade it creates exceeds the amount it diverts.

E.   Regional Economic Integration in Europe

1.   Map 8.1 identifies the member countries of the EU, and by exception, the members of EFTA. The EU is larger economically and politically, as well as having more members and having a closer degree of integration.

2.   The forerunner of the EU was the European Coal and Steel Community, which had the goal of removing barriers to trade in coal, iron, steel, and scrap metal formed in 1951. The EEC was formed in 1957 by the Treaty of Rome. While the original goal was for a common market, progress was generally very slow.

3.   Over the years the EU expanded in spurts, as well as moved towards ever greater integration.

4.   Many countries that are now members of the EU were initially members of EFTA who either felt that the EU was pushing for too much integration too fast, or were denied entry by other member states. Norway, while always a member of EFTA, has twice had its citizens vote down membership in the EU because they felt they would lose too much control to their much bigger neighbors to the south.

5.   The economic policies of the EU are formulated and implemented by a complex and still evolving political structure. The five main institutions are the European Council, the Council of Ministers, the European Commission, the European Parliament, and the Court of Justice. These are described in some detail in the book, but I have generally not felt that it was important to lecture on these administrative topics.

6.   The problems with lack of progress on the objectives of the EU resulted in a number of problems for firms and governments, and led to adoption of the Single European Act in 1987. The Single European Act called for the removal of border controls, mutual recognition of standards, open public procurement, a barrier free financial services industry, no currency exchange controls, free and open freight transport, and freer and more open competition.

7.   The Treaty of Maastricht took the EU one step further, by specially spelling out the steps to economic union and partial political union. In addition to simply spelling out the steps needed, the Treaty also laid out the future outlines of a common foreign policy, economic policy, defense policy, citizenship, and currency, as well as strengthened the role of the European Parliament. The single currency will eliminate exchange costs and reduce risk, making EC firms more efficient.

8.   How well the Treaty of Maastricht will work over time is yet to be determined. Both the British and the Danish have the option to not join in monetary union, and the absolute failure of the EU to effectively agree on a common defense and foreign policy with respect to the area formerly known as Yugoslavia underscores the difficulty in bringing together countries with such differing perspectives and histories.

9.   Future enlargement of the EU is also a concern. While the current EFTA members seem in no hurry to join, Eastern European countries are generally quite eager. Given the even more profound differences in income, development, and systems, however, makes near term integration of these countries into the EU unlikely.

10.   Many firms and countries (including the EFTA countries) are concerned that the EU will result in a "fortress Europe," where insiders will be given preferential treatment over outsiders. This clearly already exists in agriculture, although whether it will be extended to other areas is a matter of debate.

F.   Regional Economic Integration in the Americas

1.   Map 8.2 shows the primary areas of integration in the Americas.

2.   In 1988 the US and Canada agreed to form a free trade area, with the goal of gradually eliminating all barriers to the trade of goods and services between the countries. In 1991 an agreement was signed between the US, Canada, and Mexico aimed at forming a free trade area between all three countries. In all three countries the political and economic consequences of the agreement are still being felt, and politicians in all countries are able to strike a cord with workers who perceive that they lost their jobs as a result of the agreement.

3. Proponents of NAFTA argue that it will provide economic gains to all countries: Mexico will benefit from increased jobs as low cost production moves south, and will attain more rapid economic growth as a result. The US and Canada will benefit from the access to a large and increasingly prosperous market and from the lower prices for consumers from goods produced in Mexico. In addition, US and Canadian firms with production sites in Mexico will be more competitive on world markets.

4. Opponents of NAFTA argue that jobs will be lost and wage levels will decline in the US and Canada, Mexican workers will emigrate north, pollution will increase due to Mexico's more lax standards, and Mexico will lose its sovereignty.

5. Since NAFTA is an ongoing issue and process as of this writing, and as it likely will be for the next 10 years, some recent articles out of the popular press will likely be available to help illustrate the opportunities and concerns.

6. The Andean Pact, originally formed in 1969, and reformed and renegotiated several times, has made little progress to due political and economic turmoil in most of the countries. The countries are making another strong attempt again currently, and their initial progress on removing trade barriers is promising. But the tremendous differences between the countries will make agreement on many issues difficult.

7. MERCOSUR and the Central American Agreement have also had little impact, although it is positive that the countries at least have a forum to discuss regional economic issues. With a total population of over 200 million, MERCOSUR has the potential for significant economic clout.

G. Regional Economic Integration Elsewhere

1. While there was clearly economic integration with COMECON, the "agreement" between the USSR and most of Eastern Europe, it had little rational economic basis and has collapsed with the collapse of the central planning system.

2. The ASEAN pact has had little impact on trade and integration, although most of the countries have grown very quickly. APEC is a broader Pacific organization that meets yearly and includes the US, Japan, China, and 15 other countries as shown in Map 8.3. Thus far the goals of APEC and the photo opportunities for the leaders have been far more lofty than the success.

H. Implications for Business

1. Economic integration creates a number of significant opportunities for business. Larger markets can now be served, additional countries open to trade, and greater economies of scale achieved.

2. The greatest implication for MNEs is that the free movement of goods across borders, the harmonization of product standards, and the simplification of tax regimes, makes it possible for them to realize potentially enormous cost economies by centralizing production in those locations where the mix of factor costs and skills is optimal. By specialization and shipping of goods between locations, a much more efficient web of operations can be created.

3. The lowering of barriers to trade and investment between countries will be followed by increased price competition, requiring firms to rationalize production and reduce costs if they are to remain competitive.

4.   As other firms become more competitive in their home markets (now expanded), they may be able to enter additional markets and threaten local firms' positions.

5.   Firms also must be concerned that they may be "locked out" of "fortress Europe" or "fortress North America", and thus may need to establish operations with a region if they are to remain an active player in the market.

ANSWERS TO CRITICAL DISCUSSION QUESTIONS FOR CHAPTER 8

QUESTION 1: "NAFTA is likely to produce net benefits for the US economy." Discuss?

ANSWER 1: Proponents of NAFTA would agree, stating that the opening of the large and increasingly prosperous Mexican market will stimulate exports from the US, and thus jobs in the US It will also benefit US consumers by making lower priced products available. While the opponents wouldn't disagree with these contentions, they argue the job loss, income redistribution, environmental damage will more than offset the benefits.

QUESTION 2: What are the economic and political arguments for regional economic integration? Given these arguments, why don't we see more integration in the world economy?

ANSWER 2: The economic argument for regional integration proposes that free trade and movement of goods, services, capital, and factors of production allows for the most efficient use of resources. This is positive sum game, as all countries can benefit. The political argument has two main points: (i) by linking countries together, making them more dependent on each other, and forming a structure where they regularly have to interact, the likelihood of violent conflict and war will decrease, and (ii) by linking countries together, they have greater clout and are politically much stronger in dealing with other nations. These arguments for integration are not accepted by many groups within countries, especially those that are likely to be directly hurt or those that feel that their sovereignty and individual discretion will be reduced. Thus it is not surprising that most attempts to achieve integration have progressed slowly, and that there is not more integration in the world economy.

QUESTION 3: What is the likely effect of creation of a single market within the EU likely to be on competition within the EU? Why?

ANSWER 3: Competition within the EU is likely to be increased as a result of the single market. By lowering barriers to the flow of goods, services, capital, and labor firms will be better able to compete across borders than before. Thus not only will, for example, French firms begin competing with German firms in industries where they had not previously been competing, but Italian firms will also be more able to enter both the German and French markets. Additionally, competitors from outside the EU may find it now feasible to enter the markets in EU countries, due to the greater economies of scale attainable.

QUESTION 4: How should a US business firm that currently only exports to Western Europe respond to the creation of a single market?

ANSWER 4: A US business firm that is currently only exporting to Western Europe should seriously consider opening a facility somewhere in Western Europe, as the economics of a common market suggest that outsiders can be at a disadvantage to insiders. The opening of borders within Western Europe also has the potential to increase the size of the market for the firm. Of course it is possible, after careful consideration, that exporting may still be the most appropriate means of serving the market in many situations.

QUESTION 5: How should a firm that has self-sufficient production facilities to in several EU countries respond to the creation of a single market? What are the constraints on its ability to respond in a manner that minimizes production costs?

ANSWER 5: The creation of the single market means that it may no longer be efficient to operate separate duplicative production facilities in each country. Instead, the facilities should either be linked so that each specializes in the production of only certain items (as it was described that 3M has done), or several sites should be closed down and production consolidated into the most efficient locations. Existing differences between countries as well as the need to be located near important customers may limit a firm's ability to fully consolidate or relocate production facilities for production cost reasons. Minimizing production costs are only one of many objectives of firms, as location of production near R&D facilities can be critical for new product development and future economic success. Thus what is most important in location decisions is long run economic success, not just cost minimization.

STUDENT EXERCISES AND PROJECTS FOR CHAPTER 8

- If this course is being taught in a country that has some sort of regional economic agreement with its neighbors, asking students to undertake some project related to the benefits of regional economic integration makes sense. If it can also be tied to a local firm, that is even better. For example, if taught in Gothenburg Sweden, students can be asked to assess the effects of joining the EU on a Volvo. The assignment can suggest that students look at the entire value chain of the firm, and assess where regional economic integration helps the firm become more competitive.
- An alternative is to focus on a local firm, and its reaction to regional economic integration elsewhere. Students in Japan, for example, could be asked to assess how the creation of NAFTA has affected the location, investment, and marketing decisions of a firm like Sony in North America.

SUGGESTED READINGS FOR CHAPTER 8

The footnotes suggest some appropriate additional readings. The following may be of particular interest:

Cantwell, John 1992. Multinational investment in modern europe. Aldershot, UK: Edward Elgar.

Colchester, Nicholas and David Buchan 1990. Europower. New York: Random House.

Swann, D. 1990. The economics of the common market. London: Penguin Books.

World Trade Organization 1995. Regionalism and the world trading system. Geneva: World Trade Organization.

TRANSPARENCY MASTERS FOR CHAPTER 8 FOLLOW

Levels of Economic Integration

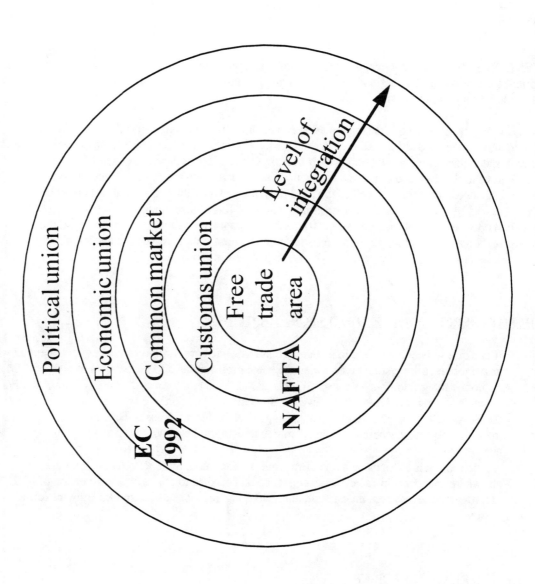

Political union

Economic union

Common market

Customs union

Free trade area

EC 1992

NAFTA

Level of integration

Figure 8.1

The European Union

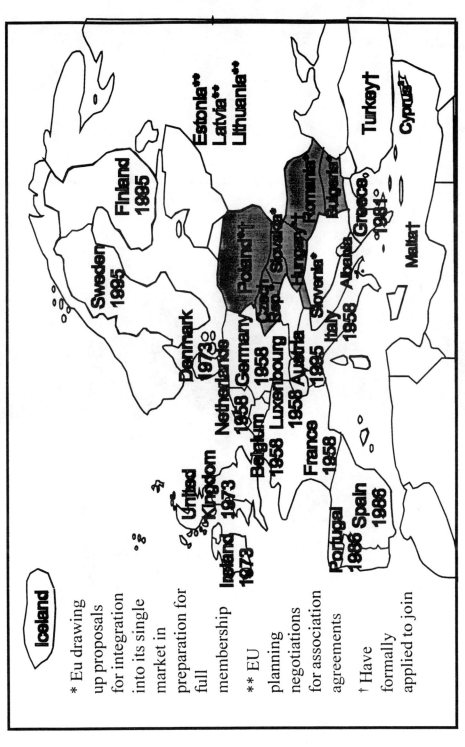

Map showing:
- Iceland
- Sweden 1995
- Finland 1995
- Estonia**, Latvia**, Lithuania**
- Denmark 1973
- United Kingdom 1973
- Ireland 1973
- Netherlands 1958
- Germany 1958
- Belgium 1958
- Luxembourg 1958
- Austria 1995
- France 1958
- Poland†
- Czech Rep.*
- Slovakia*
- Hungary*
- Romania†
- Bulgaria
- Slovenia*
- Italy 1958
- Albania
- Greece 1981
- Portugal 1986
- Spain 1986
- Malta†
- Turkey†
- Cyprus†
- Greece 1981

* Eu drawing up proposals for integration into its single market in preparation for full membership

** EU planning negotiations for association agreements

† Have formally applied to join

IRWIN © Times Mirror Higher Education Group Inc., Company 1997

 Past and present members in the European Union (with joining date)

 Potential members of the European Union towards the next century

☐ Other potential members of the European union

Map 8.1

Economic Integration in the Americas

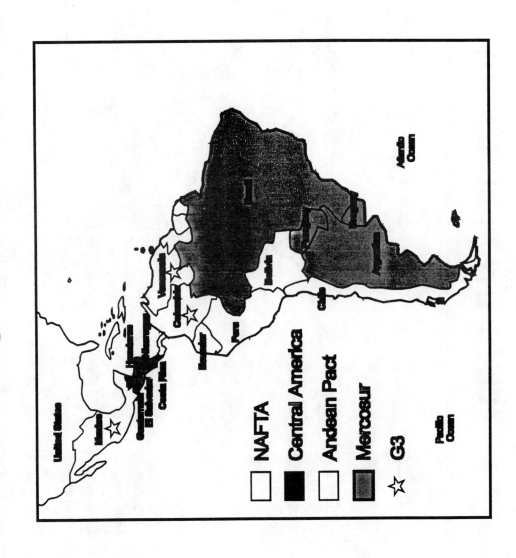

Map 8.2

Asia Pacific Economic Cooperation

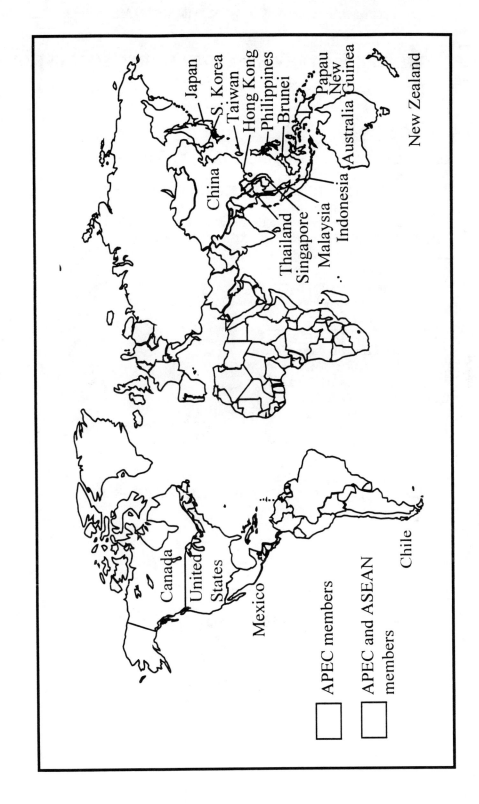

Japan
S. Korea
Taiwan
Hong Kong
Philippines
Brunei
Papau New
Australia Guinea

New Zealand

China

Thailand
Singapore

Malaysia
Indonesia

Canada
United
States

Mexico

APEC members

APEC and ASEAN
members

Chile

IRWIN © Times Mirror Higher Education Group Inc., Company 1997

Map 8.3

CHAPTER 9: OVERVIEW AND TEACHING SUGGESTIONS

OBJECTIVES OF CHAPTER 9

1.   Explain how the foreign exchange market works

2.   Explore the forces that determine exchange rates

3.   Discuss the degree to which future exchange rates can be predicted

4.   Map out the implications for international businesses of exchange rate movements and the foreign exchange market

LECTURE OUTLINE FOR CHAPTER 9

A.   Introduction

1   Different countries have different currencies. If you have examples of different currencies, these can be shown or passed around.

2.   Tourists clearly need to change money when they travel between countries, although in some border towns merchants may accept currency from both countries.

3.   Exchange rates determine the value of one currency in terms of another. It can be illustrative to right at this point show some exchange rates by writing them down or using Table 9.1. Actually going through several currency conversions provides a basis for many of the following discussions.

4.   While dealing in multiple currencies is a requirement of doing business internationally, it also creates risks and significantly alters the attractiveness of different investments and deals over time. Firms can use the foreign exchange market to minimize the risk of adverse changes, but this can prevent them for benefiting from favorable changes.

5.   Depending upon the student group, the need to go into many details will vary considerably. When teaching this topic to a group of international MBA students in Europe, it was unnecessary to cover the basics - they knew from everyday life as they converted the price of food into their own currencies to assess value. I know of other students who were surprised that a McDonald's they visited on a road trip from the US to Canada for a hockey game didn't take US dollars.

6.   One thing I have done is to bring into class a paper bills of $100, 100 NOK, 100£, and 100 Pakistani rupees, and offer to buy a student's calculator. First I usually start with the rupees, and try to convince him or her that I have a great deal. If I experience some reluctance, I might next offer the Norwegian Kroner. Depending upon the calculator, I might offer the 100£ but ask for $70 back in change. Regardless I can usually cause a little confusion and get some people flustered, thinking that they might be passing up a really good deal and just don't know it.

B.   The Functions of the Foreign Exchange Market

1.   The foreign exchange market serves two functions: converting currencies and reducing risk. There are four major reasons firms need to convert currencies.

2.   First, the payments firms receive from exports, foreign investments, foreign profits, or licensing agreements may all be in a foreign currency. In order to use these funds in its home country, an international firm has to convert funds from foreign to domestic currencies.

3.   Second, a firm may purchase supplies from firms in foreign countries, and pay these suppliers in their domestic currency.

4.   Third, a firm may want to invest in a different country from that in which it currently holds under-used funds.

5.   Fourth, a firm may want to speculate on exchange rate movements, and earn profits on the changes it expects. If it expects a foreign currency to **appreciate** relative to its domestic currency, it will convert its domestic funds into the foreign currency. Alternately stated, it expects its domestic currency to **depreciate** relative to the foreign currency. An example similar

to the one in the book can help illustrate how money can be made (or lost) on exchange rate speculation. The management focus on George Soros shows how one fund has benefited from currency speculation.

6.   Exchange rates change on a daily basis. The price at any given time is called the spot rate, and is the rate for currency exchanges at that particular time.

7.   The fact that exchange rates can change on a daily basis depending upon the relative supply and demand for different currencies increases the risks for firms entering into contracts where they must be paid or pay in a foreign currency at some time in the future.

8.   Forward exchange rates allow a firm to lock in a future exchange rate for the time when it needs to convert currencies. Forward exchange occurs when two parties agree to exchange currency and execute a deal at some specific date in the future. The book presents an example of a laptop computer purchase where using the forward market helps assure the firm that will won't lose money on what it feels is a good deal. It can be good to point out that from a firms perspective, while it can set prices and agree to pay certain costs, and can reasonably plan to earn a profit, it has virtually no control over the exchange rate. When spot exchange rate changes entirely wipe out the profits on what appear to be profitable deals, the firm has no recourse.

9.   Table 9.1 shows 30, 90, 180 day forward exchange rates for several of the major currencies. When a currency is worth less with the forward rate than it is with the spot rate, it is selling at **forward discount**. Likewise, when a currency is worth more in the future than it is on the spot market, it is said to be selling at a **forward premium**, and is hence expected to **appreciate**. These points can be illustrated with several of the currencies shown in Table 9.1.

10.   A currency swap is the simultaneous purchase and sale of a given amount of currency at two different dates and values. Figure 9.1 shows an indication of the relative importance of the different types of currency exchanges.

C.   The Nature of the Foreign Exchange Market

1.   The foreign exchange market is not a place, but a whole network of banks, brokers, and dealers that exchange currencies 24 hours/day. Figure 9.2 shows the relative size of the major international currency exchange centers.

2.   The exchange rates quoted world wide are basically the same. If different US dollar/French Franc rates were being offered in New York and Paris, there would be an opportunity for arbitrage and the gap would close. An illustrative example can be done, showing how someone could make money in arbitrage, and how this would affect the supply and demand for the currencies in both markets to close the gap.

3.   The US dollar frequently serves as a vehicle currency to ease the exchange of two other currencies.

4.   The actual mechanics of currency exchange are fairly simple, but some students seem to have difficulty with the basic algebra, not knowing when to multiply or divide by exchange rates. It is important to spend some time and make sure that they understand this. I often use the analogy of measurement, and say that currencies are just a matter of measuring the value of a good by different rulers or yardsticks. Hence converting US dollars to British Pounds is not any different from converting yards to meters, pounds to kilograms, or inches to feet. The questions in the test

bank have a number of examples that can be used directly or slightly modified to show how currency conversion works.

D.   Economic Theories of Exchange Rate Determination

1.   While at the most basic level exchange rates are determined by the supply and demand for different currencies. What affects the supply and demand is the focus of this section.

2.   The Law of One Price states that in competitive markets free of transportation costs and trade barriers, identical products sold in different countries must sell for the same price (when their price is expressed in terms of the same currency. An example can be illustrative, like the one on jackets in the book. The Purchasing Power Parity (PPP) exchange rate shows what the exchange rate would be if the law of one price held. Every April the Economist magazine prints the implied PPP and real exchange rate based on McDonalds Big Mac - a product that is virtually identical across a number of locations worldwide but priced in local currencies.

3.   To express the PPP theory in symbols, let $P_\$$ be the US dollar price of a basket of goods and P_{DM} be the price of the same basket of goods in German marks. The PPP theory predicts that the dollar/DM exchange rate should be equivalent to:

$$\$/DM \text{ Exchange Rate} = P_{DM}/P_\$$$

Thus if a basket of goods costs \$200 in the United States, and the same basket costs DM600 in Germany, PPP theory predicts that the dollar/DM exchange rate should be \$0.33 per DM (i.e. \$1=DM3).

4.   The exchange rate will change if **relative** prices change. For example, assume there is no price inflation in the US, while prices in Germany are increasing by 20% a year. At the beginning of the year a basket of goods costs \$200 in the US and DM600 in Germany, so the dollar/DM exchange rate according to PPP theory should be \$0.33=DM1. At the end of the year the basket of goods still costs \$200 in the US, but now it costs DM720 in Germany. PPP theory predicts that the exchange rate should then be \$0.27=DM1 (i.e. \$1=DM3.6). Due to price inflation the DM has **depreciated** against the dollar.

5.   There is a positive relationship between the inflation rate and the level of the money supply. When the growth in the money supply is greater than the growth in output, inflation will occur. Figure 9.3 shows the relationship for several countries. The Country Focus illustrates the extreme case of this occurring in Bolivia.

6.   Simply put, PPP suggests that changes in relative prices between countries will lead to exchange rate changes. The empirical tests suggest that this relationship does hold in the long run, but not in the short run. While PPP assumes no transportation costs or barriers to trade and investment, it also assumes that governments do not intervene to affect their exchange rates - a topic for the next chapter.

7.   Interest rates also affect exchange rates. The Fisher effect says that the real interest rates should be the same in each, while the nominal rate will include both this real rate and expected inflation. The International Fisher effect states that for any two countries the spot exchange rate should change in an equal amount but in the opposite direction to the difference in nominal interest rates between two countries. Stated more formally:

$$(S_1 - S_2)/S_2 \times 100 = i^\$ - i^{DM}$$

where $i^\$$ and i^{DM} are the respective nominal interest rates in two countries (in this case the US and Germany), S_1 is the spot exchange rate at the beginning of the period and S_2 is the spot exchange rate at the end of the period.

8.   While interest rate differentials suggest future exchange rate changes, this appears to hold in the long run but not necessarily in the short run.

9.   Investor psychology and can also affect exchange rate movements. Expectations on the part of traders can turn into self-fulfilling prophecies, and traders can join the bandwagon and move exchange rate based on group expectations. While such changes can be important in explaining some short term exchange rate movements, they are very difficult to predict. At times governmental intervention can prevent the bandwagon from starting, but at other times it is ineffective and only encourages traders.

E.   Exchange Rate Forecasting

1.   The efficient market school argues that forward exchange rates are the best possible predictors of future spot rates, as they are impounding all information available in the market. Forward rates present an unbiased, yet inaccurate prediction.

2.   The inefficient market school argues that companies can improve upon the forward rate by investing in forecasting services.

3.   Forecasters that use fundamental analysis draw upon economic theories to predict future exchange rates, including factors like interest rates, monetary policy, inflation rates, or balance of payments information.

4.   Forecasters that use technical analysis typically chart trends, and believe that past trends and waves are reasonable predictors of future trends and waves.

F.   Currency Convertibility

1.   A currency is said to be **freely convertible** when the government of a country allows both residents and non-residents to purchase unlimited amounts of a foreign currency with the domestic currency. A currency is said to be **externally convertible** when non-residents can convert their holdings of domestic currency into a foreign currency, but when the ability of residents to convert currency is limited in some way. A currency is **not convertible** when both residents and non-residents are prohibited from converting their holdings of domestic currency into a foreign currency.

2.   Free convertibility is the norm in the world today, although many countries impose some restrictions on the amount of money that can be converted. The main reason to limit convertibility is to preserve foreign exchange reserves and prevent capital flight.

3.   Countertrade, where goods are exchanged for other goods, is one way firms can work around problems in currency convertibility. A recent example of countertrade can help illustrate the point.

G.   Implications for Business

1.   Adverse changes in exchange rates can make otherwise profitable deals unprofitable. Thus firms face risks anytime they work in multiple currencies.

2.   Forward exchanges and swaps allow firms to hedge, or insure themselves against exchange rate changes.

3.   It is important that international businesses understand the forces that determine exchange rates. If a company wants to know how the value of a particular currency will change over the long-term on the foreign exchange market, it should take a close look at those economic fundamentals that appear to predict long-run exchange rate movements - i.e. the growth in a country's money supply, its inflation rate, and nominal interest rates.

ANSWERS TO CRITICAL DISCUSSION QUESTIONS FOR CHAPTER 9

QUESTION 1: In Germany the interest rate on government securities with one year maturity is 4% and the expected inflation rate for the coming year is 2%. The US interest rate on government securities with one year maturity is 7% and the expected rate of inflation is 5%. The current spot exchange rate for German marks is $1=DM1.4. Forecast the spot exchange rate one year from today. Explain the logic of your answer.

ANSWER 1: From the Fisher effect, we know that the real interest rate in both the US and Germany is 2%. The international Fisher effect suggests that the exchange rate will change in an equal amount but opposite direction to the difference in nominal interest rates. Hence since the nominal interest rate is 3% higher in the US than in Germany, the dollar should depreciate by 3% relative to the German mark. Using the formula from the book: $(S_1 - S_2)/S_2 \times 100 = i^\$ - i^{DM}$ and substituting 7 for $i^\$$, 4 for i^{DM}, and 1.4 for S_1, yields a value for S_2 of $1=1.36DM.

QUESTION 2: Two countries, France and the US produce just one good - beef. Suppose that the price of beef in the US is $2.80 per pound, and in France it is FFr3.70 per pound.
   (a)   According to PPP theory, what should be the $/FFr spot exchange rate?
   (b)   Suppose that the price of beef is expected to rise to $3.10 in the US, and to FFr4.65 in France. What should be the one year forward $/FFr exchange rate?
   (c)   Given your answers to parts (a) and (b), and given that the current interest rate in the US is 10%, what would you expect current French interest rates to be?

ANSWER 2:
   (a)   According to PPP, the $/FFr rate should be 2.80/3.70, or .76$/FFr.
   (b)   According to PPP, the $/FFr one year forward exchange rate should be 3.10/4.65, or .67$/FFr.
   (c)   Since the dollar is appreciating relative to the franc, and given the relationship of the international fisher effect, the French must have higher interest rates than the US
          Using the formula $(S_1 - S_2)/S_2 \times 100 = i^F - i^\$$ we can solve the equation for i^F, with equal to .76, equal to .67, and equal to 10, yielding a value of 23.4% for the current French interest rates. (Note, since the currency is expressed in terms of $/FFr rather than FFr/$, $i^\$$ must be subtracted from i^F. If the exchange rates were expressed as

FFr/$, then the French interest rate would be subtracted from the US interest rate. The answer would be the same either way. The algebra can get confusing, thus it is important to understand the underlying logic of what the answer should be. If you come up with a negative interest rate or an interest rate that has the wrong relationship to other interest rate, you can recognize that something must be wrong and go back.)

QUESTION 3: You manufacture wine goblets. In mid June you receive an order for 10,000 goblets from Germany. Payment of DM400,000 is due in mid December. You expect the DM to rise from its present rate of $1=DM1.5 to $1=DM1.4 by December. You can borrow marks at 6% per annum. What should you do?

ANSWER 3: The simplest solution would be to just wait until December, take the DM400,000 and convert it at the spot rate at that time, which you assume will be 1.4DM/$. In this case you would have $286,000 in mid-December. If the current 180 day forward rate is lower than 1.4DM/$, then it would be preferable since it both locks in the rate at a better level and reduces risk. If the rate is above 1.4DM/$, then whether you choose to lock in the forward rate or wait and see what the spot does will depend upon your risk aversion. There is a third possibility also. You could borrow money from a German bank that you will pay back with the 400,000 DM you will receive (400,000/1.03 = 388,350DM borrowed), convert this today to US$ (388,350/1.5 = $258,900), and then invest these dollars in a US account. For this to be preferable to the simplest solution, you would have to be able to make a lot of interest (286,000 - 258,900 = $27, 100), which would turn out to be an annual rate of 20.9% ((27,100/258,900) * 2). If, however, you could lock in these interest rates, then this method would also reduce any exchange rate risk. What you should do depends upon the interest rates available, the forward rates available, how large a risk you are willing to take, and how certain you feel that the spot rate in December will be DM1.4 = $1.

STUDENT EXERCISES AND PROJECTS FOR CHAPTER 9

- An excellent classroom exercise is outlined in: Butler, Kirt C. and Chuck C.Y. Kwok. 1994. A Classroom exercise to Simulate the Foreign Exchange Market. Journal of Teaching in International Business. Volume 6, Number 2.
- One thing I have done is to bring into class a paper bills of $100, 100 NOK, 100£, and 100 Pakistani rupees, and offer to buy a student's calculator. First I usually start with the rupees, and try to convince him or her that I have a great deal. If I experience some reluctance, I might next offer the Norwegian Kroner. Depending upon the calculator, I might offer the 100£ but ask for $70 back in change. Regardless I can usually cause a little confusion and get some people flustered, thinking that they might be passing up a really good deal and just don't know it.

SUGGESTED READINGS FOR CHAPTER 9

The footnotes suggest some appropriate additional readings. The following may be of particular interest:

Krugman, Paul and M. Obstfeld 1994. International Economics: Theory and Policy. New York: Harper Collins.

TRANSPARENCY MASTERS FOR CHAPTER 9 FOLLOW

Foreign Exchange Transactions, April 1992

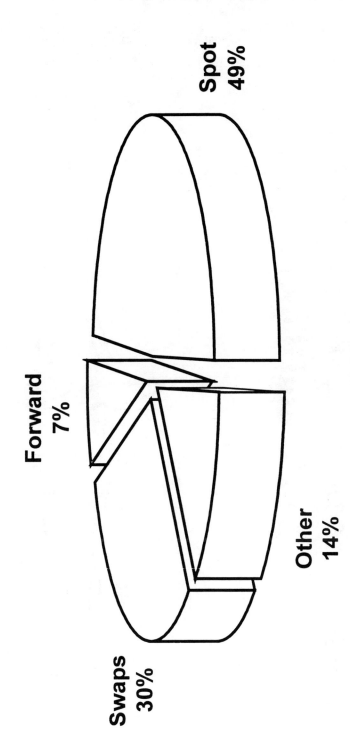

Spot 49%

Forward 7%

Other 14%

Swaps 30%

Source: Summary of Results of U.S. Foreign Exchange Market Survey, conducted April 1992 (New York: Federal Reserve Bank of New York, 1992).

Figure 9.1

Share of Global Foreign Exchange Trading Accounted for by London, New York, and Tokyo

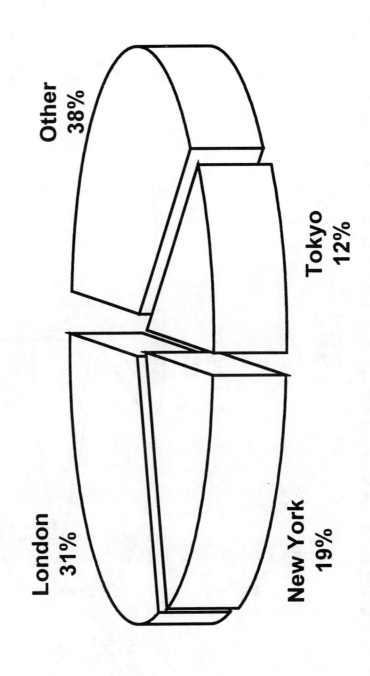

London
31%

New York
19%

Other
38%

Tokyo
12%

Source: Summary of Results of U.S. Foreign Exchange Market Survey, conducted April 1992 (New York: Federal Reserve Bank of New York, 1992).

Figure 9.2

Inflation and the Money Supply

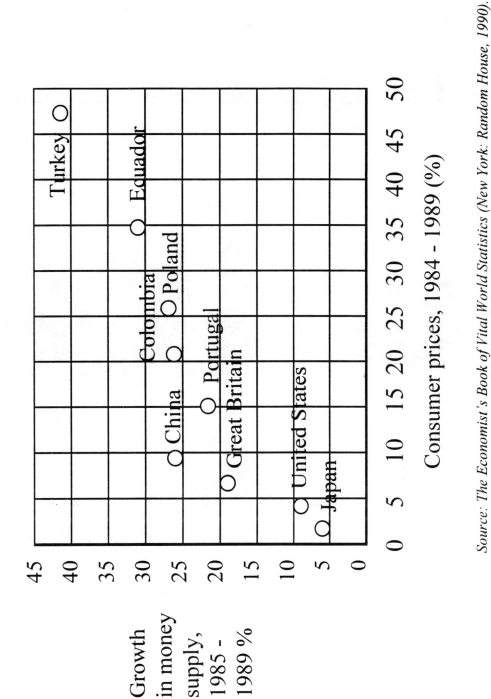

Source: The Economist's Book of Vital World Statistics (New York: Random House, 1990).

Figure 9.3

Exchange Rate Trends and Inflation Differentials, 1973 – 93

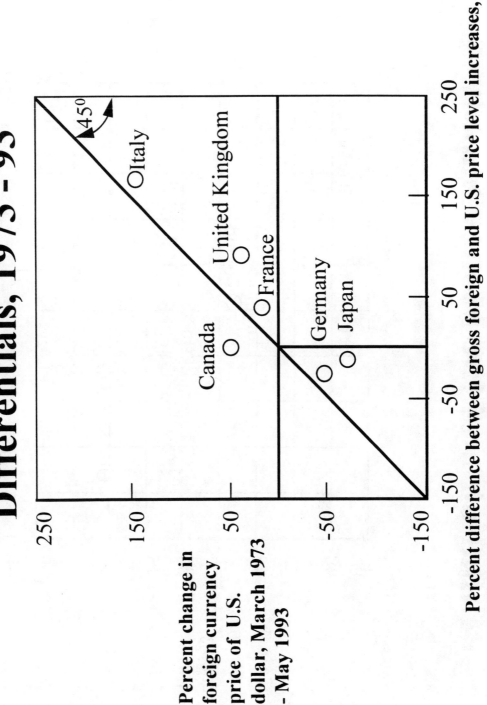

Percent change in foreign currency price of U.S. dollar, March 1973 - May 1993

Percent difference between gross foreign and U.S. price level increases, March 1973 - May 1993

Source: OECD, Main Economic Indicators.

Figure 9.4

CHAPTER 10: OVERVIEW AND TEACHING SUGGESTIONS

<u>OUTLINE OF CHAPTER 10</u>

OPENING CASE: THE TUMBLING PESO AND THE AUTO INDUSTRY
INTRODUCTION
THE GOLD STANDARD
       Nature of the Gold Standard
       The Strength of the Gold Standard
       The Period Between the Wars, 1918-1939
THE BRETTON WOODS SYSTEM
       The Role of the IMF
       The Role of the World Bank
THE COLLAPSE OF THE FIXED EXCHANGE RATE SYSTEM
THE FLOATING EXCHANGE RATE REGIME
       The Jamaica Agreement
       Exchange Rates Since 1973
FIXED VERSUS FLOATING EXCHANGE RATES
       The Case for Floating Exchange Rates
       The Case for Fixed Exchange Rates
       Who is Right?
THE EUROPEAN MONETARY SYSTEM
       The ecu and the ERM, 1979-92
       The Performance of the System, 1979-92
       The EMS after 1992
THE IMF AND WORLD BANK AFTER BRETTON WOODS
       The Third World Debt Crisis
       From the IMF Solution to the Brady Plan
       The Future of the IMF and the World Bank
IMPLICATIONS FOR BUSINESS
       Currency Management
       Business Strategy
       Corporate-Government Relations
SUMMARY OF CHAPTER
CRITICAL DISCUSSION QUESTIONS
CLOSING CASE: THE FALL AND RISE OF CATERPILLAR TRACTOR

<u>OBJECTIVES OF CHAPTER 10</u>

1.   Provide a history of the international monetary system, and describe different monetary systems.

2.   Explain how the international monetary system currently works, and thus how the real world may differ from that discussed in the previous chapter where all exchange rates were largely assumed to be flexible and based on supply and demand for different currencies.

3.   Explore the debate about the appropriateness of fixed and floating exchange rates.

4.   Suggest the implications of the current international monetary system for the practice of international Business

LECTURE OUTLINE FOR CHAPTER 10

A.   Introduction

1   The story of exchange rate determination presented in Chapter 9 was oversimplified - exchange rates are not free to move in the way we assumed. This chapter focuses on the institutional context within which exchange rates are free to and do move.

2.   Over the past 100 years the world has gone through eras with a gold standard, fixed exchange rates, and the current managed float system, with periods of high instability at several times.

3.   The opening case on the changes in the value of the Mexican peso shows how the competitive position of firms in the global market can change with changes in exchanges rates, and thus why firms have an incentive to lobby for maintaining some sort of predictability in exchange rates.

B.   The Gold Standard

1.   Under the gold standard, countries pegged their currency to gold by agreeing to exchange a particular quantity of money for an ounce or grain of gold. At one time, for example, the US government would agree to exchange one dollar for 23.22 grains of gold.

2.   The exchange rate between currencies was determined based on how much gold a unit of each currency would buy.

3.   The gold standard provides a powerful mechanism to pull trade imbalances between countries back into equilibrium - in fact this is one of the key reasons why some advocate returning to the gold standard.

4.   The gold standard worked fairly well until the inter-war years and the great depression. Trying to spur exports and domestic employment, a number of countries started regularly devaluing their currencies, with the end result that people lost confidence in the system and started to demand gold for their currency. This put pressure on countries' gold reserves, and forced them to suspend gold convertibility.

C.   The Bretton Woods System

1.   A key problem with the gold standard was that there was no multinational institution that could stop countries from engaging in competitive devaluations.

2.   The Bretton Woods system provided for two multinational institutions - the IMF and the World Bank.

3.   The US dollar was to be pegged and convertible to gold, and other currencies would set their exchange rates relative to the dollar. Devaluations were not to be used for competitive purposes, and a country could not devalue the currency by more than 10% without IMF approval.

4.   The fixed exchange rates were to force countries to have greater monetary discipline.

5.   The system also provided some flexibility, and could use short term funds from the IMF to help support currencies during temporary pressures for revaluation.

6.   The World Bank's (IBRD) major purpose was to provide funds to help in the reconstruction of Europe and the development of third world economies.

7.   The IBRD lends money at fairly generous interest rates, primarily for improvements in a country's infrastructure. During the 1960s the IBRD also lent money to support farming, education, population control, and urban development.

D.   The Collapse of the Fixed Exchange Rate System

1.   The fixed exchange rate system established in Bretton Woods collapsed mainly due to the economic management of the US Under Johnson, the US financed huge increases in welfare programs and the Vietnam war by increasing its money supply. Figure 10.1 shows presents key economic data for the US during this period.

2.   Speculation that the dollar would have to be devalued relative to most other currencies, as well as underlying economics and some forceful threats by the US forced other countries to increase the value of their currency relative to the dollar.

3.   The key problem with the Bretton Woods system was that it relied on an economically well managed US, since the dollar was the base currency. When the US began to print money, run high trade deficits, and experience high inflation, the system was strained to the breaking point.

E.   The Floating Exchange Rate Regime

1.   The Jamaica agreement called for floating exchange rates (although countries could intervene to smooth out speculative spurts), the end of gold as a reserve asset, and more funds in the IMF to help countries overcome short-term problems.

2.   Since 1973 exchange rates have been relatively volatile. Figure 10.2 shows movements in the US$ over the past two decades.

3.   The rise of the $ form 1980-5 is interesting, as this is a time where the underlying fundamentals discussed in Chapter 9 would have predicted that the $ should fall, not rise. The subsequent fall was both a result of governmental intervention and underlying market forces.

4.   The regularity of governmental intervention in the foreign exchange markets explains why the current system is sometimes referred to as a "managed" or "dirty" floating system.

F.   Fixed versus Floating Exchange Rates

1.   The case for a floating exchange rates regime claims that such a system gives countries autonomy regarding their monetary policy and that floating exchange rates facilitate smooth adjustment of trade imbalances.

2.   The case for a fixed exchange rate regime claims that: I) the need to maintain a fixed exchange rate imposes monetary discipline on a country, ii) floating exchange rate regimes are vulnerable to speculative pressures, iii) the uncertainty that accompanies floating exchange rates hinders the growth of international trade and investment, and iv) far from correcting trade imbalances, depreciating a currency on the foreign exchange market tends to cause inflation.

3. While we know that the past attempts at fixed exchange rates have not held up, perhaps there is another new approach. The floating system clearly works, but with great volatility.

G. The European Monetary System

1. The objectives of the European Monetary System (EMS) are to (i) create a zone of monetary stability in Europe, (ii) control inflation, and (iii) to coordinate exchange rate policies with third currencies.

2. The ecu is a basket of currencies that serves as the unit of account for the EMS. Each national currency in the EMS is given a central rate vis-à-vis the ecu. From this central rate flow a series of bilateral rates.

3. Currencies are not allowed to depart by more than 2.25% from their bilateral rate with another EMS currency. Countries can borrow from each other to defend their currency against speculative pressure.

4. The EMS has been fairly successful in stabilizing exchange and interest rates between countries, although a clear crisis occurred in 1992 which showed the difficulty in maintaining the bands when pressured by the currency markets. The case "Chaos in the currency markets" discusses this in much more detail. A current article on this topic could be useful - *The Economist* tends to provide very thorough and frequent coverage of European progress (or lack thereof) towards monetary union.

H. The IMF and World Bank after Bretton Woods

1. With the introduction of the floating rate system and the emergence of global capital markets, much of the original reason for the IMF's existence has gone away.

2. Hence the IMF has instead gotten significantly involved in helping third world countries out of their debt crisis's. Relatedly, the IBRD has found that economic mismanagement can make good projects turn out to be inappropriate. Thus the line between the role of the IBRD and the IMF is increasingly blurred.

I. Implications for Business

1. The present floating rate system makes it important that firms carefully manage their foreign exchange transactions and exposure to changes.

2. Given that currencies can change, and that the relative appropriateness of different locations for production and sales can change with changing exchange rates, it is important that MNEs have strategic flexibility to transfer production to locations where the exchange rates are the most favorable. Using contract manufacturing from different countries can also provide flexibility in low value added manufacturing.

3. Firms have an incentive to both encourage governments to undertake policies that provide favorable exchange rates, as well as encourage that a system of more stable exchange rates be established. The relative stability of exchange rates in Europe has clearly helped European firms in managing their cross-border activities.

ANSWERS TO CRITICAL DISCUSSION QUESTIONS FOR CHAPTER 10

QUESTION 1: Why did the gold standard collapse? Is there a case for returning to some type of gold standard? What is it?

ANSWER 1: Due to a series of competitive devaluations by countries, individuals lost confidence in what the value of a currency really was, and decided to convert their currency holdings into gold. This put pressures on the gold reserves of countries, forcing them to suspend convertibility. The case for returning to a gold standard is based on the monetary discipline this places on countries and the reduction of speculation and uncertainty that would result if currencies were pegged to gold. The automatic adjustment mechanism for balance of trade disequilibrium is also a powerful and attractive feature of the gold standard.

QUESTION 2: What opportunities might IMF lending policies to Third World nations create for international businesses? What threats might they create?

ANSWER 2: Since the conditions under which the IMF lends typically impose policies that should provide for economic stability and growth, the risk and uncertainty of investing in many countries will be reduced for international businesses. As the IMF also becomes more involved in long term developmental investments, these developmental projects also can create demand for the products and services of MNEs. A threat of the IMF's lending policies is that countries may be operating under greater monetary and budgetary restraint, and thus may not be able to make as many purchases as they had before. As was shown in the closing case on Cat, there is also added demand to make purchase decisions strictly based on price.

QUESTION 3: Do you think it is in the best interests of Western international businesses to have the IMF lend money to the former communist states of Eastern Europe to help them transform their economies? Why?

ANSWER 3: Overall it is probably favorable for Western international businesses to have the IMF lend money to Eastern Europe. For one thing, the funds are generally needed, and will provide funds for projects that help establish Western style economic systems. With the funds also come restrictions on the economic policies of the countries that help improve the predictability of governmental policies. On the other hand, the money doesn't come out of thin air, and the demand for money makes Western interest rates higher than they would otherwise be.

QUESTION 4: Debate the relative merits of fixed and floating exchange rate regimes. From the perspective of an international business, what are the most important criteria for choosing between the systems? Which system is the more desirable for an international business?

ANSWER 4: (Since there is a whole section of the chapter on this topic, this answer will be kept brief.) The case for a floating exchange rates regime is based on two elements; (i) such a system gives countries autonomy with regard to their monetary policy, and (ii) floating exchange rates facilitate the smooth adjustment of trade imbalances. The case for a fixed exchange rate regime is based upon four factors; (i) the need to maintain a fixed exchange rate imposes monetary discipline on a country, (ii) floating exchange rate regimes are vulnerable to speculative pressure, (iii) the uncertainty that exists in a world of floating exchange rates puts a damper upon the growth of international trade and investment, and (iv) far from correcting trade imbalances, the depreciation of a currency on the foreign exchange market tends to cause price inflation. One of the most important criteria for any international business is the stability and predictability of the system, allowing firms to better be able to value and make long term international investments. While in the short run a fixed rate system would seem to be better, given that long run economic fundamentals may make changes in "fixed" rates a necessity, less frequent but more significant changes may be just as difficult for businesses. And how well the internal adjustment mechanisms will work is unclear. Thus it difficult to say which is best for business, although the more stable (yet still slightly floating) system of the EMS appears to have been good for European businesses.

QUESTION 5: Imagine that Canada, the US, and Mexico, decide to adopt a fixed exchange rate system similar in form to the ERM of the European Monetary System. What would be the likely consequences of such a system for (a) international businesses, and (b) the flow of trade and investment between all three countries?

ANSWER 5: The institution of a monetary system similar to the EMS in North America, along with a "quite free" free trade agreement, would certainly make North America a more attractive place to invest for MNEs from outside North America, and increase cross border investment between the three countries. While the exchange rate has been fairly stable between the US and Canada for decades, it has not been so between Mexico and these two countries. Thus the greatest increase in the flow of trade and investment would likely be between Mexico and the US, along with some increase between Mexico and Canada. The primary effect would be to improve the attractiveness of Mexico, both as a growing market for goods and as a production location for the entire North American market.

STUDENT EXERCISES AND PROJECTS FOR CHAPTER 10

- This chapter lends itself particularly well to having students debate various topics. One topic could be whether the US (or any country) should return to a gold standard. Not only is there an intellectual debate, but business interests and other governments could be represented in the debate each providing their perspective. Another topic could be lending IMF or IBRD money to Russia. Once again, different interest groups will have their opinions as well as economists and politicians perspectives.

SUGGESTED READINGS FOR CHAPTER 10

The footnotes suggest some appropriate additional readings. The following may be of particular interest:

Eichengreen, B. 1985. The gold standard in theory and in history. London: Methuen.

Krugman, Paul 1990. The age of diminished expectations. Cambridge, MA: MIT Press.

Solomon, R. 1982. The international monetary system, 1945-1981. New York: Harper and Row.

TRANSPARENCY MASTERS FOR CHAPTER 10 FOLLOW

U.S. Macroeconomic Data, 1964–72

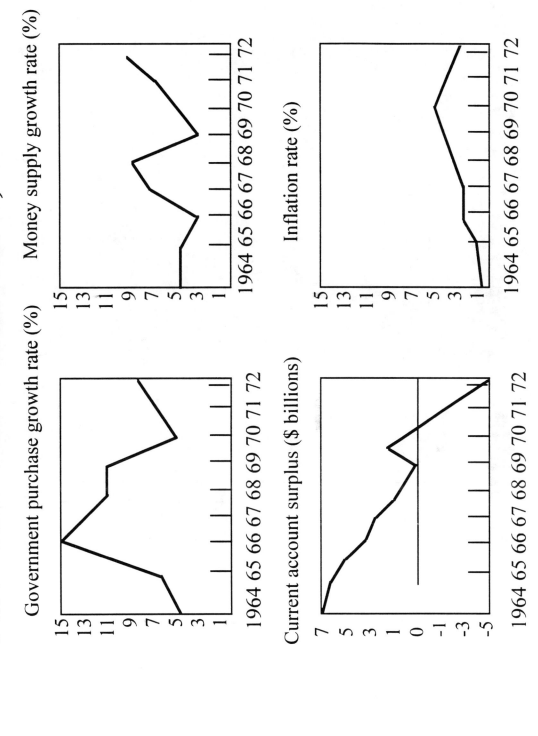

Data: Economic Report of the President, *1985.*

Figure 10.1

U.S. Dollar Movements, 1970 – 94

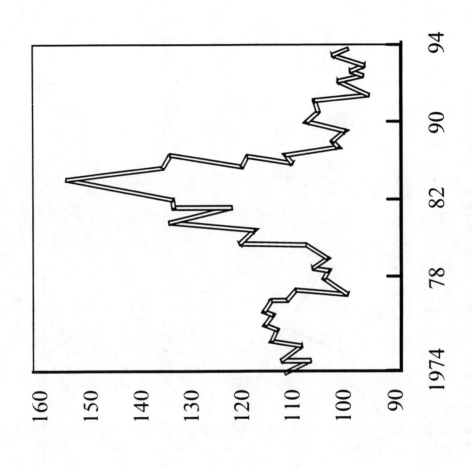

Source: Morgan Guaranty, World Financial Markets, various issues.

Figure 10.2

CHAPTER 11: OVERVIEW AND TEACHING SUGGESTIONS

OUTLINE OF CHAPTER 11

OBJECTIVES OF CHAPTER 11

1.   Describe the functions and form of the international capital market, looking carefully at some of the facilitating and inhibiting factors in the development of the market.

2.   Provide a history, as well as the attractions and drawbacks of the Eurocurrency market.

3.   Discuss the international bond and equity markets.

4.   Suggest the implications for business, paying particular attention to differences in the cost of capital and risk, of raising money on the international capital market.

LECTURE OUTLINE FOR CHAPTER 11

A.   Introduction

1   There has been a dramatic growth in the international capital market over the past 15 years. Some specific data is in the book that illustrates this growth.

2.   Companies are increasingly turning to the global capital market for funds, as the Biomedex case illustrates. By using international capital markets, firms can lower the costs and increase their access to funds.

3.   Investors are also diversifying their portfolios and reducing their systematic risk by investing internationally, although new risks are created in the process.

B.   The Nature of the International Capital Market

1.   Figure 11.1 shows who the main players are in the capital market. In the case of international capital markets, there are simply more of all of these players and a greater diversity in the players and the possible combinations.

2.   Firms can obtain funds via both debt and equity.

3.   There are two main reasons why an international capital market offers an improvement over a purely domestic capital market: (i) from a borrower's perspective, it increases the supply of funds available for borrowing and lowers the cost of capital; and (ii) from an investor's perspective, it provides a wider range of investment opportunities, thereby allowing investors to build a portfolio of international investments that diversifies risk.

4.   If there is limited liquidity in a purely domestic capital market, the cost of capital is higher relative to what would be found in an international market. Figure 11.2 shows this graphically for the Biomedex case.

5.   With an increase in the choices available to an investor, the investor is able to diversify holdings internationally, thereby reducing systematic risk below what could be achieved in a purely domestic market. Figure 11.3 shows this graphically.

6.   While the systematic risks are reduced with international portfolio investments, exchange rate risks now come into play.

C.   Growth of the International Capital Market

1.   De-regulation and improvements in technology have facilitated the growth of the international capital market.

2.   Due to advances in communications and data processing capabilities, the international capital markets are always active around the globe. Figure 11.4 shows the trading hours of the world's major financial centers. International trading is a information intensive activity that would not have been possible only a few decades ago when computing and telecommunication capabilities were much less developed.

3.   The de-regulation of capital flows, a removal of limitations on the types services that can be provided by foreign financial services firms, and a reduction in the restrictions imposed on domestic financial services firms have all contributed to the growth of the international capital market.

4.   While capital is generally free to move internationally, evidence to date suggests that most investors choose to make long term investments in their home country and only make short term opportunistic investments elsewhere.

5.   Figure 11.5 illustrates the geographic locations of the major and minor international capital markets.

D.   The Eurocurrency Market

1.   A Eurocurrency is any currency that is banked outside of its country of origin. Eurodollars, which account for about two-thirds of all Eurocurrencies, are dollars banked outside of the United States.

2.   The Eurocurrency got its origin as holders of dollars outside the US, initially communist countries but later also middle eastern countries, wanted to deposit their dollars but were afraid that they may be confiscated if deposited in the US.

3.   The lack of government regulation makes the Eurocurrency market attractive to both depositors and borrowers. Due to the lack of regulation, the spread between the Eurocurrency deposit rate and the Eurocurrency lending rate is less than the spread between the domestic deposit rate and the domestic lending rate. This gives Eurobanks a competitive advantage. Figure 11.6 shows the interest rate spreads on domestic and Eurocurrency markets.

4.   The lack of regulation is also a drawback of Eurocurrency deposits, as the risk of forfeiture is greater than for domestic deposits. There is also a risk of currency fluctuations that would not arise if funds were held domestically in the domestic currency.

E.   The International Bond Market

1.   The international bond market falls into two general classifications; the foreign bond market and the Eurobond market. . Eurobonds account for the lion's share of international bond issues.

2.   Foreign bonds are sold outside of the borrower's country and are denominated in the currency of the country in which they are issued.

3.   A Eurobond issue is normally underwritten by an international syndicate of banks and placed in countries other than the one in whose currency the bond is denominated.

4.   The Eurobond market is an attractive way for companies to raise funds due to the absence of regulatory interference, less stringent disclosure requirements than in most domestic bond markets, and the favorable tax status of Eurobonds.

5.   Ecu-denominated bonds are becoming increasingly common in the 1990s, and may be even more so as progress is made on a single European currency. One advantage of these bonds is that the risks associated with exchange rates are lower, since the ecu is actually a basket of currencies.

F.   The International Equity Market

1.   There is not an international equity market in the same sense that there are international currency and bond markets. Instead there are a number of separate equity markets that are linked via specific equities and overall market fundamentals.

2.   Foreign investors are increasingly investing in different national equity markets, primarily as a way of diversifying risk by diversifying their portfolio of stock holdings across nations.

3.   As firms are listed on multiple national exchanges and have their shares owned by an even greater number of shareholders from different nationalities, it is becoming increasingly meaningless to refer to firms as "American" or "Dutch."

4.   Companies are beginning to list their stock in the equity markets of other nations, primarily as a prelude to issuing stock in the market to raise additional capital. Other reasons for foreign listings include facilitating future stock swaps, using the company's stock and stock options to compensate local management and employees, satisfying local ownership desires, providing access to funding for future acquisitions in a country, and increasing the company's visibility to local employees, customers, suppliers, and bankers

G.   Foreign Exchange Risk and the Cost of Capital

1.   When borrowing funds from the international capital market, companies must weigh the benefits of a lower interest rate against the risks of an increase in the real cost of capital due to adverse exchange rate movements. The book presents an example showing that the true cost of capital is equal to the nominal interest rate plus the costs in interest and principal that arise from a currency change.

2.   Using forward rates cannot typically remove the risk altogether, particularly in the case of long term investments.

H.   Implications for Business

1.   By utilizing international capital markets, firms can often borrow funds at a lower cost than they could domestically - regardless of whether the funds are in the form of cash loans, equity, or bonds.

2.   The minimal regulation in international capital markets helps lower the cost of capital, but also increases risk in both currencies and security.

3.   For investors, the international capital market provides opportunities for portfolio diversification and the lowering of systematic risk. At the same time, it creates new currency risks.

ANSWERS TO CRITICAL DISCUSSION QUESTIONS FOR CHAPTER 11

QUESTION 1: Why has the international capital market grown so rapidly in recent decades? Do you think that this growth will continue throughout the 1990s? Why?

ANSWER 1: Two key trends are responsible for the rapid growth in the international capital market in recent decades - improved communication and information processing technology and deregulation. While there certainly was demand for the services provided by the international capital market earlier, government restrictions and technological limitations made globalization difficult. The growth is likely to continue. Not only is technology continuing to improve, but there are still additional governmental regulations that can be removed. While these continuing trends will facilitate further growth in the international capital market, increased demand from investors and borrowers is likely to continue as business becomes increasingly globalized.

QUESTION 2: A firm based in Mexico is finding its growth limited by the limited liquidity of the Mexican capital market. List the firm's options for raising money on the international capital market. Discuss the pros and cons of each option, and make a recommendation. How might your recommendation be affected if the Mexican peso depreciates significantly on the foreign exchange markets over the next two years?

ANSWER 2: The Mexican firm could consider foreign equity offerings, floating foreign or Eurobonds, or borrowing on Eurocurrency markets. The Eurocurrency market will certainly make additional funds available to the firm, and at a lower rate than it is likely to receive domestically. If the peso falls in the next two years, the fact that the firm will have to pay back the loan in another currency (unless the firm is able to use the forward market) would decrease the attractiveness of Eurocurrency loans. The use of both foreign bonds and Eurobonds have this same drawback - the bonds will have to be paid back in a currency that likely has appreciated significantly against the peso. Due to the minimal regulation, disclosure requirements, and tax implications the international bond market does have some strong points that make it worth considering if the currency risk can be adequately analyzed and minimized. The foreign equity market may be the most attractive for this firm, as it is not required to make payments to its shareholders and has the most autonomy over its actions. Its growth prospects have to be strong enough, however, to overcome the hesitations investors will likely have.

QUESTION 3: Happy Company wishes to raise $2 million in US dollars with debt financing. The funds, needed to finance working capital, will be repaid with interest in one year. Happy Company's treasurer is considering three options:
      (a)   Borrowing US dollars from Security Pacific Bank at 8%
      (b)   Borrowing British pounds from Midland Bank at 14%
      (c)   Borrowing Japanese yen from Sanwa bank at 5%
If Happy borrows foreign currency, it will not cover it; that is, it will simply change foreign currency for dollars at today's spot rate and buy foreign currency back one year later at the spot rate then in effect. Happy Company estimates that the pound will depreciate by 5% relative to the dollar and the yen will appreciate 3% relative to the dollar during the next year. From which bank should Happy Company borrow?

ANSWER 3: To compare the alternatives, the amount of dollars that Happy will have to repay in one year will be used as the basis of comparison.

    (a) $2 million * 1.08 = $2.160 million

    (b) $2 million * (1 + ((.14*.95) - .05)) = $2.170 million

    (c) $2 million * (1 + ((.05*1.03) + .03)) = $2.163 million

Since the US bank, Security Pacific, has both the lowest cost and no exchange rate risk, Happy should borrow from Security Pacific. Given how close these alternatives are in value, however, an only slightly different exchange rate for either the Yen or the Pound could easily change the attractiveness of these options.

STUDENT EXERCISES AND PROJECTS FOR CHAPTER 11

This chapter doesn't lend itself quite so well to most exercises, as it is rather descriptive and institutional in nature. Depending upon the overall interest in international finance, however, as well as library resources, the following projects could be developed.

- Ask students to find one or more firms that has cross listed shareholdings. SmithKline, for example, has stock listed in Japan, the US, London. Students can then be asked to look into the stock in more detail, and find out how much stock is offered where as well as the return it is generating. They might also find it interesting to look at how the stock prices move, or do not move, simultaneously in each market.

- A variant of this would be to more generally look at the foreign debt offerings of a domestic firm. This can be a little more difficult, and may require access to databases will full text financial statement disclosures. Students can be asked to look at when the debt was offered, at what interest rate, and then see how exchange rates have effected the effective interest rate over time. Some firms give rather full footnote disclosure of such information.

SUGGESTED READINGS FOR CHAPTER 11

The footnotes suggest some appropriate additional readings. The following may be of particular interest:

Aliber, Robert 1989. The handbook of international financial management. Homewood, IL: Dow Jones Irwin.

Eiteman, D.K., A.I. Stonehill, and M.H. Moffett 1992. Multinational Business Finance. Reading, MA: Addison-Wesley 1992.

TRANSPARENCY MASTERS FOR CHAPTER 11 FOLLOW

The Main Players in a Generic Capital Market

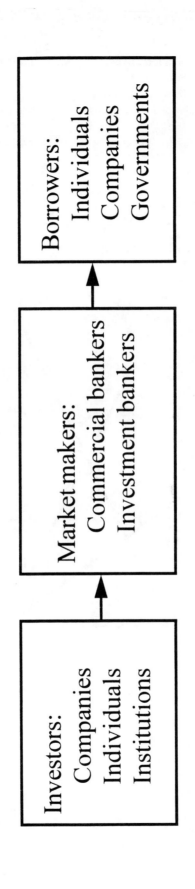

IRWIN © Times Mirror Higher Education Group Inc., Company 1997

Figure 11.1

Market Liquidity and the Cost of Capital

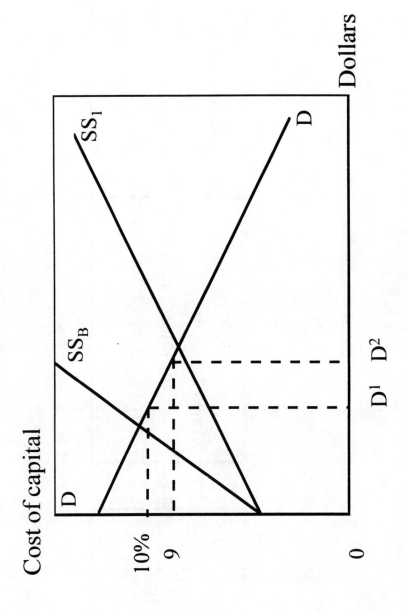

Figure 11.2

Risk Reduction Through Portfolio Diversification

(a) Risk reduction through domestic diversification

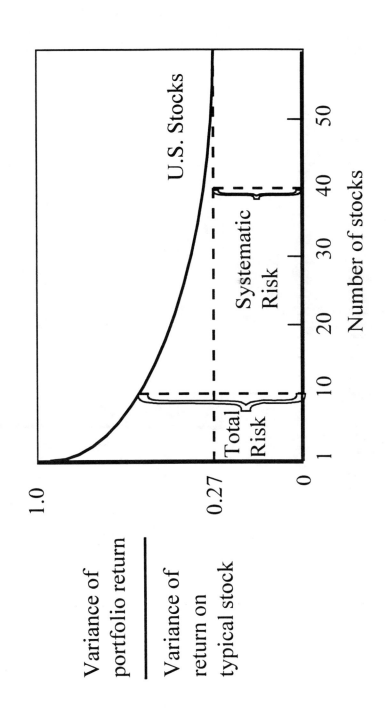

Variance of portfolio return / Variance of return on typical stock

Source: B. Solnik, "Why Not Diversify Internationally Rather than Domestically?" Financial Analysis Journal, July 1974, p. 17.

Figure 11.3a

Risk Reduction Through Portfolio Diversification *CONTINUED*

(b) Risk reduction through domestic and international diversification

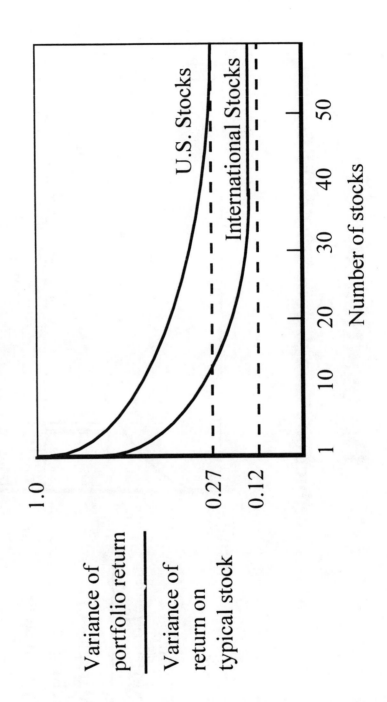

Source: B. Solnik, "Why Not Diversify Internationally Rather than Domestically?" Financial Analysis Journal, July 1974, p. 17.

Figure 11.3b

Trading Hours of the World's Major Financial Centers

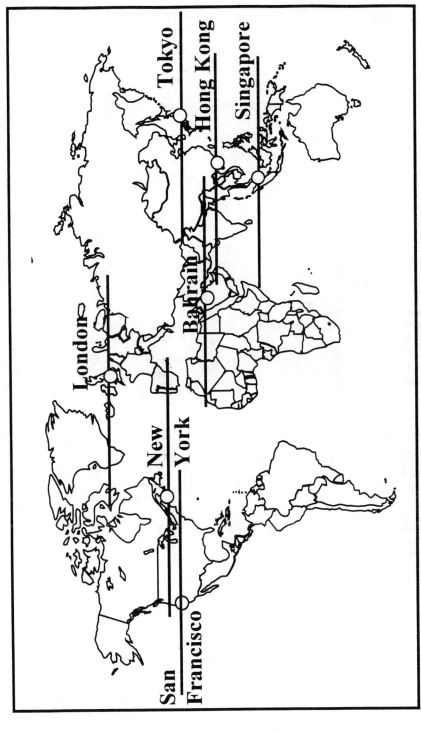

11 10 9 8 7 6 5 4 3 2 1 0 1 2 3 4 5 6 7 8 9 10 11 12

IRWIN © Times Mirror Higher Education Group Inc., Company 1997

Map 11.1

The Hierarchy of International Financial Centers, 1994

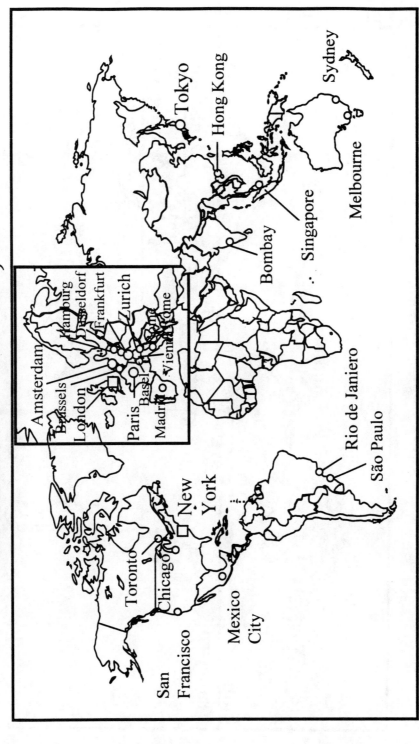

Note: *Size of dots (squares) indicates cities' relative importance*

IRWIN © Times Mirror Higher Education Group Inc., Company 1997

Map 11.2

Interest Rate Spreads in Domestic and Eurocurrency Markets

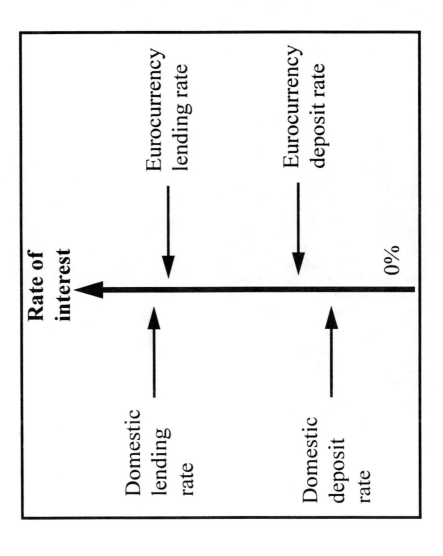

IRWIN © Times Mirror Higher Education Group Inc., Company 1997

Figure 11.4

CHAPTER 12: OVERVIEW AND TEACHING SUGGESTIONS

OUTLINE OF CHAPTER 12

> OPENING CASE: IT'S A MAC WORLD
> INTRODUCTION
> STRATEGY AND THE FIRM
> > The Firm as a Value Chain
> > The Role of Strategy
> PROFITING FROM GLOBAL EXPANSION
> > Transferring Core Competencies
> > Realizing Location Economies
> > Realizing Experience Curve Economies
> PRESSURES FOR COST REDUCTIONS AND LOCAL RESPONSIVENESS
> > Pressure for Cost Reductions
> > Pressures For Local Responsiveness
> STRATEGIC CHOICE
> > International Strategy
> > Multidomestic Strategy
> > Global Strategy
> > Transnational Strategy
> > Summary
> SUMMARY OF CHAPTER
> CRITICAL DISCUSSION QUESTIONS
> CLOSING CASE: SWEDEN'S IKEA

OBJECTIVES OF CHAPTER 12

1.   Suggest the reasons why firms may decide to enter international business, and identify the benefits from international strategies

2.   Outline the basic strategies undertaken by MNEs, and specifically focus on how they relate to the needs for local responsiveness and cost minimization

LECTURE OUTLINE FOR CHAPTER 12

A.   Introduction

1   While when we think of international businesses we often focus on the big MNEs, all of these were once small firms just beginning to expand internationally. A great deal of international business is undertaken by small firms. Some examples from local industries can help make this point.

2.   Thus far in this book we have looked primarily at the environment in which international business takes place, and suggested some implications for business. With this chapter we now move into looking more specifically at firms, and the actions that they can take to both respond to and shape their environment.

3.   As we can see from the opening case on McDonald's, successful international expansion often involves striking a balance between maintaining specific elements of domestic success while also being willing and interested in customizing for local tastes.

B.   Strategy and the Firm

1.   Firms are in the business of making profits by value creation - being able to sell what they make for more than it costs to make it. Thus they create value by either lowering the costs of production or raising the value so that consumers will pay more.

2.   To extend this, it is useful to use Porter's value chain approach, as shown in Figure 12.1.

3.   Strategy is about identifying how best a firm can go about creating value.

C.   Profiting from Global Expansion

1.   Expanding globally allows firms both large and small to increase their profitability in a number of ways not available to purely domestic enterprises.

2.   Firms that operate internationally have the ability to (i) earn a greater return from their distinctive skills or core competencies, (ii) realize location economies by dispersing individual value creation activities to those locations were they can be performed most efficiently, and (iii) realize greater experience curve economies, thereby lowering the costs of value creation.

3.   For some companies international expansion represents a way of earning greater returns by transferring the skills and product offerings derived from their *core competencies* to markets where indigenous competitors lack those skills. You could discuss what the core competencies of some local firms are.

4.   Due to national differences, it pays a firm to base each value creation activity it performs at that location where economic, political, and cultural conditions, including relative factor costs, are most conducive to the performance of that activity (transportation costs and trade barriers permitting). We refer to this strategy as focusing upon the attainment of *location economies*. MNEs that take advantage of different locational economies around the world create a *global web* of activities. In the world wide market, does your local economy have some specific locational advantages?

5.   By building sales volume more rapidly, international expansion can assist a firm in the process of moving down the experience curve. By lowering the costs of value creation, *experience economies* can help a firm to build barriers to new competition. Figure 12.2 shows a typical experience curve. It is useful to distinguish between learning effects and economies of scale when trying to analyze and predict experience economies.

D.   Pressures for Cost Reductions and Local Responsiveness

1.   Firms that compete globally typically face two types of competitive pressures: pressures for cost reductions, and the pressures for local responsiveness in the industry in which it competes. These competitive pressures place conflicting demands on firms. Figure 12.3 suggests different scenarios firms may face in balancing cost and local responsiveness pressures.

2.   Responding to cost pressures requires that a firm try to lower the costs of value creation by mass producing a standard product at the optimal locations worldwide. Pressures for cost reductions are greatest in industries producing commodity type products where price is the main competitive weapon. Pressures for cost reductions are also intense when major competitors are based in low cost locations, where there is persistent excess capacity, and where consumers are powerful and face low switching costs.

3.   Pressures for local responsiveness arise from differences in consumer tastes and preferences, differences in national infra-structure and traditional practices, differences in distribution channels, and host government demands. Pressures for local responsiveness imply that it may not be possible for a firm to realize the full benefits from experience curve and location economies.

E.   Strategic Choice

1.   Firms use four basic strategies to enter and compete in the international environment: an international strategy, a multidomestic strategy, a global strategy, and a transnational strategy. Figure 12.4 illustrates when each of these strategies is most appropriate.

2.   Firms pursuing an international strategy transfer the skills and products derived from core competencies to foreign markets, while undertaking some limited local customization. However, they may suffer from a lack of extensive local responsiveness and from an inability to exploit experience curve and location economies.

3.   Firms pursuing a multidomestic strategy customize their product offering, marketing strategy, and business strategy to national conditions. However, they may suffer from an inability to transfer skills and products between countries, and from an inability to exploit experience curve and location economies.

4.   Firms pursuing a global strategy focus on reaping the cost reductions that come from experience curve and location economies. However, they may suffer from a lack of local responsiveness.

5.   In a transnational strategy firms must exploit experience curve cost economies and location economies, transfer distinctive competencies within the firm, and pay attention to pressures for localization. To do this here need to be flows of knowledge from the parent to subsidiaries, flows from foreign subsidiary to home country, and from foreign subsidiary to foreign subsidiary - a process called **global learning**.

6.   The approach of the transnational is not appropriate in all situations, nor is it without costs. Where demands for local responsiveness is low, a global strategy may still be the most appropriate. The coordination and management challenges of a transnational also create higher costs (and sometimes benefits) than with one of the more traditional strategies.

7.   Examples of well-known firms, and particularly locally based firms can help illustrate these four strategy types.

8.   Figure 12.6 outlines the advantages and disadvantages of each of the four strategies. All are viable types of strategies for international firms, but each has particular features that make it more appropriate in some circumstances than others. It is also true that sometimes competitors and conditions make moves and changes that make once successful strategies less than optimal. The world is dynamic and no strategy may necessarily be appropriate for a long period of time.

ANSWERS TO CRITICAL DISCUSSION QUESTIONS FOR CHAPTER 12

QUESTION 1: "In a world of zero transportation costs, no trade barriers, and non-trivial differences between nations with regard to factor endowments, firms must expand internationally if they are to survive." Discuss.

ANSWER 1: Given differences in countries with respect to factor endowments, the theory of comparative advantage suggests that different activities should take place in the countries that can perform them most efficiently. If there are also no barriers or costs to trade, then it is likely that a lot of industries will be based out of the countries that provide the best set of factor endowments. For a firm that is located in a sub-optimal location, it will either have to expand internationally or switch to a different industry where the factor endowments are in its favor. For firms already located in the countries with the most favorable factor endowments for their industry, however, there may not be a need to expand internationally. Firstly, the firm may be content to simply focus on the domestic market. But if the firm does want to expand internationally, it may be able to do so via licensing or exporting, and need not necessarily undertake FDI. Thus not only in theory, but also in practice many firms are able to survive quite well without having to expand internationally.

QUESTION 2: Plot the position of the following companies on figure 12.3 - Procter & Gamble, IBM, Coca-Cola, Dow Chemicals, US Steel, McDonald's. In each case justify your answer?

ANSWER 2: (If assigning this as a discussion question, the instructor may prefer to use examples of local companies that the students are likely to have some more detailed knowledge about.) Based simply on the information in the book, it is difficult to say for sure where all these companies fit. Here is an armchair answer, which a person more knowledgeable about each company may choose to refute:
- Proctor & Gamble: They reasonably fit into the international category, although it is clear that they are becoming more transnational (see Bartlett and Ghoshal).
- IBM: Originally a classic International, but perhaps now moving more to a global strategy.
- Coca-Cola: With R&D, and the general market approach all coming from headquarters, but with subsidiaries having some discretion over the advertising message, this is probably an international.
- Dow Chemical: Given it is in a classic commodity industry, most likely a global firm
- US Steel: Given the cost pressures and commodity nature of this business, a global strategy is most likely.
- McDonalds: Given the international consistency of the product and the delivery, the slight adaptations to local tastes and requirements, and the lack of strong cost pressures, McDonalds would appear to be following an international strategy.

QUESTION 3: Are the following global industries or multidomestic industries: Bulk chemicals, pharmaceuticals, branded food products, movie making, television manufacture, personal computers, airline travel?

ANSWER 3: It is difficult, and perhaps arbitrary, to label industries as strictly one or the other. For example, there are huge economies of scale in development and manufacturing of pharmaceuticals, yet governmental regulations make it necessary to do a number of things different in various countries. Overall, however it can be said that the following are global: bulk chemicals, televisions, personal computers, pharmaceuticals, and airline travel (although in all instances some localization is required - the keyboard and software for computers, the power supplies for TVs, or the labeling and regulatory paperwork for bulk chemicals and pharmaceuticals). Branded food products and movie making are still predominantly multidomestic, although some foods have worldwide name recognition (Coke, Pepsi,

Nestle), and movies are often dubbed or subtitled for international audiences as well as developed with the interests of global customers taken into consideration.

QUESTION 4: Discuss how the need for control over foreign operations varies with the strategy and core competencies of a firm. What are the implications of this for choice of entry mode?

ANSWER 4: The need for control over foreign operations is lower when the cost pressures are lower - when firms are using a multidomestic or international strategy. There is also less need for control when the core competencies of a firm are able to be exploited without transferring to foreign operations. Thus a firm that is able to maintain its core competencies in its home country and does not require strong control over operations in a country may more likely export initially export than undertake foreign direct investment. This was clearly the case with Toyota in North America initially. Of course in the opposite situations high control and wholly owned subsidiary foreign direct investment are most appropriate.

QUESTION 5: What do you see as the main organizational problems likely to be associated with the implementation of a transnational strategy?

ANSWER 5: Simultaneously trying to achieve cost efficiencies, global learning, and local responsiveness places difficult and contradictory demands on an organization. Managing these conflicting demands requires the setting of control and motivational policies for people and organizations that force balancing of these demands at multiple levels within firms. The organizational challenges involve managing these inherent conflicts to resolutions that serve the best interests of the firm overall.

STUDENT EXERCISES AND PROJECTS FOR CHAPTER 12

The book's description of the four types of strategies paint a fairly clear distinction between each. Unfortunately, it is not necessarily so easy clearly define the position of any one firm. This can become clear by one of the following exercises:
- Suggest that students use whatever library or electronic sources are available to find out the necessary information to classify a well-known firm as employing one of the four strategy types. They should be required to cite specific information from published sources to justify why the firm should be categorized in one way, and not categorized in others.
- An alternative, and potential extension, is to explore how a firm's international strategy has changed over time. Remember that the oil industry was once very local, whereas retailing was once global (East India Company and the Hudson Bay Company).

Either of these exercises can be extended in the following chapter to look at the organizational structure of the firms.

SUGGESTED READINGS FOR CHAPTER 12

The footnotes suggest some appropriate additional readings. The following may be of particular interest:

Bartlett, Christopher and Sumantra Ghoshal 1989. Managing across borders. Boston: Harvard Business School Press.

Davidson, William H. and Jose de la Torre 1989. Managing the global corporation: Case studies in strategy and management. New York: McGraw-Hill.

Hamel, Gary and C.K. Prahalad 1994. Competing for the future. Boston: Harvard Business School Press.

Harvard Business Review 1994. Global strategies: Insights from the world's leading thinkers. Boston: Harvard Business School Publishing. This book contains reprints of a number of previous HBR articles on global strategies.

Hood, Neil and Jan-Erik Vahlne 1988. Strategies in global competition. London: Croom-Helm.

Porter, Michael E. 1985. Competitive advantage. New York: Free Press

Prahalad, C.K. and Yves L. Doz 1987. The multinational mission. New York: Free Press.

TRANSPARENCY MASTERS FOR CHAPTER 12 FOLLOW

The Firm as a Value Chain

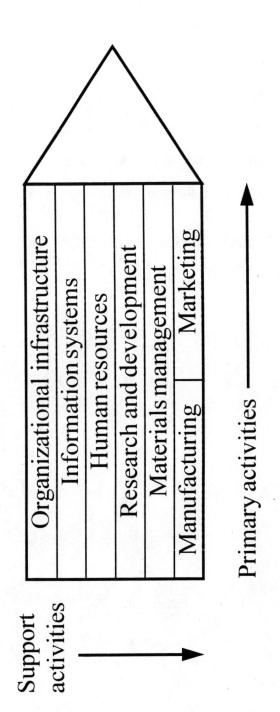

Organizational infrastructure	
Information systems	
Human resources	
Research and development	
Materials management	
Manufacturing	Marketing

Support activities →

Primary activities →

Figure 12.1

The Experience Curve

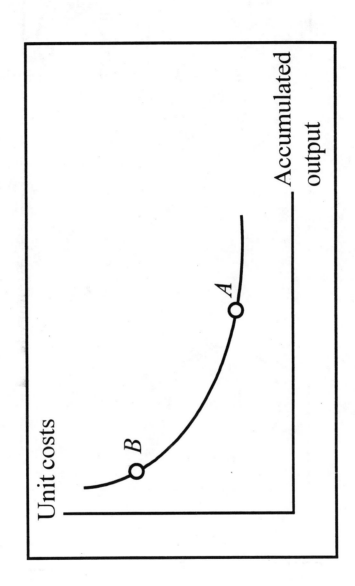

Figure 12.2

Pressures for Cost Reduction and Local Responsiveness

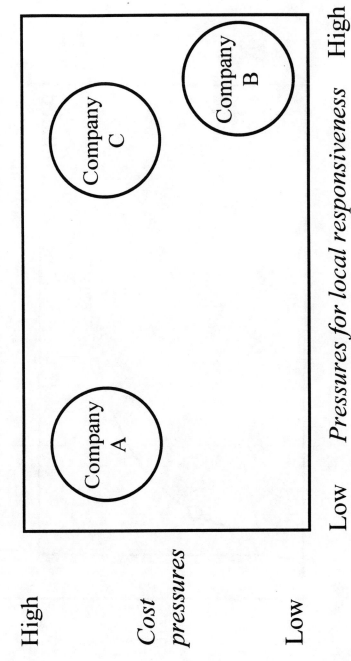

Figure 12.3

IRWIN © Times Mirror Higher Education Group Inc., Company 1997

Four Basic Strategies

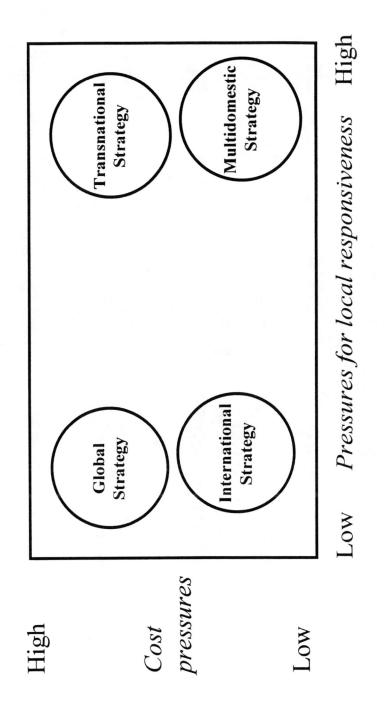

Figure 12.4

The Advantages and Disadvantages of the Four Strategies

Strategy	Advantages	Disadvantages
Global	Exploit experience curve effects Exploit location economies	Lack of local responsiveness
International	Transfer distinctive com-petencies to Foreign Markets	Lack of local responsiveness Inability to realize location economies Failure to exploit experience curve effects

Figure 12.6a

The Advantages and Disadvantages of the Four Strategies

Strategy	Advantages	Disadvantages
Multidomestic	Customize product offerings and marketing in accordance with local responsiveness	Inability to realize location economies Failure to exploit experience curve effects Failure to transfer distinctive competencies to foreign markets
Transnational	Exploit experience curve effects Exploit location economies Customize product offerings and marketing in accordance with local responsiveness Reap benefits of global learning	Difficult to implement due to organizational problems

Figure 12.6b

CHAPTER 13: OVERVIEW AND TEACHING SUGGESTIONS

OUTLINE OF CHAPTER 13

OBJECTIVES OF CHAPTER 13

1.   Identify the different kinds of organizational structures and internal control mechanisms that international businesses can use to manage global operations

2.   Discuss the advantages and disadvantages of centralized and decentralized decision systems.

3.   Present the basic types of organizational forms that multinational firms use

4.   Describe the control systems and integrating mechanisms available to multinational firms

5.   Show how the organizational forms, control systems, integrating systems, and decision making choices multinational firms have available must *fit* with their strategy and industry environment

LECTURE OUTLINE FOR CHAPTER 13

A.   Introduction

1   The basic theme of this chapter is that in order to succeed an international business must have
      the appropriate formal and informal organizational structure and control mechanisms.

2.   What is appropriate depends upon the strategy of the firm - which as we saw in the last chapter is
      inter-related with the demands of the industry environment.

3.   The opening case on Royal Dutch Shell shows how having organizational structures and control
      systems that fit with a strategy that is appropriate for an industry at one point in time may need to
      be changed as industry conditions and strategies change.

4.   Just as there were trade-offs between different strategies, there are trade-offs between different
      organizational choices - advantages and disadvantages to different approaches.

B.   Vertical Differentiation

1.   Vertical differentiation is principally about the centralization and decentralization of decision
      making responsibilities. It is concerned with identifying where in a hierarchy decision making
      power should be concentrated.

2.   There are four main arguments for centralization: (i) facilitating coordination, (ii) ensuring
      consistency between decisions and organizational objectives, (iii) providing top managers the
      means to push through major changes, and (iv) avoiding duplication of activities.

3.   There are five main arguments for decentralization: (i) overburdened and hence poor decision-
      making at the top of the organization, (ii) increased motivation at lower levels, (iii) greater
      flexibility, (iv) better decisions on the spot by the people directly involved, and (v) increased
      accountability and control.

4.   The choice between centralization and decentralization is not an absolute one. Frequently it
      makes sense to centralize some decisions and decentralize others depending upon the type of
      decision and the strategy of the firm.

5.   For firms pursuing a global strategy, there is clearly more of a need for centralized decision
      making than for firms pursuing a multidomestic strategy. For transnationals, it is less clear, as
      some decisions should perhaps be centralized while others are decentralized.

C.   Horizontal Differentiation

1.   Horizontal differentiation is basically concerned with how the firm decides to divide itself up into
      sub-units. The decision is typically made upon the basis of functions, business areas, or
      geographical areas.

2.   In many firms just one of these is predominant, while in others there are difficult trade-offs to be
      made. The opening case on Royal Dutch Shell helps illustrate how different demands can pull a
      firm in different directions.

3.   Most firms start out with no formal structure. After growth, a functional orientation usually
      develops as shown in Figure 13.1.

4.   As firms diversify into multiple product lines, a product division structure that allows autonomy responsibility in the operating units is usually chosen (as shown in Figure 13.2).

5.   Historically, when many firms began to expand abroad they typically grouped their international activities into an international division. This tended to be the case whether the firm was organized on a functional basis or on the basis of product divisions. No matter whether the domestic structure of the firm was based primarily upon functions or upon product divisions, the international division tends to be organized on geographical lines. This is illustrated in Figure 13.3 for a firm whose domestic organization is based on product divisions.

6.   This structure rarely lasts due to the inherent potential for conflict and coordination problems between domestic and foreign operations. Firms then switch to one of two structures - a world wide area structure (undiversified firms) and a world wide product division structure (diversified firms). Figure 13.4 illustrates this.

7.   A world wide area structure tends to be favored by firms that have a low degree of diversification and domestic structure based on functions as illustrated in Figure 13.5. This structure facilitates local responsiveness and is consistent with a multidomestic strategy.

8.   A world wide product division structure tends to be adopted by firms that are reasonably diversified and accordingly, originally had a domestic structure that was based on product divisions as illustrated in Figure 13.6. The great strength of such a structure is that it provides an organizational context within which it is easier to pursue the rationalization of value creation activities necessary to realize location and experience curve economies. Thus it is consistent with a global strategy.

9.   Since neither of these structures achieves a balance between the need to be both locally responsive and to achieve location and experience curve economies, many multinationals adopt matrix type structures as illustrated in Figure 13.7. However, global matrix structures have typically failed to work well, primarily due to bureaucratic problems.

10.   Transnational firms attempt to overcome the problems inherent in the matrix structure by being more flexible and working to create networks of individuals and a shared culture.

D.   Integrating Mechanisms

1.   Both formal and informal mechanisms can be used to help achieve coordination.

2.   The need for coordination (and hence integrating mechanisms) varies systematically with the strategy of the firm. It is lowest in multidomestic firms, higher in international firms, higher still in global firms, and highest of all in transnational firms.

3.   Integration is inhibited by a number of impediments to coordination, particularly different sub-unit orientations. To the extent that different sub-units have different objectives and ways of operating, integration becomes more difficult.

4.   Integration can be achieved through formal integrating mechanisms. Formal integrating mechanisms vary in complexity from direct contact and simple liaison roles, through teams, to a matrix structure. However, formal integrating mechanisms can become bureaucratic.

5.   To overcome the bureaucracy associated with formal integrating mechanisms, firms often use informal mechanisms. These include management networks and organization culture.

6.   For a network to function effectively it must embrace as many managers within the organization as possible. Information systems and management development policies (including job rotation and management education programs) can be used to establish firm wide networks.

7.   For a network to function properly, managers in different sub-units must be committed to the same goals. One way of achieving this is to foster the development of a common organization culture. Leadership by example, management development programs, and human relations policies are all important in building a common culture.

8.   Taken together, managerial networks and a common culture can serve as valuable coordination mechanisms in international firms that can help overcome the deficiencies of formal mechanisms.

E.   Control Systems

1.   One of the major tasks of a firm's headquarters is to control the various sub-units of the firm to ensure consistency with strategic goals. The headquarters' can achieve this through its use of control systems. There are four main types of controls - personal controls, bureaucratic controls, output controls, and cultural controls. In most firms all four are used, but the relative emphasis tends to vary with the strategy of the firm.

2.   Personal control involves control by personal contact with subordinates. This type of control system tends to be most widely used within small firms where it finds expression in the direct supervision of subordinates actions, but is also applicable in large international firms.

3.   Bureaucratic control involves control through the establishment of a system of rules and procedures that are used to direct the actions of sub-units. With regard to headquarters control of sub-units within multinational firms, the most important form of bureaucratic controls are sub-unit budgets and capital spending rules.

4.   Output controls involve setting goals for sub-units to achieve, expressing those goals in terms of relatively objective criteria such as profitability, productivity, growth, market share, or quality, and then judging the performance of sub-unit management by their ability to achieve these goals.

5.   Cultural controls exist when employees buy into the norms and value systems of the firm. When this occurs, employees tend to control their own behavior, which reduces the need for direct management supervision. Cultural controls require substantial investments of time and money by the firm in building organization wide norms and value systems.

6.   The key to understanding the relationship between international strategy and control systems is the concept of performance ambiguity. Performance ambiguity arises when the causes of poor performance by a sub-unit are ambiguous - when there is a high degree of interdependence between sub-units within the organization.

7.   The degree of interdependence, and hence performance ambiguity and the costs of control, is a function of the international strategy of the firm. It is lowest in multidomestic firms, higher in international firms, higher still in global firms, and highest of all in transnationals.

8.   The costs of control can be defined as the amount of time that top management has to devote to monitoring and evaluating the performance of sub-units. This will be greater the greater the amount of performance ambiguity.

9. Table 13.1 summarizes the concepts of interdependence, performance ambiguity, and costs of control for the four international business strategies outlined in the previous chapter.

F. Synthesis: Strategy and Structure

1. The key point of this chapter, and how it relates to the previous chapter, is summarized in Table 13.2. The implications of the four main strategies on organizational structure and control systems are identified. It usually is worthwhile to spend a fair bit of time going over this table, and suggesting examples of firms utilizing each strategy and its structure and controls.

2. Underlying the scheme outlined in Table 13.2 is the notion that a *fit* between strategy and structure is necessary if the firm is going to achieve high performance. For a firm to succeed two conditions must be fulfilled. First, the strategy of the firm must be consistent with the environment in which the firm operates. (Chapter 12) Second, the organizational structure and control systems of the firm must be consistent with its strategy.

ANSWERS TO CRITICAL DISCUSSION QUESTIONS FOR CHAPTER 13

QUESTION 1: "The choice of strategy for a multinational firm to pursue must depend upon a comparison of the benefits of that strategy (in terms of value creation) against the costs of implementing that strategy (as defined by organizational requirements necessary to implement the strategy). On this basis, it may be logical for some firms to pursue a multidomestic strategy, others a global or international strategy, and still others a transnational strategy." Is this statement correct?

ANSWER 1: The above statement is only partially correct. It is correct in saying that different strategies may cost the firm differently due to the differences in the costs of implementing organizational factors differently. What the statement fails to mention, and what is critical, is the importance of the environment when making choices between strategies and organizational factors. A strategy must fit with the industrial environment in which the firm is competing and the organizational structure and control systems must be consistent with its strategy. Thus while different firms may logically pursue different strategies, the industrial environment plays a critical role in determining what strategy a firm should pursue.

QUESTION 2: Discuss this statement. "An understanding of the causes and consequences of performance ambiguity is central to the issue of organizational design in multinational firms."

ANSWER 2: The statement can be interpreted as making the point that organizational design has to consider the performance ambiguities that will ultimately be created as a result of the design. Different organizational designs can remove performance ambiguities, shift them to a different level in the hierarchy, and create new performance ambiguities. Thus when crafting a new organizational design, not only must the causes of existing performance ambiguities be addressed, but the likely consequences in the form of new performance ambiguities must also be considered.

QUESTION 3: Describe what organizational solutions a transnational firm might adopt to reduce the costs of control?

ANSWER 3: A transnational, like all multinational firms, can use bureaucratic and output controls to some extent. However, the use of output controls is limited by non-trivial performance ambiguities, and bureaucratic controls have a greater difficulty in working when there are multiple lines of responsibility. As a result, we find a greater emphasis in these firms upon cultural controls. Cultural control, by encouraging managers to buy into the norms and value systems of an organization, gives managers from interdependent sub-units an incentive to look for ways of working out any problems that might arise between them. The result is a reduction in finger pointing and, accordingly, in the costs of control.

QUESTION 4: What actions must a firm take if it is to establish a viable intra-organizational management network?

ANSWER 4: The two techniques that firms have been experimenting with to try and establish firm wide networks are information systems and management development policies. With regard to information systems, firms are using their computer and telecommunications networks to provide the physical foundation for informal networks. Electronic mail, teleconferencing and high speed data systems have made it much easier for managers scattered over the globe to communicate with each other. Without an existing network of impersonal contacts, however, world wide information systems are unlikely to solve a firm's need for integration. To build an informal network firms are using their management development programs. Tactics include rotating managers through different sub-units on a regular basis so that they build up their own informal network and the use of management education programs to bring together in a single location managers from different sub-units so that they can establish contact with each other. The culture of an organization can affect how well a network will work. If firms have a culture where individuals whom have never met can develop relationships (get to know each other) over the phone and e-mail simply because someone else got them in contact with each other, then a viable intra-organizational network is more likely to develop.

STUDENT EXERCISES AND PROJECTS FOR CHAPTER 13

Building off the exercise from chapter 12 can be a good approach, thus asking students to look into the organizational and control systems utilized by the firm. An alternative is to have them find articles on multinational firms that have recently gone through, or announced, restructurings. Analyzing these decisions to restructure in light of Figure 13.4 and the fit of the structure with the strategy can be a very challenging assignment.

SUGGESTED READINGS FOR CHAPTER 13

The footnotes suggest some appropriate additional readings. The following may be of particular interest:

Bartlett, Christopher and Sumantra Ghoshal 1989. Managing across borders: The transnational solution.
     Boston: Harvard Business School Press.

Bartlett, Christopher and Sumantra Ghoshal 1992. Transnational management: Text, cases, and readings
     in cross-border management. Homewood, IL: Irwin.

Bartlett, Christopher, Yves Doz and Gunnar Hedlund 1990. Managing the global firm. London:
     Routledge.

Chandler, Alfred 1990. Scale and scope: The dynamics of industrial capitalism. Boston: Belknap Press.

Davidow, W.H. and M.S. Malone 1992. The virtual corporation. New York: Harper Collins.

Galbraith, Jay R. 1977. Designing complex organizations. Reading, MA: Addison-Wesley.

Ghoshal, Sumantra and Eleanor Westney 1993. Organization theory and the multinational enterprise. New York: St Martins Press.

Kogut, Bruce 1993. Country competitiveness: Technology and the organizing of work. New York: Oxford University Press.

Kotter, John P. and James L. Heskett 1992. Corporate culture and performance. New York: Free Press.

Stopford, John M. and Louis T. Wells 1972. Strategy and structure of the multinational enterprise. New York: Basic Books.

TRANSPARENCY MASTERS FOR CHAPTER 13 FOLLOW

A Typical Functional Structure

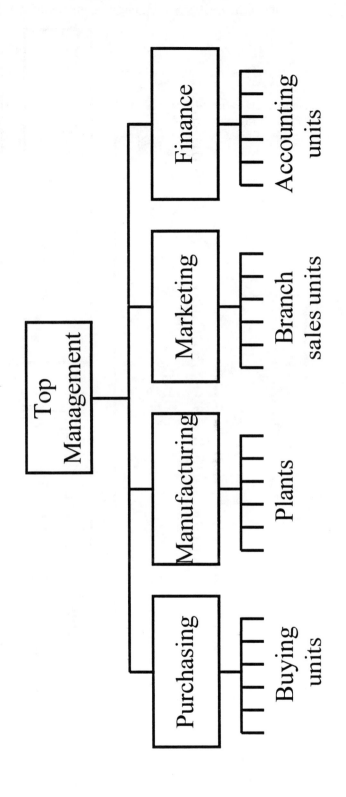

Figure 13.1

A Typical Product Division Structure

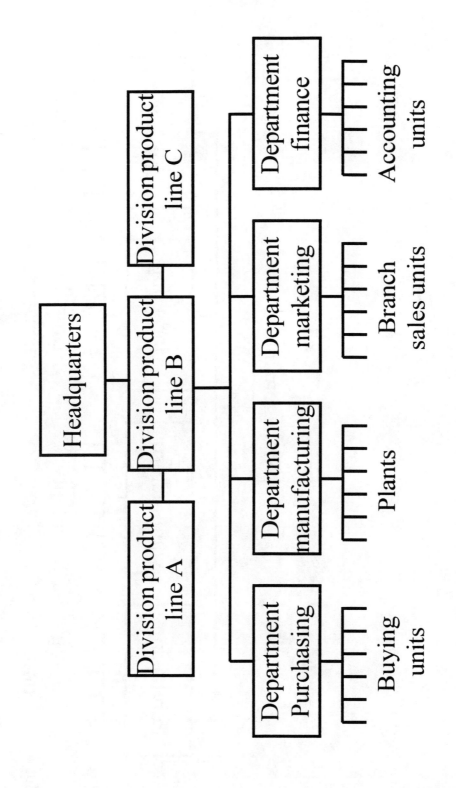

Figure 13.2

One Company's International Division Structure

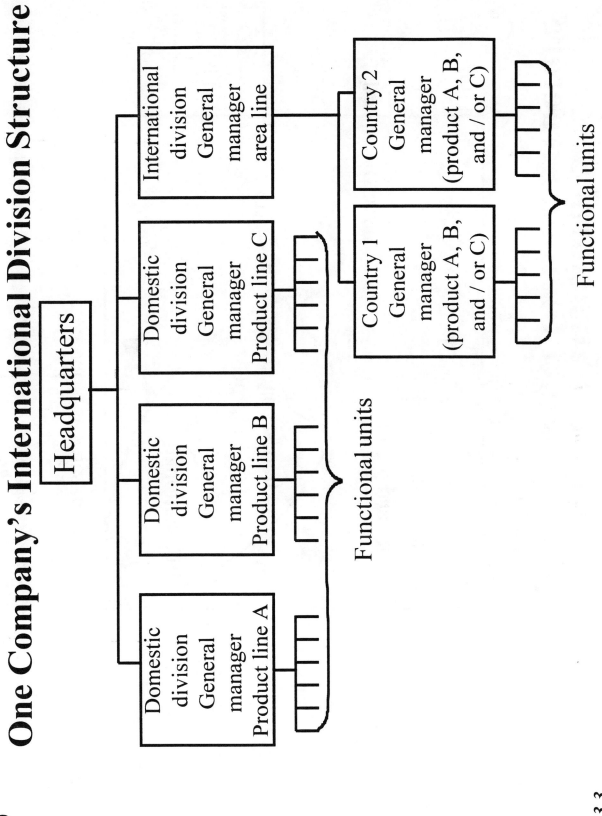

Figure 13.3

The International Structural Stages Model

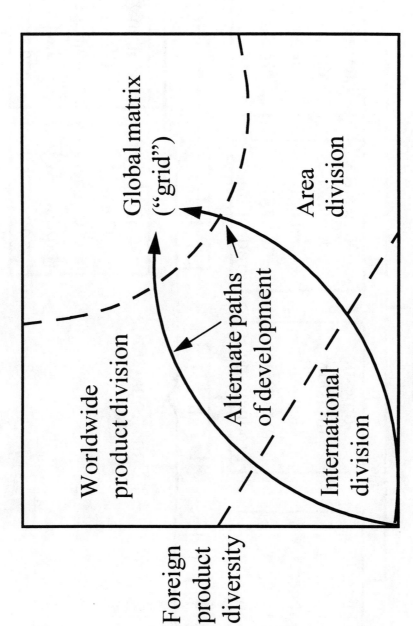

Foreign sales as a percentage of total sales

Figure 13.4

Source: Adapted from John M. Stopford and Louis T. Wells, Strategy and Structure of the Multinational Enterprise (New York: Basic Books, 1972).

Worldwide Area Structure

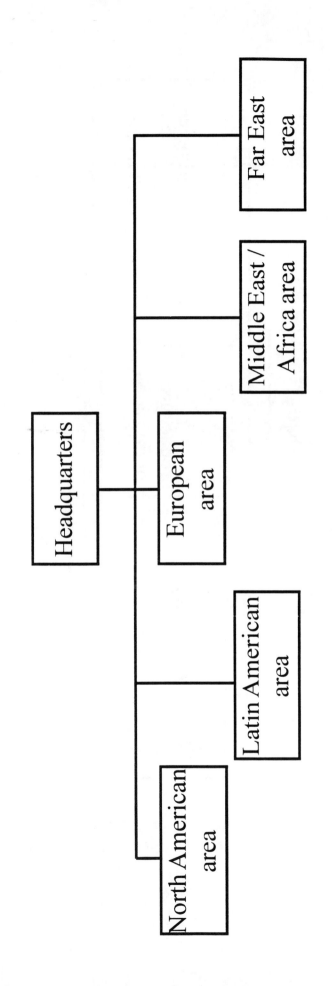

Figure 13.5

Source: Adapted from John M. Stopford and Louis T. Wells, Strategy and Structure of the Multinational Enterprise (New York: Basic Books, 1972).

A Worldwide Product Division Structure

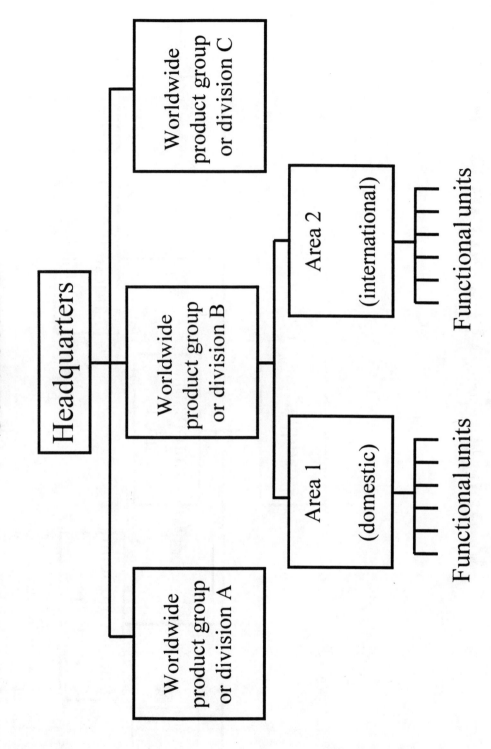

Figure 13.6

A Global Matrix Structure

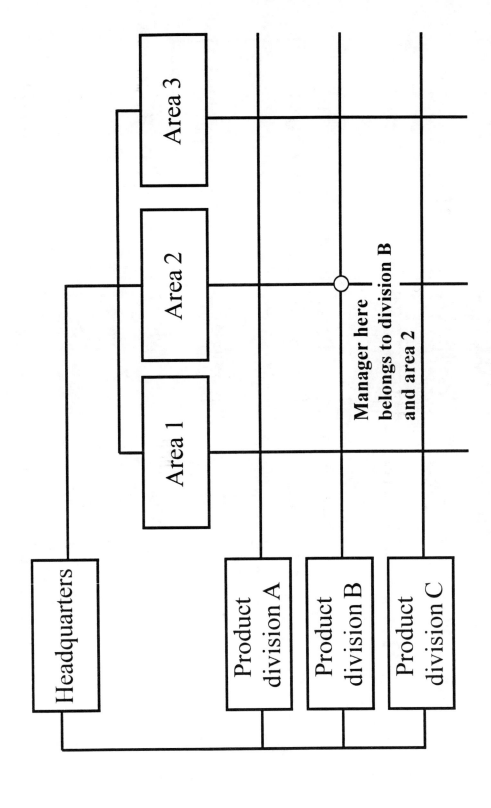

Manager here belongs to division B and area 2

IRWIN © Times Mirror Higher Education Group Inc., Company 1997

Figure 13.7

Interdependence, Performance Ambiguity, and the Costs of Control for the Four International Business Strategies

Strategy	Interdepend- ence	Performance Ambiguity	Costs of Control
Multidomestic	Low	Low	Low
International	Moderate	Moderate	Moderate
Global	High	High	High
Transnational	Very high	Very high	Very high

Table 13.1

A Synthesis of Strategy, Structure and Control Systems

Structure and control	Multidomestic	International	Global	Transnational
Vertical differentiation	Decentralized	Core competency; rest decentralized	Some centralized	Mixed centralized and decentralized
Horizontal differentiation	Worldwide area structure	Worldwide product division	Worldwide product division	Informal matrix
Need for coordination	Low	Moderate	High	Very high
Integrating mechanisms	None	Few	Many	Very many
Performance ambiguity	Low	Moderate	High	Very high
Need for cultural controls	Low	Moderate	High	Very high

Table 13.2

CHAPTER 14: OVERVIEW AND TEACHING SUGGESTIONS

OUTLINE OF CHAPTER 14

OPENING CASE: FUJI-XEROX
INTRODUCTION
ENTRY MODES
    Exporting
    Turnkey Projects
    Licensing
    Franchising
    Joint Ventures
    Wholly Owned Subsidiaries
CHOOSING AN ENTRY MODE
    Core Competencies and Entry Mode
    Pressures for Cost Reductions and Entry Mode
STRATEGIC ALLIANCES
    The Advantages of Strategic Alliances
    The Disadvantages of Strategic Alliances
MAKING ALLIANCES WORK
    Partner Selection
    Alliance Structure
    Managing the Alliance
SUMMARY OF CHAPTER
CRITICAL DISCUSSION QUESTIONS
CLOSING CASE: THE FORD/MAZDA ALLIANCE

OBJECTIVES OF CHAPTER 14

1.   Present the advantages and disadvantages of six different modes of entering new countries and markets

2.   Bring together the issues of FDI discussed chapters 6-7 and the issues of strategy and organization discussed in chapters 12-13 to better understand why different firms may make different decisions regarding the best modes of entry

3.   Discuss in some detail strategic alliances, their advantages and disadvantages, and the factors critical to making alliances work

LECTURE OUTLINE FOR CHAPTER 14

A.   Introduction

1   There are several different options open to a firm that wishes to enter a foreign market, including exporting, licensing or franchising to host country firms, setting up a joint venture with a host country firm, or setting up a wholly owned subsidiary in the host country to serve that market. Each of these options has its advantages and each has its disadvantages.

2. The magnitude of the advantages and disadvantages associated with each entry mode are determined by a number of different factors, including transport costs and trade barriers, political and economic risks, and firm strategy. The optimal choice of entry mode varies from situation to situation depending upon these various factors. Thus while it may make sense for some firms to serve a given market by exporting, other firms might serve the same market by setting up a wholly owned subsidiary in that market, or by utilizing some other entry mode.

3. We can define strategic alliances as cooperative agreements between actual or potential competitors. The term "strategic alliances" is often used rather loosely to embrace a wide range of arrangements between firms, including cross-share holding deals, licensing arrangements, formal joint ventures, and informal cooperative deals

4. Strategic alliances have both advantages and disadvantages, and require significant effort if they are to work successfully. The opening case of Fuji-Xerox and the closing case of Ford/Mazda show examples of how firms have worked together and benefited from their alliance.

B.   Entry Modes

1.   Exporting: Manufacturing in existing locations and transporting into new markets
        Advantages: avoid costs of investing in new location
                             realize experience curve and location economies
        Disadvantages: new locations may have lower manufacturing costs
                             transport costs
                             tariff and non-tariff barriers
                             agents in the foreign country may not act in exporter's best interest

2.   Turnkey Projects: Setting up a new plant ready for operation
        Advantages: obtain returns from know-how about a complex process
                             government restrictions may limit other options
                             lower risk if unstable economic/political situation in country
        Disadvantages: less potential to profit from success of plant
                             creating a competitor
                             give away technological know-how to potential competitor

3.   Licensing: Foreign licensee buys rights to manufacture a firm's product
        Advantages: do not bear the costs and risks of investment
                             avoid political/economic problems or restrictions in a country
        Disadvantages: loss of control over operations (marketing, manufacturing, strategy)
                             unable to realize experience curve and locational economies
                             limited in coordinating international strategy against competitors
                             loss of technological know-how
      Cross-licensing can minimize some of the disadvantages of direct licensing if there is a potential for two-way licensing; it creates interdependencies between the parties.

4.   Franchising: Selling limited rights to use of a brand name and service know-how
        Advantages: do not bear the costs and risks of investment
                             avoid political/economic problems and restrictions in a country
                             quicker international expansion possible
        Disadvantages: limited in coordinating international strategy against competitors
                             loss of control over quality and service

5.   Joint Ventures: Work with a local partner and share in the costs/profits of an operation
        Advantages: benefit from local firm's knowledge
                               shared costs/risks of development
                               political constraints on other options
        Disadvantages: loss of control over technology
                               limited ability to realize experience curve and locational economies
                               limited ability to coordinate international strategy against competitors
                               conflicts between partners over goals and objectives of the JV

6.   Wholly Owned Subsidiaries: 100% ownership in an operation in a country
        Advantages: control over technological know-how ensured
                               control over ability to coordinate international strategy
                               ability to realize location and experience economies
                               ability to coordinate with other subsidiaries
        Disadvantages: costly
                               risky

C.   Selecting an Entry Modes

1.   A brief summary of the advantages and disadvantages of each of the modes is shown in Table 14.1.

2.   The optimal choice of entry mode for firms pursuing an multinational strategy depends to some degree on the nature of their core competency.

3.   If a firm's competitive advantage (its core competence) is based upon control over proprietary technological know-how, licensing and joint venture arrangements should be avoided if possible in order to minimize the risk of losing control over that technology, unless the arrangement can be structured in a way where these risks can be reduced significantly.

4.   When a firm perceives its technological advantage as being only transitory, or the firm may be able to establish its technology as the dominant design in the industry, then licensing may be appropriate even if it does involve the loss of know-how. By licensing its technology to competitors, a firm may also deter them from developing their own, possibly superior, technology.

5.   The competitive advantage of many service firms is based upon management know-how. For such firms, the risk of loosing control over their management skills to franchisees or joint venture partners is not that great, and the benefits from getting greater use of their brand names can be significant.

6.   The greater the pressures for cost reductions, the more likely it is that a firm will want to pursue some combination of exporting and wholly owned subsidiaries. This will allow it to achieve location and scale economies as well as retain some degree of control over its worldwide product manufacturing and distribution.

D.   Strategic Alliances

1.   The term strategic alliances refers to cooperative agreements between potential or actual competitors

2.   The advantages of alliances are that they facilitate entry into foreign markets, enable partners to share the fixed costs and risks associated with new products and processes, facilitate the transfer of complementary skills between companies, and help firms to establish technical standards.

3.   The disadvantage of a strategic alliance is that the firm risks giving away technological know-how and market access to its alliance partner, while getting very little in return.

E.   Making Alliances Work

1.   When considering the selection of a partner, the partner must be one that can help the firm achieve its goals, share the firm's vision for the purpose of the alliances, and not act opportunistically to exploit the alliance for purely its own ends. Partner selection can be critical to success, and requires a significant investment in researching the skills and traits of potential partners.

2.   A firm should structure the alliance so as to avoid unintended transfers of know-how. This can be done by walling-off sensitive technologies, by writing contractual safeguards into alliance agreements, by agreeing in advance to engage in reciprocal swaps of technological know-how, and by seeking credible commitments from alliance partners. These are outlined in Figure 14.1.

3.   Two of the keys to making alliances work seem to be (i) building trust and informal communications networks between partners, and (ii) taking proactive steps to learn from alliance partners.

4.   Overall strategic alliances tend to have quite high failure rates. Many times this failure is a result of unrealistic expectations and conflicts between the partners. It should be noted, however, that just because an alliance is terminated it may not have necessarily failed - some perfectly acceptable alliances can serve mutual interests for short periods of time where both parties benefit, and then end when the benefits no longer exceed the costs. I sometimes make analogies between alliances and dating practices of young people to emphasize the benefits, costs, risks, and long vs. short term nature of the "alliances".

ANSWERS TO CRITICAL DISCUSSION QUESTIONS FOR CHAPTER 14

QUESTION 1: "Licensing propriety technology to foreign competitors is the best way to give up a firm's competitive advantage." Discuss.

ANSWER 1: The statement is basically correct - licensing proprietary technology to foreign competitors does significantly risk loss of the technology. Therefore licensing should generally be avoided in these situations. Yet licensing still may be a good choice in some instances. When a licensing arrangement can be structured in such a way as to reduce the risks of a firm's technological know-how being expropriated by licensees, then licensing may be appropriate. A further example is when a firm perceives its technological advantage as being only transitory, and it considers rapid imitation of its core technology by competitors to be likely. In such a case, the firm might want to license its technology as rapidly as possible to foreign firms in order to gain global acceptance for its technology before imitation occurs. Such a strategy has some advantages. By licensing its technology to competitors, the firm may deter them from developing their own, possibly superior, technology. And by licensing its technology the firm may be able to establish its technology as the dominant design in the industry. In turn, this may ensure a steady stream of royalty payments. Such situations apart, however, the attractions of licensing are probably outweighed by the risks of losing control over technology, and licensing should be avoided.

QUESTION 2: What kind of companies stand to gain the most from entering into strategic alliances with potential competitors? Why?

ANSWER 2: Firms that stand to learn much more from their competitors (or learn more important information) than they expect their competitors to learn from them stand to gain a great deal from a strategic alliance. If a firm is able to team up with a competitor that is in a good position to make significant advances in the near future (either by its own efforts or in conjunction with its partner), then an alliance can also provide significant benefits. More generally, if a strategic alliance greatly eases a firm's entry into a new market, allows it to undertake projects that would have been too risky or costly otherwise, brings together complementary skills to bear on a problem that neither firm would have been able to address individually, or provides an opportunity to set a technological standard, then a firm stands to gain a great deal from an alliance.

QUESTION 3: Discuss how the need for control over foreign operations varies with the strategy and core competencies of a firm. What are the implications of this for the choice of entry mode?

ANSWER 3: If a firm's strategy is primarily global or transnational, the need for cost reduction and coordination between different national entities - and hence control over these entities - is increased, and wholly owned subsidiaries or exporting are preferable over other alternatives. Likewise, in firm's whose core competencies suggest that it needs to carefully control the dissemination of know-how (i.e. high technology), then wholly owned subsidiaries and exporting give greater control over the competencies and decrease the possibility of loss.

QUESTION 4: A small Canadian firm that has developed a set of valuable new medical products using its own unique biotechnology know-how is trying to decide how best to serve the European Community market. Its choices are as follows. (i) Manufacture the product at home and let foreign sales agents handle marketing. (ii) Manufacture the products at home but set up a wholly owned subsidiary in Europe to handle marketing. (iii) Enter into a strategic alliance with a large European pharmaceutical firm. The product would be manufactured in Europe by a 50/50 joint venture, and then marketed by the European firm. The cost of investment in manufacturing facilities is a major one for the Canadian firm - but it is not outside of the firm's reach. If these are the firm's only options, what option would you advise it to choose? Why?

ANSWER 4: If there are no significant barriers to exporting, then option (iii) would seem unnecessarily risky and expensive. After all, the transportation costs required to ship drugs are small relative to the value of the product. Both options (i) and (ii) would expose the firm to less risk of technological loss, and would allow the firm to maintain much tighter control over the quality and costs of the drug. The only other reason to consider option (iii) would be if an existing pharmaceutical firm could also give it much better access to the market and potentially access to its products and technology, and that this same firm would insist on the 50/50 manufacturing joint venture rather than agreeing to be a foreign sales agent. The choice between (i) and (ii) boils down to a question of which way will be the most effective in attacking the market. If a foreign sales agent can be found that is already quite familiar with the market and who will agree to aggressively market the product, the agent may be able to increase market share more quickly than a wholly owned marketing subsidiary that will take some time to get going. On the other hand, in the long run the firm will learn a great deal more about the market and will likely earn greater profits if sets up its own sales operations. And if it is unable to find a sales agent who will aggressively sell the product, than this may be best alternative.

STUDENT EXERCISES AND PROJECTS FOR CHAPTER 14

- An exercise that I have used at this point in the class (with admittedly varying degrees of success) is to ask the students to identify one major purchase (over $100) they have made recently. One stipulation is that the product should either be "made" or "marketed" by a foreign firm. Things like bikes, computers, stereo equipment, autos, etc. are often identified. Then I ask them to try and figure out how that product got to them. Who "made" it where, who got it to where they bought it, how did it get the brand name it has, and who sold it to them. Sometimes this can work out great. A mountain bike, for example, may have some Japanese components put on a frame made in Indonesia, and marketed by an "local" sounding firm that is really owned by a foreign multinational. I ask them to try and explain why who licensed or exported what to whom. Sometimes it gets incredibly difficult (or impossible) to figure out what came from where and why. Other times it is a trivial problem (a VCR made in Japan by Matsushita. In any case as long as students choose some different products it is often easy to see all of the entry modes in operation. I usually ask for brief verbal reports in the next class.
- A simpler exercise is to ask students to find an example of a recent "entry" by a foreign firm by looking in the newspaper, magazines, or a database. The next step in the exercise is to see if the entry strategy would seem to fit with the advantages and disadvantages outlined in the chapter. Does a proposed joint venture, for example, seem to have the advantages outlined in the chapter, and do the other forms of entry seem less appropriate in this instance. Frequently students have wondered why an alternative wasn't chosen, but usually did not really have the information available to really get a full understanding.

SUGGESTED READINGS FOR CHAPTER 14

The footnotes suggest some appropriate additional readings. The following may be of particular interest:

Bleeke, Joel and David Ernst 1993. Collaborating to compete: Using global alliances and acquisitions in the global marketplace. New York: John Wiley and Sons.

Kogut, Bruce 1988. Joint ventures: Theoretical and empirical perspectives. Strategic Management Journal. 9(4): 319-332.

Root, Franklin R. 1980. Entry strategies for international markets. Lexington, MA: D.C. Heath

TRANSPARENCY MASTERS FOR CHAPTER 14 FOLLOW

Advantages and Disadvantages of Entry Modes

Entry Mode	Advantage	Disadvantage
Exporting	Ability to realize location and experience curve economies	High transport costs Trade barriers Problems with local marketing agents
Turnkey contracts	Ability to earn returns from process technology skills in countries where FDI is restricted	Creating efficient competitors Lack of long-term market presence
Licensing	Low development costs and risks	Lack of control over technology Inability to realize location and experience curve economies Inability to engage in global strategic coordination

Table 14.1a

Advantages and Disadvantages of
Entry Modes *CONTINUED*

Entry Mode	Advantage	Disadvantage
Franchising	Low development costs and risks	Lack of control over quality Inability to engage in global strategic coordination
Joint ventures	Access to local partner's knowledge Sharing development costs and risks Politically acceptable	Lack of control over technology Inability to engage in global strategic coordination Inability to realize location and experience economies
Wholly owned subsidiaries	Protection of technology Ability to engage in global strategic coordination Ability to realize location and experience economies	High costs and risks

IRWIN © Times Mirror Higher Education Group Inc., Company 1997

Table 14.1b

Structuring Alliances to Reduce Opportunism

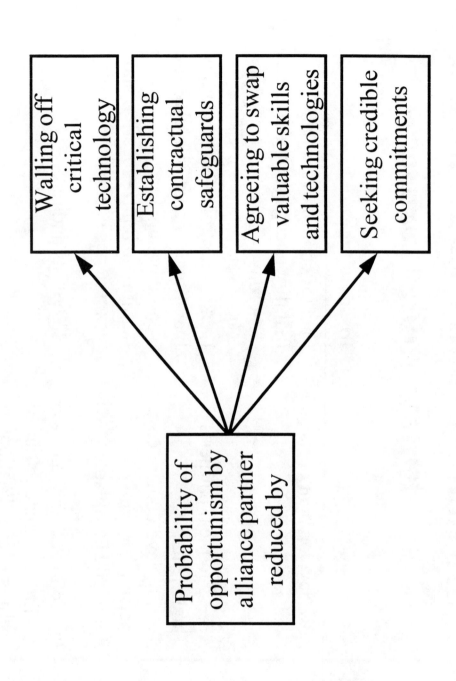

Probability of opportunism by alliance partner reduced by

- Walling off critical technology
- Establishing contractual safeguards
- Agreeing to swap valuable skills and technologies
- Seeking credible commitments

IRWIN © Times Mirror Higher Education Group Inc., Company 1997

Figure 14.1

CHAPTER 15: OVERVIEW AND TEACHING SUGGESTIONS

OUTLINE OF CHAPTER 15

OBJECTIVES OF CHAPTER 15

1.   Outline some of the tremendous advantages and common pitfalls of exporting

2.   Identify the primary sources of information available to firms interested in exporting

3.   Describe the "nuts and bolts" of exporting

4.   Suggest how firms can use the EXIM bank and insurance to facilitate exports

5.   Explain in more detail the various types of countertrade and the pro and cons of engaging in countertrade

LECTURE OUTLINE FOR CHAPTER 15

A.   Introduction

1   The previous chapter presented exporting as just one of a range of strategic options for profiting from international markets. This chapter looks more at the nuts and bolts of how to export.

2.   From the opening case we can see that exporting is not just an activity of large multinationals that do it to obtain scale and location economies, but is also an activity for small firms. Almost all large multinationals today started their expansion overseas via exporting.

3.   Exporting can be a very challenging activity for many firms - unfortunately it usually takes more effort than just placing goods in a box and slapping on foreign shipping label as we will see.

B.   The Promise and Pitfalls of Exporting

1.   The potential benefits from exporting can be great. Regardless what country a firm is based in, the rest of the world is a much larger market than the domestic market. While larger firms may be proactive in seeking out new export opportunities, many smaller firms are reactive and only pursue international opportunities when the customer calls or knocks on the door.

2.   Many neophyte exporters have run into significant problems when first trying to do business abroad, souring them on following up on subsequent opportunities.

3.   Common pitfalls include poor market analysis, poor understanding of competitive conditions, lack of customization for local markets, poor distribution arrangements, bad promotional campaigns, and a general underestimation of the differences and expertise required for foreign market penetration.

4.   If basic business issues weren't enough, the tremendous paperwork and formalities that must be dealt with can be overwhelming to small firms.

C.   Improving Export Performance

1.   National differences in the governmental and business infrastructure available for supporting exporting vary considerably. German and Japanese firms have relatively easy access to information and assistance. While US firms are not left totally to their own devices, the amount of direct and indirect assistance to them is much less developed.

2.   One of the biggest impediments to exporting is ignorance of foreign market opportunities.

3.   The best way of overcoming ignorance is to collect more information. In the US there are a number of institutions, most importantly the US Department of Commerce, that can assist firms in the information gathering and matchmaking process.

4.   Business and trade associations can also provide valuable assistance to firms.

5.   One way for first-time exporters to identify opportunities and help avoid pitfalls is to hire an Export Management Company. A good EMC will have a network of contacts in potential markets, will have multilingual employees, will have knowledge of different business mores, and will be fully conversant with the ins and outs of the exporting process and with local business regulations.

6.   One drawback of relying on EMCs is that the company fails to develop its own exporting capabilities.

7.   The probability of exporting successfully can be improved by utilizing an EMC or export consultants, focusing on only one or a few markets at first and get them working effectively, starting out on a small scale, having realistic expectations about the time and commitment required, developing good relations with local distributors, and hiring local personnel. The example of 3M helps illustrate one firm's approach.

D.   Export and Import Financing

1.   Firms engaged in international trade face a problem - they have to trust someone who may be very difficult to track down if they default on an obligation.

2.   Due to the a lack of trust, each party to an international transaction has a different set of preference regarding the configuration of the transaction. Figures 15.1 and 15.2 show the preferences for two firms - a US exporter and a French importer.

3.   The problems arising from a lack of trust between exporters and importers can be solved by using a third party who is trusted by both - normally a reputable bank. Figure 15.3 illustrates this.

4.   A letter of credit is issued by a bank at the request of an importer. It states that the bank promises to pay a beneficiary, normally the exporter, upon presentation of documents specified in the letter of credit.

5.   A draft is the instrument normally used in international commerce to effect payment. It is an order written by an exporter instructing an importer, or an importer's agent, to pay a specified amount of money at a specified time. Drafts fall into two categories - sight drafts and time drafts. Time drafts are negotiable instruments.

6.   The bill of lading is issued to the exporter by the common carrier transporting the merchandise. It serves three purposes; it is a receipt, a contract, and a document of title.

7.   The entire 14 step process for conducting an export transaction is summarized in Figure 15.4. One professor we know goes through the entire 14 step process by describing how a foreign brewery gets a bottle of his favorite beer to from the factory to him - progressively moving a bottle across the board in the front of the room. After the last step, he drinks it.

E.   Export Assistance

1.   Exporters in the US can draw upon two types of government backed assistance to help finance their exports; the Export-Import bank and export credit insurance provided by the FCIA.

2.   The Export-Import Bank is an independent agency of the US government whose mission is to provide aid in financing and facilitate exports and imports and the exchange of commodities between the US and other countries.

3.   In the US, export credit insurance is provided by the Foreign Credit Insurance Association (FCIA). The FCIA provides insurance policies protecting US exporters against the risk of nonpayment by foreign debtors as a result of commercial and political risks.

F.   Countertrade

1.   Countertrade is a term that covers a whole range of barter like agreements. It is primarily used when the firm is exporting to countries whose currency is not freely convertible, and who may lack the foreign exchange reserves required to purchase the imports.

2.   By some estimates, countertrade accounted for 20% of world trade by volume in 1990.

3.   There are five distinct types of countertrade - barter, counterpurchase, offset, switch trading, and buy back.

4.   Barter is the direct exchange of goods and services, or both, between two parties without a cash transaction. Although in theory barter is the simplest arrangement, in practice it is not that common.

5.   Counterpurchase is a reciprocal buying agreement. It occurs when a firm agrees to purchase a certain amount of materials back from a country to which a sale is made.

6.   Offset is similar to counterpurchase in so far as the exporter is required to purchase goods and services with an agreed percentage of the proceeds from the original sale. The difference is that the exporter can fulfill this obligation with any firm in the country to which the sale is being made.

7.   The term "switch trading" refers to the use of a specialized third-party trading house in a countertrade arrangement. When a firm enters into a counterpurchase or offset agreement with a country it often ends up with what are called "counterpurchase credits". These should be used to purchase goods from that country. Switch trading occurs when a third party trading house buys the firm's counterpurchase credits and sells them to another firm that can make better use of them.

8.   A buyback occurs when a firm builds a plant in a country, or supplies technology, equipment, training, or other services to the country, and agrees to take a certain percentage of the plant's output as partial payment for the contract.

9.   The main attraction of countertrade is that it gives a firm a way to finance an export deal when other means are not available. A firm that insists on being paid in hard currency may be at a competitive disadvantage vis-à-vis one that is willing to engage in countertrade.

10.   The main disadvantage of countertrade is that it may involve the exchange of unusable or poor quality goods that cannot be disposed of profitably.

11.   As an option, countertrade is most attractive to large, diverse, multinational enterprises that can use their world wide network of contacts to profitably dispose of goods acquired in a countertrade agreement. It is less attractive to small and medium sized exporters who lack a similar network.

ANSWERS TO CRITICAL DISCUSSION QUESTIONS FOR CHAPTER 15

QUESTION 1: A firm based in Washington State wishes to export a shipment of finished lumber to the Philippines. The would be importer cannot get sufficient credit from domestic sources to pay for shipment, but insists that the finished lumber can quickly be resold in the Philippines for a profit. Outline the steps that the exporter should take to effect the export of this shipment to the Philippines?

ANSWER 1: (If the exporter feels confident that it can completely trust the Philippines purchaser, then a much simpler procedure than that outlined below can be utilized.)

Step 1: The Philippine importer places an order with the American exporter, and asks the American if he would be willing to ship under a letter of credit.

Step 2: The American exporter agrees to ship under a letter of credit, and specifies relevant information such as prices, delivery terms, and the like.

Step 3: The Philippine importer applies to the Bank of Manila (or some other international bank) for a letter of credit to be issued in favor of the American exporter for the merchandise the importer wishes to buy.

Step 4: The Bank of Manila issues a letter of credit in the Philippine importer's favor and sends it to the American exporter's bank, the Bank of Seattle.

Step 5: The Bank of Seattle advises the American exporter of the opening of a letter of credit in his favor.

Step 6: The American exporter ships the goods to the Philippine importer on a common carrier.

Step 7: The American exporter presents a 90 day time draft to the Bank of Seattle, drawn on the Bank of Manila in accordance with the Bank of Manila's letter of credit and accompanied by the bill of lading. The American exporter endorses the bill of lading such that the title to the goods goes with the holder of the document - which at this point in the transaction is the Bank of Seattle.

Step 8: The Bank of Seattle presents the draft and documents to the Bank of Manila. The Bank of Manila accepts the draft, taking possession of the documents and promising to pay the now accepted draft in 90 days.

Step 9: The Bank of Manila returns the accepted draft to the Bank of Seattle.

Step 10: The Bank of Seattle tells the American exporter that they have the accepted bank draft, which is payable in 90 days.

Step 11: The exporter sells the draft to the Bank of Seattle for a discount from the face value and receives the discounted cash value of the draft in return.

Step 12: The Bank of Manila notifies the Philippine importer of the arrival of the documents. It agrees to pay the Bank of Manila in 90 days. The Bank of Manila releases the documents so that the Philippine importer can take possession of the shipment.

Step 13: In 90 days the Bank of Manila receives the importer's payment so that it has funds to pay the maturing draft.

Step 14: In 90 days the holder of the matured acceptance, in this case the Bank of Seattle, presents it to the Bank of Manila for payment. The Bank of Manila pays.

QUESTION 2: You are the assistant to the CEO of a small textile firm that manufactures high-quality, premium priced, stylish clothing. The CEO has decided to see what the opportunities are for exporting and has asked you for advice as to the steps the company should take. What advice would you give to the CEO?

ANSWER 2: The first steps are clearly to get additional information regarding about export opportunities. Getting in contact with EMCs, textile and fashion consultants experienced in exporting, industry trade associations, and potentially your country's commerce or export assistance departments would be some of the best ways to gather information about potential markets.

QUESTION 3: An alternative to using a letter of credit is export credit insurance. What are the advantages and disadvantages of using export credit insurance as opposed to a letter of credit for (a) exporting a luxury yacht from California to Canada, and (b) exporting machine tools from Seattle to the Ukrainian Republic?

ANSWER 3: In the case of exporting a luxury yacht from California to Canada, either a letter of credit or credit insurance is likely to be available, and the choice for the exporter would simply rest on which was the least expensive - neither is entirely costless in effort nor expenditures. If the exporter is under severe cash constraints, an advantage of the letter of credit is that it can sell it at a discount from face value and get some cash immediately without having to wait until the importer pays. However given the close proximity, similarity, and close legal relations of the US and Canada, the importer may think that a letter of credit is an unnecessary requirement by the exporter, and choose to only do business with a firm that does not require a letter of credit. In such a situation the exporter's only choices would be to bear the risks or purchase credit insurance. In the case of exporting machines tools to the Ukraine, credit insurance may be the best alternative since it insures not only against commercial risk, but political risk as well. Given the current turmoil in the Ukraine, a US bank may also find it difficult to find a Ukrainian bank that it is confident will be able to pay in a convertible currency.

QUESTION 4: What are the reasons for the growing popularity of countertrade? Can you see any scenarios under which the popularity of countertrade might increase still further by the year 2000? Can you see any scenarios under which the popularity of countertrade might decline by the year 2000? What are they?

ANSWER 4: During the 1980s countertrade became increasingly popular among many developing nations who lacked the foreign exchange reserves required to purchase all necessary imports. Today, reflecting their own shortages of foreign exchange reserves, many of the countries of the Commonwealth of Independent States are engaging in some degree of countertrade to purchase their imports. As long as many former communist and developing countries lack hard currencies and foreign exchange reserves, yet have an interest in increasing trade, countertrade is likely to continue. If countries start to erect trade barriers that decrease world trade, or the monetary systems of many countries strengthen significantly, then countertrade may decrease - but this does not seem as likely.

STUDENT EXERCISES AND PROJECTS FOR CHAPTER 15

One interesting exercise for students that deals directly with the material in this chapter, and can be related to material in other chapters, has students visit a small local retailer that sells some imported goods. They are to select one particular good, and attempt to follow its trail back to the foreign manufacturer. Unless students are very persistent they usually loose the trail somewhere. On occasion, however, they have been able to describe the entire process described in this chapter looking backwards through the steps (although the specific financial details can be most difficult to obtain). If a student has close contacts (and is an employee) at a shop, this can be a very interesting exercise. For other students, however, it can be rather frustrating.

SUGGESTED READINGS FOR CHAPTER 15

The footnotes suggest some appropriate additional readings. The following may be of particular interest:

Tuller, L.W. 1991. Going global. Homewood, IL: Irwin.

TRANSPARENCY MASTERS FOR CHAPTER 15 FOLLOW

Preference of the U.S. Exporter

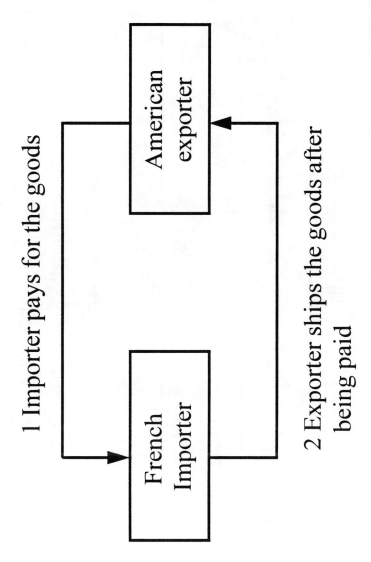

1 Importer pays for the goods

French Importer

American exporter

2 Exporter ships the goods after being paid

Figure 15.1

Preference of the French Importer

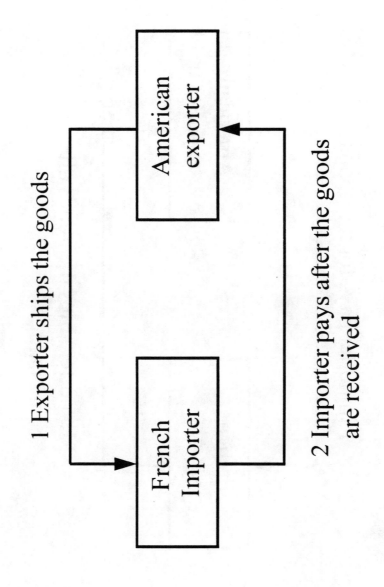

1 Exporter ships the goods

French
Importer

American
exporter

2 Importer pays after the goods
are received

Figure 15.2

A Typical International Trade Transaction

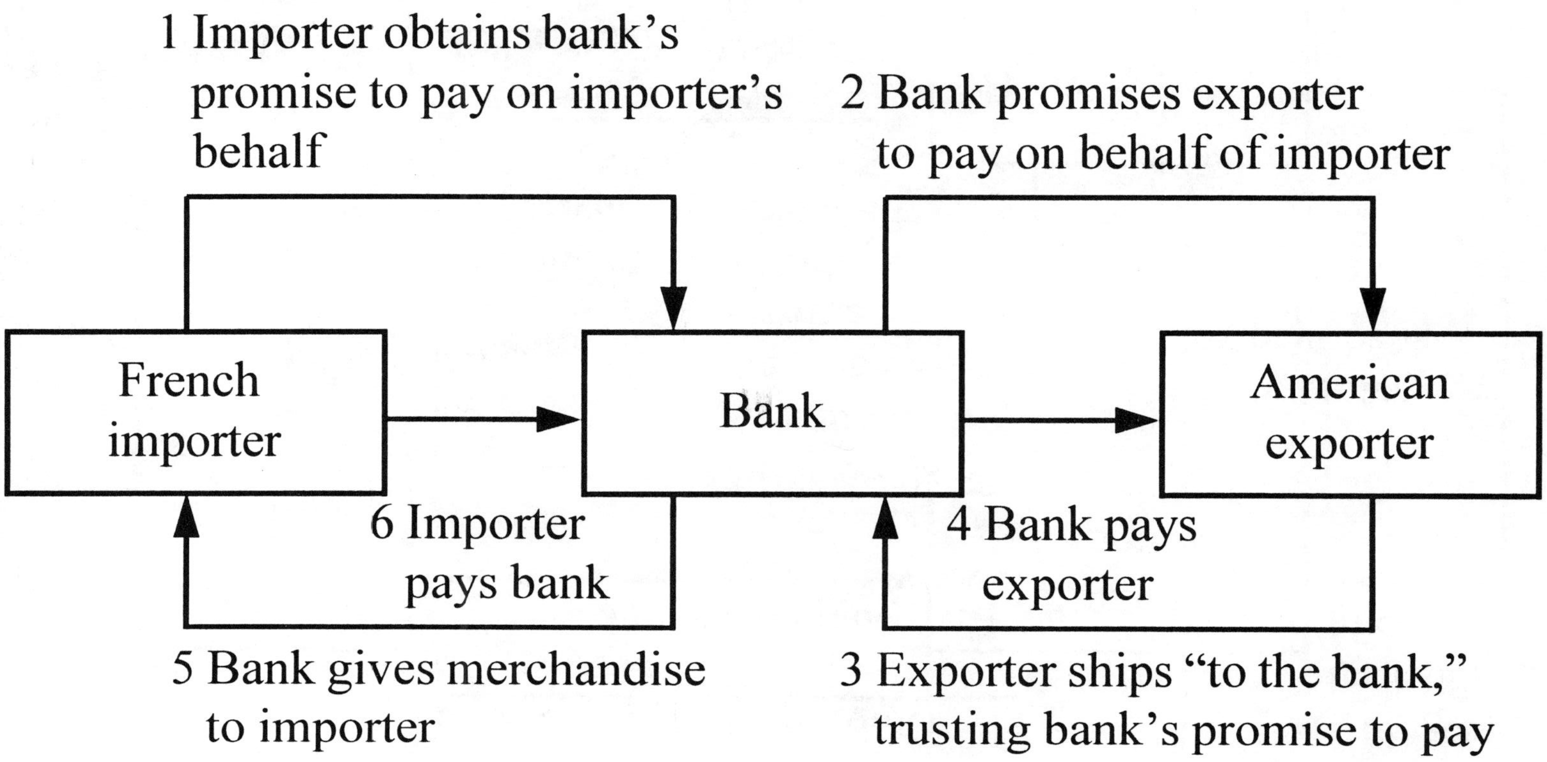

1 Importer obtains bank's promise to pay on importer's behalf

2 Bank promises exporter to pay on behalf of importer

French importer	Bank	American exporter

6 Importer pays bank

5 Bank gives merchandise to importer

4 Bank pays exporter

3 Exporter ships "to the bank," trusting bank's promise to pay

IRWIN © Times Mirror Higher Education Group Inc., Company 1997

Figure 15.3

The Use of a Third Party

Figure 15.4

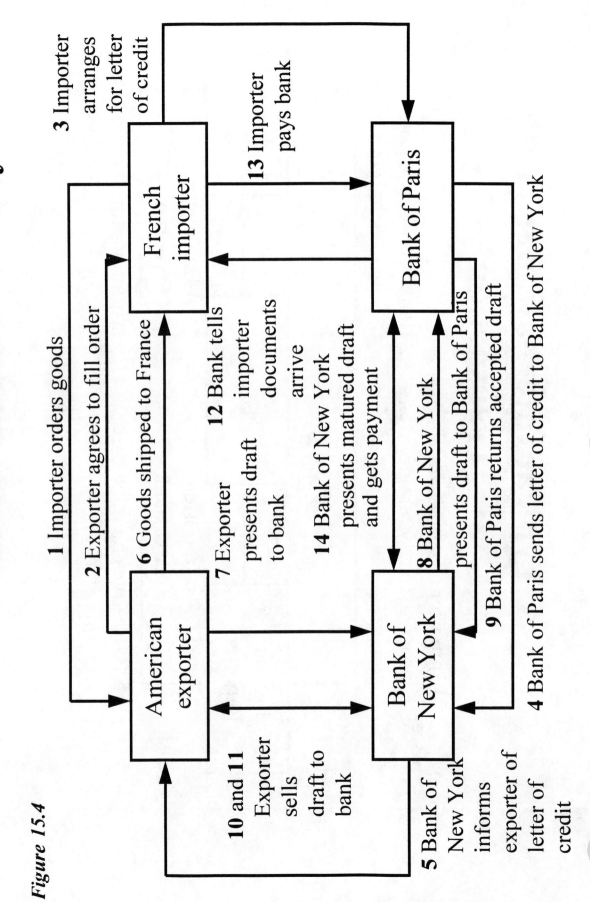

CHAPTER 16: OVERVIEW AND TEACHING SUGGESTIONS

OUTLINE OF CHAPTER 16

OBJECTIVES OF CHAPTER 16

1.   Discuss the factors that firms should consider when deciding where particular goods should be manufactured

2.   Identify the issues associated with deciding what products or component parts should be manufactured in-house by a firm and what should be out-sourced to independent suppliers

3.   Illustrate the advantages, disadvantages, and problems associated with coordinating a tightly linked global manufacturing system

LECTURE OUTLINE FOR CHAPTER 16

A.   Introduction

1.   In this chapter we will be looking at three questions:
        Where in the world should productive activities be located?
        Decide how much production should be performed in-house, and how much outsourced?
        How best to coordinate a globally dispersed supply chain?
      The opening case on Timberland helps illuminate these questions.

B.   Strategy, Manufacturing, and Materials Management

1   The objectives of manufacturing and materials management are to lower costs and to increase
      product quality by eliminating defective products both from the supply chain and from the
      manufacturing process. These objectives are **not** independent of each other.

2.   There are three ways in which improved quality control reduces costs. First, productivity
      increases because time is not wasted manufacturing poor quality products that cannot be sold.
      This saving leads to a direct reduction in unit costs. Second, increased product quality means
      lower re-work and scrap costs. Third, greater product quality means lower warranty and re-work
      costs. The net effect is to lower the costs of value creation by reducing both manufacturing and
      service costs. Figure 16.1 illustrates this.

3.   Added to the objectives of lowering costs and improving quality are two further objectives of
      manufacturing and materials management that take on particular importance for international
      businesses. First, manufacturing and materials management must be able to accommodate
      demands for local responsiveness. Second, manufacturing and materials management must be
      able to respond quickly to shifts in customer demand.

C.   Where to Manufacture

1.   For the firm that considers international production to a feasible option, three broadly defined
      factors need to be considered when making a location decision; country factors, technological
      factors, and product factors

2.   As discussed earlier in the book, country factors suggest that a firm should locate it various
      manufacturing activities in those locations where economic, political, and cultural conditions,
      including relative factor costs, are most conducive to the performance of that activity. However,
      regulations affecting FDI and trade can significantly affect the appropriateness of specific
      countries, as can expectations about future exchange rate changes.

3.   Technological factors include the fixed costs of setting up manufacturing facilities, the minimum
      efficient scale of production, and the availability of flexible manufacturing technologies.

4.   The adoption of flexible manufacturing technologies can help improve the competitive position of
      firms. Most importantly, from the perspective of an international business, flexible
      manufacturing technologies can assist in the process of customizing products to different national
      markets in accordance with demands for local responsiveness.

5.   When fixed costs are substantial, the minimum efficient scale of production is high, and/or
      flexible manufacturing technologies are available, the arguments for concentrating production at

a few choice locations are strong. Alternatively, when both fixed costs and the minimum efficient scale of production are relatively low, and when appropriate flexible manufacturing technologies are not available, the arguments for concentrating production at a few choice locations are not as compelling.

6.   Product factors include the value to weight ratio of the product and whether or not the product serves universal needs.

7.   Two location strategies are possible - concentration of manufacturing and decentralization of manufacturing. The choice between these two strategies should be made in light of country, technological, and product factors. These are summarized in Table 16.1. Figure 16.3 shows the network of production for the Ford Fiesta in Europe.

D.   Make or Buy Decisions

1.   A key issue in many international businesses is identifying which component parts should be manufactured in-house, and which should be out-sourced to independent suppliers.

2.   The advantages of making components in-house are that it facilitates investments in specialized assets, helps the firm protect its proprietary technology, and improves scheduling between adjacent stages in the value chain. Cost is obviously also an important, and not independent factor.

3.   When substantial investments in specialized assets are required to manufacture a component part, the firm will prefer to make that component internally rather than contract out to an independent supplier.

4.   In order to maintain control over its technology, a firm might prefer to make component parts that contain proprietary technology in-house, rather than have them made by independent suppliers.

5.   When a firm needs to tightly control scheduling, planning, and coordination of adjacent production processes, vertical integration can be preferable to being dependent on independent suppliers.

6.   The advantages of buying components from independent suppliers are that it helps preserve strategic flexibility and it helps the firm to avoid many of the organizational problems associated with extensive vertical integration.

7.   The great advantage of buying component parts from independent suppliers is that the firm can maintain its flexibility, switching orders between suppliers as circumstances dictate. This is particularly important in the international context where changes in exchange rates and trade barriers might alter the attractiveness of various supply sources over time.

8.   Vertical integration into the manufacture of component parts involves an increase in the scope of the organization. The resulting increase in organizational complexity can be costly. There are three reasons for this. First, the greater the number of sub-units within an organization, the greater the problems of coordinating and controlling those units. Second, the firm that vertically integrates into component part manufacture may find that because its internal suppliers have a captive customer in the firm, internal suppliers lack an incentive to reduce costs. Third, leading directly on from the previous point, vertically integrated firms have to determine the appropriate price for goods transferred between sub-units within the firm. Setting appropriate transfer prices

is a problem in any firm. The firm that buys its components from independent suppliers can avoid all of these problems.

9.   Several firms have tried to capture some of the benefits of vertical integration, without encountering the associated organizational problems, by entering into long-term strategic alliances with key suppliers. Although alliances with suppliers can help the firm to capture the benefits associated with vertical integration without dispensing entirely with the benefits of a market relationship, alliances do have their drawbacks. The firm that enters into a strategic alliance may find its strategic flexibility limited by commitments to alliance partners.

E.   Coordinating a Global Manufacturing System

1.   Materials management encompasses the activities necessary to get materials to a manufacturing facility, through the manufacturing process, and out through a distribution system to the end user. The materials management function is complicated in an international business by distance, time, exchange rates, customs barriers, and the like. Efficient materials management can have a major impact upon a firm's bottom line.

2.   Just-in-time systems generate major cost savings from reduced warehousing and inventory holding costs. In addition, JIT systems help the firm to spot defective parts and take them out of the manufacturing process - thereby boosting product quality.

3.   For a firm to establish a good materials management function it needs to legitimize materials management within the organization. It can do this by putting materials management on an equal footing with other functions in the firm.

4.   Information technology and particularly electronic data interchange, play a major role in materials management. EDI facilitates the tracking of inputs, allows the firm to optimize its production schedule, allows the firm and its suppliers to communicate in real time, and eliminates the flow of paperwork between a firm and its suppliers.

5.   The closing case on Digital Equipment shows how one firm restructured and reconfigured its global supply chain.

ANSWERS TO CRITICAL DISCUSSION QUESTIONS FOR CHAPTER 16

QUESTION 1: An electronics firm is considering how best to supply the world market for micro-processors used in consumer and industrial electronic products. A manufacturing plant costs approximately $500m to construct. A manufacturing plant costs approximately $500 million to construct and requires a highly skilled workforce. The total value of the world market over the next ten years for this product is estimated to be in the $10-15 billion range. The tariffs prevailing in this industry are currently low. What kind of manufacturing strategy do you think the firm should adopt - concentrated or decentralized? What kind of location(s) should the firm favor for its plant(s)?

ANSWER 1: Given the low tariff barriers, high fixed costs, high value to weight ratio, and universal needs served, a concentrated manufacturing strategy would be favored. As for location, the availability of a highly skilled workforce, relatively stable economic and political environment, and availability advanced manufacturing technologies would be key considerations in choosing a plant location.

QUESTION 2: A chemical firm is considering how best to supply the world market for sulfuric acid. A manufacturing plant costs approximately $20m to construct and requires a moderately skilled workforce. The total value of the world market over the next ten years for this product is estimated to be in the $20-30 billion range. The tariffs prevailing in this industry are moderate. Should the firm favor concentrated manufacturing or decentralized manufacturing? What kind of location(s) should the firm seek for its plant(s)?

ANSWER 2: Given the moderate tariffs, fairly low fixed costs and minimum efficient scale, lack of a need for flexible manufacturing, low value to weight ratio, and volatility of the product, a decentralized manufacturing strategy seems most appropriate. Given the demands for low cost in the commodity chemicals industry, locations that minimize the costs of manufacturing and materials management would be preferred.

QUESTION 3: A firm has to decide whether to make a component part in-house, or to contract out manufacturing to an independent supplier. Manufacturing the part requires a non-recoverable investment in specialized assets. The most efficient suppliers are located in countries with currencies that many foreign exchange analysts expect to appreciate substantially on the foreign exchange market over the next decade. What are the pros and cons of (a) manufacturing the component in-house, and (b) out-sourcing manufacture to an independent supplier? Which option would you recommend? Why?

ANSWER 3:
 Manufacturing in-house:
   reduce risk of currency appreciation - rising costs from independent suppliers
   specialized asset investment would make firm dependent on specific suppliers
   protect technological know-how
   improved scheduling
 Out-sourcing:
   if the product using the component fails in the market, the supplier will bear the cost of
     the non-recoverable investment
   preserve flexibility in case a better component can be designed or bought
   lower organizational and coordination costs
Based on what we know, manufacturing in house may be slightly preferred, but other information could tip the decision the other way.

QUESTION 4: Explain how an efficient materials management function can help an international business to compete more effectively in the global market place?

ANSWER 4: Given the complexity involved in coordination of material and product flows in a multinational enterprise (purchases, currency exchange, inbound and outbound transportation, production, inventory, communication, expediting, tariffs and duties), a materials management function can help to assure that these flows take place in the most efficient manner possible. A related advantage is that by having a materials management function, a firm may obtain improved information about the costs of different transport alternatives, and choose to reconfigure some of its flows to better take advantage of these costs. By being better able to utilize just in time techniques, the cost of production can be lowered while the quality is increased. The materials management function can also help an international business to develop information technology systems that allow it to better track the flow of goods throughout the firm.

STUDENT EXERCISES AND PROJECTS FOR CHAPTER 16

- Many of the practitioner-oriented periodicals in industrial engineering and materials management frequently carry articles like those in the chapter on Bose, Digital, and Timberland. Having students use one or more of these as a basis of a written report or class presentation can often prove very interesting.
- Where available, visiting a local firm with worldwide logistics operations can be very interesting. Sometimes manufacturing and materials personnel are very receptive to class or small group visits, and it can be very interesting for students to actually see the boxes and goods that come from all over the world.

SUGGESTED READINGS FOR CHAPTER 16

The footnotes suggest some appropriate additional readings. The following may be of particular interest:

Dicken, Peter 1992. Global shift. New York: Guilford Press.

Stalk, G. and T.M. Hout 1990. Competing against time. New York: Free Press.

TRANSPARENCY MASTERS FOR CHAPTER 16 FOLLOW

The Relationship Between Quality and Costs

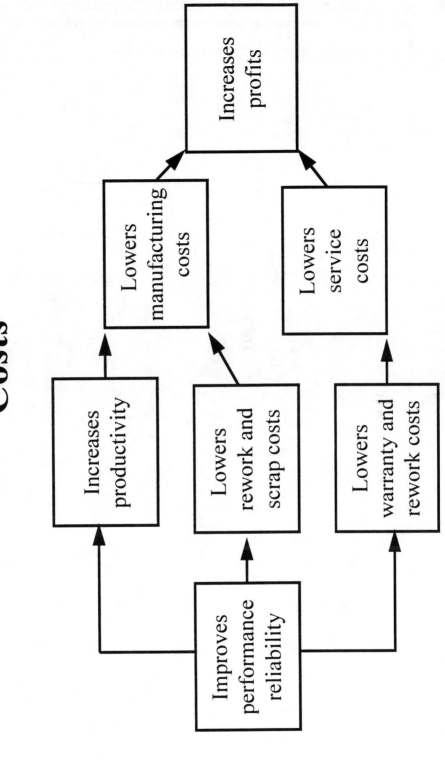

Figure 16.1

The Ford Fiesta Production Network in Europe

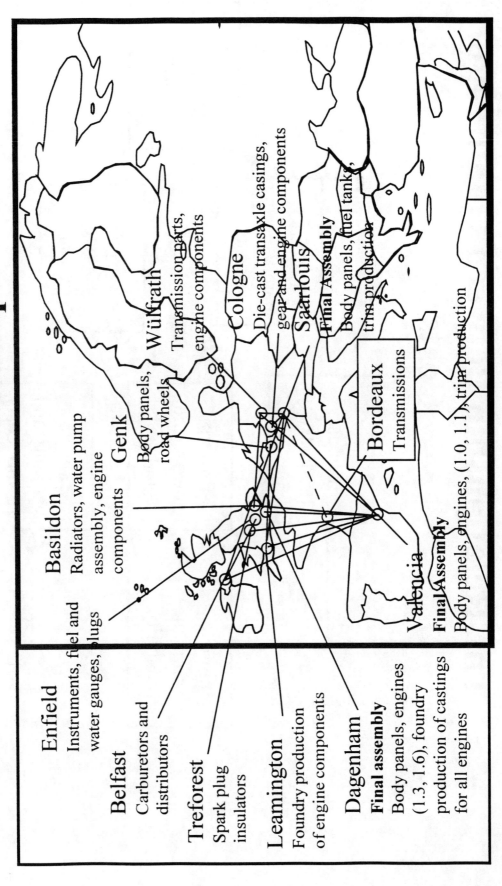

Enfield
Instruments, fuel and
water gauges, plugs

Belfast
Carburetors and
distributors

Treforest
Spark plug
insulators

Leamington
Foundry production
of engine components

Dagenham
Final assembly
Body panels, engines
(1.3, 1.6), foundry
production of castings
for all engines

Basildon
Radiators, water pump
assembly, engine
components

Genk
Body panels,
road wheels

Wülfrath
Transmission parts,
engine components

Cologne
Die-cast transaxle casings,
gear and engine components

Saarlouis
Final Assembly
Body panels, fuel tanks,
trim production

Bordeaux
Transmissions

Valencia
Final Assembly
Body panels, engines, (1.0, 1.1), trim production

Source: Peter Dicken, Global Shift (New York. The Guilford Press, 1992). p. 300.

Map 16.1

CHAPTER 17: OVERVIEW AND TEACHING SUGGESTIONS

OBJECTIVES OF CHAPTER 17

1.   Review the debate on the globalization of markets - are all customers the same? or are there distinct and significant differences?

2.   Better understand the factors that cause firms to alter the marketing mix across countries.

3.   Discuss issues related to the location of R&D facilities and linking marketing and R&D in new product development

<u>LECTURE OUTLINE FOR CHAPTER 17</u>

A.   Introduction

1   The focus of this chapter is on how marketing and R&D can be performed in order to (i) lower the costs of value creation, and (ii) add value by better serving customer needs

2.   The tension that exists in most international businesses between, on the one hand, the need to reduce costs, and on the other hand, the need to be responsive to local conditions is particularly predominant in this chapter as we look at the development and marketing of products

3.   The opening case on MTV illustrates the importance of this network as a conduit to, and creator of, one global market segment. Map 17.1 illustrates MTV's reach. As a contrast, the closing case describing Proctor and Gambles experiences in serving international markets with products developed specifically for the US market illustrates both how underlying products and marketing of these products often must be customized to local requirements. It is interesting to note, however, that Proctor & Gamble was noted as one of the big advertisers on MTV.

B.   The Globalization of Markets?

1.   This topic isn't new - it was discussed several times in earlier chapters. Having students read the passage from Levitt (or reading aloud), and then asking for comments and critique can get a good discussion going. Having students give examples of truly global products, products that have become global recently, as well as those that will likely continue to be quite different in different countries also stimulates discussion.

2.   The general view is usually that while Levitt overstates the case, he does identify a clear trend.

C.   Product Attributes

1.   A product can be viewed as a bundle of attributes. Different customers value different attributes, and value the same attributes differently.

2.   A product can be viewed as a bundle of attributes. Product attributes have to be varied from country to country to account for differences in consumer tastes and preferences. In classes with "foreign" students, I have sometimes asked them what products they have found to be different in their home country from the country they are studying - what products that they thought would be the same did they find to be different. Sometimes they report even the same brand to be notably different. On occasion this has led into a nice discussion of why these differences exist.

3.   Differences in consumer tastes and preferences between countries are a function of differences in culture and economic development.

4.   Differences in product and technical standards may require the firm to customize product attributes from country to country. Within the EU the need to meet differing technical standards is being reduced - but some of these previous technical standards have shaped consumer preferences as well. Even in advanced products like cellular phones, the new "global" GSM standard for digital communication (which allows customers to travel in many countries and still receive calls) has not been approved in North America.

D.   Distribution Strategy

1.   Distribution strategy is about choosing the best channel to deliver a product to the consumer.
        Figure 17.1 illustrates a typical distribution strategy.

2.   Significant country differences with regard to distribution systems exist. In some countries the
        retail system is very concentrated, whereas in others it is very fragmented. In some countries
        channel length is short, whereas in others it is long. And in some countries distribution channels
        may be difficult to gain access to.

3.   In countries with concentrated retail systems, a few retailers supply most of the market. In
        Germany, for example, 4 retail chains control 65% of the food market. In nearby Italy, no chain
        controls more than 2% of the market. Such differences clearly affect how a firm gets its products
        to consumers.

4.   The longer the channel the greater the aggregate mark-up and the higher the price that
        consumers are charged for the final product. Despite this, the benefits of using a longer channel
        may outweigh the drawbacks, particularly if the retail market is very fragmented. The benefits of
        using a longer channel are that longer channels may economize on selling costs and assist the
        firm to gain market access.

5.   When there are exclusive distribution channels, it can be difficult for outsiders to obtain access to
        markets. Exclusive channels are often based on long established and successful relationships.

6.   Occasionally in order to gain market access a firm may have to devise an entirely new
        distribution strategy. While costly, this may be the only way to obtain access, and it may even
        give the firm a competitive advantage.

E.   Communication Strategy

1.   A critical element in the marketing mix is communication strategy; which is the process of
        communicating the attributes of a product to prospective customers.

2.   A number of different communications channels are available to a firm. These include direct
        selling, sales promotion, direct marketing, and advertising via many different media.

3.   A firm's communications strategy is partly defined by its choice of channel.

4.   The effectiveness of international communication can be hindered by three potentially critical
        variables - cultural barriers, source effects, and noise levels.

5.   Cultural barriers arise from the difficulty of communicating messages across cultures. The best
        way for a firm to overcome cultural barriers is for it to develop cross-cultural literacy.

6.   Source effects occur when the receiver of the message (the potential consumer) evaluates the
        message based upon the status or image of the sender. Source effects can be either positive or
        negative. The class can be stimulated to think of some positive and negative source effects
        (German autos vs. German wine, Italian cuisine vs. British cuisine).

7.   Noise tends to reduce the chance of effective communication. In this context, noise refers to the
        amount of other messages that are competing for a potential consumer's attention.

8. The main choice with regard to communication strategy is between a push strategy and a pull strategy. A push strategy emphasizes personnel selling whereas a pull strategy emphasizes mass media advertising. The choice between push and pull strategies depends upon product type and consumer sophistication, channel length, and media availability.

9. Push strategies tend to emphasized more in the following circumstances; (i) for industrial products and/or complex new products, (ii) when distribution channels are short and (iii) when few print or electronic media are available. Pull strategies tend to be emphasized more in the following circumstances; (i) for consumer goods products, (ii) when distribution channels are long and when (iii) sufficient print and electronic media are available to carry the marketing message.

10. A globally standardized advertising campaign is one in which the same marketing message is used the world over. The major benefits of standard advertising are lower costs of ad creation, better utilization of creative talent, avoiding confusion created by differences in message. While a standardized campaign has economic advantages, it fails to account for differences in culture and advertising regulations between countries.

F. Pricing Strategy

1. Price discrimination exists whenever consumers in different countries are charged different prices for the same product. Price discrimination can assist a firm in the process of maximizing its profits.

2. For price discrimination to work the firm must be able to keep national markets separate and different price elasticities of demand must exist in different countries.

3. The elasticity of demand is determined by a number of factors, of which income level and competitive conditions are probably the most important. In general price elasticities tend to be greater in countries with lower income levels and greater numbers of competitors.

4. Figures 17.2 and 17.3 can be used to illustrate how price elasticity can affect pricing strategies and allow firms to maximize profits.

5. Predatory pricing involves using the profit gained in one market to support aggressive pricing in another market. The objective being to drive competitors out of the market.

6. Experience curve pricing involves aggressive pricing to build up accumulated global volume as rapidly as possible, thereby moving the firm down the experience curve as rapidly as possible.

7. The ability of a firm to engage in price discrimination or strategic pricing is limited by antidumping regulations and nation competition policy. Antidumping regulations limit firms ability to price below cost or below the price in its domestic market. Competition regulations can limit firm's ability to charge monopoly prices.

G. Configuring the Marketing Mix

1. Standardization versus customization is not an all or nothing concept. In reality most firms standardize some things and customize others. When looking at the overall marketing mix and message, one often finds some aspects of standardization and some aspects of customization in all products depending on local requirements and overall cost structures.

H.   New Product Development

1.   New product development is a high risk but high return activity. In order to build up a competency in new product development the international business must do two things; (i) disperse R&D activities to those countries where new products are being pioneered, and (ii) integrate R&D with marketing.

2.   Innovations can make established products obsolete overnight. At the same time, innovations can create a host of new product possibilities. To stay abreast of competitors innovations, as well as develop their own, firms should have R&D activities in locations that are on the cutting edge of technology.

3.   The need to adequately commercialize new technologies poses special problems in international businesses, since commercialization my require different versions of the product be produced for different countries.

ANSWERS TO CRITICAL DISCUSSION QUESTIONS FOR CHAPTER 17

QUESTION 1: Imagine you are the marketing manager for a US manufacturer of disposable diapers. Your firm is considering entering the European market, concentrating on the major EU countries. Your CEO believes the advertising message that has been effective in the United States will suffice in Europe. Outline the possible objections to this strategy.

ANSWER 1: While babies behinds serve the same function in all cultures, and the product's technical standards may be similar, sensitivity to bodily functions does vary across cultures. Thus the advertising message may need to be changed for different attitudes towards what is appropriate advertising. Likewise, where it might be progressive to show an ad with a male changing a diaper in some countries, in other countries this message could be lost or misinterpreted. Another consideration would be the noise level created by the advertising message of competitor's products, which may well be different across the continent.

QUESTION 2: "By the end of this century we will have seen the emergence of enormous global markets for standardized consumer products." Do you agree with this statement? Justify your answer.

ANSWER 2: One could either choose to agree or disagree, while the best answer would likely hedge it somewhere in the middle. There clearly already are enormous global markets already for products like Coke and Levis, while it is questionable whether there will ever be a global consumer market for Norwegian lutefisk. More global consumer markets will likely emerge, but there will continue to be national distinctions for many products.

QUESTION 3: You are the marketing manager of a food products company that is considering entering the South Korean market. The retail system in South Korea tends to be very fragmented. Moreover, retailers and wholesalers tend to have long-term ties with South Korean food companies, which makes it difficult to get access to distribution channels. What distribution strategy would you advise the company to pursue? Why?

ANSWER 3: Given the fact that one is marketing a consumer good in a country with long (and seemingly blocked) distribution channels and where there are many different types of media advertising available, a pull strategy would probably be the best.

QUESTION 4: "Price discrimination in indistinguishable from dumping." Discuss the accuracy of this statement?

ANSWER 4: In some specific instances this statement is correct, but as a general rule it is not. When a firm is pricing lower in a foreign country than it is in its domestic market, it can be difficult to distinguish dumping from price discrimination unless it is clear that the firm is selling at below cost in the foreign market. Yet when costs are reasonably well known and all prices are above these, or if the firm is pricing lower in its domestic market than in foreign markets, it can reasonably concluded that price discrimination rather than dumping is occurring.

STUDENT EXERCISES AND PROJECTS FOR CHAPTER 17

- A relatively simple and interesting exercise for this chapter is to ask students to devise an advertising strategy for a product for different countries. In a very short version of this exercise, you can take a product that the students know well (a local product is particularly good), divide the students in groups, and ask each group to develop an advertising strategy and message for the product in a specific country. This can be done as a 15-20 minute break in the class where they must just rely on their own perceptions of the country. Then each group should present their advertising message to the rest of the class - who are sitting an overall corporate board that must approve local advertising and consider the potential for a single global message. What often results are fairly divergent marketing messages - which illustrates the advantages of local adaptation as well as the difficulty of trying to harmonize these for a worldwide message. Alternatively, this could be given as an exercise to be done between classes or over a week's period, when then it would be possible to gather more country specific information and evaluate positioning relative to local products. (I ran an exercise like this when teaching a 3 hour lecture on global marketing to students in Latvia. A famous local alcoholic beverage made from roots and berries with purported medicinal value was used. The students developing the message for France decided this was a "Latvian Cognac", that should be sipped, enjoyed, and be expensive. The group responsible for Japan suggested that it be marketed as an "ancient medicinal drink" that had positive health benefits and promoted longevity. The group focused on Finland wanted to market it as a cheap way to get very intoxicated. Each group felt the local message would be most appropriate for its market, and as a class we found it difficult to find a message that would be successful in all markets.)
- Students can be asked to look at publications from other countries, and see how products are advertised similarly or differently. For example, students in a class taught in the US could be asked to look at copies of Der Spiegel, La Monde, The Economist, The Financial Times, or other newspapers or magazines that are locally available but published in a foreign country. While some ads will look identical to those they would see in Time or Newsweek (and in fact they may be seeing a "North American Edition" of the publication), others will seem rather strange. They can be asked to find examples of similar or different ads in foreign and local publications, and discuss why the similarities and/or differences exist based on ideas from the chapter.
- One in-class exercise I have done is to play different musical selections, and ask students to identify the source. I have used the "Nirvana Unplugged in New York" album to illustrate how a "local" Seattle band has gained worldwide recognition (distributed at the time by MCA from Japan and pressed by Bertlesmann in Germany), and also played other "local" US, Swedish,

British, and Icelandic artists that the students may or may not have ever heard before. I have used not only modern rock, but also folk, classical, and Jazz depending upon the audience.

SUGGESTED READINGS FOR CHAPTER 17

The footnotes suggest some appropriate additional readings. The following may be of particular interest:

Bartlett, Christopher A. and Sumantra Ghoshal 1989. Managing across borders: The transnational solution. Boston: Harvard Business School Press.

Clark, Kim B. and Steven C. Wheelwright 1993. Managing new product and process development. New York: Free Press.

Douglas, Susan P. and Yoram Wind 1987. The myth of globalization. Columbia Journal of World Business. 22: 19-29

Levitt, Theordore 1983. The globalization of markets. Harvard Business Review. 61(3): 92-102

Any one of the many "International Marketing" text books would also be a useful reference.

TRANSPARENCY MASTERS FOR CHAPTER 17 FOLLOW

MTV: Rocking All over the World

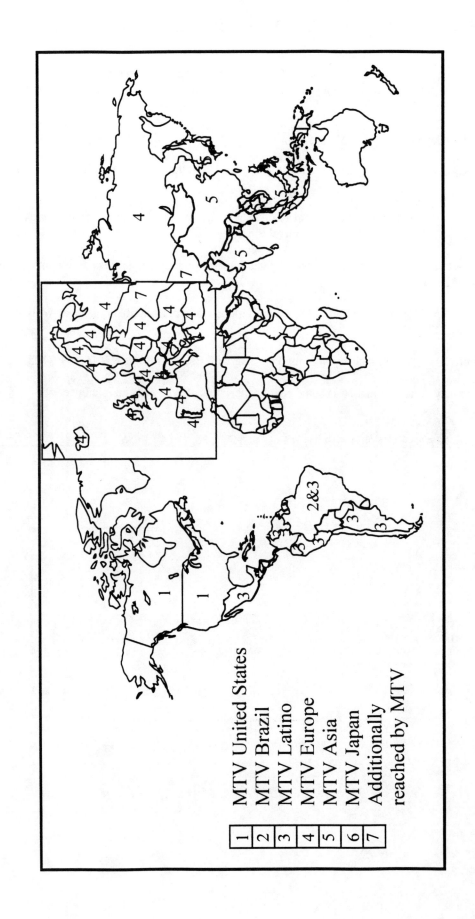

1	MTV United States
2	MTV Brazil
3	MTV Latino
4	MTV Europe
5	MTV Asia
6	MTV Japan
7	Additionally reached by MTV

Source: Industry estimates

Map 17.1

A Typical Distribution System

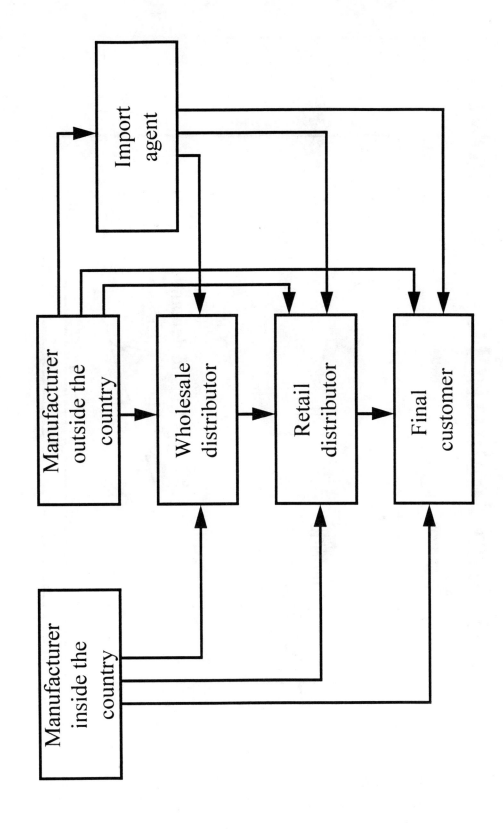

Figure 17.1

Elastic and Inelastic Demand Curves

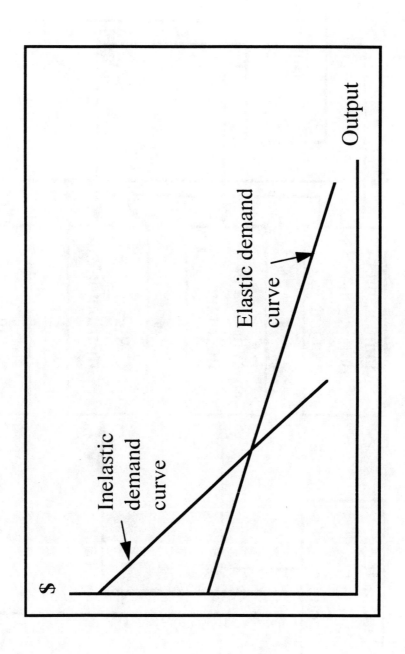

$ — Inelastic demand curve — Elastic demand curve — Output

Figure 17.2

Price Discrimination

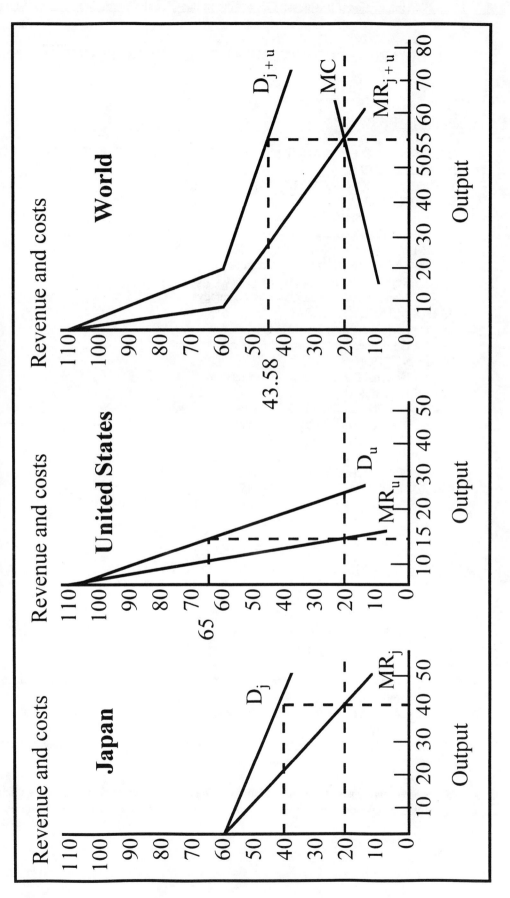

Figure 17.3

CHAPTER 18: OVERVIEW AND TEACHING SUGGESTIONS

OUTLINE OF CHAPTER 18

OPENING CASE: GLOBAL HUMAN RESOURCE MANAGEMENT AT COCA-COLA
INTRODUCTION
THE STRATEGIC ROLE OF INTERNATIONAL HRM
STAFFING POLICY
        Types of Staffing Policy
        The Expatriate Problem
TRAINING AND MANAGEMENT DEVELOPMENT
        Training for Expatriate Managers
        Repatriation of Expatriates
        Management Development and Strategy
PERFORMANCE APPRAISAL
        Performance Appraisal Problems
        Guidelines for Performance Appraisal
COMPENSATION
        National Differences in Compensation
        Expatriate Pay
INTERNATIONAL LABOR RELATIONS
        The Concerns of Organized Labor
        The Strategy of Organized Labor
        Approaches to Labor Relations
SUMMARY OF CHAPTER
CRITICAL DISCUSSION QUESTIONS
CLOSING CASE: GLOBAL HRM AT COLGATE-PALMOLIVE, INC.

OBJECTIVES OF CHAPTER 18

1.   Discuss briefly the strategic role of HRM

2.   Identify the issues and problems with expatriate staffing in particular, and more generally
        rotating managers through international assignments

3.   Suggest some actions for managerial training and development for international firms

4.   Present some of the problems and guidelines relating to the performance appraisal of expatriates

5.   Discuss the issue of compensation in the context of international firms, where differing standards
        across countries can create problems within firms

6.   Show how relations with organized labor can vary across countries, and how organized labor has
        attempted to develop a more international approach to labor negotiations with multinationals

LECTURE OUTLINE FOR CHAPTER 18

A.   Introduction

1   In general, HRM refers to those activities undertaken by an organization to effectively utilize its human resources. These activities include human resource strategy, staffing, performance evaluation, management development, compensation and labor relations.

2.   Firm success requires that HRM policies are congruent with the firm's strategy, and with the firm's formal and informal structure and controls.

3.   The opening case on Coca-Cola and the closing case on Colgate both illustrate some of the practices firms take to increase the international orientation of management.

B.   The Strategic Role of International HRM

1.   For a firm to undertake any of the basic strategies outlined earlier, and have their organization fit with this strategy, the staffing and other HRM functions must also fit with and complement the strategy and organization. Table 18.1, taken from chapter 13, summarizes the relationships among international strategies, structures, and controls.

2.   In particular, we will explore how firms with transnational strategies place different demands on the HRM function than other strategies.

3.   Slogans like "think globally and act locally" sound good, but it requires effective HRM policies for these slogans to be put into action.

C.   Staffing Policy

1.   Staffing policy is concerned with the selection of employees who have the skills required to perform a particular job. Staffing policy can be viewed as a major tool for developing and promoting a corporate culture.

2.   In firms pursuing transnational and global strategies we might expect the HRM function to pay significant attention to selecting individuals who not only have the skills required to perform a particular job, but who also "fit" with the prevailing culture of the firm.

3.   Research has identified three main approaches to staffing policy within international businesses. These have been characterized as an ethnocentric approach, a polycentric approach and a geocentric approach.

4.   An ethnocentric approach to staffing policy is one in which all key management positions in an international business are filled by parent-country nationals. The policy makes most sense for firms pursuing an international strategy. However, ethnocentric firms can suffer from cultural myopia.

5.   A polycentric staffing policy is one in which host country nationals are recruited to manage subsidiaries in their own country, while parent country nationals occupy the key positions at corporate head quarters. While this approach may minimize the dangers of cultural myopia, it may also help create a gap between home and host country operations. The policy is best suited to firms pursuing a multidomestic strategy.

6.   A geocentric staffing policy is one in which the best people are sought for key jobs throughout the organization, regardless of nationality. This approach is consistent with building a strong unifying culture and informal management network. It is well suited to firms pursuing either a global or transnational strategy. The immigration policies of national governments may limit the ability of a firm to pursue this policy.

7.   The advantages and disadvantages of each of the three main approaches to staffing policy are summarized in Table 18.2

8.   A prominent issue in the international staffing literature is expatriate failure, which may be defined as the premature return of an expatriate manager to his or her home country.

9.   The costs of expatriate failure can be substantial. The main reasons for expatriate failure among Western firms seems to be 1) an inability of an expatriate's spouse to adapt to a foreign culture, 2) inability of the employee to adjust, 3) other family-related reasons.

10.   Expatriate failure can be reduced by selection procedures designed to screen out inappropriate candidates. The most successful expatriates seem to be those who have a high self-esteem and self confidence, who get on with others and are willing to communicate in a foreign language, and who can empathize with the behavior of foreigners.

D.   Training and Management Development

1.   Selection is just the first step in matching a manager with a job. The next step involves training the manager to do the job. Training begins where selection ends and it focuses upon preparing the manager for a specific job.

2.   Management development is a rather broader concept. Management development is concerned with developing the skills of the manager over his or her career with the firm.

3.   Training can lower the probability of expatriate failure. Training should include cultural training, language training, and practical training. It should be provided to both an expatriate and her spouse.

4.   As important as selection and training is for expatriate employees, much of the benefit from such assignments can be lost on firms if they are not careful in the repatriation of the expatriates. The Management Focus box on Monsanto describes this firms repatriation program.

5.   Management development programs are designed to increase the overall skill levels of managers through a mix of on-going management education and by rotating managers through a number of different jobs within the firm to give them varied experiences.

6.   Management development is often used as a strategic tool to build a strong unifying culture and informal management network, both of which are supportive of a transnational and global strategy.

E.   Performance Appraisal

1.   It can be difficult to objectively evaluate the performance of expatriate managers due to the intrusion of unintentional bias on the part of those doing the appraisal.

2.   Frequently home country managers must rely more on hard data when evaluating expatriates, and host country managers can be biased towards their own frame of reference.

3.   Involving former expatriates and other expatriates in the evaluation process can help reduce biases.

F.   Compensation

1.   Substantial differences exist between the average pay for executives at the same level in different countries. US executives generally receive substantially more than executives of a similar rank in other countries. Figures 18.1 and 18.2 illustrate this.

2.   Differences in compensation practices raise a difficult problem for an international business. Should the firm pay executives in different countries according to the standards that prevail in each country, or should it equalize pay on a global basis? The problem does not really arise in firms pursuing either an ethnocentric or polycentric staffing policy, but it can be serious in firms pursuing a geocentric staffing policy.

3.   The most common approach to expatriate pay is known as the balance sheet approach. The aim of this approach is to equalize purchasing power so that employees can enjoy the same living standard in their foreign posting that they enjoyed at home. Figure 18.3 illustrates the balance sheet approach.

4.   A further component of the balance sheet approach is to provide financial incentives and allowances to offset qualitative differences between assignment locations.

G.   International Labor Relations

1.   A key issue in international labor relations is the degree to which organized labor is able to limit the choices available to an international business. A firm's ability to pursue a transnational or global strategy can be significantly constrained by the actions of labor unions.

2.   A principal concern of organized labor is that the multinational can counter union bargaining power by threatening to move production to another country. Another concern is that multinationals will try to import and impose unfamiliar labor practices from other countries.

3.   Organized labor has responded to the increased bargaining power of multinational corporations by taking three actions; (1) trying to set-up their own international organizations, (2) lobbying for national legislation to restrict multinationals, and (3) trying to achieve regulations of multinationals through international organization such as the United Nations. However, none of these efforts have been that successful.

4.   Traditional labor relations have been decentralized to individual subsidiaries within multinationals. Now there is a trend towards greater centralization. This enhances the bargaining power of the multinational via-a-vis organized labor.

5.   There is a growing realization that the way in which work is organized within a plant can be a major source of competitive advantage.

ANSWERS TO CRITICAL DISCUSSION QUESTIONS FOR CHAPTER 18

QUESTION 1: What are the main advantages and disadvantages of the ethnocentric, polycentric and geocentric approaches to staffing policy? When is each approach appropriate?

ANSWER 1: An ethnocentric approach to staffing policy is one in which all key management positions in an international business are filled by parent-country nationals. The policy makes most sense for firms pursuing an international strategy, helps a firm maintain a corporate culture, and can be very appropriate when attempting to transfer competencies. However, ethnocentric firms can suffer from cultural myopia, and the limited opportunities available to host country nationals can harm morale. A polycentric staffing policy is one in which host country nationals are recruited to manage subsidiaries in their own country, while parent country nationals occupy the key positions at corporate head quarters. While this approach may minimize the dangers of cultural myopia, it may also help create a gap between home and host country operations and also limits opportunities available to host country nationals. The policy is best suited to firms pursuing a multidomestic strategy. A geocentric staffing policy is one in which the best people are sought for key jobs throughout the organization, regardless of nationality. This approach is consistent with building a strong unifying culture and informal management network, puts all labor to its best use, and minimizes cultural myopia. It is well suited to firms pursuing either a global or transnational strategy. The immigration policies of national governments may limit the ability of a firm to pursue this policy.

QUESTION 2: Research evidence suggests that many expatriate employees encounter many problems that limit both their effectiveness in a foreign posting and their contribution to the company when they return home. What are the main causes and consequences of these problems, and how might a firm reduce the occurrence of such problems?

ANSWER 2: The primary causes of expatriate problems are the inability of the spouse to adjust, inability of the employee to adjust, and other family problems. The consequences of such problems are that an employee can be ineffective or detrimental overseas, and/or may return prematurely before the assigned job tasks are completed. A firm can reduce the occurrence of expatiate problems by developing an effective training and repatriation program. An expatriate training program should include cultural, language, and practical training. Cultural training seeks to foster an appreciation of the host country's culture so that the expatriate behaves accordingly. Language training involves training in local language both from a business and personal perspective. Practical training is aimed at assisting the expatriate manager and her family to ease themselves into day-to-day life in the host country. The sooner a day-to-day routine is established, the better the prospects are that the expatriate and family will adapt successfully. Before leaving, however, specific plans and procedures should be in place for the repatriation of the employee.

QUESTION 3: What is the link between an international business's strategy and its human resource management policies, particularly with regard to the use of expatriate employees and their pay scale?

ANSWER 3: In firms pursuing a multidomestic strategy, a polycentric staffing approach is most common and there are relatively few expatriates or the associated pay issues. Expatriates are more common in firms with international strategies, and an ethnocentric staffing approach is utilized. In this situation the pay is often based on home country levels, with adjustments as required for differing living costs and taxes as outlined by the balance sheet approach. Firms pursuing global or transnational strategies most often use a geocentric approach to staffing, where the best individuals (regardless of nationality) are chosen fill positions in any country. Here the pay issues for expatiates can become particularly complex, as allowance must be made for home country norms, host country costs and expectations, and global norms across the company.

QUESTION 4: In what ways can organized labor constrain the strategic choices of an international business? How can an international business limit these constraints?

ANSWER 4: Organized labor can significantly constrain the choices firms make with respect to location. International firms (or domestic ones for that matter) often choose to locate new facilities in places where there is relative labor peace and harmonious working relations. Labor can also raise objections and threaten disruptive behavior if a firm decides to move some activities to other locations - which in some cases only reinforces the need for relocating the activities. Organized labor has also attempted to (i) set-up their own international organizations, (ii) lobby for national legislation to restrict multinationals, and (iii) achieve regulation of multinationals through international organization such as the United Nations. However, none of these broader efforts have been that successful. International businesses have the advantage of being able to provide or take away jobs, and in today's labor market that gives them considerable power. As a condition of opening or expanding a facility, firms can negotiate favorable conditions with local unions and force unions to compete against each other for the gains in membership.

STUDENT EXERCISES AND PROJECTS FOR CHAPTER 18

•   For this chapter students can be asked to look into the international human resource practices of a multinational firm. Some might be able to gather information from published articles, like many of those referenced in the text and used in writing the opening and closing cases, and the management focus boxes. Others who are working could inquire at their employer - if that employer has operations in other countries. Others may be able to ask a parent or family friend who works in a multinational firm. While sometimes there is initial resistance to such requests, many HRM departments have extensive information on cross-national HRM and expatriate policies in written manuals.

SUGGESTED READINGS FOR CHAPTER 18

The footnotes suggest some appropriate additional readings. The following may be of particular interest:

Adler, Nancy J. 1986. International dimensions of organizational behavior. Boston: Wadsworth.

Black, J. Stewart, and Mark E. Mendenhall 1992. Global assignments: Successfully expatriating and repatriating international managers. San Francisco: Josey-Bass.

Dowling, P.J. and R.S. Schuler 1990. International dimensions of human resource management. Boston: PSW-Kent.

Lane, Henry, Joseph DiStefano, and Martha Mavnezski 1996. International management behavior. Cambridge, MA: Blackwell.

TRANSPARENCY MASTERS FOR CHAPTER 18 FOLLOW

Compensation of General Managers of $30 Million Firms in Selected Countries (in $000)

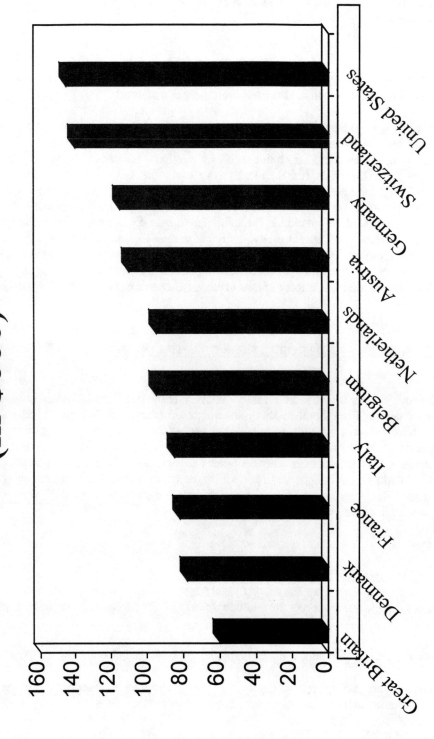

Source: Data from G. Oddou and M. Mendenhall, "Expatriate Performance Appraisal: Problems and Solutions." International Human Resources Management, ed. M. Mendenhall and G. Oddou (Boston: PSW-Kent, 1991)

Figure 18.1

Average Remuneration of CEOs of Firms with More Than $250 Million in Sales, 1991 (in $000)

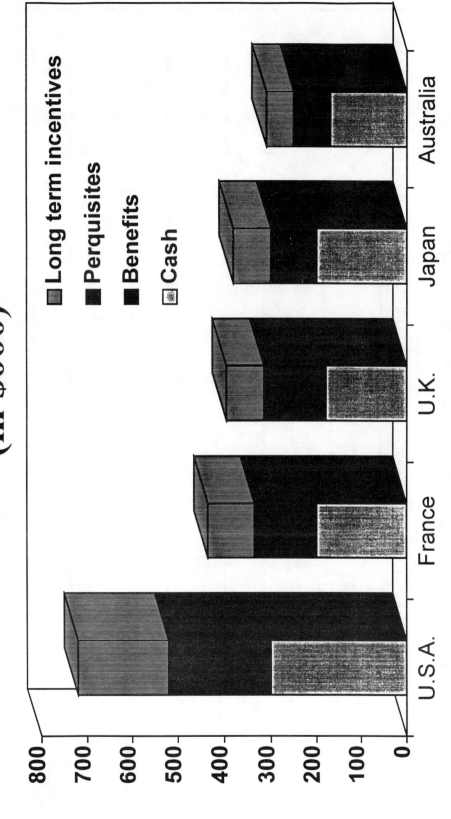

Source: Data estimates from Towers Perrin.

Figure 18.2

A Typical Balance Sheet

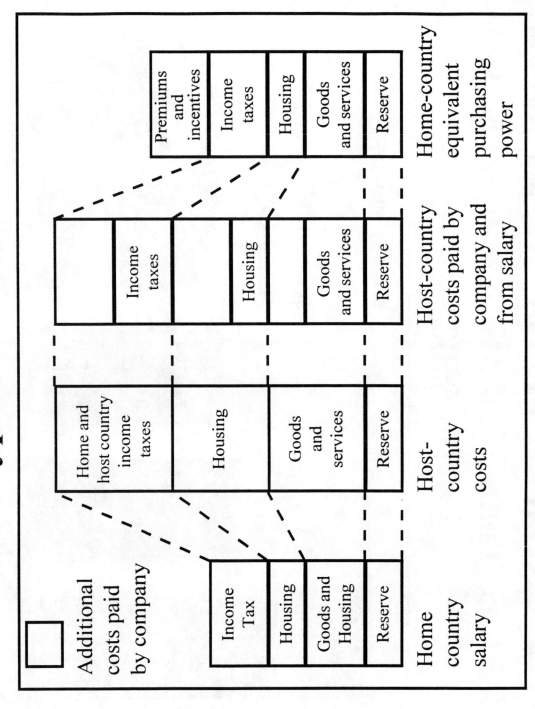

Source: C. Reynolds. "Compensation of Overseas Personnel," in Handbook of Human Resource Administration.
2nd ed. ed J. J. Famularo (New York: McGraw-Hill, 1986), p.51

Figure 18.3

CHAPTER 19: OVERVIEW AND TEACHING SUGGESTIONS

OBJECTIVES OF CHAPTER 19

1.   Describe differences in the accounting policies of different countries

2.   Identify problems associated with these differences, and how international standards are trying to
      address these problems

3.   Show how multinationals need to consolidate financial information across subsidiaries

4.   Explore alternate approaches to currency translation for financial reporting and managerial
      control and evaluation

5.   Emphasize the importance of separating the issue of subsidiary performance from managerial
      performance

LECTURE OUTLINE FOR CHAPTER 19

A.   Introduction

1   Accounting is the language of business. Accounting information represents the means by which firms communicate their financial position to the providers of capital - investors, creditors, the government. Figure 19.1 illustrates the use of financial information in making resource allocations.

2.   International businesses are confronted with a number of accounting problems that do not arise in the case of domestic businesses. They must prepare different reports for different international constituencies and translate and consolidate information across countries and currencies.

3.   The opening case illustrates on example - preparing statements for different investors.

B.   Country Differences in Accounting Standards

1.   Accounting is shaped by the environment in which it operates. In each country the accounting system has evolved in response to the nature of the demands for accounting information.

2.   Five main factors seem to influence the development of a country's accounting system. These are (i) the relationship between business and the providers of capital, (ii) political and economic ties with other countries, (iii) levels of inflation, (iv) the level of a country's development, and (v) the prevailing culture in a country. These are shown in Figure 19.2.

3.   There are three main external sources of capital for business enterprises; (1) individual investors, (2) banks, and (3) government. In most advanced countries all three sources are of some importance, but the form and content of accounting information provided depends upon the relative importance of each of these sources of capital.

4.   Similarities between the accounting systems of two countries may be due to close political and/or economic ties between the two countries. For example, due to geographical proximity and close economic ties, the US accounting system has influenced accounting practices in Canada and Mexico. Many former British colonies have adopted standards similar to the British system.

5.   Differing levels of inflation also have caused countries to take different postures relative how the effects of inflation should affect reporting.

6.   Accounting in developed countries tends to be far more sophisticated than accounting in less developed countries, where fairly primitive accounting standards may prevail.

7.   Map 19.1 identifies the major accounting clusters - groups of nations that have similar standards.

C.   National and International Standards

1.   One result of national differences in accounting and auditing standards is that there is a general lack of comparability of financial reports from one country to the next. The chapter points out a number of specific examples.

2.   The lack of comparability matters due to the rapid growth in transnational financing and transnational investment in recent decades - which is a consequence of the globalization of capital markets. Due to the lack of comparability, a firm may have to explain to investors why its

financial position looks very different when financial reports are prepared under two different sets of accounting principles.

3.   There have been substantial efforts to harmonize accounting standards across countries in recent years. The most significant body pushing for harmonization has been the International Accounting Standards Committee (IASC). IASC has made progress towards harmonization, and for many issues it now allows two alternative reporting scenarios. While this still allows for many differences overall in aggregate financial statements, it represents some progress towards harmonization.

4.   Within the EU, there has been more progress on harmonization, but significant differences still exist.

D.   Multinational Consolidation and Currency Translation

1.   A consolidated financial statement combines the separate financial statements of two or more companies to yield a single set of financial statements as if the individual companies were really one. Most multinational firms are composed of a parent company and various subsidiary companies located in different countries around the globe. Typically, such firms issue consolidated financial statements that cover the whole group of companies, as opposed to issuing individual financial statements for the parent company and each subsidiary

2.   The purpose of consolidated financial statements is to provide financial accounting information about a group of companies that recognizes the economic interdependence between companies within the group.

3.   Transactions among the members of a corporate family are not included on consolidated financial statements; only assets, liabilities, revenues, and expenses with external third parties are shown.

4.   The foreign subsidiaries of multinational firms normally keep their accounting records and prepare their financial statements in the currency of the country in which they are located. When a multinational prepares consolidated accounts, these financial statements must be translated into the currency of the multinational's home country. Some firms use a currency other than the home country's for consolidation; ABB uses US dollars, although its headquarters are in Switzerland. Translation is usually done by either the current rate method or the temporal method.

5.   Under the current rate translation method, the exchange rate at the balance sheet date is used to translate the financial statements of a foreign subsidiary into the home currency. This has the drawback of being incompatible with the historic cost principle.

6.   Under the temporal method, assets valued in a foreign currency are translated into the home currency using the exchange rate that existed when the assets were originally purchased. One problem with this approach is that the balance sheet of the multinational may no longer balance.

7.   Firms pursuing a multidomestic or international strategy are the ones most likely to have self-sustaining subsidiaries, whereas firms pursuing global or transnational strategies, by the very nature of those strategies, are the ones most likely to have integral subsidiaries. Under US FASB regulations, a self-sustaining subsidiary is said to have its own local currency as its functional currency. The balance sheet for such subsidiaries is translated into the home currency using the exchange rate in effect at the end of the firm's financial year, while the income statement is

translated using the average exchange rate in effect during the firm's financial year. On the other hand, an integral subsidiary has US dollars as its functional currency.

E.   Accounting Aspects of Control Systems

1.   In most international businesses the annual budget is the main instrument by which the headquarters controls foreign subsidiaries. Throughout the year the headquarters compares performance against the financial goals incorporated in a subsidiary's budget, intervening selectively in the operations of a subsidiary when short-falls occur. Table 19.1 lists various financial criteria.

2.   Most international businesses require that all budgets and performance data within the firm be expressed in one corporate currency. While this enhances comparability, it leads to distortions in the control process if the relevant exchange rates change between when a foreign subsidiary's budget was initially set and when the subsidiary's performance is evaluated.

3.   According to the Lessard-Lorange model suggesting 9 possibilities, the best way to deal with this problem is to use a projected spot exchange rate to translate both the budget and actual performance figures into the corporate currency. Figure 19.3 illustrates the Lessard-Lorange model.

4.   Transfer prices can also introduce significant distortions into the control process. Thus the transfer price must be taken into account when setting budgets and evaluating a subsidiary's performance.

5.   Foreign subsidiaries do not operate in uniform environments. Some are much tougher than others. Accordingly, it has been suggested that the evaluation of a subsidiary should be separate from the evaluation of the subsidiary manager. The manager's evaluation should involve a degree of subjectivity that considers how hostile or benign the countries environment is for the business and makes allowances for items over which managers have no control (e.g. exchange rates, inflation, interest rates).

ANSWERS TO CRITICAL DISCUSSION QUESTIONS FOR CHAPTER 19

QUESTION 1: Why do the accounting systems of different countries differ? Why do these differences matter?

ANSWER 1: Accounting systems are shaped by the environment of the country, and have evolved to meet the nature of demands for accounting information. Five factors seem to influence the type of accounting system that a country ends up with. These are (i) the relationship between business and the providers of capital, (ii) political and economic ties with other countries, (iii) levels of inflation, (iv) the level of a country's development, and (v) the prevailing culture of a country. These differences do not really matter much at all if one is only concerned with domestic firms (a domestic firm selling to domestic customers and competing with other largely domestic firms), but with increasing trade and the globalization of capital markets the need to compare and evaluate firms from different countries is increasing. And in the case of multinational firms with operations in different countries, and hence different reporting requirements in different countries, differences in accounting systems can significantly impact the way a firm collects and reports information.

QUESTION 2: Why are transactions among members of a corporate family not included in consolidated financial statements?

ANSWER 2: To outside investors, the transactions among members of a corporate family are of limited interest, as the main interest is in the overall economic viability of the combined enterprise. Internal transactions are typically not undertaken at a market rate (although firms may try to get as close to a true market rate as possible), and governmental regulations may induce firms to undertake internal transactions at unrealistic transfer prices. Beyond this, the internal transactions often just even out in any case (a profit in one subsidiary is removed by a loss in another from their transactions, an account payable is a liability in one subsidiary that is offset by an equal account receivable asset in another subsidiary). Thus consolidated financial statements exclude intra-firm transactions since these may be of limited use in understanding the overall financial situation of the corporate family and may include misleading or immaterial information. At times, however, the performance of individual businesses within a diversified firm is of interest in evaluating the overall viability of the enterprise. Thus it is not uncommon for large diversified firms to publish both consolidated accounts and separate accounts for some of its businesses.

QUESTION 3: The following are selected amounts from the separate financial statements of a parent company (unconsolidated) and one of its subsidiaries:

	Parent	Subsidiary
Cash	$180	$80
Receivables	$380	$200
Accounts payable	$245	$110
Retained Earnings	$790	$680
Revenues	$4,980	$3,520
Rent Income	$0	$200
Dividend Income	$250	$0
Expenses	$4,160	$2960

Additional Info   (i) Parent owes subsidiary $70
                   (ii) Parent owns 100% of subsidiary. During the year subsidiary paid parent a dividend
                        of $250.
                   (iii) Subsidiary owns the building that parent rents for $200
                   (iv) During the year parent sold some inventory to subsidiary for $2,200.
                        It had cost Parent $1,500. Subsidiary, in turn, sold the inventory to an
                        unrelated party for $3,200.

Given this information
(a) What is the parent's (unconsolidated) net income?
(b) What is the subsidiary's net income?
(c) What is the consolidated profit on the inventory that the parent originally sold to the subsidiary?
(d) What are the amounts of consolidated cash and receivables?

ANSWER 3:
(a) Parent's unconsolidated net income: Revenues (4980-2200) + Rent Income (0) + Dividend Income
        (250 - 250) - Expenses (4160 -1500-200) = 320
(b) Subsidiary's net income: Revenues (3520) + Rent Income (200) + Dividend Income (0) - Expenses
        (2960) = 490
(c) Consolidated profit on the inventory: 3200 - 1500 = 1700
(d) Cash: 180 + 80 = 260, Receivables: 380 - 70 +200 = 510

QUESTION 4: Why might an accounting based control system provide headquarters management with biased information about the performance of a foreign subsidiary? How can these biases be best corrected?

ANSWER 4: There are three primary reasons why accounting based control systems may provide headquarters management with biased information about the performance of a subsidiary; exchange rate changes, transfer prices, and general economic conditions. Because exchange rates can change over the course of a budget, translated financial data can be misleading - an increase in domestic sales could actually show up as a decrease after translation due to home currency appreciation. By using a common exchange rate for both budget setting and evaluation (i.e. the initial rate or a forecast rate), this problem can be addressed. Since multinational firms often have significant intra-firm transactions, prices have to be set on these transactions. Due both to the difficulty of setting such prices fairly, and the incentives to set prices in order to minimize tax or import duties, profitability of units can be distorted by unrealistic transfer prices. Since it can be impossible and inefficient to use only fair transfer prices, the effects of transfer prices have to be taken into consideration when evaluating the performance of a subsidiary. Lastly, different foreign subsidiaries may be operating in vastly different business environments. The subsidiary that is growing and barely showing a profit in an economy that is in recession is clearly doing better than one that is growing quickly and profitable, but in country where the GDP is growing twice as fast as the subsidiary. Thus when comparing the results of separate subsidiaries, the economic environment in which they are operating should be taken into consideration.

STUDENT EXERCISES AND PROJECTS FOR CHAPTER 19

The availability of financial statement information for international firms has increased dramatically in recent years. Many firms provide annual reports on world wide web sites, for example. In addition, the SEC provides electronically filed EDGAR data on its home page. Fee based services like Lexis and Compact Disclosure are available at many libraries, and it is possible to pull a significant amount of financial information on firms from these services. In addition to basic financial statements, these services also include firms' filings of SEC Form 20F, which provides information on foreign consolidations. Depending upon data and computer availability, a general project would involve gathering information on international companies' reporting and consolidation practices. More specifically:

- Students could be asked to identify firms that have listings on multiple international stock exchanges, and examine the financial reports available to all investors.
- Students could be asked to carefully examine the financial statements of a particular international firm, and pay specific attention to the various footnote disclosures and Form 20F disclosures relating to accounting of foreign subsidiaries.

This sort of a project could obviously be developed into an extensive report, or be a minor project depending upon an instructor's preferences. I have frequently been quite surprised by the amount and quality of information students have gathered on firms. The more open-ended the assignment, the more likely they are to search around on the internet and find analysts reports and other sources of information.

SUGGESTED READINGS FOR CHAPTER 19

The footnotes suggest some appropriate additional readings. The following may be of particular interest:

Choi, Frederick D.S., Gerhard Mueller 1992. International accounting. Englewood Cliffs, NJ: Prentice-Hall

Mueller, Gerhard G, Helen Gernon, and Gary Meek 1991. Accounting: An international perspective. Homewood, IL: Irwin.

Nobes, B.W. and R.H. Parker 1991. Comparative international accounting. Englewood Cliffs, NJ: Prentice-Hall

Samuels, J.M., R.E. Brayshaw, J.M. Craner 1995. Financial statement analysis in Europe. London: Chapman and Hall.

Wallace, R.S., O. Gernon, and Helen Gernon 1991. Frameworks for international comparative financial accounting. Journal of Accounting Literature. 10: 209-264.

Any one of the many textbooks on "International Accounting" would also serve as a useful reference.

_____ TRANSPARENCY MASTERS FOR CHAPTER 19 FOLLOW _____

Accounting Information and Capital Flows

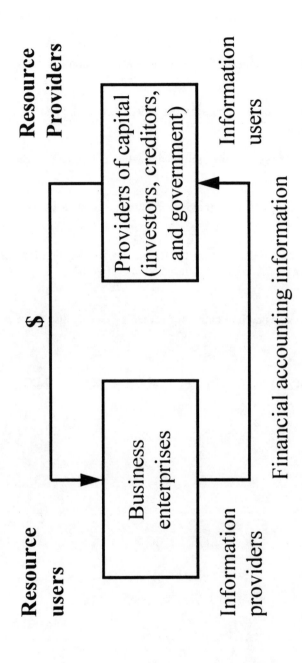

Figure 19.1

Determinants of National Accounting Standards

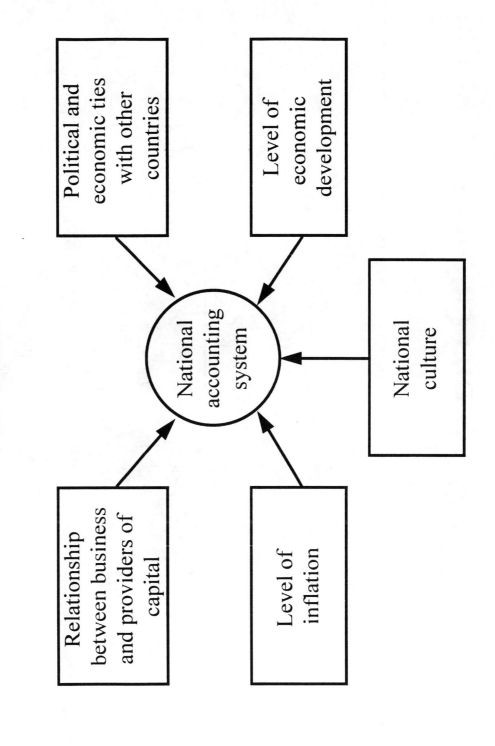

Figure 19.2

Accounting Clusters

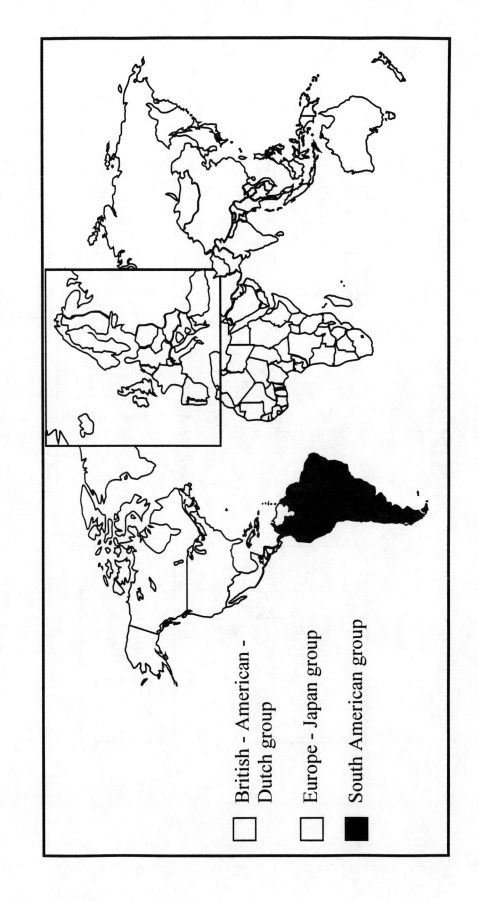

British - American - Dutch group

Europe - Japan group

South American group

IRWIN © Times Mirror Higher Education Group Inc., Company 1997

Map 19.1

Possible Combinations of Exchange Rates in the Control Process

Rate used to translate actual performance for comparison with budget

		Initial (I)	Projected (P)	Ending (E)
Rate used for translating budget	**Initial (I)**	(II) Budget at initial Actual at initial	Budget at initial Actual at projected	(IE) Budget at initial Actual at ending
	Projected (P)	Budget at projected Actual at initial	(PP) Budget at projected Actual at projected	(PE) Budget at projected Actual at ending
	Ending (E)	Budget at ending Actual at initial	Budget at ending Actual at projected	(EE) Budget at ending Actual at ending

Figure 19.3

IRWIN © Times Mirror Higher Education Group Inc., Company 1997

CHAPTER 20: OVERVIEW AND TEACHING SUGGESTIONS

OBJECTIVES OF CHAPTER 20

1.   Discuss how political and economic risk complicate capital budgeting decisions in multinationals

2.   Show how the capital structure of firms from different countries differs, and explore what this means for how a firm should structure the capitalization of its subsidiaries in different countries

3.   Suggest how firms can and should adjust their international management of money to increase efficiency, minimize expenses, and move money across borders

4.   Consider alternatives for managing and minimizing foreign exchange risk

LECTURE OUTLINE FOR CHAPTER 20

A.   Introduction

1.   Financial management focuses on three types of decisions: investment decisions, financing
       decisions, and money management decisions. In an international business all of these decisions
       are complicated by the fact that different countries have different currencies, different tax
       regimes, different regulations concerning the flow of capital across their borders, different norms
       regarding the financing of business activities, different levels of economic and political risk, and
       so on.

2.   Good financial management can be a source of competitive advantage by lowering the cost of
       activities or enhancing the value of activities of a firm.

3.   The opening case illustrates how P&G has improved their competitive position by improving
       their international financial management.

B.   Investment Decisions

1.   The process of using capital budgeting techniques to evaluate proposed foreign investments is
       complicated by several factors that are unique to an international business. While the basic
       process is the same (estimating cash outflows and inflows), in an international business it is
       necessary to: 1) make a distinction between cash flows to the project and cash flows to the parent
       company; 2) weigh how political and economic risks, including foreign exchange risk, can
       significantly change the value of a foreign investment; and 3) understand the connection between
       cash flows to the parent and the source of financing.

2.   When using capital budgeting techniques to evaluate a foreign project, a distinction must be
       made between cash flows to the project and cash flows to the parent. The two will not be the
       same thing when a host governments blocks the repatriation of cash flows from a foreign
       investment. While this problem is not as much an issue as it was in the past, it can still be an
       important consideration.

3.   When using capital budgeting techniques to evaluate a foreign project, the firm needs to
       explicitly recognize the risks that arise from its foreign location. Political and economic risks
       can be incorporated into the capital budgeting process either by using a higher discount rate to
       evaluate risky projects, or by lowering future cash flows forecasted for such projects. Table 20.1
       shows country risk ratings.

C.   Financing Decisions

1.   When considering options for financing a foreign investment, an international business has two
       factors to consider. The first is the issue of how to finance the foreign investment? Most
       importantly, if external financing is required, the firm has to decide whether to borrow from
       sources in the host country, or to borrow from sources elsewhere. The second factor that has to
       be considered is how to configure the financial structure of a foreign affiliate?

2.   The cost of capital is typically lower in the global capital market than in many domestic markets.
       Consequently, other things being equal, firms would prefer to finance their investments by
       borrowing from the global capital market.

3.   Borrowing from the global capital market may be restricted by host government regulations or demands. In such cases, the discount rate used in capital budgeting must be revised upwards to reflect this.

4.   The firm may wish to consider local debt financing for investments in countries where the local currency is expected to depreciate.

5.   Local financing can also help integrate the subsidiary into the local business community, providing it additional contacts for business, and protecting it somewhat from adverse governmental action (including at the extreme, expropriation).

6.   There is a striking difference between the financial structure of firms based in different countries. This may be due to differences in tax regimes and cultural practices. Despite the existence of such differences, the arguments for conforming to local debt norms are not that strong. Table 20.2 illustrates the differences in the financial structure of firms.

D.   Global Money Management: The Efficiency Objective

1.   The principle objectives of global money management are to utilize the firms cash resources in the most efficient manner, and to minimize the firm's global tax liabilities.

2.   Efficient cash management involves 1) minimizing the necessary cash balances held by a firm - which is often best done by centralizing cash reserves and 2) reducing transaction costs by multilateral netting.

E.   Global Money Management: The Tax Objective

1.   Different countries have significantly different corporate tax rates as illustrated in Figure 20.1.

2.   Firms typically want to minimize taxes paid. If countries do not have tax treaties, a firm can end up paying income taxes in both the foreign and the home country on profits earned in the foreign country. Firms can make use of tax havens to minimize tax liability. For US firms, the advantages of incorporating in tax havens is minimal.

F.   Moving Money Across Borders: Attaining Efficiencies and Reducing Taxes

1.   There are a number of techniques that firms use to transfer liquid funds across borders. These include dividend remittances, royalty payments and fees, transfer prices, and fronting loans.

2.   Dividend remittances are the most common method used. However, royalty payments and fees have certain tax advantages over dividend remittances.

3.   There is evidence that the manipulation of transfer prices is frequently used to move funds out of a country in order to minimize tax liabilities, hedge against foreign exchange risk, circumvent government restrictions on capital flows, and reduce tariff payments. However, manipulating transfer prices in this manner runs counter to government regulations in many countries, may distort incentive systems within the firm, and may rest upon ethically dubious foundations.

4.   Fronting loans involve funds being channeled from a parent company to a foreign subsidiary through a third party - normally an international bank. Fronting loans are a way of

circumventing host government restrictions on the remittance of funds. Fronting loans also have certain tax advantages. Figure 20.2 diagrams how a fronting loan works

G.   Techniques for Global Money Management

1.   By holding cash at a centralized depository the firm may be able to invest its cash reserves more efficiently.

2.   First, by pooling cash reserves centrally the firm will be able to deposit larger amounts, and interest rates offered on such cash deposits normally increase with the size of the deposit.

3.   Second, if the centralized depository is located in a major financial center , it will have the advantage of information about short-run investment opportunities that the typical foreign subsidiary might lack and be able to be staffed with financial experts with investment skills and know-how that managers in the typical foreign subsidiary might also lack.

4.   Most importantly, it can reduce the total size of the cash pool that it needs to hold in highly liquid accounts, thereby freeing money up for investment in higher interest bearing (less liquid) accounts or in tangible assets.

5.   These advantages of a centralized depository must be weighed against the fact that a firm's ability to establish a centralized depository might be limited by government imposed restrictions on capital flows across borders. Moreover, the transaction costs of moving money in and out of different currencies can place a limit upon the advantages of such a system.

6.   Multilateral netting is a way of reducing the transaction costs that arise when a large number of transactions occur between the subsidiaries of the firm in the normal course of business. Figure 20.3 shows how a firm can significantly reduce the amount of currency exchanged by using multilateral netting.

H.   Managing Foreign Exchange Risk

1.   While some issues of foreign exchange risk were described in chapter 9, the focus in this chapter is on the various strategies that international businesses use to manage their foreign exchange risk.

2.   There are three types of exposure to foreign exchange risk; transaction exposure, translation exposure, and economic exposure.

3.   Firms can adopt a number of tactics to insure against transaction and translation exposure. These include buying forward, using currency swaps, leading and lagging payables and receivables, manipulating transfer prices, using local debt financing, accelerating dividend payments, and adjusting capital budgeting to reflect foreign exchange exposure.

4.   Reducing economic exposure requires strategic choices about the distribution of the firm's productive assets in various countries around the globe.

5.   In order to effectively manage foreign exchange exposure, the firm must exercise centralized oversight over its foreign exchange hedging activities, recognize the difference between transaction exposure and economic exposure, forecast future exchange rate movements, establish good reporting systems within the firm to monitor exposure positions, and produce regular foreign exchange exposure reports that can then be used as a basis for action.

ANSWERS TO CRITICAL DISCUSSION QUESTIONS FOR CHAPTER 20

QUESTION 1: How can the finance function of an international business improve the competitive position of the firm in the global market place?

ANSWER 1: Good financial management can be an important source of competitive advantage, as is illustrated in the opening case in the chapter. While this is true in a purely domestic business, due to the added complexity of competing in multiple markets, it is even more true in the case of an international business. Chapter 12 described the value chain and about how creating a competitive advantage requires the firm to lower the costs of value creation and/or add value by improving customer service. Good financial management can help the firm both to lower the costs of value creation and to add value by improving customer service. By lowering the firm's cost of capital, eliminating foreign exchange losses, minimizing the firm's tax burden, minimizing the firm's exposure to unduly risky activities, and managing the firm's cash flows and reserves in the most efficient manner, the finance function in an international business can lower the costs of value creation.

QUESTION 2: What actions can a firm take to minimize its global tax liability? On ethical grounds, can such actions be justified?

ANSWER 2: The complexity of the various national tax laws and tax treaties between countries makes minimizing global tax liability a considerable challenge. The first step is to become familiar with the appropriate regulations. The use of tax havens can be used by many multinationals to limit their tax liability. Charging royalties and fees to lower the taxable income in high tax nations can lower taxes by shifting profits to countries with lower tax rates. The level of transfer prices set can also shift profits between different national entities, although there are laws that require that these prices be reasonable in some countries. Fronting loans can also be used to minimize tax liability by treating invested funds as independent loans that incur interest expense rather than using equity and earning profits. Most of the actions outlined above can be justified on ethical grounds as long as they are done "reasonably". Of course what one person or firm considers reasonable may not be reasonable to another, what is ethical to one may not be ethical to another - particularly in international contexts. Transfer prices that bear no relation to the true value of a good would clearly be unreasonable and unethical, but short of this there is a great deal of gray area in taking actions to minimize global tax liability.

QUESTION 3: You are the CFO of a US firm with a wholly owned subsidiary in Mexico that manufactures component parts for your US assembly operations. The subsidiary has been financed by bank borrowings in the United States. You have just been told by one of your analysts that the Mexican peso is expected to depreciate by 30% against the US dollar on the foreign exchange markets over the next year. What actions, if any, should you take?

ANSWER 3: This issue suggests that some interest and principal will have to be repaid in US dollars in the near future, but the plan was likely to pay this off out of earnings from the Mexican subsidiary. If the overall amount outstanding is relatively small, simply paying off the entire loan in advance before the peso depreciates would be a good option. At least funds could be transferred out of Mexico now and invested in the US to pay off the loan later. Alternately it may be possible to use a forward rate to lock in an exchange rate now for future remittances, but unless the analyst has some information that is not generally available in the market, the efficacy of this approach will be limited since the forward rate will likely already reflect the expected depreciation. Another option available is to simply pay off the loan with funds already in the US over time, and retain the pesos in Mexico for reinvestment if needed. The actual action taken would likely depend upon the size of the loan, any restrictions on the loan, and where funds are most efficiently available for paying off the loan. In any case it would probably be unlikely that the best solution would be to wait and exchange pesos for dollars later to pay off the loan.

QUESTION 4: You are the CFO of a Canadian firm that is considering building a $10 million factory in Russia to produce milk. The investment is expected to produce net cash flows of $3 million every year for the next ten years, after which the investment will have to close down due to technological obsolescence. Scrap values will be zero. The cost of capital will be is 6% if financing is arranged through the Eurobond market. However, you have an option to finance the project by borrowing funds from a Russian bank at a 12% interest rate. Analysts tell you that due to high inflation in Russia, the Russian ruble is expected to depreciate against the Canadian dollar. Analysts rate the probability of violent revolution occurring in Russia within the next ten years as high. How would you incorporate these factors into your evaluation of the investment opportunity? What would you recommend that the firm do?

ANSWER 4: In considering this investment there are three basic steps to be taken: making a basic analysis, adjusting for economic/political risk, and deciding on the source of capital (which involves a more careful analysis of exchange rate risk). There are several different ways of doing this problem, and the method outlined below is just one. By making different assumptions, or by playing with the sensitivity of the decision based on different assumptions, different answers would likely be obtained. In a finance course a sophisticated approach would be required, but for this book more of a "back of the envelope" approach is probably appropriate unless all students have had a finance course.

(1) Make a basic analysis of the investment:
    a quick analysis of the basic problem, a $10m investment that pays $3m/year for 10 years shows a ROI of 27%, suggesting that in general this is a good opportunity.
(2) Adjust for risk
    In the case of Russia, the likelihood of violent revolution which could damage the plant irreparably or cause the firm to effectively lose ownership is probably as likely to occur in the first year as it is in any future year. Hence treating later cash flows different than earlier cash flows is inappropriate. By adjusting the $3m cash flows down by some percentage for each year (the risk that there will be a violent revolution that will cause the plant to close in any given year), probability that the plant will still be available to the firm can be factored into the yearly cash flows.
(3) Determine whether it would be better to fund the project from Canada or Russia or not at all.
    (i) Russian Funds: If we assume that if there is a violent revolution we would neither earn money nor have to pay back the bank (let them have the plant if they are around to get it from the revolutionaries), the financing in Russia looks very good. Having a 27% ROI while having to pay only 12% shows this to be a very profitable investment. And even if it does fail in the first year due to revolution, the bank is at risk not the firm. The main issue is being able to get funds out of Russia and back to Canada. The yearly cash flows that could be repatriated would be $3m less interest and principal (which is still leaves over $1millon), followed by an adjustment for economic/political risk and anticipated exchange rate changes. The net present value of these cash flows in Canadian dollars could then be calculated.
    (ii) Eurobond Funds: Unfortunately Eurobond investors would still want to be paid even if the plant goes out of production. They will also want to be paid most likely in US dollars or some European currency; it is unlikely that the Eurobonds would be denominated in either rubles or Canadian dollars. Hence the approach would be to discount the cash flows for economic/political risk, discount them for the currency depreciation, make payments on the Eurobonds, and then determine the net present value of the remainder. The quick calculation shows that this is still a positive net present value option.
After more careful analysis both choices would likely yield a positive net present value, although which one is higher is not obvious. While one can make estimates for the risks and include them as suggested, it is clear that the Eurobond option exposes the firm to higher economic/political and exchange rate risks. It also requires that funds be repatriated to pay off the bonds, while with the bank financing the firm could just keep the funds in Russia if foreign exchange controls were instituted. Thus unless the Eurobond option has a significantly higher net present value, the Russian bank financing has some strong advantages that are difficult to fully quantify.

STUDENT EXERCISES AND PROJECTS FOR CHAPTER 20

- One of the best exercises that deals directly with many of the issues in this chapter (as well as touching on others from early in the text) is the FINS simulation described in Part II of this manual.

SUGGESTED READINGS FOR CHAPTER 20

The footnotes suggest some appropriate additional readings. The following may be of particular interest:

Eiteman, D.K., A.I. Stonehill, and M.H. Moffett 1992. Multinational Business Finance. Reading, MA: Addison-Wesley.

Levi, Maurice 1990. International Finance. New York: McGraw-Hill.

Shapiro, Alan C. 1982. Multinational Financial Management. Boston, MA: Allyn and Bacon.

TRANSPARENCY MASTERS FOR CHAPTER 20 FOLLOW

OECD Corporate Income Tax Rates

Country	Top Tax Rate (%)	Note
Australia	33	
Austria	34	1
Belgium	40.17	2
Canada	44.3	3
Denmark	34	4
Finland	25	5
France	33.33	6
Germany	58.95/46.13	7
Greece	40	8
Iceland	33	9
Ireland	40	10
Italy	52.2	

Source: Organization of Economic Cooperation and Development.

Figure 20.1a

OECD Corporate Income Tax Rates
CONTINUED

Country	Top Tax Rate (%)	Note
Japan	51.6	11
Luxembourg	40.29	12
Mexico	34	
Netherlands	35	13
New Zealand	33	14
Norway	28	15
Portugal	39.6	16
Spain	35	
Sweden	28	
Switzerland	28.5	17
Turkey	42.8	18
UK	33	19
US	40	20

Source: Organization of Economic Cooperation and Development.

Figure 20.1b

An Example of the Tax Aspects of a Fronting Loan

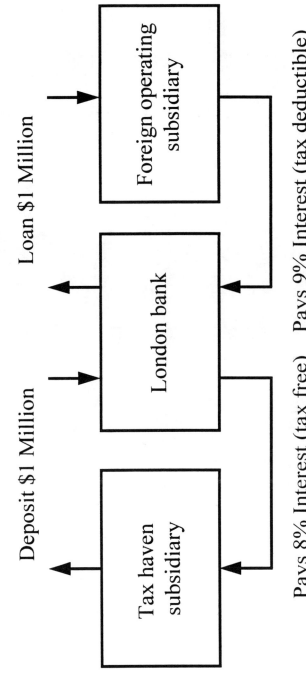

Loan $1 Million

Deposit $1 Million

Foreign operating subsidiary

London bank

Tax haven subsidiary

Pays 8% Interest (tax free)   Pays 9% Interest (tax deductible)

IRWIN © Times Mirror Higher Education Group Inc., Company 1997

Figure 20.2

PART IV

CASE NOTES

CASE: RUSSIAN PRIVATIZATION

SYNOPSIS

The Russian government is in the process of trying to transform a centrally planned economy in which almost all productive assets were owned by the state into a vibrant market economy. The hope is that by putting state enterprises into private hands, and making them accountable for their performance to their new owners, that major gains in efficiency will result leading to a more productive economy.

The privatization process was driven by three goals. The first was to move quickly to break up the old Soviet system before opposition could build, primarily by privatizing most state assets within two years. The second goal was to "divide and conquer" the potential opposition splitting the ministries from the enterprises, and putting former communist directors in charge of the enterprises while giving them an ownership stake. The third goal was to create a broad base of property owners who would be opposed to reversing the changes.

For small enterprises the privatization went quickly and seemed to be effective, as workers generally took charge simply and easily. For midsized and large enterprises, a voucher system for shares of stock was established, although workers and managers generally still kept a large share of the business. More recently large investors have been allowed to take bigger stakes in firms, especially those that will need additional investment in restructuring.

While the privatization process was effective in quickly transferring control away from the government and the ministries, there have been a number of criticisms of the process. Firstly, control has tended to fall into the hands of the managers and employees who were running the enterprises before, and they are not necessarily keen on restructuring, nor in many cases do they have the expertise to do so. Secondly, because of the voucher system the government did not raise much money in its transfer of ownership, and the government is in great need of some source of revenue. Thirdly, foreign investors were not given much of an opportunity to invest, and this type of investment may be needed in order to tap into both sufficient funds and management expertise for restructuring. Additional problems for foreign investors included poor property rights protection and a non-existent stock market for their investments.

Questions about the longevity of the reforms, and what might happen in future elections has also made many foreign firms leery of investing in Russia. By the time you are using this case some of these issues may be resolved, but then the latest news will also help frame the uncertainty inherent at the time of the case.

TEACHING OBJECTIVES

The main teaching objectives of the case are:

1. Suggest some of the difficulties countries face in trying to change their political and economic systems.
2. Show how these difficulties create uncertainties for foreign investors interested in acquiring or developing assets in the country.
3. Better understand the complex internal political issues within countries that affect their ability to undertake various forms of change.

This case could be used either after chapter 2 (National Differences in Political Economy) or chapter 7 (Political Economy of Foreign Direct Investment). If used after chapter 2 the case can illustrate the difficulties in changing economic and political systems, suggest how these changes are complex and involve many inter-related elements in a countries economic and political systems, and introduce to students how this process of change causes uncertainty for firms interested in investing in the country. If held for use until after students have read chapter 7, the a more detailed look at the risk factors in FDI in a country such as Russia can occur. The answers to the questions below, however, assume it is being used after chapter 2.

STRATEGIC ISSUES AND DISCUSSION QUESTIONS

1.   What are the strengths and weaknesses of the Russian privatization process? Could a better process have been devised?

As always it is easy to criticize after the fact, and a better process could have perhaps been devised. How a plan will really work can't be fully predicted, and any alternative plan suggested would likely have its own unintended consequences that we wouldn't (and can't) fully anticipate. Whatever alternatives students suggest (e.g. less control given to existing managers), they should also discuss the potential side effects (e.g. more resistance to the changes from these managers), and what should be done to minimize these side effects.

2.   Do you think that the privatization of formerly state owned enterprises is sufficient to induce foreign companies to invest in Russia? If not, what else needs to be put in place before Russia becomes an attractive location for inward investment

Privatization alone would appear to be an insufficient condition to encourage foreign direct investment. Investors need some sort of assurances with respect to property rights, or more bluntly that their investments won't be taken away. In addition, many investors will be leery until they believe that the economy is on track and that they will be able to find adequate suppliers and customers in Russia. Unfortunately all of these factors and others are intertwined, as investment will help bolster the economy and decrease the threat of a return to communism.

3.   What are the nature of the political and economic risks confronting foreign investors in the Russian economy in late 1995? Given the nature of these risks, and the existence of attractive investment opportunities elsewhere in the world, what approach do you think foreigners should adopt towards investing in Russia?

Political risks include the potential for social unrest, failure to protect property rights, or reversion to a more controlled economy. Economic risks include the potential for mismanagement of the economy, inadequate wealth on the part of customers, inadequate suppliers, and a poorly functioning economic infrastructure (transportation, communication, etc.). Given these risks, investors would appear to be rightly reluctant to invest heavily in Russia at this time. Cautious approaches, however, that allow firms to gain knowledge of the market and potentially reap first mover advantages should not be ignored.

CASE: MULTIGAMA

SYNOPSIS

Along with the fall of the other Eastern European countries in the late 1980s, Romania underwent a revolution that toppled the communist government and installed 'reformers.' Along with freeing the economy of governmental controls, private enterprises began to spring up and privatization of national enterprises begun.

In this context, a group of engineers at a pump manufacturer (Aversa) decided to start their own business. They had had contact with Western business as part of the design process of pumps for a nuclear power plant, and felt that Romanian managerial practices lagged far behind those in the West. Due to the lack of private financing for full scale companies, they began modestly by working their regular jobs and importing and distributing products from a Syrian exchange student. Working out of an empty house, the business proved successful, they were able to leave their jobs to work at the new venture full time, and were able to develop the working capital necessary to begin manufacturing pumps. Their first products, while designed for use on farms, also proved ideal for improving the water pressure in buildings. Multigama (as the pump manufacturing firm was called) originally had difficulty obtaining production space and additional financing, however.

It appears that Multigama may be in a position to finally take off. They have arranged for a building to be built, are planning on leasing out extra space, and are considering diversification into other product lines. Yet there are clearly issues in working with the Romanian workforce, and a great deal of inertia and managerial deficiencies that need to be overcome. They also are concerned about the effects of privatization of the state-owned firms, and realize that Aversa may team up with a foreign partner.

TEACHING OBJECTIVES

The main teaching objectives of the case are:

1.   Illustrate the difficulty faced by firms and entrepreneurs in the former communist countries.
2.   Highlight the importance of well working capital markets for funding firms' growth, and the challenges of targeting international lending to help in the rebuilding of Romania.
3.   Explore some HRM issues that will arise as Eastern European firms and countries try to become more free market-like.
4.   Show how firms in highly dynamic environments have a great deal of challenges and opportunities, and explore whether they should focus their strategy on a particular business or simply be flexible in order to take advantage of the opportunities they see.

This case is a bit eclectic and could be used in several places. If used at the end of Part II (Chapter 3), the challenges of working in a business environment very different from that which most students are familiar can be highlighted. If used at the end of Part IV (Chapter 11), the discussion could be similar with an additional discussion on how Multigama may be able to raise additional funds and why foreign MNEs might find an investment in Multigama attractive. A portion of the discussion could also address how international agencies like the World Bank and the IMF can best help the growth of the Romanian economy. If used at the end of Part V (Chapter 14), this same discussion can be extended to discuss the strategic issues of how Multigama should focus its activities. Although the HRM issues alluded to in the case are not in the same vein as those discussed in Chapter 18, after reading this chapter students may be in a better position to explore how a MNE might try to address the HRM issues that it would face if it invested in Multigama or Aversa.

STRATEGIC ISSUES AND DISCUSSION QUESTIONS

1.   As an executive of a MNE, would you consider investing in Multigama? What would be the main issues you would want to consider?

The most attractive reason to invest in Multigama would be for the entrepreneurial management. One has to give them credit for the initiative to start their own business, begin by selling bubble gum, curtains and shoes, and now manufacture pumps and arrange for buildings to be built. An investment in Multigama would be high risk, however. Not only could it fail from lack of managerial talent and strategic direction or political turmoil in Romania, but as more attention towards Multigama may cause additional governmental regulation or pressures from the state-owned Aversa. When investing in Multigama, it would be important to ascertain whether governmental officials were overall supportive and excited about the investment as one that could attract additional interest, or if they were more interested in remaining protective of state-owned enterprises and the status quo. Regardless, an investment in Multigama would have to be considered a high risk gamble that the MNE is prepared to lose, but one that could have good upside if nurtured and provided with some direction.

2.   What about investing in Aversa? What are the advantages and disadvantages of investing in each.

By investing in Aversa, a MNE is likely to have the support of the government that is looking to privatize and find investors for its firms. But unfortunately Aversa would appear to be significantly overstaffed and poorly managed, and changing this might not be easy. Hence an investment in Aversa could take a long time to pay off and require significant effort and further investment over time. While the biggest risk in Multigama is likely business failure, Aversa is unlikely to fail, but it may never pay off either and continue to absorb resources for a long time. Clearly the labor and management team are more favorable in Multigama, but the series of governmental contacts and access to other state owned firms that Aversa could provide may bring to light new opportunities that would not be apparent otherwise. Whether either can profitably make pumps for export is unclear, but Multigama's management would more likely find new opportunities if the pump business went dry. Thus, based on what we know and a few assumptions, Multigama may be a more viable business investment where the return will be known relatively soon, while Aversa may provide the MNE with a better set of contacts and access to other firms owned by the government.

3.   Given the industries in which Romania had invested under the communist regime, how likely are these industries to help lead Romania out of its mess and towards economic prosperity?

It would not appear that the industries Romania has invested in are likely to help it much today. There is over capacity in the world wide steel industry, and the source of Romania's crude oil for its refineries is the troubled fields in the southern countries of the former USSR.

4.   As an IMF or World Bank official, how would you target lending to assist in the development of Romania?

To help Romania develop, investments in agriculture and labor intensive manufacturing may be the most appropriate. While providing funding to private enterprises like Multigama is certainly risky, it may be more likely to pay off than investments to modernize the existing state-owned enterprises.

5.   Given their success to date, and the opportunities they have, what advice would you give
        Multigama's management?

Multigama's management has to be given a great deal of credit for their success to date. Yet it would
appear that some focus of their energies would be best right now. Selling bubble gum, making pumps,
and serving as a landlord are a pretty diverse set of activities. Given the engineering background of the
founders, staying with equipment like pumps and food processing machinery would perhaps be a good
idea. As far as international sales, Multigama may want to work out an arrangement with a MNE that
already has worldwide distribution activities to market its products.

CASE: THE CHINA STRATEGY: A TALE OF TWO FIRMS

SYNOPSIS

This case describes the differing success, and success factors of two different firms in China in the late 1980s : Western Energy, and American Copier. The case separately describes the history of each firms' dealings in China, and allows for an examination of the factors that worked to the favor and disadvantage of each firm. The case is set with individuals from each firm discussing their experiences in China on an airplane ride from the US. (In the first edition of this book these were two separate cases: "Arnold Tanner" and "American Copier Company".)

Western Energy Inc. (WEI) is a oil and natural resources firm that conducts business in over 100 countries, has sales around $10 billion, and is vertically integrated from the fields to the pumps. It also is involved in chemicals and coal exploration. Arnold Tanner is the chairman and CEO. Tanner is a well respected and charismatic leader, and had been active in the East European markets and the Soviet Union since the 1930s. When China started its "open door policy" in 1979, China's leaders naturally looked to Tanner for investment.

Tanner took a high profile approach, visited Beijing often, and befriended China's leader, Deng Xiapoing. Tanner sensed that if WEI penetrated China early, it might be able to capitalize on some first mover advantages - particularly if it gained preferential access to China's natural energy resources. WEI bid upon, and won, the right to work on the development of the Taibao coal mine. While WEI clearly brought some technological expertise to the venture, and its American ownership appealed to the Chinese who wanted to show US firms that it was open for business, Tanners connections with Chinese leaders played an important role. A 30 year renewable 50/50 joint venture was signed with a consortium of Chinese organizations.

As WEI was working out the details with its Chinese partners, it made a number of important promises and commitments to the success of the product. The Chinese, noted for their preference for "general principles" in the negotiations, took these commitments seriously and treated them as a foundation upon which details could be worked out with WEI later. However, shortly after the agreement was signed and feasibility studies began, a fall in world coal prices caused WEI to pressure the Chinese for further concessions. On several occasions during more detailed negotiations, disputes at the working level came close to derailing the project. But Tanner and the Chinese political leadership always intervened to force a solution.

Tanner was very skillful in cultivating *guanxi* (connections) with the central leadership in Beijing and was able to use his central *guanxi* influence to make his Chinese partners grant him concessions. However, WEI failed to develop close *guanxi* relations with local partners, which caused many operational problems.

Inside WEI, as the company's financial situation worsened in the late 1980s with increasing debts, discussions of withdrawing form the Taibao venture were ongoing. In a similar manner to how Deng Xiaoping ruled China, Tanner dismissed such ideas and urged a "long term perspective." The Chinese leadership had a strong desire to save its political face (in light of Tiananmen Square) and avoid the failure of a flagship project. Therefore, despite huge financial losses which depleted WEI's cash flow, the Taibao venture continued until Tanner's sudden death in August 1990.

Ray Schon, Tanner's successor, decided to re-evaluate all of WEI's operations with an eye on improving profitability and reducing debt. Schon announced WEI's intention to withdraw from the Taibao venture, which was Tanner's favorite project but never part of WEI's core business. As Schon planned a trip to China, he faced two options: (1) sell its share to the Chinese partners, or (2) sell to another foreign investor. In either case he was going to have some difficulties in dealing with his Chinese contacts. While he could decide to stay with the project, his mind seemed to be made up.

American Copier Company (ACC) is a $10 billion sales MNE with sales in over 100 countries and development and manufacturing sites worldwide. ACC began exporting copiers to China in the early 1980s, although the market at that time was dominated by Japanese firms that were also exporting. After four years of careful and long negotiations and considering a number of different sites and partners, ACC set up a joint venture in Shanghai which was intended to manufacture and develop copiers for the Chinese market. ACC's Shanghai venture partners included Bank of China (5%), Shanghai Photo Industry Co. (44%) and ACC (51%) in a 30 year renewable joint venture contract. ACC Shanghai was intended to produce low-end and mid-range copiers suitable for the Chinese market and would be capable of switching to produce more advanced designs.

Despite the Chinese preference to have a high percentage of the venture's output exported, the ACC negotiation team persuaded the Chinese that the models ACC would introduce to China would be low to mid-range products specifically suited to the Chinese market. In return ACC accepted a stipulation which insisted that 70% of the venture's components be sourced locally by the end of 1992. To make this successful, ACC Shanghai spent a great deal of time, energy, and resources on vendor development and quality assurance. ACC Shanghai also developed a close working relationship with the Shanghai Foreign Investment Commission, which provided funding to local companies to enable them to upgrade their plants and purchase new technology required for ACC Shanghai's products and standards.

ACC Shanghai developed a dealer network throughout China, and aggressively advertised the product - 'a combination of Shanghai beauty and American technology.' Vigorous quality standards, extensive dealer networks, and an aggressive and skillfully executed advertising campaign accompanied with reasonable prices lead ACC Shanghai to become the number one copier seller in China. The fact that it was made in China also helped, especially since many customers were directly or indirectly tied to the government.

Yet all was not rosy. Costs were higher than expected and the government's austerity program led to a much smaller market than ACC had expected. In addition, the paper feeders originally shipped tended to jam frequently due to the lower quality paper used in China. While this was remedied by a redesign, it illustrates some of the other unexpected problems ACC faced.

At the time of the case, ACC Shanghai was still producing only one copier, but was considering developing and manufacturing a new lower end copier and a higher end copier. Yet for this to be really practical the market had to expand, and the only way this would happen is if the Chinese government lifted its stringent austerity program and purchase controls. Unfortunately ACC Shanghai had little influence over government policy. Secondly, costs would have to come down further by making additional investments in the local supplier network. Given the existing good relations with its local suppliers, this seemed feasible.

The case does not leave the reader with burning questions that need to be answered nor problems that need to be addressed for either firm. It does, however, provide a good opportunity to look at each firm in isolation as well as allow comparison across the firms.

TEACHING OBJECTIVES

The main teaching objectives of the case are:

1.   Show the importance of taking a long term perspective when undertaking some international ventures.
2.   Illustrate the importance of personal relations, with governmental leaders both centrally and locally, in host countries, and what a huge factor governmental relations can be in some countries.
3.   Illustrate how different cultures perceive negotiations and important elements of success in a venture.
4.   Present a chance to compare and contrast the experiences of two different firms in China.

This case can go well either after chapter 3 (National Differences in Culture), chapter 7 (The Political Economy of FDI), or chapter 14 (Mode of Entry and Strategic Alliances). Depending upon where it is used, and thus the amount of background students have to cover various issues, the focus and assigned discussion questions will obviously differ.

STRATEGIC ISSUES AND DISCUSSION QUESTIONS

These discussion questions suggest an approach where one would look at each situation individually first, and then finally undertake a comparison of the two companies' approaches. Depending upon where in the course this case is used, different questions will be more (and less) relevant.

1.   What were the perceived "first mover advantages" for WEI? How did WEI exploit these advantages?

The most important first mover advantage available to WEI was to have preferential access to China's energy resources. At the time Tanner was cultivating the relationship he may not have known what project(s) WEI might become involved with, but knew that the best way to get to know China and potentially obtain access to resources was to get to know the leaders. Once WEI had worked on one project and established rapport with the Chinese, it may be in a much better position to have preferential access to additional natural resources. The connections WEI developed had an important role in its subsequent success in winning the Taibao project.

2.   Why didn't Arnold Tanner's connections with the Chinese leadership lead to successful cooperation with WEI's Chinese partners.

While Tanner had developed strong connections with the upper echelons of the Chinese government, successful cooperation on the Taibao coal mine required a good working relationship and rapport with much lower level officials. It appears that Tanner's employees directly involved with the project were not able to develop a good working relationship. This may have been due to cultural differences, a lack of understanding of the Chinese and their objectives, or a failure to appreciate the long term importance of developing a working relationship - their goal may have been to get the most out of this project for WEI rather use this project as a learning opportunity and a chance to develop *Guanxi*. *Guanxi* is difficult to develop, and perhaps it is even unrealistic for someone other than the very senior (elderly) and respected Tanner to be able to do this with the Chinese. WEI cannot be entirely responsible however, as their Chinese counterparts also likely did not understand the style and objectives of the WEI employees.

3.   If you were Ray Schon, would you decide to pull out from the Taibao venture? Is Schon being shortsighted in his current plans?

Pull out:- we're losing money, and it doesn't look better anytime soon
            - this does not fit with the strategy
            - the limited success to date was due to Tanner, and he is no longer around to help
            - the Chinese are difficult to work with, and there are better places to invest energy and money

Stay: - the economics of this project could turn around
            - we've perhaps just gotten the relationship working, so we should now be able to benefit
            - given China's huge energy reserves, there are many other potential projects if we stay with it
            - all that's invested so far could give us a first mover advantage on other projects

4.   Why did ACC choose to joint venture with the Chinese? What are the advantages and disadvantages to use the joint venture mode as compared to the export mode or the wholly owned subsidiary mode?

Joint Venture	Advantages:	- risks are shared
		- partners bring expertise (i.e. business and marketing in China)
		- investment is lower than wholly owned subsidiary
		- more integrated into local business culture
		- less exchange risk than exporting, low risk of nationalization
	Disadvantages:	- less autonomy in decision making
		- upside profits must be shared
		- additional constituencies must be considered
		- can lose control over technology
Export	Advantages:	- less investment in new manufacturing
		- more economies of scale in centralized manufacturing
		- work with known existing suppliers
	Disadvantages:	- labor costs are less in China
		- higher transport costs
		- are not an insider in China, and may have less access
		- not as close to the customer, less able to know demands
Wholly Owned	Advantages:	- maintain tight control over manufacturing and technology
		- can better coordinate international activities across subsidiaries
		- more autonomy in decision making
		- are part of the Chinese business network - eventually are "locals"
	Disadvantages:	- highest expense
		- highest risk, both of failure and nationalization
		- are not able to tap into the Chinese business network easily

5.   In your assessment, how would ACC Shanghai achieve its goals? Facing obstacles, what would be your recommended course of action?

ACC Shanghai seems to on a good track with its present course of action. It has developed good local relations with suppliers, the government, and probably the bank, and is producing and marketing products that meet the needs of the market. Whether it should expand production and produce two new models seems less clear, given the constraint on demand. Perhaps beginning development and limited production on one additional model would be o.k., but additional resources should perhaps instead be focused on getting the costs down for current suppliers. ACC may also consider exporting in order to increase volume, lower costs, and develop additional goodwill with the government. For this to be feasible, however, costs need to be competitive internationally.

6.   Describe the primary similarities and differences in approach of WEI and ACC?

Similarities: - need for re-negotiation and changes from original plan
                                       - external factors cause problems (world coal prices, exchange rate)
                                       - poor up-front research on some issues (coal quality, paper quality,
                                               local supplier sophistication)

Differences: - local vs central *guanxi*
                                       - high vs medium or low visibility
                                       - high vs low level problem solving

CASE: THE RISE (AND STALL) OF THE JAPANESE SEMICONDUCTOR INDUSTRY

SYNOPSIS

US enterprises dominated the world semiconductor market from the 1950s until the early 1980s. During the 1980s, however, the market share of US firms plummeted, falling to 29% by 1990, while the share held by Japanese producers rose from 24% at the end of the 1970s to 49% by 1990. By the end of the 1980s the US was a net importer of semiconductors, while 5 of the 10 largest semiconductor producers were Japanese. By the mid 1990s, however, US firms had regain global market share (to 42%) while the Japanese share had dipped to 41%.

Japanese industrial policy may have had a great deal to do with the success of Japanese firms. Japan denied direct access to the Japanese market, and had firms aggressively pursue technology licensing agreements from US manufacturers. While these agreements were financially attractive for US firms in the short run, they were not these firms' first choice for accessing the Japanese market, and they resulted in a significant transfer of technology to Japanese firms.

As a result of political pressure from US semiconductor manufacturers, trade agreements were signed by the US and Japan in 1986 and 1991 that attempted to increase free trade in semiconductors. While different interest groups and politicians on both sides of the Pacific clearly have differing opinions on the appropriateness and effectiveness of these two agreements, the US manufacturers did improve their worldwide and Japanese market share during this time period. Of course the increasing strength of the Yen also contributed to this, and South Korean manufacturers made significant inroads in addition.

TEACHING OBJECTIVES

The main teaching objectives of the case are:

1.   Show how governmental policies can affect trade and industrial development.
2.   Suggest that industries can work to correct perceived inequities through lobbying and working with the government.
3.   Illustrate how short term decisions on the part of US manufacturers can have long term impacts.

This case fits well after chapter 7, as it ties together material from chapters 4-7 of the political economy of international trade and foreign direct investment.

STRATEGIC ISSUES AND DISCUSSION QUESTIONS

1.   What factors account for the rise of Japan's semiconductor manufacturers during 1970s and 1980s?

The case suggests that Japanese industrial policy was a significant contributor to the success of the Japanese semiconductor industry. These policies included requiring majority Japanese ownership in joint ventures, instituting high import tariffs, applying restrictive quotas on imports, requiring open licensing agreements, stipulating technology transfer requirements, and encouraging vigorous cost competition among Japanese firms. The growing demand within Japan and the strong competition within the country certainly also contributed. Some students will often try to apply the Porter diamond to this question, but unfortunately we do know enough about the elements of this model to undertake a full analysis.

2.   Does the rise of the Japanese semiconductor companies during the 1970s and 1980s indicate that governmental industrial policy can play an important role in facilitating national competitiveness in industries targeted by that policy?

The answer to question 1 suggests that this is true - governmental industrial policy can play a role. How big a role, however, it is hard to say. There are certain other Japanese industries where governmental policy has been less effective and even inhibiting. Other factors may have also played a critical role, including domestic demand conditions and the existence of related and supporting industries.

CASE: THE COMMERCIAL AIRCRAFT INDUSTRY IN 1995:
AIRBUS INDUSTRIE, BOEING, AND MCDONNELL DOUGLAS

SYNOPSIS

The key issue is whether there is fair competition in the commercial aircraft industry, and if the Europeans or Americans are subsidizing their commercial aircraft industries to the detriment of each other. While the US (Boeing and McDonnell-Douglas) criticize the direct subsidies European governments pay to their companies that comprise Airbus, the Europeans note the level of US government support for military programs - programs that certainly have spill over effects into the commercial aircraft industry.

Until the 1980s the US had a virtual monopoly in the commercial aircraft industry, and Boeing was the single largest exporter in the US While Airbus Industrie was formed in 1970 as a consortium of several European companies, it was not until the mid-1980s and early 1990s that it started to make a significant impact on the world market. The combination of high development costs, break-even levels that account for a substantial percentage of world demand, significant experience curve effects, and volatile demand makes for an industry that can only support a few major players. While Airbus clearly required and received some subsidies to break into the market, it also had a very good product strategy and has developed some truly state of the art planes.

In 1992 the US and the four European governments backing Airbus entered into an agreement that was intended to equitably solve the disputes about subsidization and unfair practices. The US industry generally thought the agreement was fair, and had for the most part "leveled the playing field". The industry was also aware that this is a very complex international business, as there are important international suppliers that sell to both the US companies and Airbus. Thus raising too much rancor over the issue potentially politicizes it more than is in the best interest of the firms involved.

TEACHING OBJECTIVES

The main teaching objectives of the case are:

1.   Show how cases of subsidies and government interference in trade are not always very straight forward. It is difficult to determine just how much a domestic firm is being helped by protectionist policies, or how much a foreign competitor is being helped by its government.
2.   Show the difficulty of complaining about foreign subsidies when it is clear that the complainer is not standing on the high moral ground and has also subsidized in the past.
3.   US firms like Pratt & Whitney and General Electric are also significant suppliers to Airbus as well as Boeing, and by being too strident in its dealing with Airbus governments the US government could hurt other US aerospace firms (that also supply the aircraft manufacturers) while trying to help the aircraft manufacturers. The net result could be that the aircraft manufacturers are worse off if their suppliers are worse off.
3.   Present a situation where one possible option can be to take an aggressive stance and threaten to escalate the dispute. While this can lead to both parties backing down, what if it leads to an even more vicious trade war.

This case fits well after chapter 5, as it includes elements of the political economy of international trade. Since this is really an ongoing issue, the case may be able to be augmented by recent articles from periodicals.

STRATEGIC ISSUES AND DISCUSSION QUESTIONS

1.   Do you think that Airbus could have become a viable competitor without subsidies?

While Airbus clearly developed new technology and had a very good product strategy, either the governments or the parent firms would have had to provide subsidies for quite some time for Airbus to be able to develop its new aircraft and get sales volume up to a break-even level. Given the large investments, long break-even, significant experience curve effects, and volatile demand, it is inconceivable that a firm like Airbus could have successfully entered the industry without subsidies.

2.   Why do you think the European governments agreed to subsidize the establishment of Airbus.

The aircraft industry provides a large number of direct jobs, and even greater number of indirect jobs. The aircraft industry also creates a number of spillover effects into other industries that can use the technology developed for aircraft. The European governments are also owners (or part owners) of domestic airlines, would rather give the aircraft business to domestic firms and are perhaps even concerned about the balance of payments effects of having to purchase all aircraft from US manufacturers.

3.   Is Airbus' position with regard to the dispute over subsidies reasonable?

Airbus' position is reasonable. It does not deny any of the subsidies it receives, but says that the US government provides significant subsidies to the US firms indirectly via NASA and Defense spending. Beyond this, the development of the US aircraft industry was largely funded by the government in the first half of this century. Hence since the US industry was given a head start through government funding and continues to receive indirect subsidies from government contracts, the subsidies Airbus has received more recently simply allow it to catch up. Its contention that another reason for its success is a smart product strategy and state of the art technology is also valid.

4.   Given the 1992 agreement, what additional action (if any) should the US government take with
         respect to Airbus?

At this time it does not appear that there would be much reason to take action other than monitor compliance with the 1992 agreement and take action only to address deviance from the agreement.

5.   Why do you think that the US industry reacted with caution to attempts by US politicians to
         reopen the trade dispute in 1993?

One can think of a couple of aspects to the industry's reaction. One, the upturn in business and marketshare diminished the immediate importance of the issue. Secondly, there may simply an interest in seeing how well the 1992 agreement works before suggesting changes. Thirdly, politicians can as easily screw things up as help, and may actually make more of a mess than help. Fourth, the international interconnectedness of this industry is substantial, and while the aircraft manufacturers may compete, they also collaborate with suppliers and don't want to disrupt other well functioning international relations. Finally, they realize that Airbus isn't going to go away, and in many ways it is better to have a healthy competitor that acts rationally than a struggling competitor that may take desperate measures that hurt the entire industry.

CASE: ACTIVE MATRIX LIQUID CRYSTAL DISPLAYS (A): 1990-91 TRADE DISPUTE

SYNOPSIS

This case highlights both some of the administrative mechanisms available to the US government to intervene in trade, and how these mechanisms may have unintended side effects and still not meet the original objectives. Active matrix liquid crystal displays (AM-LCDs) were pioneered in the US, but Japanese firms have become the major suppliers today (95% worldwide market share). They represent a significant advance over the passive matrix LCDs that are most common in watches, calculators, and laptop computers. Attaining success is difficult, with high up front investment in technology, a potential loss for 5-6 years, and a difficult production process in which 80% of production must currently be scrapped. No large US firms are in the business (with the exception of an IBM-Toshiba joint venture in Japan), but several small entrepreneurial US firms serve specific market niches - primarily for military applications.

In 1990 this small group of US manufacturers filed an anti-dumping action against the Japanese suppliers, claiming they were selling AM-LCDs at below market value and at half of the cost of production. The International Trade Commission in the Commerce Department sided with the producers, and levied a 62.67% duty on the import of AM-LCDs from Japan. (In 1987 a 100% tariff on laptop computers from Japan had also been levied.) A key point is that both of these tariffs were very specific - they applied only to imports from Japan.

While the US AM-LCDs manufacturers may have been pleased, computer manufacturers were not. They had been importing the screens from Japan, and then assembling products in the US (To some extent, the earlier imposition of duties on lap top computers had encouraged MNEs to perform assembly in the US rather than Japan, since the individual components were not subject to the earlier duties.) Now they faced a significant increase in the price of one of the computer's critical and expensive components - the screen. The computer manufacturers responded by launching formal protests to have the duty revoked, and secondly began to move production out of the US Apple decided to locate lap top production in Ireland, while Compaq announced that it would produce laptop computers in Scotland. Thus an effect of the duties on AM-LCDs was that computer manufacturing jobs were exported to other countries where there were no duties on either the computers nor the screens, and were not subject to the duties that were specific to Japan.

Japanese companies also appealed for a reversal of the decision. They argued that the reason they were not making profit was due to the high start up costs, and that profits would only come once the production process was perfected and economies of scale are able to realized.

If the goal of the duties was to "save the US AM-LCD industry," it may have come too late. The companies involved are all very small, and the prospect of a high investment, losses for several years, and difficult production may deter entry by other US firms. While the Defense department is interested in assuring the viability of US producers, the size of this business is potentially too small to be economically viable.

TEACHING OBJECTIVES

The main teaching objectives of the case are:

1.   Provide some insight into a policy option available to the US government - countervailing duties.
2.   Show how in some industries there are significant first mover advantages, economies of scale, and high start-up costs - all factors that fit with prescriptions for a strategic trade policy.
3.   Show how governmental actions in regulating trade can have serious and significant side effects on other industries, and hence how the "cure" can be worse than the "illness."
4.   Introduce how easy it is for firms to work around policies that have very specific targets.

This case fits well right after chapter 5, which describes the political economy of international trade. According to the arguments in both chapters 4 and 5, this situation seems to be one where "strategic trade policy" makes sense - yet it clearly does not appear to work out the way theory suggests.

STRATEGIC ISSUES AND DISCUSSION QUESTIONS

1.   Evaluate the decision by the Department of Commerce to impose anti-dumping duties upon Japanese manufacturers of AM-LCDs? On balance, has this decision helped or harmed American industry? What is the likely impact upon the American consumer?

The decision to impose duties on Japanese AM-LCDs seems to generally fit with the goals of countervailing duties - Japanese producers were selling goods at a loss. By imposing a duty that priced the screens at what is calculated to be their fair price, at least US producers do not have to compete against subsidized imports. (Given the amount of guessing and estimation that must go into these calculations, that they came up with 62.67% seems ridiculous.) Whether US AM-LCD manufacturers will truly benefit is less clear, since they are primarily selling to the Defense department, and probably have a price disadvantage of much more than 62.67% based on their lower investment and lesser scale economies. For US industry in general, however, the decision unambiguously harms it in the near term. US firms that import AM-LCDs and then use these in products will face higher costs than, for example, European competitors that import the screens to Europe and then export the entire product to the US. US consumers are clearly worse off, since they will have to pay more for the same products than they did before the imposition of the duties. Employees may also lose their jobs as manufacturers move production overseas in order to avoid the specific duties. In the long run, if US manufacturers are to become successful partially as a result of these duties, US industry and consumers may end up recovering these initial costs and become better off; but this is a very big if, and fairly unlikely given the facts presented.

2.   What, in anything, might the US government do to stop US computer manufacturers from moving their manufacturing operations offshore? Should the government take such action?

The US government really can do very little to stop US manufacturers from moving manufacturing offshore. While a number of options are available, like a broad tariff on any product that has an AM-LCD screen, another country would stand a reasonable chance if they challenged this under GATT rules, and it could provoke even more creative and unintentional side effects. While students will likely be able to come up with a number of options, these are likely to be either easily circumvented or completely contrary to GATT. Hence, by its actions, the government is causing a behavior that was not of its intentions, and a behavior that may in fact be more damaging than the problem that the government was trying to remedy.

3.   What criteria should the US government use to target industries for anti-dumping protection?

The key criteria are relatively simple - that firms from other countries are dumping products in the US below cost. Yet while a domestic industry may be harmed by this, a criteria that is not used is whether on the whole the US is better off when it has access to goods at below cost.

4.   If you were the CEO of a small US firm interested in AM-LCD manufacturing, what factors would be important in your decision to enter the AM-LCD market? Under what conditions might you enter the market?

   a. availability of financial resources
   b. ability to run deficits for a number of years
   c. likelihood of getting long term contracts, either from the government or other firms
   d. availability of technological expertise to design and manufacture AM-LCDs
   e. permanence and level of future duties on imports

Points a-d are critical before entering the market. While it would be nice to also be able to expect to be protected from foreign competition for quite some time by import duties, it would be foolish to count on point e - government policy can change.

5.   Should the US government urge the Pentagon to support production of AM-LCDs? Explain the reasoning behind your answer?

   Yes: Why?
               this technology can be critical for national defense - we should not be dependent on
                     foreigners
               this is an infant industry with huge start-up costs - with support it may become a world
                     leader
               we need to break down the entry barriers that will give the Japanese a monopoly

   No: Why?
               the game is over, the Japanese have moved too far down the learning curve already
               our government should get the best deal possible on the parts it needs - taxpayers should
                     not be supporting inefficient manufacturers
               if we want to spend money subsidizing industries, we should choose one where we
                     already have a lead that just needs to be solidified

CASE: ACTIVE MATRIX LIQUID CRYSTAL DISPLAYS (B): 1992-94

SYNOPSIS

After finding that there is virtually no support for its 62.67% duty on AM-LCDs from Japan, and that it is actually causing US computer manufacturers to move assembly operations overseas, the US government revokes the duty. Yet there are strong feelings within the government that the US should be in the LCD industry, and if not by tariffs, perhaps there is some other way to encourage entry by US manufacturers.

In 1993 the defense department announced that it would fund up to $100 million in LCD research grants for some US manufacturers. In addition, well over $1 billion in additional funds would potentially be available to firms interested in setting up LCD manufacturing facilities. While companies like AT&T and Xerox are interested in this industry, the government has argued that because of the high set up costs (~$300 million) and risks, US firms might not participate without assistance.

Critics are concerned with this sort of industrial policy. Historically the US has limited subsidies to military technologies - subsidizing the start-up costs of commercial operations would be a new step. Taking such an approach might encourage other governments to do the same, something which the US has objected to in the past (e.g. Airbus). The ability of the US to criticize such actions by other countries (which can be detrimental to US firms) will be severely compromised if the US starts subsidizing industries. Others are concerned that taking such an action presumes that government bureaucrats are more able to pick winners and losers, and allocate money more efficiency, than the capital markets.

TEACHING OBJECTIVES

The main teaching objectives of the case are:

1.   Show more clearly the fallacies of some forms of governmental interaction in markets.
2.   Suggest a situation where subsidies may be more appropriate than tariffs.
3.   Question the appropriateness of governmental industrial policy.

This case builds on the previous A case, and looks at the subsequent three years. While it is possible to assign only the B case (since the introduction summarizes the A case), I would recommend that you ask students to read both cases (skimming the A case), even if you want to focus the discussion on the B case. This case, as well as the A case, fits well after chapter 5.

STRATEGIC ISSUES AND DISCUSSION QUESTIONS

1.   Do you think that the Commerce Department was correct to revoke the 62.67 percent tariff on imports of flat panel displays from Japan?

The case makes it seem that this should have been a pretty straightforward decision in light of the fact that there were no US domestic suppliers at the time as well as the trade and investment distorting nature of the tariff. The only reasonable argument against would seem to be that it takes time to develop a new domestic industry, and not enough time had elapsed.

2.   Does it make sense for the US government to subsidize the development of technology and establishment of manufacturing facilities by US firms in the flat panel display industry?

This question is really one where one's personal political and economic philosophy drives the answer. The libertarians would say that the government has no business interfering in such an industry, and that if capital markets that fund new firms and the designing of new billion dollar airplanes and autos don't think the investment will pay off, it probably doesn't make sense. In their view, governments will only fund things that don't make sense because otherwise the private sector would have done it long before the bureaucrats got around to it. Believers in big government, however, will say that this is precisely the situation where the government will have a longer term perspective than the private sector, and support of such industries make sense. Some students will be more pragmatic, and suggest that since other governments do it, the US should too.

3.   Assuming that the government does aggressively subsidize US companies in this area, what do you think might be the reaction from the governments of other countries where firms are active in this industry.

The two most likely reactions are the governments will express their displeasure, and potentially attempt to get the US to reverse this action, or that they take this as a signal to do likewise in their country.

4.   Do you think it is possible for the government, by drawing upon the advice of private sector experts, to pick winners and losers in this field?

Answers to this question will likely also display a philosophical belief. The skeptics will strongly feel that any group of experts will be less efficient the capital markets, and even if almost as good, the subsequent political process would likely obscure the decision (i.e. Senator Y will support it only if the plant is located in his district, but Representative X thinks that the university in his state should be involved in the research, and Senator B (who heads the subcommittee) has received significant contributions from company A and thinks they should be involved as a joint venture partner, etc., and hence something inherently inefficient will result). Others will say that the government does this all of the time in defense procurement, and the performance of the defense industry in assuring national defense is unquestionable. Hence the government has already shown its ability to pick winners and losers in the defense industry, and can do likewise in other industries.

CASE: RISKY BUSINESS: NICK LEESON, GLOBAL DERIVATIVES TRADING, AND THE FALL OF BARINGS BANK

SYNOPSIS

In February 1995 the financial world was shaken by the revelation that unauthorized derivatives trading by Nick Leeson had caused a loss of over $1 billion for Barings Bank. This loss essentially caused the bankruptcy of Barings, and it was purchased for 1 British Pound by ING. Unfortunately this loss was not entirely unique, but it helped call into question the fragility of international markets and the destructive potential of derivatives. The case contains a fairly long description of derivatives that can be skimmed or ignored by those familiar with financial instruments.

Barings Bank was one of the oldest and most respected banks in Britain, and for most of its life had stuck strictly to banking. As the financial world became more complex, however, and clients required securities trading capabilities, Barings opened a securities trading arm. The securities business was quite different from the traditional banking business, and the business cultures of the two parts of the bank differed significantly. The trading arm managed to make some fairly strong profits, and was this left relatively alone. A series of management changes and personnel turnover in Asia left Barings trading expertise in Asia quite thin by late 1994.

Nick Leeson was a successful arbitrage trader in Singapore, and had devised a trading strategy that had made Barings a nice stream of profits. He had also set up a couple of fictitious accounts over the years that he used when needed to help cover positions. The success of his strategy depended upon the Nikkei average moving within a fairly narrow range. In the aftermath of the Kobe earthquake and questions over the strength of the Japanese economy, the Nikkei started to fall. At first Nick tried to cover, then he tried to drive the price of his derivatives higher, and in the process just dug himself deeper and deeper into the hole. After he had exhausted all of the funds under his control, he requested and received more from Barings. His superiors thought he was trading on behalf of clients, and claimed to have no idea he was taking these positions for the bank. When the losses from his unsuccessful strategy and failed cover-up was tallied, he had blown through $1.33 billion of Barings capital. (And other traders were correspondingly better off.)

TEACHING OBJECTIVES

The main teaching objectives of the case are:

1.   Provide an understanding of derivatives and global capital markets.
2.   Show how wide open and wild international securities trading can be, and how important it is to carefully monitor exposure to potential losses.
3.   Illustrate a situation where the resilience of the global capital market can be discussed, along with options for evaluating potential oversight mechanisms.

This case fits nicely after chapter 11, The Global Capital Market.

STRATEGIC ISSUES AND DISCUSSION QUESTIONS

1.   Why do you think critics are worried that the rapid growth in the use of derivatives might de-stabilize global financial markets?

The simplest answer would be that critics do understand derivatives, and that fear of the unknown is driving these worries. While this is likely part of the answer, the size of losses that have occurred in several companies gives some call for concern. And in spite of assurances, the potential exists that a significant loss could start a unpredictable chain of events leading to de-stabilization of multiple international markets. Yet no loss so far has come close to really destabilizing the global financial markets. The critics, however, don't want to wait until something catastrophic happens before making changes.

2.   Do you think that derivatives are risky and speculative financial instruments, or instruments that can be used to reduce an investors risk?

Derivatives are both. They can be used to reduce risk when used in appropriate ways, but can be risky and speculative if used uncovered.

3.   Does the collapse of Barings expose a fundamental flaw in the global financial system? If so, how might this flaw be fixed?

Rather than exposing a fundamental flaw, the collapse and quick absorption of the loss by ING suggests the strength of the global financial system in being able to minimize the impact of any particular loss. An alternative perspective is that the global financial system contains too many independent markets and players, and that some sort of global oversight of the financial system is called for. Advocates of this latter perspective suggest that there should be a UN or GATT type organization to oversee international financial markets.

4.   What is your view on the basic causes of the collapse of Barings' Bank?

Lack of oversight and internal controls in Barings is the obvious cause of the collapse of Barings. Some of this had to do with the personnel turnover at Barings, the inability of the 'bankers' to understand the 'traders', and greed (or blindness) based on the past success of the traders. Even the controls that were in place were ignored by Leeson's bosses when he asked for additional funds to try to recover from his position.

CASE: CHAOS IN THE CURRENCY MARKETS

<u>SYNOPSIS</u>

The case begins with some of the same background material that is in Chapter 10 - the debate on fixed vs. floating exchange rates and information about the ERM. It then describes in more detail the challenge to the ERM that occurred in September 1992.

With the unification of Germany, the German money supply increased dramatically, causing the Bundesbank to raise interest rates. At the same time the US government was pushing interest rates down to help get the US out of its recession. Thus investors were selling dollars and buying marks, pushing the dollar lower and the mark higher. This put pressure on the Italy, Britain, and Spain, all of whom needed to raise their interest rates in order to avoid devaluation within the ERM.

Speculators began to bet that these countries would have to devalue, and knew that a lot of money could be made if they now dumped these currencies and bought marks in advance of the devaluation. This of course put added pressure on the currencies, accelerating the need to devalue. The Lira was the first to get hit, and eventually had to undergo a 7% devaluation. Next the speculators focused on the Swedish krona and the pound. Sweden responded by raising interest rates first to 30%, and then 500%, and beat back the speculation at a huge cost. Britain responded by raising interest rates to 12% and then 15%, and spent over $15 billion supporting the pound. In the end it proved useless, and Britain withdrew from the ERM, lowered interest rates back to 10%, and allowed the pound to float freely. Attention of the speculators switched back to Italy, which also then pulled out of the ERM.

Speculation then focused on the French franc. In a concerted effort by both Germany and France, they remained steadfast and bought francs to support the ERM. Thus the speculative splurge was stopped, and the ERM remained tattered but still in place for the other currencies.

Foreign exchange trading had grown 50% between 1989 and 1992, and the current reserves held by most central banks may not be enough to stop speculative pressures like this in the future.

<u>TEACHING OBJECTIVES</u>

The main teaching objectives of the case are:

1.   Show how the EMS really works, and what can happen when speculators dump a currency in anticipation of a devaluation.
2.   Suggest that while a stable EMS can be very good for business, when adjustments have to be made they can be fairly large and dramatic.
3.   Illustrate how fixed exchange rates can be prey for speculators, and how difficult it can be for countries to defend their currencies.

This case fits well after Chapter 10 or 11, and illustrates how dramatic exchange rate movements can really be.

STRATEGIC ISSUES AND DISCUSSION QUESTIONS

1.   What does the crisis of September tell you about the relative ability of the currency markets and national governments to influence exchange rates?

The crisis of September 1992 suggests that currency markets are in a very strong position to influence exchange rates. While governments can take actions to limit the influence of speculators, it comes at a great cost. The governments (and taxpayers) of Britain, Italy, Germany, and France put a great deal of money in the pockets of speculators, and business was certainly hurt by the high interest rates imposed to support the currencies. Only concerted multi-governmental action seems to have been effective, as was true in both the Plaza Accord and the actions of Germany and France in this case. Whether such action will be as effective in the future is less clear.

2.   What does the crisis of September 1992 tell you about the weaknesses of fixed exchange rate regimes?

The crisis suggests that fixed exchange rates can only remained fixed if the economic fundamentals are strong enough to discourage speculation and support the exchange rate as fixed. When the underlying economics (i.e. interest rate disparities) suggest an imbalance in the supply and demand for currencies, fixed rates are difficult to maintain.

3.   Assess the impact of the events of September 1992 upon the ability of the EC to establish a common currency by 1999?

The reason the events of September 1992 occurred was because different countries were undertaking different economic policies. As long as the countries of Europe desire this autonomy, including the ability to set their own interest rates and maintain different inflationary levels, establishing a common currency will be impossible. If, however, the events force countries to realize that they need to further harmonize their economic policies, then the net effect may be a strengthening of the EC's ability to establish a common currency.

4.   "The crisis of September 1992 occurred because the ERM system was too inflexible." Discuss.

While greater flexibility in exchange rates (i.e. wider bands) could have prevented the problem by allowing the countries more time to align their economic policies, widening the bands to increase flexibility isn't necessarily a solution. Firstly, if the economic fundamentals are truly out of line, a wider band will simply extend the time to realignment, not remove the need for realignment. Secondly, as bands become wider, the costs of doing business and the risk of exchange rate changes will increase. Thus the advantage for business of having the ERM goes away if bands are set too wide.

5.   If you were an executive working for a company that undertook substantial intra-EC trade, what would your reaction to the events of September 1992 be?

My reaction to the events would depend upon how much my firm currently covers exchange rate changes. Given the relative stability of the ERM, my firm may have become more complacent and not insured against exchange rate changes. These events would lead me to looking more carefully at how my firm manages intra-EC exchange rate risk, and consider the need to hedge risks when currencies are nearing the limits of the exchange rate bands.

CASE: PHILIPS NV

SYNOPSIS

Philips is one of the world's largest electronics enterprises. As of the late 1980s, Philips had several hundred subsidiaries in sixty countries, operated manufacturing plants in over 40 countries, employed approximately 300,000 people, and manufactured thousands of different products in lighting, consumer electronics, computers, medical equipment, and basic electronic components like chips. However, despite its global reach, by 1990 Philips was a company in deep trouble. After a decade of deteriorating performance, in 1990 Philips lost $2.2 billion on revenues of $28 billion. A major reason for this seems to have been the inability of Philips to adapt to the changing competitive conditions in the global electronics industry during the 1970s and 1980s.

While Philips had traditionally been run out of its head office, during WWII the various national entities were cut off from headquarters and each began to operate independently as a self contained entity. After the war, Philips decided to keep the multidomestic structure due to trade barriers, differing local demands, and the success of the present structure. At the same time it did create several world wide product divisions to achieve some coordination between national organizations. Most national organizations top management responsibilities were split between two managers - one responsible for technical affairs and the other commercial affairs.

From the 1960s onwards a number of significant changes took place in Philips' competitive environment that were to profoundly affect the company. First, due to the efforts of GATT, trade barriers fell world wide. In addition, in Philips' home base, Europe, the emergence of the European Economic Community, of which the Netherlands was an early member, led to a further reduction in trade barriers between the countries of Western Europe. Second, during the 1960s and 1970s a number of new competitors emerged in Japan that utilized standardization and economies scale to lower the costs. Third, due to technological changes, the cost of R&D and manufacturing increased rapidly. Finally, as the world moved from a series of fragmented national markets and towards a single global market, so uniform global standards for electronic equipment were beginning to emerge.

By the early 1980s Philips realized that if it was to survive it was going to have to radically restructure its business. Its cost structure was high due to the amount of duplication across national organizations, particularly in the area of manufacturing. In the early 1980s Philips tried to rationalize manufacturing, enter more alliances to share the costs of development, move away from the dual leadership structure, and give more power to the product divisions.

In the latter 1980s Philips took further autonomy away from national divisions, specifically that of North America. It established four product divisions and gave these much more power over country managers, and decided to cut its world wide work force. Yet losses continued.

The current situation is unclear, but slightly positive. Philips has sold off its unprofitable mini-computer division, announced plans to cut costs by $1.2 billion by cutting the workforce by 55,000, and entered into a strategic alliance with Matsushita to market the digital compact cassette. Whether this is enough, only time will tell.

TEACHING OBJECTIVES

The main teaching objectives of the case are:

1.   Show how a changing environment affects the strategy and structure of an organization.
2.   Illustrate how an inappropriate strategy and structure, given the environment, can be devastating.
3.   Describe the difficulty a firm faces when trying to change its strategy and structure.

This case fits well either after chapter 12 or 13. The primary point is to show how the strategy, structure, and environment of an organization must fit together if it is to be successful. The environmental change brought about by WWII necessitated a strategic and structural change, and Philips appears to have made this change quite successfully. The change required by the competitive environment of the 1980s was not as easy, however.

STRATEGIC ISSUES AND DISCUSSION QUESTIONS

1.   What were the drawbacks of Philips' post World War II organization?

Philips post WWII organization fit with a multidomestic strategy - with all the advantages and disadvantages this form typically has. The primary were drawbacks were a lack of coordination across national entities, duplication of facilities, and difficulty in undertaking the very large costs of new product development. The top management was also organized so that two people headed every major national organization.

2.   What international strategy was Philips pursuing in the 1960s? What strategy should it have
      been trying to pursue?

Philips was basically pursuing a multidomestic strategy in the 1960s when either an international or global strategy would have been preferable. Although in theory a global strategy would make a great deal of sense, it would be difficult to make the necessary organizational changes to go directly from multidomestic to global.

3.   Why did Dekker and van de Klugt try to tilt Philips' matrix away from the national organizations
      and towards the product divisions?

The need for greater coordination and sharing of development expenses was a primary motive for tilting Philips' matrix away from the national organizations and towards the product divisions. A related reason was to lower costs and rationalize manufacturing.

4.   Identify the forces opposed to change at Philips?

The primary forces opposed to change at Philips were the heads in national organizations. Not only would they lose autonomy in decision-making, they might lose manufacturing plants and R&D organizations in the re-organization. Even lower level managers in the national organizations may have opposed the changes, since they would be less responding to local demands and more to directives from senior managers in other countries and at headquarters.

5.   Is Philips correct to enter into an alliance with Matsushita to manufacture and market the DCC?
          Wouldn't it be better to go it alone?

Its hard to tell whether this is the correct decision for certain, but it looks good. For Philips to make any
money from the DCC, it has to be accepted by the market. This market acceptance is greatly enhanced by
teaming up with Matsushita - both because of Matsushita's market presence and its excellent low cost
manufacturing capabilities. While Philips may be able to make more money in the long run by going it
alone, the risks that the DCC will not be accepted (i.e. V2000) are much greater if Philips goes it alone.
Given the high development costs, the potential losses from a DCC failure are significant.

CASE: HONDA MOTOR COMPANY

SYNOPSIS

Honda was established in 1948 to manufacture motorcycles, and started manufacturing autos in the 1960s. MITI strongly objected to Honda's entering of the auto market, and Honda had a great deal of difficulty setting up a domestic supply and distribution system in Japan. Consequently, Honda found that its growth in Japan was limited, and turned its attention overseas. So successful was this strategy that by 1990 more than 60% of Honda's total sales were made outside Japan; Honda also had 77 manufacturing plants in 40 countries outside Japan.

Honda's initial international expansion was in a motorcycle factory in Belgium in 1962. It took almost a decade for this plant to make a profit - its mopeds did not match European needs, it was not able to find the necessary suppliers, and it had a series of labor disputes. Honda's first major US investment was a motorcycle plant in Ohio in 1979. This was followed by two auto plants and an engine plant in Ohio, and a auto plant in Canada. In total, by 1992 Honda had invested over $3 billion in US manufacturing facilities and created more than 11,000 jobs in the Ohio region and 3,000 elsewhere in the US.

Honda claims that its strategy for operating overseas consists of four target concepts; localization of products, profit, production, and management. Localization of products means developing, manufacturing, and marketing products that are best suited to the demands of local consumers. To localize products so that they appeal to local consumer tastes and preferences, Honda has invested in R&D centers in North America, Europe, and Southeast Asia. Localization of profits means reinvesting profits earned in a country in that country. Localization of production means establishing significant production centers in each major market (country or region) where Honda does businesses. Localization of management means a number of things. First, it means that local people should play a major role in the management of foreign subsidiaries. In the US, for example, Honda's operations are headed by an American. Second, it means that local managers and employees should have a good understanding of Honda's corporate philosophy. And third, it means that managers dispatched from Honda's head office (in Japan) should be encouraged to become part of the local community by understanding local culture and ways of thinking.

Despite the substantial investments in Ohio, Honda has recently run headlong into a potentially serious dispute with the US Customs department. In 1992 Customs researchers argued that Honda overstated the local content of the cars it built in Ohio. At the heart of the dispute lies the claim that Honda cars are mostly a collection of Japanese parts handled by Americans, but designed, engineered and fabricated in Japan. The US Customs service has also criticized Honda for overstating the US content of the engines produced at its Anna, Ohio plant. When these engines are shipped to Canada to be included in Canadian assembled autos, and then shipped back to the US, the net effect is avoid a significant import duty if these engines were classified as having a lower domestic content.

Honda's response is to point out that the US Custom's service is ignoring the input of local labor, depreciation, and overheads in the Anna engines. When this is added in, the total the figure for US content is over 50%. Honda also points out that the US Customs service has not yet adopted rules for calculating local origin - a point which the US Customs service acknowledges. Thus, according to Honda, there is nothing to say that they can't count labor inputs and parts supplied by US based Japanese suppliers as being of US origin. Moreover, Honda notes that it is ironic that the Customs Service has chosen to focus on an engine produced by Honda in Ohio at a time when Chrysler, GM, and Ford all import small engines for their cars. Honda is, in fact, the only auto maker that manufacturers a small fuel efficient engine in the US. Honda also argues that in 1992 it spent $2.9 billion purchasing parts from more than 240 American parts suppliers, and by 1995 its plans call for the company to purchase $5 billion worth of parts per year from American suppliers.

TEACHING OBJECTIVES

The main teaching objectives of the case are:

1.   Show how Honda has expanded internationally, adapting to local demands while maintaining a
        focus on minimizing costs.
2.   Illustrate how governmental policies can significantly affect the strategy of firms.
3.   Suggest how governmental policies intended to benefit "local" firms can be convoluted, difficult
        to interpret, and have a negative impact on some "local" firms.

This case fits well after Chapter 12, as it brings together the issues of strategy discussed in this chapter
with the topics of Part III on global trade and investment. It could, in fact, be also used after Chapter 7 by
placing more emphasis on the effects of trade and investment policies and less emphasis on Honda's
strategy.

STRATEGIC ISSUES AND DISCUSSION QUESTIONS

1.   In terms of the strategies discussed in Chapter 12, what kind of strategy is Honda pursuing?
        What are the benefits of Honda's strategy? What are the costs?

Honda is pursing essentially a transnational strategy - trying to carefully coordinate activities between
countries in order to minimize costs while simultaneously being responsive to local demands. The
benefits of this strategy can be enormous, as it allows a firm to create products that provide high value to
different domestic consumers while keeping costs low by developing experience curve and locational
economies. The costs are the high costs of coordination that are required to achieve these goals, and the
significant organizational problems that can arise due to conflicting demands and performance ambiguity.

2.   What are the reasons behind Honda's decision to establish production facilities outside of the US?

Of course Honda already had significant production facilities outside the US prior to the opening of its
Canadian and subsequent international plants in Europe and elsewhere. Honda's primary reasons for
establishing new international production facilities seem to be three fold: firstly, governmental
restrictions can necessitate investment in facilities if a market is to be served economically, secondly, in
order to realize locational economies, and thirdly to minimize transportation costs.

3.   Honda's Ohio plants are reportedly among the most efficient in the US. How do you think that
        Honda has achieved this in such a short space of time?

The fact that these are new plants may be part of the explanation. By being able to build new and not be
hampered by past investments and employment practices, Honda can build in efficiencies more easily than
other plants can be adapted. By importing mass production techniques developed in Japan and adapted in
other countries (transferring a core competence), Honda also be better able to learn and improve the
efficiency of its plants.

4.   Is the Honda Civic an American car? Is it more or less "American" than a car like the GM's Pontiac Le Mans, which while designed in the US is built by Dawoo Motors of Korea, largely using parts manufactured in South East Asia?

This is a good question for debate, but with no clear answer. The key question revolves around what should be considered in "domestic content" and what should not. Key items to discuss are R&D time, overhead allocation, depreciation, direct labor, the domestic content of parts supplied, and ownership of facilities.

5.   Should parts produced in the US by Japanese owned suppliers be counted under "US content"?

Again, this is a good question for debate but with no clear answer. The simple answer would be that the domestic content of each part be used - parts should not classified as strictly 100% American or 100% foreign, but each have a calculated domestic content percentage. This of course would keep many accountants and government bureaucrats employed for a long time.

6.   Does Honda's presence in Ohio benefit the American economy?

Honda's presence in Ohio clearly benefits the American economy by creating jobs and efficiently produced products that provide value to US consumers. The fact that Honda exports autos from Ohio also benefits the American economy.

7.   Do you think the US customs service was correct to focus attention of Honda?

It is hard to know the rationale behind the customs service's focus on Honda. If it was simply trying to enforce rules written by Congress on what should be taxed and what shouldn't, and collect taxes if taxes were due, then it was entirely justified to try and collect the additional revenue. If it was simply trying to point out the difficulty inherent in calculating domestic content in order to provide an impetus for more explicit rules, then its actions may also be warranted. Similarly, if by making an example out of Honda it encourages other firms to comply voluntarily with domestic content rules, its actions may be appropriate. If however it focused on Honda as a foreign firm, while domestic firms like Ford and GM are also involved in similar cross shipments of goods between countries, then perhaps it was wrong to focus on Honda instead of other firms.

CASE: FORD 2000

<u>SYNOPSIS</u>

In 1994 Ford announced a massive restructuring that transformed it from an area division structure into a worldwide matrix. With this restructuring the world wide responsibility for developing a particular class of vehicles was given to a particular vehicle program center (VPC). In the case of small and medium cars, this VPC was to be headquartered in Europe, while the other four were in the US. While different areas of the world could make minor alterations in cars in order to fit local tastes, there was a strong desire to minimize the amount of duplicitous design activities that had been occurring around the world.

With the matrix structure many employees will report to two or more managers, one within a vehicle center team and one within a functional discipline. Given the well known problems with matrix organizations, Ford has tried to minimize these by taking the following steps:
*   Making doubly sure that objectives are agreed upon precisely between the vehicle centers and the functional side of the organization.
*   Specifying clearly the respective roles and responsibilities of individuals towards each side of the matrix.
*   Changing appraisal and reward systems accordingly.
*   Only appointing senior executives who have shown they can work collaboratively.
*   Training everyone involved in the art of developing a cooperative matrix perspective which largely replaces the need for policing.
*   Introducing much more intensive and open communications.

Ford made these changes quickly, and when Ford was extremely profitable. This is in sharp contrast to a more common "go slow" approach, and only undertaking major changes when times are difficult and dictate the need for change. Ford believes that it is best to make changes when things are going well, so that things can be done for the right reason rather than simple expediency. The potential gains from this restructuring are great, but it won't be easy to pull off.

<u>TEACHING OBJECTIVES</u>

The main teaching objectives of the case are:

1.   Show how one firm is attempting to change organizational structure.
2.   Suggest the amount and type of benefits that may be possible from restructuring and re-setting priorities.

This case fits very well after chapter 13, The Organization of International Business.

STRATEGIC ISSUES AND DISCUSSION QUESTIONS

1.   What other possible obstacles might Ford encounter as it becomes a global organization?

One potentially big obstacle is resistance to the change from individuals and organizations worldwide that feel their autonomy is being threatened. Another is that the increase in coordination costs, and the need for coordination, will be greater than existing systems and personnel can handle, and the firm will be unable to make decisions efficiently. It is also unclear whether it will make sense to have one group of individuals responsible for the design and production of a particular model worldwide, and whether they will be able to adequately understand and respond to the differing demands in different areas. Finally the matrix type organization has some well known problems as suggested in the book, and while Ford is trying to address these problems, others have tried and not done well.

2.   How important will the new matrix system be in the success or failure of Ford 2000?

The new matrix structure is an integral part of the Ford 2000 program. In order to fulfill all the objectives of Ford 2000 as listed in the case, it is unlikely that any other type of organization could meet the competing demands. Thus the success or failure of the matrix system will be instrumental in the success or failure of the Ford 2000 program.

3.   What is Trotman forgetting in restructuring?

While it is unlikely that he is forgetting anything, he is counting on a great ability and willingness to change the *modus opperandi* of organizations, systems, and individuals.

4.   What other efficiencies might also be a byproduct of Ford 2000?

While the specific directives of cheaper, faster, and worldwide are pretty inclusive, by creating new connections among people and organizations Ford my foster some new creativity and problem solving that could result in new products or solutions to problems that can create a competitive advantage for Ford.

5.   How successful do you think this program will be in preparing Ford to enter emerging markets?
         What will be the key factors for success in entering these markets?

In many emerging markets cost considerations and the ability to adapt to unexpected demands are critical. To the extent the program brings Ford's cost to be among the lowest in the industry, Ford will be able to effectively compete on cost. It is less clear whether Ford 2000 can make Ford more flexible and adaptable. While the ability to reduce development and manufacturing time can help, decision-making could be hindered in the matrix structure.

CASE: THE GLOBALIZATION OF XEROX CORPORATION

SYNOPSIS

During the 1960s and 1970s Xerox dominated the world copy machine industry as a result of its patents. The parent company, Xerox Corporation, designed and produced products in the US for the North American market; Rank-Xerox, a 51% owned Xerox company developed and manufactured products for the European market; and Fuji-Xerox, a 50/50 joint venture between Xerox and Fuji, developed and manufactured products for the Japanese market. Each Xerox company controlled its own suppliers, manufacturing plants, and distribution channels. Each was, in effect, a self-contained entity.

However, by 1980 Xerox was a company facing problems. Xerox's patents had expired and many new competitors were entering Xerox's market. Xerox learned first hand how far they had fallen behind when they began to produce and market a copier in the US that had been designed by their Japanese affiliate, Fuji-Xerox. To their surprise, Xerox found that the reject rate for Fuji-Xerox parts was only a fraction of the reject rate for American produced parts. Xerox decided that it needed to focus on quality and launched a series of initiatives to improve its quality.

Xerox focused on its suppliers, and reduced it suppliers from over 5,000 to 325. It then worked with these suppliers to lower the defect rate on incoming parts. The net effect of this was to increase the level of cooperation between Xerox and its suppliers and the development of long term relationships.

Within Xerox, "quality of work life circles" and a "leadership through quality" programs were implemented. Xerox also began competitive bench marking, looking at LL Bean for distribution, Deere for central computer operations, etc. To improve new product development, multifunctional teams were put together. The development of the 5100 copier was done jointly between Xerox US and Fuji-Xerox. It also decided to link its worldwide ordering system in order to try to reduce the amount of inventory held in stock.

In 1988 Xerox created a multinational task force to review its progress towards global integration. This task force identified three levels of integration and used them as a basis for restructuring various operations at all facilities. Xerox plants were required to do the following; (1) adopt global standards for basic processes that apply to all operations (e.g. use standard data bases for materials management); (2) maintain common business processes but, where necessary, tailor them to local needs (e.g. just-in-time programs); and (3) set site-specific processes for only those systems that must conform to local needs (e.g. government reporting requirements).

As a result of the various steps discussed above Xerox's competitive position improved markedly during the 1980s. Due to its improved quality, lower costs and shorter product development time Xerox was able to gain market share back from its Japanese competitors and to boost its profits and revenues. Xerox's share of the US copier market increased from a low of 10% in 1985 to 18% in 1991.

TEACHING OBJECTIVES

The main teaching objectives of the case are:

1.   Look at the importance of *fit* between the environment, strategy, and organizational design.
2.   Show how this fit affects functional areas, and how changing strategies requires changes in the functional areas - including inter-functional coordination.
3.   Identify some of the concrete steps Xerox took to improve its competitive position.

This case fits well after chapter 18, and helps bring together topics from chapters 12, 13, 16, 17, 18.

STRATEGIC ISSUES AND DISCUSSION QUESTIONS

1.   What strategy was Xerox pursuing in 1979? What strategy was it pursuing in 1989?

Xerox was essentially pursuing a multidomestic strategy in 1979, although a bit of an unusual one. Perhaps it would be more appropriate to call it a multi-regional, as Rank-Xerox served all of Europe. By 1989 the strategy would probably best be described as transnational.

2.   From what source did Xerox draw upon to transform its own organization in the 1980s? What does this tell you about the advantages of a multinational firm?

Xerox looked to Fuji-Xerox for ideas on transforming its organization. One of the advantages of being a multinational was that Xerox had very good access to Fuji-Xerox and insight into the Japanese market and its Japanese competitors. If Xerox would not have had the opportunity to learn from Fuji-Xerox, it is questionable whether it would have been able to deal nearly as well with Canon and Ricoh's competitive threat.

3.   To what extent did taking a global rather than local perspective help Xerox to improve its competitive position?

The global approach clearly helped Xerox improve its relations with suppliers, as chosen suppliers could serve Xerox's world wide needs better and increase their economies of scale, and Xerox would have more uniform parts worldwide. By globalizing aspects of product development so that a large number of parts were used world wide, development time could be cut and individuals familiar with different markets could be brought together to design products and parts that would serve larger needs. The global perspective on customer orders, while not fully implemented, should allow Xerox to reduce its world wide inventory holdings.

4.   Evaluate the role played by global manufacturing, materials management and R&D in Xerox's improved performance during the 1980s?

Clearly all functions have played a role in Xerox's improved performance. R&D has worked internationally to improve new product development and work together to lower the cost of developing individual products. Manufacturing operations have clearly tried to learn from each other and improve the quality of the products. Materials management has played an important role in working with suppliers to reduce inventory and improve quality. Although there is no specific information on finance and accounting, it is reasonable to expect that they played an important role in helping Xerox identify the areas where it could focus attention.

CASE: METALFABRIKEN BRAZIL

SYNOPSIS

Metalfabriken Brazil was the Brazilian subsidiary of a German firm (MFK) that had been fairly successful through the early 1980s. Its success came from exploiting parent company technology in Brazil and by exporting intermittently elsewhere in Latin America. MFK Brazil produced the parent company's line of specialized automatic lathes, importing key components and attachments from the parent company in Germany. The more advanced the model, the more dependent the Brazilian operation was on imported components.

Because of worsening foreign exchange problems, the Brazilian government had imposed a 25% tax on foreign currency that was used for purchasing imported components. Yet if a firm increased its exports (thus earning hard currency), there was a 25% bonus added onto the exchange of foreign currency into cruzados.

MFK Brazil started off producing the basic model (X20), and gradually began producing and assembling parts of 3 more advanced models that were demanded by Brazilian customers. While MFK Brazil was able to make all the models, more complex models used a much higher content of German parts, and the special attachments used on the more advanced models for specialized purposes were all made in Germany. The marketing of the machines took a highly skilled and specialized sales force that could go into factories and help identify where and how MFK machines could be used. When a sale was close, technical marketing specialists would usually get involved to be certain that all the right attachments were quoted and the model would best serve the customer's needs. Due to high inflation there were price controls on the basic machines, but not on attachments or other customized features.

MFK Brazil was committed to exporting throughout Latin America, as it contributed to scale economies and helped the firm earn foreign currency needed for its imported components from Germany. However, the instability of most Latin American nations (including Brazil) made sales difficult. While it was true that the German factories had even lower costs than the Brazilian factory, an inter-Latin American agreement added extra import duties on products shipped directly from Germany that could be avoided if the lathe was produced and sold from Brazil.

Given declining profitability, the limitations on imports due to the 25% tax, and tough economic conditions throughout Latin America, it was time to reconsider or reconfirm the basic strategy of MFK Brazil. Thus a meeting was called of the top management team in Brazil. Along the possibility of just continuing as is, two other options came up. The first was to increase the technical capabilities of MFK Brazil so it could manufacture more of the components and rely less on imports. This of course would require some additional technical support from headquarters, who would have to be convinced that further investment was warranted. The second option would be to scale back and focus only on production of the low end X20, attain additional scale economies, and export it world wide. Seemingly this would make MFK Brazil less of an independent operating company and more just a manufacturing plant for one of MFK's models.

TEACHING OBJECTIVES

The main teaching objectives of the case are:

1.   Show how government policies and local economic/political considerations can significantly impact the strategic choices available to firms.
2.   Explore, from a subsidiary's viewpoint, the advantages and disadvantages of being part of a firm with an "international" or "global" strategy.
3.   Consider how the various options for MFK Brazil may look from both the Brazilian and the German perspectives.

This case fits well after either chapter 14 or chapter 16. A discussion could explore any or all of the following topics: mode of entry; understanding, anticipating, and dealing with country level economic and political problems; choices of the best multinational strategy for MFK; functional and organizational implications of different strategic options; and global manufacturing and materials management strategy. This is a particularly good case for students to write up a 4-6 page case write-up with some quantitative analysis.

STRATEGIC ISSUES AND DISCUSSION QUESTIONS

1.   Why is Brazil implementing exchange controls and taxes? What are the objectives of these policies? What are the likely consequences?

Brazil has a great deal of foreign debt to pay off, and the only way to pay it off is to earn foreign exchange reserves, which requires exporting more than it imports. Unfortunately the opposite is occurring. Thus the government decided to place a 25% tax on the purchase of foreign reserves (it takes 25% more cruzados to purchase foreign currencies than the stated exchange rate price), the net effect being an increase in the price of imports, and therefore hopefully a decline in imports. Likewise, a firm that increased its exports would receive a 25% bonus in cruzados of any foreign exchange it earned. The net effect is that a firm can lower the foreign currency prices it charges on exports and still receive additional cruzados as long as the total value of exports increases. An unfortunate consequence of this is that purchases of foreign capital equipment that could be used to increase domestic output are discouraged by the 25% higher price of the imported machinery.

2.   How do the Brazilian government's foreign exchange policies impact MFK Brazil?

The foreign exchange policies hurt the viability of MFK Brazil since it imports more than it exports (it is part of the problem). MFK Brazil has to increase its prices (some of which it can't since they are under government control) if it is to remain profitable. It clearly increases the incentives for MFK Brazil to push the low end machines that have a higher domestic content, and decreases incentives to sell the previously more profitable upper end machines. It is also causing MFK Brazil to reconsider its strategy.

3.   Why does MFK Brazil need to consider a change in strategic direction?

MFK Brazil's current situation (importing more than it exports) is incompatible with the wishes, incentives, and restrictions imposed by the Brazilian government. It either has to figure out how it can maintain its strategy and still remain profitable in spite of the governmental policies, or change its strategy so that it no longer imports more than it exports. Obviously this can be done by some combination of increasing exports and/or decreasing imports.

4.   What are the primary options facing MFK Brazil? What are the advantages and disadvantages of each?

The null option is that MFK Brazil just continue its current policies, recognizing that its profits will be hurt, but hoping that the present exchange controls are only temporary. This would require no strategic changes, but both MFK Brazil and its German parent would have to agree to "tough it out" until the economic situation in Brazil turned around. This strategy could work in the short term, but if the government's policies persisted, MFK Brazil's viability could be threatened.

A second option would be to invest in additional technical expertise in Brazil so that it could become more self sufficient and would need to import less. It appears that MFK Brazil can repatriate some additional dividends to Germany as an incentive for Germany to invest in the additional technical training that would be required. The advantage of this is that MFK Brazil becomes more self-sufficient and would reduce imports. The disadvantage, as put so kindly by Kruger, "You are building a bigger, stronger Brazilian company with more assets and more profit just as the country is going to blow up. Everything will be trapped here. What good is that to the company?"

The third option is to only manufacture the low end X20 in Brazil. By reaping additional economies of scale, MFK Brazil may be able to then lower its costs below those of Germany and export the product world wide. This strategy would probably not lower the demand for imports, since there is strong customer demand for the higher end products in Brazil and the entire products would now have to be imported from Germany. The net effect, however, could be to bring MFK Brazil's imports and exports more into line. An advantage would be that MFK Brazil would be the world wide leader in the production of one product, and not be a poor imitation of the German operation. The disadvantages could be the loss of technical expertise and a loss of independence from Germany, as it would be more dependent upon the rest of the company for sales success world wide.

5.   What would recommend to Simon Kirsch? What changes in the organization and personnel would this recommendation precipitate? What changes would have to take place at the functional level? How reasonable is it for MFK Brazil to make the functional level changes needed to support the strategic choice you recommend?

Recommending the null option would probably not be a great idea unless you were an optimist and had reason to believe that Brazil's economy and exchange rate policies will turn around.

Recommending further investment in technical expertise to make MFK Brazil more autonomous would be the best option if one felt the present multidomestic strategy was the best. This really involves reconfirming the current strategy and strengthening MFK Brazil. This would mean improving the technical expertise of production and factory based technical support, something that Kruger does not seem to support. While it might be good to try to send him back to Germany, he may cause more problems for MFK Brazil there than he will if he is in Brazil and has to help implement the strategy. This option really does not involve a change in functional strategies, just a reinforcement of the current strategy.

Recommending that MFK Brazil become focused on production of the X20 has more serious organizational implications. First of all, it would probably make sense to split MFK Brazil into two pieces: one focused on production and development of the X20, the other focused on the sales of all MFK products into the Brazilian market. The marketing piece would then be just like any other national sales organization of MFK, and focused on trying to satisfy the needs of domestic consumers. It would have an advantage over some other domestic sales subsidiaries in that it would have access to a local factory for "plant tours" and showing how MFK was a good Brazilian citizen. It would also have closer access to a strong technical support staff, and some of the current technical support staff in the factory would probably be transferred out of the factory and into the sales organization. The X20 production and development piece would have few ties directly to Brazil, and would be more tightly integrated with the world wide manufacturing and marketing functions. It would need to work with the manufacturing function in Germany to improve its efficiency in production of the X20, and would want to become more involved the design of successors to the low end product offerings. It would need to work with the world wide marketing organization to have its production schedule and product features sensitive to the world wide demand for the product. In essence this recommendation would mean that MFK Brazil move from being a semi-autonomous subsidiary of a multi-domestic firm and become two integrated subsidiaries in a global firm. While this option is probably do-able, it requires much greater organizational changes.

PART V

VIDEO NOTES

VIDEO: COCA-COLA IN JAPAN

SYNOPSIS

The history of Coke's expansion in Japan is described, with a special emphasis on how it has responded to the local business environment and tastes. The importance of working with experienced local companies is emphasized. Yet Coke maintained some procedures that, while not previously done in Japan, had proven to be successful in its worldwide operations. A loyal Coke employee from another culture would likely see some things that seem very Coke-like and reflect standard operating procedures, and some things that seem very foreign. The key to Coke's success in Japan is attributed patience - gaining consensus and gradually expanding.

TEACHING OBJECTIVES

The main teaching objectives of the video are:

1.   Illustrate how a firm must adapt to the local environment, while simultaneously trying to maintain and promote some practices that have lead to its success - in spite of the fact that they seem unusual to locals.
2.   Show the importance of working with local partners in Japan.
3.   Emphasize the importance of patience when making overseas expansions, and realizing that great success is possible even if initially illusive.

This video fits well with chapters 2-3 on the differences between countries. It could also be used in the last section of the book to highlight how marketing, HRM, managerial control, and distribution activities had to be adapted to the Japanese environment.

STRATEGIC ISSUES AND DISCUSSION QUESTIONS

1.   How did Coke enter the Japanese market?

While Coke was available on US military bases after WWII, it was not until the 1950s that it began to enter the Japanese domestic market. It did this by setting up partnerships with a number of experienced local firms for the bottling and distribution of Coke in different parts of Japan.

2.   What are the key factors in Coke's continued success and growth in Japan?

Local partners, a patient approach to growth, developing products for the local market, and adapting (while maintaining the essential features) of its distribution system are the primary success factors outlined in the video.

3.   What are the major changes Coke had to make for the Japanese business environment?

It relied much more on local partners for the overall business. It also had to adapt its receivables policy. With regard to personnel practices, morning exercises, lifetime employment, consensus decision making, and assistance in employee's home buying were all implemented.

VIDEO: DIFFERENCES IN POLITICAL ECONOMY

SYNOPSIS

This video discusses many of the issues related to differences in political economy outlined in Chapter 2 of the text. It describes in some detail how various firms are dealing with investment, operations, and the marketing of products in China and the nations of the former Soviet Union.

TEACHING OBJECTIVES

The main teaching objectives of the video are:

1.   Visually present basic concepts from Chapter 2.
2.   Show how Western business must adapt practices when entering markets of totalitarian (or previously totalitarian and reforming) countries.
3.   Suggest that while there may be significant difficulties in undertaking business in these countries, the opportunities are also too good to completely ignore.

This video fits best as a supplement to Chapter 2.

STRATEGIC ISSUES AND DISCUSSION QUESTIONS

1.   Why is there a general trend towards market based economics in many previously socialist and communist countries?

This is obviously a question that one cannot begin to fully explain. And in fact some people would question the basic premise. The simplest (and clearly incomplete) answer is that market economies seem to be more efficient at allocating resources and contributing to the economic well-being of individuals. One could spend time discussing differences in market approaches within the former Soviet sphere of influence, compare these to the approach in China, and also consider how many socialist nations in Western Europe are privatizing enterprises and trying to reduce direct governmental involvement in economic activities.

2.   Why do Western firms invest in countries like China and Russia, given the significant unrest, governmental control of economic activity, and experiences like piracy?

There is both a short term and long term explanation. It is clear that some firms are interested in making short term returns, and treat investments in these countries very opportunistically. In some cases they do very well, in others they fail. But the returns can be great. The long term explanation is more appropriate for large multinational businesses. In general they see large markets that will eventually develop, and believe that it is important to enter early, establish a presence, learn about the market and country, and be well positioned for future growth.

VIDEO: FOREIGN TRADE DISPUTES

<u>SYNOPSIS</u>

Several contemporary trade issues between the US and Japan are highlighted in this video. The video starts out with some basic cultural differences between the countries, and then moves into a discussion of trade. It describes how the rice market has been traditionally protected in Japan, even though domestic prices are several times those available on world markets. Yet rice farming has important cultural values in society, and protecting these values (as well as the farmers) is viewed as important in Japan. Multiple views of this trade dispute are presented, as well as trade issues relating to logs and lumber.

<u>TEACHING OBJECTIVES</u>

The main teaching objectives of the video are:

1.   Show how cultural issues can impact the political economy of trade.
2.   Review basic instruments of trade policy available to governments.
3.   Suggest that an understanding of cultural differences will aid us understanding motivations
        behind various trade disputes.

This video fits well with chapter 5, the political economy of international trade. It also builds on issues from chapter 3.

<u>STRATEGIC ISSUES AND DISCUSSION QUESTIONS</u>

1.   Given the theory of comparative advantage, does it make sense for there to be a large and
        persistent trade imbalance between the US and Japan? What can account for this imbalance?

While this issue isn't directly addressed in the video, the video can be used to have students think about this issue. Regarding the theory of comparative advantage, the persistent trade imbalance would seem to be inconsistent with the theory. (While the US and Japan operate in a world more complex than the two-good-two-country model, this doesn't detract from the bilateral trade imbalance analysis.) The text would suggest that formal and informal trade barriers must contribute to this imbalance. From the video one might conclude that cultural differences, and differing acceptance of things foreign, may also be part of the explanation.

2.   By increasing cultural understanding on both sides, will the US-Japan trade dispute go away?

While increased cultural understanding can minimize conflict and help each side better understand the other's position, cultural, economic, and political differences will still exist. As a comparison, the US and Canada typically have some sort of trade dispute going at any given time - whether it is agriculture, fishing, lumber of something else. And the cultural differences between these countries are small compared to those between the US and Japan. Hence improving cultural understanding will not likely make the trade dispute go away.

VIDEO: FOREIGN CURRENCY

SYNOPSIS

This video provides a brief overview of the development of the current international monetary system. The primary emphasis is on how in today's world, currency is exchanged around the clock. Traders are active in the market not only to execute specific transactions for multinational firms, but attempt to make profits by predicting future exchange rate movements. The role of information technology is highlighted.

TEACHING OBJECTIVES

The main teaching objectives of the video are:

1.   Illustrate the role of technology in creating a global monetary trading system.
2.   Describe the history and evolution of the world's monetary system.
3.   Show how the existence of liquid financial markets ease firms' ability to undertake international transactions.

This video fits well as an introduction to Part 4 (chapters 9-11) on the global monetary system. Showing the film while discussing chapter 9 can illustrate the context within which firms undertake transactions, and provide a good lead into chapter 10.

STRATEGIC ISSUES AND DISCUSSION QUESTIONS

1.   In the video, a trader speculating on the British Pound makes a $32000 profit in three minutes. How, if at all, does this sort of speculation help small businesses and manufacturers that need to execute currency transactions?

The current level of international monetary transactions is much greater than that required to support firms' specific transactions. Yet it is the existence of such a large and liquid market that allows firms to be able to easily undertake international transactions and do business internationally with ease.

2.   Are international financial markets much more efficient now than they were 30 years ago? Why or why not?

While some would prefer the much more stable environment of thirty years ago, the dramatic exchange rate shifts that occasionally occurred had significant impacts and were difficult to predict. The timing of exchange rate changes was more driven by politics than economics. Exchange rates used to be controlled to a much greater extent by governments' fiscal policies, the actions of central banks, and the dealings of large banks. In today's world traders working from their homes influence the prices of various currencies, along with other traders around the world. Exchange rates are always moving and changing according to supply and demand, with direct governmental intervention having less influence. Thus while some would prefer the near term stability in exchange rates that prevailed most of the time in the past, the disruptions were extreme and severe. Hence most economists would argue that financial markets are more efficient today, although speculation and bandwagon effects do introduce new inefficiencies.

VIDEO: GLOBAL STRATEGY - FORD

SYNOPSIS

This is a video produced by Ford on the challenges it is facing and the changes it is making in its own internal organization. It describes the need to work more closely across borders, make better use of scarce worldwide resources, and engage in simultaneous engineering across countries and continents. It identifies the future importance of the Asian market for Ford, and the need for Ford to be competitive in this market.

TEACHING OBJECTIVES

The main teaching objectives of the video are:

1. Put pictures, voices, and colors on the issues described in the Ford 2000 case in the text.
2. Illustrate the changing demands on Ford's development and manufacturing capabilities

This video fits best if used in conjunction with the Ford 2000 case after chapter 13.

STRATEGIC ISSUES AND DISCUSSION QUESTIONS

1. Why is Ford trying to transform its worldwide processes and undertake simultaneous engineering when it is already quite profitable?

Ford is in the fortunate situation that it is doing very well. Yet as it looks ahead, it sees the need for changes the opportunity for efficiencies. The development of the Mondeo is one example where it developed a car for a worldwide market. In future it sees important markets in Asia, but most of its developmental and manufacturing resources are in the US and Europe. The most efficient way for it to be able to address these markets is to tap into existing capabilities and not replicate existing resources in Asia. Thus to operate as a transnational organization it needs to make better use of information technology and worldwide resources in order to work effectively to develop new products quickly. It is better able to make these investments now, and undertake the difficult and expensive learning tasks, when things are going well. These investments in process change are expensive, although they do not show up as simple accounting entries that can be easily assessed.

Questions from the case note on Ford 2000 would also be appropriate for this video.

VIDEO: DOING BUSINESS IN TAIWAN

SYNOPSIS

This video gives an overview of the development of business and competitive advantage in Taiwan. It shows the progression from farming, to cheap manufacturing, to high technology development and manufacturing. The experiences of one successful American entrepreneur in Taiwan are highlighted.

TEACHING OBJECTIVES

The main teaching objectives of the video are:

1.   Show the evolution and development of Taiwan's economy.
2.   Provide some suggestions for successful foreign businesses in Taiwan.

This video fits well after chapter 14.

STRATEGIC ISSUES AND DISCUSSION QUESTIONS

1.   Describe the development of Taiwan's economy. How has its source of competitive advantage changed.

Not that long ago Taiwan was a poor farming based island nation. Gradually industrialization was encouraged, and Taiwan earned a reputation as a location for cheap manufacturing and exporting. The high level of education, however, allowed it to develop expertise in heavier manufacturing. Now it is active at the forefront of many high technology industries. Meanwhile, it has lost its advantage as a cheap manufacturing location to other less developed nations. One of the things affecting its continued innovation is a culture supporting entrepreneurship and business success.

2.   Why does it make sense for a firm to consider doing business in Taiwan today?

First, Taiwan is a relatively rich country with a large number of highly educated consumers. Second, the pace of business in Taiwan is very fast. This can help a firm develop its skills and products. Relatedly, there are important related and supporting industries for many types of firms. Additionally, experience in Taiwan could prove useful for firms eyeing the much larger mainland Chinese market.

3.   According to the video, what are the keys to achieving success in Taiwan's market?

First, know the market thoroughly by being in it. Second, work with a strategic partner or agent who can help with local market knowledge and contacts. Third, adapt to the market. And fourth, provide excellent after sales service and support.

PART VI

TEST BANK

CHAPTER 1

Students should be encouraged to choose the BEST answer, as more than one may be technically correct. Following each question is the answer, estimated difficulty, and page reference.

#1-1 When in 1984 Kodak decided to re-enter the Japanese market, the primary motive was to
A   capture the growing and lucrative Japanese market
B.   give it an advantage for sponsoring the Japanese Olympic team
C.   take advantage of the lowered trade barriers with Japan
D.   attack Fuji's home market in order to better defend itself from Fuji's attacks on its markets
E.   develop its own *keiretsu* in Japan

D, medium, 26

#1-2 The environmental context within which international business takes place
A   goes through phases of stability and rapid change
B.   is rapidly changing
C.   remained fairly stable from World War II until the fall of the Soviet Union
D.   is unaffected by the level of economic development in each country
E.   is governed by the rules in the General Agreement on Tariffs and Trade (GATT)

B, hard, 4

#1-3 With the globalization of markets, the tastes and preferences of consumers in different countries
A   are becoming more like Americans'
B.   are being forced by multinational firms to be the same worldwide
C.   are converging upon a global norm
D.   is less important than the price of the product
E.   can be ignored by firms

C, medium, 5

#1-4 The Pontiac Le Mans can most accurately be described as
A   an American car
B.   a car that has been very successful in international markets, but received poorly in the US
C.   a Korean car with an American GM nameplate
D.   an example of the globalization of production
E.   car that can be sold in many countries with a standard advertising message and sales program

D, easy, 6

#1-5 The original goal of the GATT
A   was to remove barriers to the free flow of goods
B.   promote world peace and prevent war
C.   establish a system of stable exchange rates
D.   protect vital industries from unfair foreign competition
E.   was unrealistic, so the subsequent failure of the initial treaty is not surprising

A, medium, 7

#1-6 An international firm may design a product in one country, produce component parts in other countries, assemble the product in yet another, and then export it worldwide. This is an example of:

A   how political pressures to locate plants in certain countries makes overall production inefficient
B.   an adaptive, not proactive, approach to international business
C.   the increasing global village of consumers
D.   the globalization of production
E.   how firms can limit exposure to exchange rate fluctuations

D, medium, 7

#1-7 For international businesses, the single most important technological innovation over the past thirty years has been the

A   advent of international telephone service
B.   development of the micro-processor
C.   introduction of the jet engine
D.   building of super freighters
E.   fax machine

B, hard, 9

#1-8 The term global village refers to:

A   the convergence of consumer tastes and preferences
B.   increasing concern worldwide over the health of the planet
C.   how modern communication makes it as easy to talk to someone around the world as it is your neighbor
D.   how individuals worldwide watch the same television shows and movies
E.   a move towards world peace where neighbors can settle conflict without war

A, easy, 4

#1-9 From 1960 to 1990, the US

A   experienced an absolute decline in manufacturing output
B.   economy grew more rapidly than most other industrialized countries' economies
C.   dramatically increased its share of world manufacturing output
D.   suffered a relative decline in its share world manufacturing output
E.   along with Western Europe declined economically, while Japan and Southeast Asia grew

D, hard 13

#1-10 The relative decline of the US in its share of world exports reflects

A   increasing trade barriers against US products
B.   the inability of US managers to respond to changes in the world economy
C.   the growing strength African and South American countries
D.   how exchange rate changes affect international export flows
E.   the growing industrialization of much of the rest of the world

E, easy, 13

#1-11 The World Wide Web:
A   is not set up to facilitate international business
B.   was originally conceived by the UN to improve worldwide military cooperation
C.   helps businesses in developed countries, but does nothing for firms from developing countries
D.   could be the background of the global economy in the 21st century
E.   is useful only if you know exactly who it is you want to communicate with

D, medium, 10

#1-12 Which statement best states Japan's recent experience regarding foreign direct investment (FDI).
A   Its FDI outflow has grown while its FDI inflow has decreased
B.   Its FDI inflow has grown while its FDI outflow has decreased.
C.   Japanese firms have invested heavily in Western countries.
D.   Formal barriers are responsible for the low level of FDI inflow presently entering Japan.
E.   The high FDI inflow into Japan may be responsible for much of Japan's economic growth.

C, hard, 15

#1-13 The increasing number of major non-US multinationals suggests that
A   most US multinationals will be forced to retreat from foreign markets
B.   US businesses failed to recognized the threat of foreign entry into the US
C.   US businesses now face a more competitive environment in the US and abroad
D.   today small US firms will not be able to expand overseas
E.   as consumers most US citizens will be worse off than before

C, medium, 17

#1-14 Which of the following statements about doing business in Eastern Europe is NOT true?
A   The countries' commitment to democracy and free markets cannot be taken for granted.
B.   The risks of doing business in these countries is high.
C.   Individuals in these countries are interested in and financially well able to buy many Western products.
D.   The potential returns from investments in Eastern Europe are high.
E.   The economies of these countries are generally in poor condition relative to their western neighbors.

C, medium, 18

#1-15 China
A   has been much more accessible to international business since the Tiananmen Square incident.
B.   seems to be moving progressively towards free market reforms.
C.   is unlikely to ever rival Japan's economic strength due to its small population.
D.   has experienced a drop in inward FDI since 1983.
E.   has been stagnating economically since the communist government was overthrown in 1989.

B, hard, 19

#1-16 For decades most Latin American countries

A   were ruled by dictators, many of whom seemed to view Western international businesses as instruments of imperialist domination.

B.   welcomed foreign direct investment in order to spur their economies.

C.   experienced very low inflation and debt, attracting foreign direct investment

D.   have been the largest market for US exports.

E.   have had much closer ties with Japan than with the US.

A, easy, 20

#1-17 Currency exchange rates between countries

A   have remained fairly stable for the past 20 years

B.   are not affected by political changes

C.   fluctuate in response to changing economic conditions

D.   are set by the United Nations in consultation with the World Bank

E.   have few, if any, implications for firms' decisions on where to invest or expand internationally

C, medium, 21

#1-18 Individual national governments' regulation of cross border trade and investment

A   has never materially impacted the flows of FDI

B.   is limited severely by the United Nations

C.   is inconsequential for most multinational businesses

D.   has tended to increase gradually since the "free trade era" in the 1920s and 1930s

E.   is substantial

E, medium, 21

#1-19 Kodak re-evaluated its strategy for the Japanese market after

A   Fuji captured over 80% of the market away from Kodak

B.   its joint venture with Nagase Sangyo failed to meet expectations

C.   it realized that Fuji was outspending it 3 to 1 in promotion in Japan

D.   Agfa's vigorous attacks were severely eroding Kodak and Fuji's profits

E.   it realized it faced a global challenge from Fuji

E, easy, 26

#1-20 In today's competitive global environment, country differences

A   rarely matter any more for international businesses

B.   still have a profound effect on international business

C.   can usually be overcome with proper "global" advertising

D.   have all but disappeared in the European Community

E.   are primarily legal trade matters that can be handled by skilled attorneys and trade consultants

B, easy, 5

#1-21 The lowering of trade barriers
A   allows most firms to profitably sell the same product for the same price in different countries
B.   was tried just after World War I, but with disastrous results for the world economy
C.   has made it increasingly possible for firms to base production activities at optimal locations
D.   is prohibited unless approved by GATT
E.   has rarely occurred since World War II

C, medium, 5

#1-22 Which statement best describes the relationship between the volume of world trade and the volume of world output between 1980 and 1990?
A   Both grew significantly, but trade grew faster than output.
B.   Both stagnated during these tough economic years.
C.   While output grew slowly, trade actually declined slightly.
D.   While trade grew slowly, output actually declined slightly.
E.   Trade grew slowly, but output grew more quickly.

A, medium, 9

#1-23 Which statement best describes the recent relationship between the volume of international trade and the volume of foreign direct investment (FDI)?
A   Trade is growing much faster than FDI.
B.   While both have been growing, FDI is growing much faster.
C.   Protectionist policies have significantly limited trade growth, but there are few political concerns about FDI.
D.   While trade has remained rather stagnant, FDI has grown considerably.
E.   While FDI has remained rather stagnant, trade has grown considerably.

B, hard, 8

#1-24 Which countries have dramatically increased their share of world output over the past 30 years?
A   South Korea and Taiwan
B.   Canada and the US
C.   France and Great Britain
D.   Japan and the US
E.   Australia and New Zealand

A, hard, 13

#1-25 Which of the following countries was the largest recipient of FDI between 1988-92:
A   Argentina
B.   Malaysia
C.   Mexico
D.   Singapore
E.   China

E, medium, 16

#1-26 Which of the following countries was the largest recipient of FDI between 1988-92:
A   Mexico
B.   Hong Kong
C.   Brazil
D.   Taiwan
E.   Indonesia

A, hard, 16

#1-27 As of 1994, firms from which country accounted for the largest percentage of the world's 500 largest multinationals.
A   The US
B.   The Netherlands
C.   Japan
D.   Germany
E.   Great Britain

A, easy, 17

#1-28 For a US manager considering investment in a foreign country, which of the following countries would likely entail the lowest risk investment.
A   China
B.   Poland
C.   Brazil
D.   Russia
E.   France

E, easy, 18-20

#1-29 National culture
A   is largely irrelevant for international businesses
B.   can be managed by hiring only local personnel for foreign operations
C.   is rapidly becoming unimportant as a worldwide global culture is taking hold
D.   has significant implications for international business
E.   is important for a few products like food, but doesn't affect the way most products are marketed

D, easy, 20

#1-30 The structure of a firm
A   is determined by the country in which it is headquartered
B.   much match the strategy of the firm if it is to survive
C.   rarely varies from country to country
D.   is strictly regulated by GATT for multinationals, but not for domestic firms
E.   has little impact on the overall success or failure of firms

B, medium, 23

#1-31 Countertrade involves

A   the exchange of goods for goods
B.   exchanging currencies in foreign markets
C.   negotiations between countries to assure that the trade flows between their countries are even
D.   trading only in "black market" goods
E.   trading goods for foreign currencies

A, medium, 24

#1-32 Deutsche TeleKom is in an alliance with:

A   AT&T
B.   British Telecom
C.   Telia of Sweden
D.   France Telecom
E.   all of the above

D, hard, 3

#1-33 Historically, Deutsche Telekom's competitive situation can best be described as:

A   under fire from low cost domestic competitors
B.   continually challenged by international competitors
C.   non-existent, since it is a new company
D.   easy, since it had a government approved monopoly
E.   a duopoly with Daimler-Benz

D, medium, 3

#1-34 Which of the following best describes the reason(s) why Deutsche Telekom decided to develop a new strategy.

A   Changing technology and legal changes that opened individual country's markets in the EU
B.   The hostile takeover bid it received forced management changes.
C.   The opening of Eastern Germany necessitated new approaches to business.
D.   France Telecom announced that it was going to enter the German market
E.   It was losing money with its previous strategy.

A, medium, 3

#1-35 Which country is the home base of the *chaebol*?

A   Bolivia
B.   South Korea
C.   Brazil, although they migrate north every summer into Canada
D.   Japan
E.   Indonesia

B, easy, 18

#1-36 Historically, what accounted for the success of the *chaebol* in exporting:
A   low labor costs
B.   Japanese protectionism
C.   high import barriers
D.   innovative product design
E.   their symbiotic relationship with the Soga Shosha

A, medium, 18

#1-37 The *chaebol*:
A   rarely invest in overseas facilities
B.   do not respond to governmental pressures
C.   are likely to cease to exist given the increased global trade
D.   all of the above
E.   none of the above

E, medium, 19

#1-38 The investment pattern of South Korean multinationals has, since 1985, favored investments in:
A   USA
B.   Mexico
C.   Western Europe
D.   Asia
E.   Russia

D, medium, 19

#1-39 According to a study by the International Institute of Management Development in Switzerland, the following countries were ranked the highest in terms of national competitiveness:
A   USA, Singapore, Japan
B.   Switzerland, Sweden, Norway
C.   South Korea, Thailand, Indonesia
D.   Germany, France, Mexico
E.   Japan, Thailand, Mexico

A, hard, 18

#1-40 Harry Ramsden's Fish and Chips is headquartered in:
A   Japan
B.   Hong Kong
C.   Britain
D.   Canada
E.   USA

C, medium, 6

#1-41 Which country currently serves as Harry Ramsden's largest target market:
A   China
B.   USA
C.   Australia
D.   South Korea
E.   Japan

E, medium, 6

#1-42 In 1913, which of the following countries had the highest average tariff rates on manufactured products:
A   Japan
B.   USA
C.   Sweden
D.   France
E.   Germany

B, hard, 8

#1-43 In 1990, which of the following countries had the lowest average tariff rates on manufactured products:
A   France
B.   Germany
C.   Sweden
D.   Japan
E.   USA

C, hard, 8

#1-44 Which of the following countries experienced a growth in their share of world output between 1963 and 1993:
A   Italy
B.   Canada
C.   Germany
D.   France
E.   USA

A, hard, 13

#1-45 Of the following countries, which one has the fewest headquarters of the top 500 multinationals in the world:
A   USA
B.   Japan
C.   Britain
D.   France
E.   Germany

C, hard, 17

#1-46 The economic theories of foreign direct investment
A   have no practical use in understanding actual patterns of foreign direct investment
B.   outline the conditions under which it makes sense for a firm to establish foreign operations
C.   suggest the best way for firms to get around regulatory barriers
D.   all of the above
E.   none of the above

B, easy, 22

#1-47 The global capital market
A   recently became more volatile when Germany moved its capital from Bonn to Berlin
B.   is becoming increasingly irrelevant with the growth of multinational firms
C.   is now closely regulated by the World Trade Organization after the crash in the 1980s
D.   is inaccessible to US firms due to governmental regulations
E.   has grown very rapidly over the past twenty years

E, easy, 23

#1-48 Accounting standards
A   differ from country to country
B.   are being changed so that they are more similar across countries
C.   provide great challenges for multinational firms that need to keep different records in different countries
D.   all of the above
E.   none of the above

D, easy, 24

#1-49 Fuji claims that
A   Kodak's large neon signs are equivalent to "American cultural pollution"
B.   Kodak unfairly hired away many of its top executives in an attempt to break Fuji patents
C.   Kodak bribed Japanese officials to get around the trade barriers Fuji had imposed
D.   Kodak has unfairly locked up portions of the US market

D, easy, 27

#1-50 GATT stands for
A   German Accounting Tabulation Technology
B.   General Agreement on Tariffs and Trade
C.   General Agreement to Talk and Talk
D.   German Association of Trade and Transportation
E.   General Administration of Tariffs and Transport

B, medium, 7 (although the skeptics have often thought it meant C)

#1- 51Q: Why did Kodak decide to re-enter the Japanese market in 1984? What tactics and attitudes did it take?

#1-51A: Because Fuji enjoyed a lucrative home market with little competition in Japan, it had been able to expand aggressively overseas into Kodak's markets. Believing that an attack on Fuji's home market would provide the best defense against Fuji's global challenge, Kodak decided to take control of its own distribution and marketing channels in Japan and established a joint venture with a Japanese firm. Kodak also realized that it would not succeed in Japan unless it thought and acted just like a Japanese company.

#1- 52Q: What is meant by the term "globalization of markets?"

#1-52A: In many situations the tastes and preferences of consumers in different nations are beginning to converge upon some global norm. Products like Levi's, Walkmans, and Pepsi are sold to the same sorts of customers via the same methods throughout much of the world.

#1- 53Q: What is meant by the term "globalization of production?"

#1-53A: Many firms are now dispersing parts of their production process to different locations around the globe to take advantage of national differences in the cost and quality of factors of production. Hence many products are not simply produced in a single country, but are assembled in one country from parts that may have been produced in a number of countries.

#1- 54Q: What two factors have been primarily responsible for the increasing globalization of markets and production?

#1-54A: A decline in barriers to the free flow of goods, services, and capital has made it feasible for many industries to be more global than previously possible. Technological advances in communications, transportation, and information processing have turned these possibilities into realities, allowing firms to work in a global environment in ways not possible prior to these advances.

#1-55Q: How has the GATT (General Agreement on Tariffs and Trade) contributed to the internationalization of business?

#1-55A: The fundamental goal of GATT has been to lower barriers to the free flow of goods. As more governments have supported GATT, and made changes to their own regulations regarding trade and investment, firms have been able to expand their activities overseas into previously restricted areas.

#1-56Q: How have developments in transportation technology aided firms in expanding internationally?

#1-56A: The introduction of commercial jet aircraft, large ocean going ships, and containerized transport have made it easier for firms to move goods and people around the globe more quickly, economically, and safely than ever before. Not only can goods be shipped overnight across the oceans, but business people can travel and visit customers and production facilities around the world.

#1-57Q: Is the world a "global village?"

#1-57A: Since US TV networks like CNN, MTV, HBO and CNBC are now seen in many countries, and Hollywood movies are shown worldwide, American culture affects many other cultures. Thus for many products, a "global customer" exists. Yet there are still very significant differences between countries in culture, tastes, and the conduct of business, and firms (and individuals) that ignore these differences believing that all customers and suppliers are the same risk making major errors.

#1-58Q: Describe the changing position of the US in the world economy over the past 30 years, and its current status.

#1-58A: Thirty years ago the US was the dominant economic power, with a substantial share of the world manufacturing output, exports, and FDI. While the US is still the largest economic power, other industrialized countries dominate many industries worldwide, and many developing countries have developed a significant presence in many industries.

#1-59Q: "International business is dominated by large US multinationals." Critically evaluate this statement.

#1-59A: During the 1960s this statement was basically correct. Yet a number of European and Japanese multinationals have emerged in the past 30 years, and mini-multinationals and small exporters account for a large portion of international business activity.

#1-60Q: Is the job of a manager of a international business different from that of a manager of a domestic business? If so, how? If not, why?

#1-60A: While both managers have to deal with budgets, people, customers, problems, and opportunities, the range of issues confronting a manager in an international business is wider and the problems themselves are more complex than those confronted by a manager in a purely domestic business.

CHAPTER 2

Students should be encouraged to choose the BEST answer, as more than one may be technically correct. Following each question is the answer, estimated difficulty, and page reference.

#2-1 At the time it was purchased by General Electric, Tungsram was
A.   controlled by the Russian Mafia
B.   understaffed and unable to meet the market demand
C.   insolvent.
D.   owned the Czech-German joint venture Budvar.
E.   widely regarded as one of Hungary's strongest companies.

e, medium, 31

#2-2 Who is most likely to believe that private property is more productive than communal property?
A   A leader of a Social Democratic party.
B.   Karl Marx
C.   A communist dictator
D.   Plato
E.   Adam Smith

e, easy, 35

#2-3 Which of the following is NOT common in a representative democracy?
A   individual freedom of expression
B.   a free press
C.   single party elections
D.   universal adult suffrage
E.   an independent judiciary

c, easy, 36

#2-4 Social Democratic governments
A   tend support individualism over collectivism.
B.   have, like those of Eastern Europe in the 1960s, refused to subsidize industry.
C.   look to John Stuart Mill as their intellectual founder.
D.   often nationalized private companies so they could be run for the public good rather than profit.
E.   are most common in Latin America and Africa.

d, medium, 33

#2-5 The ideas expressed in the US Declaration of Independence are closely aligned with
A   individualism
B.   socialism
C.   totalitarianism
D.   communism
E.   anarchism

a, easy, 35

#2-6 In a representative democracy
A   the interests of all individuals are represented
B.   citizens periodically elect individuals to represent them
C.   individuals vote directly on most issues that affect them by referendum
D.   individual's rights to freedom and expression are repressed
E.   the court system is usually under the control of elected representatives

b, medium, 36

#2-7 Right wing totalitarian dictatorships have been most common in
A   the nations of the former Soviet Union
B.   The Middle East
C.   Western Europe
D.   Eastern Europe
E.   Latin America

e, hard, 38

#2-8 A country that has a large number of state owned enterprises
A   will score quite high on a measure of political freedom.
B.   most likely espouses a individualist philosophy.
C.   will probably not score highly on a measure of economic freedom.
D.   is always a totalitarian state.
E.   is rarely a democracy.

c, hard, 39

#2-9 Which of the following would NOT contribute to a high rating on political freedom?
A   recent free and fair elections
B.   significant opposition to the party in power
C.   a legislative body with effective power
D.   centralized political power
E.   shifts in power following elections

d, medium, 36

#2-10 The role of government in a market economy is to
A   set prices at fair market value
B.   control the quantity of goods produced
C.   discourage imports in order to protect domestic producers
D.   manage state owned enterprises for the good of the people
E.   encourage vigorous competition

e, easy, 39

#2-11 A nation with a large number of state owned enterprises
A   can be classified as a free market economy
B.   would not be a democracy
C.   is often a command economy
D.   is never a communist country
E.   would be consistent with Aristotle's concept of an ideal nation

c, hard, 39

#2-12 Gross National Product
A   measures the total value of goods and services produced
B.   is equal to total exports minus total imports
C.   per head is usually highest in command economies
D.   reflects differences in costs of living
E.   is higher in Mexico than the US

a, easy, 45

#2-13 Which country likely has the highest GDP per head after adjusting for the PPP Index?
A   Spain
B.   Mexico
C.   China
D.   Japan
E.   Canada

e, medium, intuition and page 46

#2-14 Which country achieved the highest annual growth rate in GDP during the last decade?
A   India
B.   France
C.   USA
D.   Brazil
E.   Zambia

a, medium, 48

#2-15 Countries with low scores on the Human Development Index
A   include Hungary and Mexico
B.   usually have rapidly growing populations
C.   are generally communist dictatorships
D.   have little capacity for growth
E.   are likely to have high scores on PPP adjusted measures of GDP per head

b, medium, 49

#2-16 Countries that appear to achieve greatest sustained economic growth rates are typically
A   market economies
B.   totalitarian states
C.   command economies
D.   pure democracies
E.   those that also have a large number of state owned enterprises

a, easy, 51

#2-17 Laws enacted by governments in democratic states where individualism is the dominant political philosophy tend to
A   favor the interests of consumers and heavily regulate business activity.
B.   favor the interests of producers and provide few, if any, protections for consumers.
C.   support the "common good" over the interests of individuals.
D.   set prices and quantities of goods produced so that individuals are not taken advantage of.
E.   be pro-private enterprise and pro-consumer.

e, medium, 40

#2-18 Which of the following is NOT an example of an intellectual property that can be protected by law?
A   software
B.   brand name
C.   drug
D.   animal
E.   book

d, easy, 40

#2-19 Intellectual property rights
A   grant inventors the right to capitalize on their ideas into perpetuity.
B.   are standardized worldwide by the United Nations
C.   provide an incentive for people to search for novel ways of doing things and reward creativity.
D.   are most strict in South East Asian countries like China and Thailand.
E.   can not be applied to brand names or company names.

c, medium, 41

#2-20 Product liability laws
A   are common under civil law systems, but not under common law systems.
B.   can assess civil, but not criminal damages.
C.   are typically more lax in the US than in other countries.
D.   are standardized worldwide by the United Nations.
E.   hold firms and their officers responsible if a product causes injury.

e, medium, 43

#2-21 When faced with different levels of product standards in different countries,
A   a firm should customize its products so it just meets the standards in each country.
B.   appeal to the United Nations to settle the differences.
C.   ethical tradeoffs must be made regarding the best interests of consumers, shareholders, and employees.
D.   a firm should produce products only to the highest standards.
E.   refuse to do business in countries with poor consumer protection.

c, hard, 61

#2-22 A document that specifies the conditions under which an exchange is to take place
A   should specify a great number of contingencies under a civil law system.
B.   is a contract.
C.   can be written quite loosely under a common law system.
D.   is covered under intellectual property law.
E.   is needed to make sure that bribes are not paid.

b, medium, 44

#2-23 Common law is
A   enunciated in a clear and concise code of law.
B.   based on tradition, precedent, and custom.
C.   utilized in Germany, France, and Japan.
D.   "common" or uniform across all countries adhering to this standard.
E.   more easily interpreted and applied than laws drawn from civil law systems.

b, easy, 44

#2-24 A contract written in a country under a civil law system would
A   likely be long and spell out many possible contingencies.
B.   be also enforceable in a country with a common law system.
C.   be required if intellectual property rights are to be preserved.
D.   likely be shorter than a contract covering the same issue in a common law system.
E.   would be treated as invalid if it came before the International Court in The Hague

d, medium, 45

#2-25 A firm that invested in South Korea in the 1960s probably
A   has reaped significant first mover advantages.
B.   had many of its assets seized after the violent revolutions of the 1970s.
C.   has had its operations taken over by state owned enterprises.
D.   had to pull out during the years of rampant inflation during the 1980s.
E.   was from India, due to their historic trading ties and relationship.

a, hard, 58

#2-26 McDonalds, when opening its Moscow restaurant

A   did not hire any Russian employees, since Russian labor unions would not let workers work for a capitalist firm.

B.   could not use the name "McDonalds", since this was already the trademark of a tire company.

C.   had to vertically integrate and develop its own farms and food processing plants.

D.   had to promise to provide free "Big Macs" on the opening day of each parliament.

E.   found it would always have to import potatoes from Idaho, since the entire Russian crop was being used to produce Vodka for export in order to earn foreign exchange.

c, medium, 59

#2-27 The likelihood that social unrest could alter the balance of power in a country's government is an example of what type of risk?

A   economic

B.   legal

C.   theocratic

D.   political

d, easy, 59

#2-28 The most visible indicator of economic mismanagement of an economy is a county's

A   frequency of elections

B.   Human Development Index

C.   GDP/capita

D.   growth rate

E.   inflation rate

e, hard, 60

#2-29 The risks associated with doing business in a country are typically lower when countries

A   are politically stable developing nations with mixed economies.

B.   are economically advanced and politically stable democratic nations.

C.   are underdeveloped, politically unstable, and managed as a command economy.

D.   have a high capacity for growth.

E.   have a large number of state owned enterprises, as these firms tend to be much more stable and predictable than private enterprises.

b, hard, 60

#2-30 All other things being equal, when firms consider investing overseas, the benefit/cost/risk tradeoff is likely to be most favorable in the case of

A   politically unstable, mixed economy, developing nations.

B.   developing, command based, totalitarian nations.

C.   developing, politically stable, free market nations.

D.   politically stable, developed, mixed economy nations.

E.   free market, theocratic totalitarian, developed nations.

c, medium, 60

#2-31 Why did many multinationals either pull out of or refuse to invest in South Africa in the 1970s and 1980s?
A   South Africa's failure to ratify the GATT agreements
B.   the apartheid system
C.   economic mismanagement of the economy, and hence high risk
D.   the brutal repression by the communist dictatorship that controlled South Africa
E.   the declining GDP suggested that was little demand for more goods

b, hard, 60

#2-32 After gaining its independence from Britain in 1947, India
A   took over Pakistan in a bloody coup.
B.   was ruled by the former tribal emir.
C.   adopted theocratic totalitarianism.
D.   became a mixed economy under a democratic political system.
E.   was run by a brutal right wing dictator who abolished all commercial enterprises.

d, medium, 56

#2-33 By 1994, India had
A   a population of over 1 billion.
B.   a lower GDP/capita than Nepal
C.   more telephones than any other Asian country
D.   a policy that forbid foreign firms from investing in local firms
E.   a smaller economy than Belgium

e, hard, 56

#2-34 Which words best Desiree the current climate for FDI in India
A   strong potential, but not insignificant political and economic risks
B.   very risky with low potential economic benefit
C.   politically very risky with minimal economic opportunity
D.   low political and economic risk, high legal risk, low benefits, low costs
E.   it is almost impossible to invest in India because of governmental restrictions

a, easy, 57

#2-35 Trinity Motors
A   pays over 100% in import duties
B.   has 40 dealers throughout Russia
C.   have seen steadily rising sales since opening in 1992
D.   sell BMW, Mercedes, and Cadillacs to the Russian Mafia
E.   has to pay "protection money" to the Russian Mafia

a, medium, 62

#2-36 Which statement best reflects the sentiment of GE managers regarding the challenges they faced in their Hungarian joint venture.

A   You can't make a profit when paying bribes that are greater than net income.
B.   We completely underestimated the difficulties we would face in hiring people.
C.   Joint ventures won't work when the two parties don't agree on fundamental objectives.
D.   Human engineering was more difficult than product engineering.
E.   You can lead a horse to water, but you can't make him drink.

d, medium, 31

#2-37 The "political economy" of a country reflects its
A   political system
B.   economic system
C.   legal system
D.   all of the above
E.   A and B only

d, easy, 32

#2-38 Collectivism is most closely associated with the writings of
A   Plato
B.   Smith
C.   Mills
D.   Aristotle
E.   Hill

a, easy, 33

#2-39 Which country today best reflects the ideals of social democracy
A   USA
B.   Sweden
C.   Cuba
D.   Saudi Arabia
E.   Singapore

b, medium, 34

#2-40 Which of the following is the best example of a public action to abrogate property rights.
A   piracy
B.   blackmail
C.   theft
D.   bribery
E.   obfuscation

d, hard, 41

#2-41 Which country is generally viewed as the worst violator of intellectual property rights.
A   Russia
B.   France
C.   India
D.   Chile
E.   China

e, medium, 42

#2-42 What is the greatest source of difficulty for Microsoft as it tries to increase sales in China.
A   the Chinese character-based written language
B.   software piracy
C.   bribery of public officials by foreign competitors
D.   inability to hire computer literate personnel
E.   inadequate supply of materials from domestic sources

b, medium, 44

#2-43 Most Microsoft products used in China
A   are incompatible with the hardware available locally
B.   do not meet Microsoft's environmental standards
C.   have a virus installed that will "eat" the program if it is copied illegally
D.   are produced in the US, since manufacturing labor costs are insignificant for software
E.   are illegal copies

e, easy, 44

#2-44 Which of the following is NOT included in calculating the Human Development Index
A   education spending as a percentage of GDP
B.   life expectancy
C.   literacy rate
D.   average income
E.   purchasing power parity

a, hard, 46

#2-45 Which country has the lowest PPP index
A   USA
B.   Australia
C.   China
D.   Poland
E.   Japan

c, medium, 48

#2-46 Which country had the greatest annual change in real GDP between 1985-1993
A   Zambia
B.   Brazil
C.   France
D.   Nigeria
E.   Hungary

d, hard, 48

#2-47 Which country had the largest population in 1994
A   Indonesia
B.   Britain
C.   Mexico
D.   Japan
E.   Hungary

a, hard, 49

#2-48 Which country had the lowest Human Development Index in 1994
A   Thailand
B.   Malaysia
C.   Pakistan
D.   Mexico
E.   Brazil

c, hard, 49

#2-49 In a planned economy, who captures the gains from an innovation in that country
A   individuals
B.   private enterprise
C.   foreign multinationals
D.   the state
E.   no person, group, or organization

d, hard, 50

#2-50 Which has been a common trend in Western Europe for the past 10 years
A   nationalization of firms
B.   movement toward more centralized planning of industry
C.   restriction of intellectual property rights
D.   privatization of state owned firms
E.   re-regulation of renegade industries

d, medium, 53

#2- 51Q: Describe the differences between collectivism and individualism.

#2-52A: While collectivism believes that the needs of society can be best met if the government takes actions on behalf of and in the best interests of all its citizens by making their rights secondary, individualism states that the good of society is best promoted if individuals have freedom to make individual decisions and pursue economic self interest.

#2- 52Q: Are all totalitarian governments communist? Are communist regimes the most repressive of individual freedoms?

#2-52A: Not all totalitarian governments are communist. While much of eastern Europe was under communist rule for the last half of this century, anti-Communist totalitarian rulers have held power in many South East Asian, middle Eastern, and Latin American countries. Besides communist totalitarianism, there is also theocratic, tribal, and right wing totalitarianism. While communism generally represses individual freedom, the theocratic totalitarianism in Iran and right wing totalitarianism in Chile was arguably more repressive of individual freedom than the communist variety in Eastern Europe. Hence, we cannot say that communism is more repressive than other forms of totalitarianism, although it is generally more repressive than most democracies.

#2- 53Q: "Countries with high political freedom also have high economic freedom, while countries with low tolerance for economic freedom also repress political freedom." Critically evaluate this statement.

#2-53A: While it is generally true that countries tend to either support or repress both political and economic freedoms, there are a number of exceptions. While China has very low political freedom, id does grant some economic freedom. Meanwhile, India with high political freedom, has had a highly controlled economy. And Taiwan, with a vibrant free economy has a heavily controlled political environment. Thus it is incorrect to completely equate economic with political freedom.

#2- 54Q: Who determines the prices charged for goods in a market-based economic system?

#2-54A: Consumers and producers together, via the market, determine both the price and quantity of goods supplied in a market economy. If consumer demand for goods exceeds the supply currently being produced, prices will rise, signaling for producers to produce more. If the supply is greater than the demand, prices will fall.

#2- 55Q: What determines a countries economic growth rate?

#2-55A: Innovation is the primary engine of long run economic growth. Innovation thrives in a market economy, and also requires that there are adequate protections of property rights.

#2- 56Q: Why are there intellectual property laws? Why might a firm not invest in country that did not recognize patents?

#2-56A: Intellectual property laws are intended to award the inventor or originator of an idea or product the rights to the profits benefits from his/her work. Without these rights, individuals and firms would have less incentive to undertake inventions or take the risks to develop new ideas, and economic development would likely be inhibited. A firm may choose not to invest in a country where patent rights were not recognized, as any other firm could simply copy its inventions and market the same product without having to undertake the initial investment. In this case, the firm may never recover the initial costs of developing the product.

#2- 57Q: Does the US have too many lawyers? Does the legal system in the US put US firms at a relative competitive disadvantage internationally?

#2-57A: While Dan Quayle characterized the US as having too many lawyers, leading to higher costs in the US and competitive disadvantage, it is perhaps inappropriate to blame it all on the number of lawyers. After all, in a free market economy we would expect the supply of lawyers to be equal to the demand for their services. While compared to most other countries the ratio of lawyers to citizens is high in the US, society must gain some benefit from their services or their would be oversupply and the ratio would decrease. Thus while the liability laws in the US may put some American companies at a disadvantage globally, they also can use this same legal system to seek damages from other firms that cause them to incur a loss.

#2- 58Q: Describe how the contracts a firm writes with another firm may differ depending upon whether the other firm is in a country governed by a common law or civil law system.

#2-58A: Since common laws tend to be relatively ill-specified, contracts drafted under a common law framework tend to be very detailed with many possible contingencies spelled out. In civil law systems, however, contracts tend to be much shorter and less specific, since many issues typically covered in a common law contract are already covered in a civil code.

#2-59Q: What are the key factors that determine the long run potential benefits of doing business in a country?

#2-59A: In the most general sense the long run monetary benefits of doing business in a country are a function of the size of the market, the present wealth (purchasing power) of consumers in that market, and the likely future wealth of consumers. Hence not only do current conditions matter, but so does the economic growth of the country.

#2- 60Q: Why may it be more expensive to do business in a less developed country?

#2-60A: The most obvious additional cost of doing business in a less developed country is that additional investments may have to be made in infrastructure or in developing suppliers. If the country has less developed protection of property rights and systems of legal recourse, the costs of assuring that property can not appropriated can also raise the cost of doing business.

#2- 61Q: Are there any situations when it is ethically correct to pay bribes to governmental officials in other countries in order to secure a business contract? What factors should enter into such an ethical decision?

#2-61A: As with most ethical considerations there no clear answers. To refuse to ever pay bribes, while an acceptable position to take, necessarily limits the potential to do business and may detract from the potential welfare of citizens. Refusing to pay bribes also shows a lack of sensitivity to the way business is routinely conducted in other societies, and suggests that one cultural tradition is superior to that of the other country. An unwillingness to pay a bribe may also make the residents of a country worse off, at least in the short run. (If by refusing to pay a bribe a pharmaceutical firm's products "spoil" before they can reach sick citizens, diseases could kill or spread unnecessarily.) Given a firm's ethical responsibilities to its shareholders, employees, customers, etc., it is not easy to say that the ethical responsibilities regarding bribes are so strong that they subsume all other ethical considerations.

CHAPTER 3

Students should be encouraged to choose the BEST answer, as more than one may be technically correct. Following each question is the answer, estimated difficulty, and page reference.

#3-1 The Euro Disneyland theme park is located in which country
A   Britain
B.   Germany
C.   Belgium
D.   France
E.   Spain

d, easy, 65

#3-2 What were the primary factors affecting the decision of where to locate Euro Disneyland
A   proximity to "hard-core" Mickey Mouse fans
B.   demographics and subsidies
C.   similarity between local and American culture
D.   availability of skilled employees
E.   workers' culture being receptive to teamwork and group achievement

b, medium, 65

#3-3 Class conflict within the society may have the greatest negative impact on the costs of doing business in
A   Switzerland
B.   Norway
C.   Germany
D.   Britain
E.   Japan

d, medium, 67

#3-4 Cultural differences
A   are minimized by today's interconnectedness of the world.
B.   remain deep and profound.
C.   are less important than economic and political differences for international business.
D.   affect business decisions of individual firms but not the overall competitive advantage of a nation.

b, hard, 66

#3-5 "That complex whole that includes knowledge, belief, art, morals, custom, and other capabilities acquired by man as a member of society" is a definition for
A   Norms
B.   Values
C.   Mores
D.   Culture
E.   Ethics

d, medium, 67

#3-6 Abstract ideas about what a society believes to be good, right, and desirable are
A   Norms
B.   Values
C.   Mores
D.   Culture
E.   Folkways

b, medium, 67

#3-7 Attitudes about love, marriage, sex, social obligations, and truth
A   do not change over time within a society, but do vary across societies
B.   are often very quite different between different people in a homogeneous society
C.   can change in a society, but usually only in conjunction with political turmoil and unrest
D.   are reflected in values
E.   affect culture, but do not impact economic or political philosophy

d, hard, 67

#3-8 Generally, folkways are actions
A   of little moral significance
B.   steeped in tradition and values
C.   that are codified into the law of a country
D.   that, if violated by a foreigner, are likely to lead to immediate ostracization
E.   that are integrally linked to spoken language

a, easy, 67

#3-9 People who violate folkways
A   will likely end up in jail.
B.   are always considered crude and usually perceived to be from a lower social class.
C.   are treated more severely than people who violate mores.
D.   may be considered eccentric or ill-mannered, but usually not considered bad or evil.
E.   are likely to have their visas revoked and will be thrown out of the country.

d, medium, 68

#3-10 The consumption of alcohol in a Islamic country like Saudi Arabia is
A   common and consistent with a pursuit of happiness on Earth, since there is not an after-life.
B.   considered a violation of a social more.
C.   not illegal, but is not generally done out of respect for the clergy.
D.   much more accepted among the lower social strata than upper class people.
E.   not permitted for Saudi citizens, but since foreigners are considered infidels, foreigners are
        allowed to import alcohol and consume it in their own homes or hotel rooms.

b, hard, 68

#3-11 A high level of entrepreneurial activity in a society is generally associated with
A   theism
B.   Buddhism
C.   Hinduism
D.   Confucianism
E.   individualism

e, medium, 70

#3-12 Job and company switching, and a high level of managerial mobility in a society may lead to
A   low levels of entrepreneurship
B.   lack of company specific knowledge
C.   loyalty and commitment to a firm
D.   more personal contracts throughout and within a firm
E.   better team building within a firm

b, easy, 70

#3-13 High social mobility
A   is common in caste systems
B.   is inconsistent with a class system with open stratification
C.   in Britain is primarily between the 'working class' and the 'upper class' rather than other classes
D.   permits individuals to change social class out of their own initiative, inability, or luck
E.   generally leads to a competitive disadvantage

d, medium, 72

#3-14 The class system in Britain
A   ensures that the brightest students are assured entrance into the most prestigious universities
B.   was abolished by an act of parliament in 1994
C.   is much less rigid than the class system in the United States or Canada
D.   tends to perpetuate itself and limits mobility
E.   leads to harmony in workforce relations within firms

d, hard, 73

#3-15 Which is the most widely practiced religion in the world?
A   Christianity
B.   Islam
C.   Hinduism
D.   Buddhism
E.   Confucianism

a, easy, 74

#3-16 The caste system is supported by
A   Christianity
B.   Islam
C.   Hinduism
D.   Buddhism
E.   Confucianism

c, medium, 79

#3-17 Adherents of which religion are encouraged to follow the *Noble Eightfold Path*, which includes things like undertaking only "right living" and being considerate in ones actions?
A   Christianity
B.   Islam
C.   Hinduism
D.   Buddhism
E.   Confucianism

d, medium, 80

#3-18 Loyalty, reciprocal obligations, and honesty are all central to the ethics of
A   Christianity
B.   Islam
C.   Hinduism
D.   Buddhism
E.   Confucianism

e, easy, 80

#3-19 The payment of interest is frequently considered illegal under which religion?
A   Christianity
B.   Islam
C.   Hinduism
D.   Buddhism
E.   Confucianism

b, easy, 78

#3-20 Writing in 1904, Max Weber suggested that which set of religious beliefs were most consistent with capitalism?
A   Confucianism
B.   Christianity
C.   Protestantism
D.   Catholicism
E.   Islam

c, easy, 75

#3-21 Which set of religious beliefs are most likely to lead to economic development and growth
A   Hinduism and Buddhism
B.   Christianity and Confucianism
C.   Confucianism and Hinduism
D.   Hinduism and Islam
E.   Islam and Christianity

e, medium, 75 & 78

#3-22 Which language is the "mother tongue" of the most individuals?
A   Arabic
B.   Hindi
C.   English
D.   Chinese
E.   Russian

d, easy, 82

#3-23 Which may be the best way to develop a cadre of cosmopolitan executives that have a great deal of cross cultural literacy?
A   international transfers and overseas assignments
B.   language courses
C.   cross cultural sensitivity classes
D.   ethnocentric development programs
E.   understanding the background and values of different religions

a, hard, 92

#3-24 Ethnocentrism
A   mainly affects business in less developed countries.
B.   is a belief in the superiority of one's own ethnic group or culture.
C.   describes the difference between social classes.
D.   is uncommon in ethnically diverse societies like Russia and the US
E.   describes the degree to which a country is ethnically homogenous or diverse.

b, medium, 92

#3-25 It has been argued that a variety of factors in culture affect the competitive advantage of a nation. Which of these statements is least likely to be true as a result of cultural influences on the cost of business?
A   The US has an advantage over Britain.
B.   Pakistan is at a disadvantage to the US
C.   Saudi Arabia has an advantage over Sweden.
D.   Japan has an advantage over China.
E.   China has an advantage over India.

c, hard, 93

#3-26 An emphasis on loyalty, group affiliation, reciprocal obligations, honesty, and education all tend to boost the competitiveness of firms from

A   Japan
B.   Canada
C.   Saudi Arabia
D.   India
E.   Sweden

a, easy, 93

#3-27 Free market economics, Confucian ideology, group oriented Social structures, and relatively advanced education can be found in all of the following EXCEPT:

A   South Korea
B.   Taiwan
C.   Japan
D.   India
E.   portions of China

d, medium, 93

#3-28 Class conscious societies

A   are characterized by high social mobility and a low degree of stratification.
B.   tend to have few conflicts between labor and management and low mobility.
C.   typically have a high degree of stratification and low mobility.
D.   are characterized by a low degree of stratification and more frequent labor/management conflicts.
E.   usually have a competitive advantage over less class conscious societies.

c, hard, 72

#3-29 Countries with more than one major language

A   have frequent civil unrest
B.   have more than one major religion also
C.   should be avoided by international businesses
D.   also have the greatest levels of management/labor conflict
E.   tend to have more than one culture

e, easy, 81

#3-30 Which of the following statements about Asea Brown Boveri is true

A   It is headquartered in Sweden
B.   Its CEO, Percy Barnevik, is British
C.   It uses the Swiss Franc for reporting all financial information
D.   All of the above
E.   None of the above

e, hard, 95

#3-31 Which of the following is the LEAST common as a person's first language
A   French
B.   Russian
C.   Portuguese
D.   Arabic
E.   English

a, easy, 82

#3-32 Which of the following is the official language of ABB
A   French
B.   English
C.   Swedish
D.   German
E.   it has no official language

b, medium, 95

#3-33 Multinational firms, by their very nature, include people from different cultures. Percy Barnevik, CEO of ABB believes the best way to deal with these cultural differences is to
A   let everyone know what Swedish culture is, so that the foreign employees can adapt to the Swedes and establish one clear common corporate culture
B.   broaden understanding and recognition of differences
C.   ignore them and just focus on the business of making money
D.   have extensive "group encounter" meetings where employees from different cultures can openly discuss the difficulties they have with their co-workers from other countries
E.   tell everyone to leave their culture in their own country, and act like a local when visiting or working in another country

b, hard, 95

#3-34 According to Percy Barnevik, CEO of ABB, a culturally diverse set of managers
A   can really make a mess out of things
B.   rarely can reach consensus on an important issue
C.   can be a source of strength for ABB
D.   make ABB "a real pain in the behind" to manage
E.   makes ABB a very interesting place to work

c, medium, 95

#3-35 Hitachi
A   has consistently been resisting the movement in Japan away from consensus decision making
B.   brings foreign managers back to Japan for assignments
C.   admonishes workers from spending time after work in bars with co-workers
D.   recently had to install a fence around the company compound to keep others from "crashing" the company's popular bath house
E.   believes that it is important to maintain its unique Japanese corporate culture if it is to remain successful

b, hard, 91

#3-36 Saudi Arabia is a
A   democracy
B.   theocratic totalitarian state
C.   monarchy
D.   communist totalitarian state
E.   Bhuddist theocracy

c, easy, 76

#3-37 The major dissident movement in Saudi Arabia believes that
A   the House of Saudi has been corrupted by wealth and monopolized political power
B.   the House of Saudi has been too soft on the Islamic fundamentalists who want more power
C.   women should have the right to drive cars
D.   there should be violent overthrow of the government by Western governments
E.   Saddam Hussein should take over as rule of all of Arabia

a, medium, 77

#3-38 The relation between culture and a country is
A   less important than between a language and a country
B.   rarely significant
C.   only exists when the country is dominated by one religion
D.   is very strong, with only minor cultural differences existing within a country
E.   often ambiguous

e, hard, 68

#3-39 The ability to identify good business practices and techniques and transfer these capabilities to
other firms within a society
A   is promoted in societies with high managerial mobility
B.   is inherent a society dominated by Confucianism
C.   can be enhanced through cross-cultural awareness training
D.   is strong in societies with rigid social strata
E.   cannot be developed in monocultural societies

a, hard, 71

#3-40 In traditional Japanese society
A   women were the primary income earners for a family
B.   individuals could improve their *karma* by undertaking noble acts
C.   the written language was an adaptation of that brought by Marco Polo
D.   an individual was strongly bonded to the family or village
E.   the caste prevented Japanese from marrying foreigners

d, hard, 71

#3-41 In which of the following countries or regions do the differences among people, as represented by having different languages, seem to be least threatening to the unity of the country or region
A   Yugoslavia
B.   Canada
C.   Spain
D.   Cyprus
E.   Switzerland

e, medium, 81

#3-42 Formal education does all of the following EXCEPT:
A   plays a key role in society
B.   affects socialization of individuals
C.   teaches cultural norms
D.   diminishes national competitive advantage
E.   reduces illiteracy

d, easy, 83

#3-43 After defeat in World War II, Japan
A   was able to quickly convert munitions factories to computer manufacturing
B.   needed to entirely build a new educational system
C.   turned its navy into one of the worlds best merchant marine fleets
D.   formally changed its national religion to Confucianism
E.   had almost nothing except a well educated work force

e, medium, 83

#3-44 Which one of these was NOT part of one of Hofstede's dimensions of culture
A   uncertainty avoidance
B.   masculinity
C.   individualism
D.   spirituality
E.   collectivism

d, medium, 86

#3-45 Hofstede's "power distance" measures
A   inequalities between the most and least powerful in terms of power and wealth
B.   the distance between two people that yields the "most powerful" negotiating position in a culture
C.   the difference in salary between the highest and lowest paid person in a firm
D.   mobility of individuals between different social strata
E.   tends to be greater in societies where there is high consumption of hard liquor

a, hard, 86

#3-46 Which of the following countries exhibits the weakest uncertainty avoidance according to Hofstede
A   Germany
B.   Belgium
C.   USA
D.   Denmark
E.   New Zealand

d, hard, 89

#3-47 Hofstede's study
A   is generally regarded as sexist as it promotes stereotypes about masculine cultures
B.   is biased as it relies too heavily on data from manual laborers
C.   confirms many stereotypes held by Asian cultures, but is less appropriate for European cultures
D.   dispels many stereotypes that were common in earlier studies during the 1960s and 1970s
E.   included employees from only one company

e, hard, 89

#3-48 Many observers claim that a major culture shift is currently taking place in Japan that
A   strengthens the importance of the firm and fellow employees for group identification
B.   has increased the abuse of alcohol among factory workers
C.   suggests a move towards greater individualism
D.   abhors Western goods and is causing people to return to traditional Japanese dress
E.   is causing Japanese workers to spend less time with their families

c, medium, 90

#3-49 Which statement best describes the relation between individualism and power distance
A   Virtually all countries with low individualism have a large power distance score
B.   Countries with large power distance also all exhibit high individualism
C.   Individualism and power distance are independent constructs, with no clear relation between them
D.   Countries with small power distance are almost always countries that also exhibit low individualism
E.   Most all English speaking countries exhibit both high individualism and large power distance

a, hard, 88

#3-50 The best culture in the world
A   is American
B.   is French
C.   is yogurt
D.   depends upon who you ask
E.   depends upon the objectives society wants culture to contribute to
F.   (your school's name here)

e, easy. This s a joke question. There is no right answer, at least not in the book.

#3-51Q: What is the difference between a value and a norm?

#3-51A: Values are abstract ideas about what is right or wrong, good or bad, desirable or undesirable. Values reflect the overall attitude of a society to philosophical issues. Norms are more specific rules and guidelines that individuals follow, whether prescribed by law or simply routines followed out of habit. Norms reflect a codification of a society's values.

#3-52Q: What are the consequences to a foreigner of ignoring or being insensitive to the folkways of a country?

#3-52A: As a foreigner, people are often give some slack if they fail to adhere to a country's folkways. Being on time, when you're supposed to be "late", or referring to someone by the wrong name or title will often be ignored if it is clear that someone is a foreigner. (Someone may be slightly insulted if they are referred to as John or Abdul rather than Herr Doktor Professor Gruner or Your Highness Sheik Ramajam.) Repeated violation of folkways, however, may lead one to be ostracized or not invited back to work on future business opportunities.

#3-53Q: In what ways does a focus on the group rather than the individual help and hinder productivity?

#3-53A: Strong group identification can lead to better collective action, team problem solving, and mutual self help. It may also limit job and company hopping, leading to a greater network of contacts and knowledge of a particular firm. However it also suppresses individual initiative and entrepreneurship.

#3-54Q: How does the immobility of people between classes affect hiring and promotion decisions of international businesses in some societies?

#3-54A: In some societies, the immobility of people between classes can severely restrict hiring and promotion practices. Restrictions on the types of jobs people from different classes can hold can affect who it is appropriate to hire for a particular post. In international sales positions it can be important to hire people that are of the same class or one class higher than most of the customers. It may also not be possible to promote someone from a lower class into a position with higher class individuals. Someone promoted above a position of his/her class may not have the respect of employees, peers, or superiors, even if they are quite capable and otherwise superbly qualified for the position.

#3-55Q: Why did Weber suggest that there was a link between Protestantism and capitalism?

#3-55A: According to Weber, there was clearly a relation between Protestantism and the emergence of modern capitalism. Weber argued that Protestant ethics emphasize the importance of hard work and wealth creation (for the glory of God) and frugality (abstinence from worldly pleasures). According to Weber, this was just the kind of value system needed to facilitate the development of capitalism. Protestants worked hard and systematically to accumulate wealth. However, their ascetic beliefs suggested that rather than consuming this wealth by indulging in worldly pleasures, they should reinvest it in the expansion of capitalist enterprises. Thus, the combination of hard work and the accumulation of capital which would be used to finance investment and expansion, helped pave the way for the development of capitalism in Western Europe, and subsequently in the US. In contrast, Weber argued that the Catholic promise of salvation in the next world, rather than this world, did not foster the same kind of work ethic among members of the Catholic religion.

#3-56Q: What are some of the similarities between Islam and Christianity, specifically as they relate to the practice of business?

#3-56A: Having the same roots, Islam and Christianity share many similarities regarding the conduct of business. Many of the economic principles of Islam are pro free enterprise and hostile to socialist ideals. It is appropriate to earn a profit through trade and commerce, as long as the profit is justly earned and not based on the exploitation of others. The principles of honesty, respect of the rights of others, and dealing justly and equitably with others are found in both religions, although many practitioners of each religion may not always behave this way in business dealings.

#3-57Q: What aspects of the Hindu religion may run counter to capitalism?

#3-57A: The Hindu belief that advancement comes through spiritual growth and not material gains may limit initiative towards entrepreneurship, and even make material achievement and impediment to spiritual growth. Hinduism also supports the caste system, limiting personal advancement and opportunities for responsibility and influence. The caste system may also require that some people be promoted over others regardless of their abilities.

#3-58Q: How does a country's education system affect its a) competitive advantage, and b) desirability for international investment?

#3-59A: The availability of a pool of skilled and educated human resources, the product of a good educational system, seems to be one of the major determinants of the likely economic success of a country. The nature of the educational system can also guide decisions on facility location. Having a ready pool of people trained with the needed skills can significantly decrease the initial costs of beginning operations in a country. Firms are much more likely to invest in a country where the job applicants will already have the requisite skills and will require minimal additional training.

#3-59Q: What is ethnocentrism? How can it affect business dealings internationally?

#3-59A: Ethnocentrism is a belief in the superiority of one's own ethnic group or culture, and hence a disregard or contempt of the culture of other countries. A firm or individual that acts ethnocentrically may lack cross-cultural sensitivity and take actions that are embarrassing, insult others, limit success, or ultimately lead to failure with respect to particular deals or operations in a country.

#3-60Q: In the case of Japan, how does culture influence its national competitive advantage?

#3-60A: It can be argued that the culture of modern day Japan lowers the costs of doing business in that country, relative to the costs of doing business in most western nations. Japanese culture emphasizes group affiliation, loyalty, reciprocal obligations, honesty, and education, all of which may boost the competitiveness of Japanese companies. The emphasis upon group affiliation and loyalty encourages individuals to identify strongly with the companies in which they work. In turn, this tends to foster an ethic of hard work and cooperation between management and labor "for the good of the company". Similarly, the concepts of reciprocal obligations and honesty help foster an atmosphere of trust between companies and their suppliers. In turn, this encourages them to enter into long-term relationships with each other to work on factors such as inventory reduction, quality control, and joint design - all of which have been shown to improve the competitiveness of an organization. In addition, the availability of a pool of highly skilled labor, and particularly engineers, has undoubtedly helped Japanese enterprises develop a number of cost reducing process innovations that have boosted their productivity. Thus, cultural factors may help explain the competitive advantage enjoyed by many Japanese businesses in the global marketplace. Indeed, the rise of japan as an economic superpower during the second half of the twentieth century may be in part attributed to the economic consequences of its culture.

#3-61Q: Consider a hypothetical case when a company has to choose between two countries, "A" and "B", for locating a production facility. Both countries are characterized by low labor costs and good access to world markets. Both countries are of roughly the same size (in terms of population) and currently both are at a similar stage of economic development. In country "A" the education system is undeveloped, the society is characterized by a marked stratification between the upper and lower classes, the dominant religion stresses the importance of reincarnation, and there are three major linguistic groups. In country "B" the education system is well developed, there is a lack of social stratification, group identification is a value that is stressed by the culture, the dominant religion stresses the virtue of hard work, and there is only one linguistic group. Which country, "A" or "B" makes the best investment site? Why?

#3-61A: Country B is the preferable investment site. This is because the culture of country B is supportive of the capitalist mode of production and social harmony, whereas the culture of country A is not. In country A conflict between management and labor, and between different language groups, can be expected to lead to social and industrial disruption, thereby raising the costs of doing business. The lack of a good education system, and the dominance of a religion that stresses ascetic behavior as a way of achieving advancement in the next life can also be expected to work against the attainment of business goals.

CHAPTER 4

Students should be encouraged to choose the BEST answer, as more than one may be technically correct. Following each question is the answer, estimated difficulty, and page reference.

#4-1 After achieving independence from Great Britain, Ghana adopted policies
A   that discouraged its businesses from engaging in exports.
B.   designed to encourage foreign investment.
C.   with low import tariffs, which decimated its domestic businesses.
D.   with a strong pro-trade bias.
E.   that led to huge increases in the prices paid to cocoa growers.

a, medium, 121

#4-2 Ghana's
A   policies were more outward oriented in South Korea's.
B.   farmers resorted to subsistence farming after world cocoa prices collapsed.
C.   reliance on cocoa exports led to its declining international competitiveness.
D.   import substitution policy redirected resources towards inefficient uses.
E.   subsidization of cocoa production led to a decrease in the competitiveness of its cocoa industry.

d, hard, 121

#4-3 Mercantilism
A   encourages high imports and exports.
B.   discourages trade with other countries.
C.   suggests that exports should have a greater value than imports.
D.   explains why countries should specialize in production of goods where they have a comparative
         advantage.
E.   encourages imports while discouraging exports.

c, easy, 124

#4-4 Which of the following writers is not associated with the theory that follows his name?
A   Adam Smith / Absolute Advantage
B.   David Ricardo / Comparative Advantage
C.   Michael Porter / National Competitive Advantage
D.   Eli Hecksher & Bertil Ohlin / Product Life Cycle Theory
E.   Wassily Leontief / Leontief Paradox

d, easy, 136

#4-5 Mercantilism views trade as
A   a negative sum game.
B.   a detriment to domestic producers.
C.   a zero sum game.
D.   beneficial only to importers.
E.   something that should be avoided except for trade of rare metals like gold and silver.

c, medium, 125

#4-6 Assume that in Finland it takes 10 units of resources to produce a barrel of wine and 15 units of resource to produce a ton of paper. Also assume that in Italy it takes 7 units of resource to produce a barrel of wine and 20 units of resource to produce a ton of paper. Which of the following statements is NOT true?

A   Finland has an absolute advantage in paper production.
B.   Finland has a comparative advantage in paper production.
C.   Italy has a comparative advantage in paper production.
D.   Both countries can gain from specialization in production and trade.

c, easy, 129

#4-7 Assume that in Poland one unit of resource can produce either 12 ships or 50 trucks. Also assume that in Hungary one unit of resource can produce either 10 ships or 30 trucks. Which of the following statements is true?

A   Hungary has a comparative advantage in ships.
B.   Hungary has an absolute advantage in both ships and trucks.
C.   Poland has a comparative advantage in ships.
D.   There is no reason for Hungary and Poland to trade ships for trucks.

a, hard, 129

#4-8 Assume that in Tahiti 10 units of resource can produce either 2 tons of bananas or 6 tons of pineapples. Also assume that in Fiji 2 units of resources can produce either 1 ton of bananas or 3 tons of pineapples. Which of the following statements is NOT true?

A   There is no reason for Tahiti and Fiji to trade bananas for pineapples.
B.   Fiji has an absolute advantage in bananas.
C.   Fiji has an absolute advantage in pineapples.
D.   Fiji has an comparative advantage in pineapples.

d, hard, 129

#4-9 Which theory first identified that even if a country has an absolute advantage in all goods, it can benefit from trade with other countries?

A   Leontief Paradox
B.   Absolute Advantage
C.   Hecksher-Ohlin
D.   National Competitive Advantage
E.   Comparative Advantage

e, medium, 129

#4-10 Which of the following is NOT an assumption of the theory of comparative advantage?

A   zero transportation costs
B.   factors of production are equally productive in both countries for the same goods
C.   resources are mobile within countries, but not between countries
D.   constant returns to scale
E.   fixed stocks of resources in each country

b, medium, 130

#4-11 Assume the republic of Borscht can produce 10 million board feet of lumber per year with 800 workers and another 5 million board feet per year with an additional 600 workers. Worldwide demand for lumber is greater than 20 million board feet, and other countries can also produce lumber. Using only this information, which of the following statements is true?
A   Borscht should specialize in lumber production and trade for other goods.
B.   Borscht should produce no more than 10 million board feet of lumber.
C.   Borscht should produce at least 15 million board feet of lumber.
D.   Borscht experiences diminishing returns to specialization in lumber production.
E.   Borscht should not produce lumber, and utilize its workers in other industries.

d, medium, 132

#4-12 Dynamic gains in both the stock of a country's resources, and the efficiency with which resources are utilized, will cause a country's production possibilities frontier to
A   shift outwards.
B.   become more convex.
C.   shift inwards.
D.   become more concave
E.   contract.

a, hard, 134

#4-13 Diminishing returns and dynamic effects
A   contradict the theory of comparative advantage.
B.   are inconsistent with Porter's theory of national competitive advantage.
C.   complement and supplement the work of Ricardo.
D.   diminish the case for unrestricted free trade leading to economic growth.
E.   do not affect the productivity of resources.

c, medium, 134

#4-14 Which theory specifically suggests that differences in national factor endowments lead to comparative advantage?
A   Absolute advantage
B.   Hecksher-Ohlin
C.   Leontief Paradox
D.   New Trade Theory

b, easy, 134

#4-15 Leontief postulated that
A   the US would be an exporter of technologically intensive products.
B.   the US had an absolute advantage in both agricultural and industrial goods.
C.   industrialized countries would import agricultural products.
D.   Britain should trade textiles for wine from France.
E.   the US should export capital intensive goods and import labor intensive goods.

e, hard, 135

#4-16 According to the product life cycle theory, new products
A   should be produced in low cost countries to build economies of scale.
B.   will be primarily consumed in and exported from the US
C.   will be exported from industrialized European countries to the US and developing countries.
D.   will be competitive only if low priced.
E.   should be produced in the lowest cost countries to minimize the uncertainty and risks.

b, medium, 136

#4-17 Which theory of international trade suggests that the production of products is likely to switch from advanced countries to developing countries over time.
A   New Trade Theory
B.   Absolute Advantage
C.   Product Life Cycle Theory
D.   Comparative Advantage
E.   Hecksher-Ohlin

c, easy, 136

#4-18 The relevance of luck in explaining the international location of certain industries is noted in
A   Absolute and Comparative Advantage theories.
B.   New Trade Theory and Porter's Theory of National Competitive Advantage.
C.   only Leontief's Paradox.
D.   only Porter's Theory of National Competitive Advantage.
E.   Leontief's Paradox and New Trade Theory.

b, medium, 140

#4-19 Strategic trade policy
A   should be focused on encouraging exports and limiting imports in all industries.
B.   explains the failure of DeHavilland in passenger jet aircraft.
C.   is at variance with new trade theory.
D.   suggests that judicious use of government subsidies can give firms first mover advantages.

d, medium, 139

#4-20 The focus of Porter's theory of national competitive advantage is to
A   explain why a nation achieves international success in a particular industry.
B.   identify which industries should be targeted for government subsidies.
C.   understand the role of government in making its industries competitive.
D.   show why a country may import products that it could produce for itself.
E.   explain how a cluster of related and supporting industries is necessary for firms to be competitive.

a, hard, 140

#4-21 What theory does the best at explaining why Japan is strong in automobiles, Switzerland in precision instruments and pharmaceuticals, and Germany in chemicals?
A   Comparative advantage
B.   Absolute advantage
C.   New trade theory
D.   Porter's theory of national competitive advantage
E.   Leontief's paradox

d, easy, 140

#4-22 Which of the following is not one of the four attributes or corners in Porter's diamond?
A   Related and supporting industries
B.   Demand conditions
C.   Factor endowments
D.   Trade policies
E.   Firm strategy, structure, and rivalry

d, easy, 141

#4-23 What, according to Porter's theory of national competitive advantage, is the relationship between basic and advanced factors?
A   basic factors are more important than advanced factors
B.   if a country has advanced factors, then basic factors are not important
C.   the level of basic factors can influence the development of advanced factors
D.   advanced factors cannot be developed without supporting and complementary basic factors

c, hard, 141

#4-24 According to Porter's theory of national competitive advantage, domestic firm rivalry
A   stifles innovation.
B.   lowers profits and competitiveness.
C.   leads to a short term financial emphasis.
D.   should be regulated and reduced by the government to encourage cooperation.
E.   should be vigorous to create better international competitors.

e, medium, 143

#4-25 New trade theory, the theory of comparative advantage, and the Hecksher-Ohlin theory
A   all do little to truly explain the nature of trade in the real world.
B.   are superseded and encompassed in Porter's theory of national competitive advantage.
C.   typically lead to different conclusions in similar situations, and are thus competitive.
D.   are complementary and supplemented by Porter's theory of national competitive advantage.
E.   are only applicable for industrialized economies.

d, medium, 143

#4-26 Which theory has the least to say about what the most appropriate place might be for a firm to locate facilities
A   Porter's theory of competitive advantage
B.   Hecksher-Ohlin theory
C.   Mercantilism
D.   Comparative advantage
E.   Absolute advantage

c, medium, 135

#4-27 What might the effect of US import tariffs on LCD screens (used in computers) be on firms?
A   US computer manufacturers will face higher costs for LCD screens.
B.   US LCD manufacturers will become more competitive in world markets.
C.   Foreign computer manufacturers will become less competitive in world markets.
D.   Foreign LCD manufacturers will become less competitive in world markets.

a, medium, 147

#4-28 "Voluntary" restrictions or restraints on imports
A   are typically more effective than import tariffs.
B.   have often been self-defeating.
C.   usually precede formal restrictions.
D.   of machine tools has led to a resurgence in the US machine tool industry.
E.   can be targeted so that only one industry is affected.

b, hard, 146

#4-29 Which of the following theories does not lead to the conclusion that unrestricted free trade is in the best interest of all countries?
A   Hecksher-Ohlin theory
B.   New trade theory
C.   Absolute advantage
D.   Comparative advantage

b, easy, 140

#4-30 The key variable for explaining the pattern of world trade under the Hecksher-Ohlin theory is
A   phase of product life cycles
B.   resource productivity
C.   government subsidies
D.   factor endowments

d, medium, 134

#4-31 The Leontief Paradox casts doubt on the accuracy of which author's theory?
A   Porter
B.   Hecksher-Ohlin
C.   Ricardo
D.   Smith
E.   Vernon

b, medium, 135

#4-32 The increasingly integrated global economy has significantly decreased the predictive power of which author's theory?
A   Hume
B.   Ricardo
C.   Vernon
D.   Porter

c, medium, 138

#4-33 Which of the following was NOT one of the trade policies generally held by South Korea over the past 40 years
A   general reduction of import tariffs from an initial level of around 60%
B.   abolition of all import quotas
C.   reduction of subsidies given to exporters
D.   rapid reduction of tariffs or trade barriers on agricultural products

d, hard, 121

#4-34 A strongly inward oriented trade policy is generally associated with
A   South East Asian nations
B.   low or negative annual GNP growth per person
C.   high annual GNP growth per person
D.   high GNP per person
E.   industrialized European nations

b, medium, 121

#4-35 The current production pattern of a laptop computer
A   suggests a global web of production that takes advantage of the expertise of different countries.
B.   highlights how significant transportation costs limit the globalization of production.
C.   shows how final assembly is done in highly automated high-skilled countries.
D.   completely contradicts the theory of comparative advantage.
E.   is consistent with the product life cycle theory, since laptop computers are relatively new products.

a, easy, 144

#4-36 Mercantilism was advocated
A   by Eli Heckscher
B.   during the 16th century
C.   by importers of textiles in England
D.   along with violent revolution by Hume
E.   during the years after World War II in South Korea

b, hard, 122

#4-37 Hume argued that mercantilism wouldn't work in the long term because of
A   product shortages
B.   the effects of a positive sum game
C.   the limited ultimate supply of gold and silver
D.   political pressure from consumer groups
E.   changes in prices

e, hard, 125

#4-38 Neo-mercantilism equates
A   political power with economic power which derives from a balance of trade surplus
B.   absolute advantage with economic power
C.   factor endowments with political power
D.   a positive sum game with benefits to exporters
E.   Japanese exports with unfair trade as a result of Yen appreciation

a, hard, 125

#4-39 What has been Japan's general posture towards international free trade agreements
A   It attempts to block most international agreements, preferring bilateral agreements
B.   It is fine for other countries to enter them, but Japan would prefer to avoid such agreements
C.   It will enter them only if the US puts pressure on Japan
D.   It is a strong supporter
E.   It opposes all free trade agreements on neo-mercantilist grounds

d, hard, 126

#4-40 In a 1994 study by three Japanese economists cited in the text, they found that
A   the US had unjustly accused Japan of protecting its agriculture industry
B.   the Japanese government protected the cosmetics, food products, and chemicals industries from
       more efficient foreign competitors
C.   Japan would have exported more wheat, oilseeds, leaf tobacco, and cosmetics if free trade were
       practiced with the US and other trading nations
D.   the US was unfairly protecting its aerospace industry and preventing imports of Japanese
       passenger aircraft
E.   US politicians usually used flawed data in order to justify tariffs on Japanese goods

b, hard, 126

#4-41 The Japanese government argues that the primary reason US auto producers have not been successful in Japan is
A   because they do not make cars suited to the Japanese market
B.   the US government refuses to provide export credits
C.   the Japanese producers are just more efficient, as evidenced by their export success
D.   of the oversupply in the Japanese market
E.   they try too hard to sell in Europe and the US, and have not made the required sales effort in Japan

a, medium, 127

#4-42 Wassily Leontief tested the Heckscher-Ohlin theory on the
A   exports of Sweden
B.   imports of Poland
C.   exports and imports of the US
D.   imports and exports of Germany
E.   imports of Sweden

c, easy, 135

#4-43 According to the product life cycle theory
A   the country that invents a product will have an competitive advantage in its production throughout the lifecycle of the product
B.   consumption will end up being highest in developing countries
C.   there are significant first mover advantages in industries with high economies of scale
D.   the country that initiated production of a product will become a net importer by the end of the product life cycle
E.   in the maturing phase of a product life cycle the country that initiated the product will be a net importer

d, medium, 137

#4-44 Which of the following products best illustrates the product life cycle theory of trade patterns
A   laptop computers
B.   photocopiers
C.   compact discs
D.   electronic cameras
E.   bread

b, easy, 138

#4-45 Nokia is headquartered in
A   Japan
B.   South Korea
C.   US
D.   Finland
E.   Sweden

d, medium, 144

#4-46 The success of Nokia can be best explained by which theory
A   Porter's Diamond
B.   Absolute Advantage
C.   Product Life Cycle Theory
D.   New Trade Theory and strategic governmental intervention
E.   none of the above

a, medium, 145

#4-47 Which geographic region has the highest number of cellular phones per capita
A   South East Asia
B.   North America
C.   European Union
D.   Scandinavia
E.   Australia

d, easy, 145

#4-48 Which country is the world leader in ceramic tiles
A   Greece
B.   Italy
C.   Brazil
D.   Portugal
E.   Venezuela

b, easy, 148

#4-49 Which word(s) best describes the nature of competition in the Italian ceramic tile industry
A   non-existent
B.   minimal
C.   controlled by the government
D.   oligopolistic
E.   intensely vigorous

e, medium, 148

#4-50 Which theory best explains the success of the Italian ceramic tile industry
A   Porter's Diamond
B.   Absolute Advantage
C.   Product Life Cycle Theory
D.   New Trade Theory and strategic governmental intervention
E.   none of the above

a, easy, 148

#4-51Q: Describe Ghana's policies that led to a decrease in the production of cocoa and an increase in the production of subsistence foods. What was the effect of these policies on Ghana's standard of living?

#4-51A: Ghana did not pay its farmers the going world price for their cocoa crops, and did not raise the prices it paid fast enough to keep up with the costs of other goods. Hence, Ghana's farmers switched out of production of cocoa (where Ghana had an absolute advantage) into the production of basic foods (where it did not even have a comparative advantage). Thus exports fell, and inefficient manufacturing and basic food production grew, although these industries were not competitive in world markets and could not supply Ghana's citizens with the same standard of living as had been achievable when cocoa was traded for food and manufactured goods.

#4-52Q: What does mercantilism advocate?

#4-52A: Mercantilism suggests that countries can benefit from always having a positive balance of trade. Hence exports should be encouraged and imports discouraged.

#4-53Q: Most lawyers and doctors, could if they needed to, type their own memos on a typewriter or computer, address an envelope, and mail it. Yet most professionals employ secretaries to do these tasks. Using theories of international trade, why do lawyers and doctors employ secretaries to do tasks they could do themselves. If a particular doctor could type faster than the fastest typist she could hire, why might she still hire a typist? (Again, use what you learned from international trade theory in answering this question.)

#4-53A: Lawyers and doctors have invested in a specialized expertise, the law or medicine. Thus they have an absolute advantage in these services, and can likely earn more by spending time seeing extra clients and patients than it costs for them to hire a secretary. Thus they can benefit from performing those tasks where they have an absolute advantage, and letting others specialized in secretarial services provide these services. Even if a doctor had an absolute advantage in medicine and typing, she would have a comparative advantage only in medicine, and would likely be better off hiring a typist whose comparative advantage is in typing.

#4-54Q: Define "diminishing returns to specialization." Give an example where there likely are diminishing returns to specialization.

#4-54A: Diminishing returns to specialization suggests that the more of a good a country produces, the greater the units of resources required to produce each additional unit of the item. For example, Canada is able to produce a great deal of wheat. Yet at some point, when farmers started to try to grow wheat in the northern tundra or the western rain forests, the wheat output per acre or per hour of work would fall.

#4-55Q: What is the Leontief paradox?

#4-55A: Since the US had abundance of capital relative to most other nations, using the theory of comparative advantage Leontiff postulated that the US should be exporting more capital intensive goods than it imported. His findings, however, showed that US exports were less capital intensive than US imports.

#4-56Q: In today's linked global economy, is the product life cycle theory still valid?

#4-56A: The product life cycle theory, while apparently valid during the time of US dominance, is less relevant today. It may be harsh to say that the theory is no longer at all valid, but its usefulness and appeal has certainly declined as the world has become more linked and US dominance has declined.

#4-57Q: Why might world demand support only three commercial aircraft producers, even though hundreds of planes are sold annually?

#4-57A: In the commercial aircraft industry there are huge economies of scale. Given the high costs of designing a new aircraft and the significant investment that must be made in manufacturing facilities, training, and technology, a firm must produce several hundred aircraft just to recover these costs. Thus given world demand and the substantial economies of scale, only a few companies are likely to be viable.

#4-58Q: New trade theory emphasizes the importance of first mover advantages and economies of scale. Do these aspects of new trade theory contradict the theory of comparative advantage? Why?

#4-58A: First mover advantages often lead to economies of scale. Since economies of scale allow a firm or nation to increase the efficiency of resource utilization, the new trade theory identifies an important source of comparative advantage. Thus new trade theory complements rather than contradicts the theory of comparative advantage.

#4-59Q: What does Porter's theory of national competitive advantage suggest are important attributes of domestic demand conditions for firms and nations interested in improving their competitive advantage?

#4-59A: Domestic customers should be more sophisticated and demanding, since this pressures local firms to meet high standards.

#4-60Q: What position should government policy take with respect to domestic firm rivalry if, based on Porter's theory of national competitive advantage, it wants to improve the international competitiveness of its domestic firms?

#4-60A: According to Porter's theory of national competitive advantage, governments should pursue policies that encourage rivalry and domestic competition among firms.

#4-61Q: Why might a tariff designed to "protect" a domestic industry actually hurt that industry? How might this tariff hurt the competitiveness of domestic firms that use the products of a "protected" industry?

#4-61A: A tariff designed to protect a domestic industry can eventually hurt that industry if firm do not have to face the rigorous demands of international competition. These firms may not be able to effectively compete internationally for customers outside their protected market, and may fall further behind foreign competitors. If the tariffs are eventually lifted, these firms may quickly lose their domestic market. Even if the tariffs remain, foreign competitors may increase their competitiveness to the point that the tariffs no longer deter entry into the domestic market. Customers of protected industries may also suffer in international markets if they have to pay higher prices for inferior goods that are an important component of their final products. They may not be as competitive in world markets, since foreign competitors can use components produced by the best worldwide suppliers.

#4-62Q: In Bazookistan it takes 40 units of input to make one ton of pretzels and 30 units of input to produce in one ton of peanuts. In neighboring Fargbuk, 40 units of input can make either one ton of peanuts or one ton of pretzels. Which country has the absolute advantage in peanut production? Which country has the comparative advantage in pretzel production. According to the theory of comparative advantage, what should Bazookistan export to Fargbuk?

#4-62A: Since it takes less input to produce peanuts in Bazookistan than in Fargbuk, Bazookistan has an absolute advantage in peanut production. Fargbuk has a comparative advantage in pretzel production. Bazookistan should specialize in the production of peanuts and export these to Fargbuk, while Fargbuk should specialize in the production of pretzels and trade these to Bazookistan for peanuts.

#4-63Q: "Americans should buy American products whenever possible to help save US jobs." Critically discuss this statement.

#4-63A: The American economy may gain overall if Americans bought certain products from foreign manufacturers that they could buy from American manufacturers. The gains arise because international trade allows the American economy to specialize in the manufacture and export of products that can be produced more efficiently than in other countries. By "buying American" consumers are supporting industries that may be inefficient, and cause resources to be used in ways which are less efficient than alternative uses. Rather than saving US jobs, "buying American" can cause workers to remain in inefficient industries rather than seeking better opportunities in industries where there is greater potential for growth and the creation of even more jobs. "Buying American" can also divert other resources (including capital) away from emerging industries that could create additional jobs and exports if they had access to these resources.

CHAPTER 5

Students should be encouraged to choose the BEST answer, as more than one may be technically correct. Following each question is the answer, estimated difficulty, and page reference.

#5-1 What is "Super 301"
A   a US trade law
B.   a cellular phone technology
C.   a section of the GATT regulations
D.   a Toyota model that was only built in Japan until trade pressures forced foreign production
E.   a model of cellular phone built by Motorola that was denied access to the Japanese market

a, medium, 151

#5-2 What is the general position of the Japanese government with respect to numerical targets for levels of inputs of particular products
A   targets are the best way of managing bi-lateral trading relationships
B.   targets should be incorporated into GATT regulations, so that all countries can participate
C.   targets should only be used in very limited and specific situations
D.   targets should be agreed to only as a stand of last resort
E.   targets are contrary to the ideals of a free market economy and free consumer choice

e, hard, 151

#5-3 Protectionism
A   can be justified on political, but not economic, grounds.
B.   has been given intellectual respectability in certain circles by the rise of the new trade theory.
C.   always benefits foreign producers at the expense of consumers.
D.   benefits domestic producers in both the short term and the long term.

b, hard, 160

#5-4 The Smoot-Hawley tariff
A   was focused on stemming unemployment growth and diverting consumers from foreign products.
B.   allowed to US to finally run a balance of payments surplus and become a net creditor.
C.   was a retaliatory measure against Britain's "Campbell" tariff.
D.   was shortly followed by the stock market collapse of 1929.
E.   followed the failure of the Moxon Round of the GATT negotiations.

a, hard, 163

#5-5 GATT membership includes
A   only the primary economic powers: the US, Britain, Russia, and China.
B.   only the permanent members of the United Nations Security Council.
C.   all the members of the United Nations.
D.   is open to any country that will agree to the terms and conditions of GATT treaties.
E.   most economic powers except Japan, which was expelled in 1991 for its unfair policies.

d, medium, 173

#5-6 GATT
A   has been generally quite unsuccessful in achieving its original goals.
B.   regulations are enforced by the World Court in The Hague.
C.   relies on a mutual monitoring mechanism to identify possible violations.
D.   was superseded by CAP in 1992.
E.   has ruled that VERs are an illegal restraint on trade.

c, medium, 163

#5-7 The US trade deficit
A   has been growing at an increasing rate since the early 1980s.
B.   peaked in 1987 and is now again close to zero.
C.   on a cumulative basis keeps growing, and growing, and growing.
D.   is caused by the fact that US exports are greater than US imports.
E.   with Japan is actually close to zero, and much larger with lesser developed countries with low
           labor costs.

c, easy, 164

#5-8 Japanese markets have been effectively closed to many imports and foreign investment by
A   high taxes
B.   voluntary import restraints
C.   quotas
D.   tariffs
E.   administrative trade barriers

e, easy, 164

#5-9 Why would exporting countries impose VERs?
A   To keep the GATT bureaucrats from intervening.
B.   To avoid more damaging punitive tariffs.
C.   To protect their domestic producers.
D.   To protect consumers.
E.   To punish firms for unfair practices.

b, medium 164

#5-10 Why did the US choose to focus attention on the cellular phone market in its dispute with Japan
A   the rapid growth of Motorola in the market
B.   the high ad valorem tariff significantly harmed US producers
C.   tremendous growth of IDO in the US without corresponding success by US firms in Japan
D.   it was a fairly obvious example of an administrative barrier
E.   pressure by Motorola

d, medium, 151

#5-11 What is IDO
A   International Dispute Organization
B.   Industrial Development Organization
C.   a British organization that invested in Malaysia
D.   a side agreement of the 1993 GATT accord
E.   a Japanese phone service company

e, hard, 151

#5-12 If an firm imports 500 pounds of tea valued at $20/pound into a country with an ad valorem import tariff of 5%, how much will it have to pay in tariffs?
A $1,000
B. $4
C. $25
D. $10,000
E. $500

e, medium, 153

#5-13 If an agricultural products firm imports 50 tons of rutabagas valued at $20,000, and faces a specific tariff of $4 per ton, how much will it have to pay in tariffs?
A $80,000
B. $800
C. $10,000
D. $200
E. $4

d, medium, 153

#5-14 Which statement best describes the winners and losers from a tariff?
A   The gains to the government and producers exceed the loss to consumers.
B.   Producers gain in the short and long run.
C.   The gains to the government and producers are equal to the consumer's loss.
D.   Consumers end up paying more for products covered by import tariffs.
E.   The gains to the government and producer are less than the loss to consumers.

d, hard, 153

#5-15 Subsidies typically
A   make it easier for foreign firms to import into a subsidizing country.
B.   lower costs for domestic producers.
C.   benefit domestic consumers, who do not have to pay the costs of the subsidy.
D.   harm domestic producers.
E.   prevent firms from attaining first mover advantages.

b, medium, 154

#5-16 Which of the following statements is NOT true about the effects of a quota?
A   Domestic consumers typically pay more for products.
B.   Foreign producers can enjoy higher profits.
C.   Domestic producers benefit.
D.   The government enjoys increased tax revenue on imports.
E.   Firms may change facility location decisions.

d, hard, 154

#5-17 The effects of a VER are most similar to those of a
A   tariff
B.   subsidy
C.   quota
D.   local content requirement

c. easy, 156

#5-18 Which of the following is NOT an example of an administrative barrier to trade?
A   time consuming inspection of express mail packages for pornography
B.   cutting tulip bulbs down the middle to inspect them
C.   requiring that all imports of certain products go through small and remote customs posts with
            "specially trained" inspectors
D.   assessing a tax equal to 25% of the value of light truck
E.   holding bananas at customs for inspection so long that they spoil

d, medium, 157

#5-19 How have Toyota and Honda responded to possible local content requirements for cars
manufactured in the US?
A.   They have agreed to buy more manufactured parts from plants in the US
B.   They have shifted vehicle production from Japan to the US
C.   They have ignored them, knowing that the requirements are unenforceable.
D.   They have lobbied to have Japanese vehicles specifically exempted from the requirements.

a, medium, 156

#5-20 The most common political argument for government intervention in trade is probably
A   to protect jobs and industries from foreign competition.
B.   assure national security
C.   invest in infant industries
D.   retaliation for other country's policies
E.   protect consumers from inferior foreign products

a, medium, 157

#5-21 Based on experience in a number of countries, protecting infant industries
A   has been highly successful in allowing firms to develop first mover advantages
B.   has tended to create inefficient industries that are not internationally competitive.
C.   has allowed developing countries to establish competitive industries, but has been unsuccessful industrialized countries.
D.   has benefited domestic consumers and spurred economic growth
E.   has improved the efficiency of international capital markets

b, hard, 159

#5-22 If global capital markets are efficient,
A   subsidies would still be economically appropriate under most conditions.
B.   local content requirements would have no effect on business location decisions.
C.   tariffs would be ineffective in restricting trade.
D.   quotas would have a greater effect on consumer losses than tariffs.
E.   the only industries that would require government protection would be those that are not economically efficient.

e, hard, 159

#5-23 It is argued that Boeing's success and first mover advantages may be the result of US
A.   import tariffs
B.   VERs
C.   subsidies
D.   local content requirements
E.   import quotas

c, easy, 160

#5-24 Airbus Industrie may have never been able to successfully compete in the world market without the help it has received, primarily in the form of
A   import tariffs
B.   VERs
C.   subsidies
D.   local content requirements
E.   import quotas

c, medium, 160

#5-25 While strategic trade policies are nice in theory, why may they fail in reality?
A   quotas are much simpler than the prescriptions of strategic trade policy
B.   retaliation by other countries and the influence of political groups domestically
C.   only the most politically powerful groups will have access to strategic trade policies
D.   other governments may enact policies that counteract strategic trade policies
E.   strategic trade policy assumes perfect markets, and there are no perfect markets

b, hard, 161

#5-26 Who has benefited from the CAP?
A   domestic consumers
B.   foreign producers
C.   farmers and politicians
D.   textile workers and cotton mills
E.   machine tool and auto manufacturers

c, medium, 161

#5-27 What was one of the most important consequences of the Japanese auto VERs on the US auto consumers?
A   US auto firms had to lower their prices.
B.   Prices were raised on Japanese autos
C.   US consumers were able to get better value for their money.
D.   The US government was able to use the increased revenues it raised to lower taxes on US autos.
E.   The "big 3" US manufacturers were able to recapture the market share they had previously lost.

b, hard, 156

#5-28 Which of the following is NOT a significant drawback of government intervention in trade?
A   Intervention can be self defeating since in practice it tends to protect the inefficient.
B.   Intervention can invite retaliation and trigger a trade war.
C.   The industries targeted for intervention are as likely to be chosen for political rather than economic reasons.
D.   Domestic consumers will likely end up paying more for goods.
E.   Intervention can help firms establish first mover advantages.

e, easy, 160

#5-29 The Corn Laws
A   placed a high tariff on corn imported into Britain
B.   were enacted by the US government shortly after defeating Britain in the War of Independence
C.   were repealed after a stinging speech parliament by David Ricardo where he outlined the theory of comparative advantage
D.   were repealed after record harvests in Britain
E.   placed on imported corn into the US provided American farmers the chance to recover from a disastrous harvest

a, medium, 162

#5-30 During the 1980s and early 1990s the world trading system developed under GATT underwent strain for all of the following reasons EXCEPT:
A   Japan's rise as the world's largest exporter
B.   Increase in the use of VERs by US exporters
C.   The west's perception that Japan's market was closed because of administrative trade barriers
D.   The large US trade deficit
E.   Increase in the number of ways countries circumvented GATT agreements with non-tariff barriers

b, hard, 164

#5-31 Import tariffs on goods into the US
A   are zero for all goods
B.   average 15% of the value of all imported goods
C.   have been a significant factor in the creation of the huge US trade deficit
D.   cost US consumers over $30 billion a year
E.   are generally pro-consumer

d, medium, 155

#5-32 What is the cost to the US economy of US import tariffs
A   about $50,000 for every job saved
B.   over $30 billion a year
C.   almost zero, as the tax revenue gains by the government offset the loss to consumers
D.   almost zero, since the US has virtually no import tariffs
E.   around $1 billion

a, hard, 155

#5-33 In the view of most analysts, what accounts for Toyota's success
A   value of the Yen
B.   price leadership strategy
C.   superior styling
D.   world renowned reliability
E.   manufacturing and design skills

e, hard, 170

#5-34 NUMMI is
A   a new type of gummi bear made with artificial sweeteners
B.   an acronym for an automobile joint venture
C.   a model of cellular phone
D.   the 20% numerical target for semiconductor imports in Japan
E.   a mechanism in the dispute resolution process of WTO

b, medium, 170

#5-35 Toyota's operation with General Motors in California
A   was originally focused on improving the styling and design characteristics of Toyota
B.   proved the unfeasibility of applying Toyota's manufacturing processes in US plants
C.   proved to be a dismal failure for GM, but was successful by Toyota's standards
D.   outperformed Toyota's Takaoka factory as early as 1986
E.   allowed Toyota to circumvent Japanese VERs

e, hard, 170

#5-36 The voluntary export restraints imposed by the Japanese auto industry in 1981
A   led to lower average profits per auto for US dealers
B.   gave European auto firms some "breathing room" and time to catch up
C.   led to lower average profits per auto for Japanese manufacturers
D.   resulted in stagnant export growth
E.   all of the above

d, medium, 170

#5-37 By 1990, the local content of Toyota cars produced overseas was
A   less than 10%
B.   around 20%
C.   around 40%
D.   around 70%
E.   over 85%

c, hard, 171

#5-38 What has been one of Toyota's greatest difficulties in its foreign assembly operations
A   disappointing sales
B.   cheap local component parts
C.   resistance by foreign governments in countries where it has set up operations
D.   resistance by labor unions to the new jobs
E.   inability to find local suppliers that meet price and quality expectations

e, medium, 171

#5-39 In Europe,
A   the Common Agricultural Policy helps assure that food prices are kept low
B.   Japanese auto manufacturers have set a limit on their share of the market
C.   the cellular telephone service market is effectively controlled by 3 multinational firms
D.   the semiconductor market is controlled by numerical targets for firms from different countries

b, hard, 171

#5-40 The trade dispute between Britain and Malaysia in early 1994
A   involved a British government development grant for a dam
B.   revolved around the British press' portrayal of bribe seeking on the part of Malaysian officials
C.   caused the Malaysian government to ban all governmental purchases of British products
D.   all of the above
E.   none of the above

d, medium, 173

#5-41 Which statement best describes the growth of the Malaysian economy since 1989
A   sluggish
B.   severely depressed
C.   average for an developed economies
D.   average for a developing country
E.   extremely fast

e, hard, 173

#5-42 Government subsidies to industry are the highest in
A   Sweden
B.   Germany
C.   Britain
D.   US
E.   Japan

a, hard, 154

#5-43 An EU Commission study found that government subsidies to manufacturing were the lowest in
A.   Greece
B.   Germany
C.   Portugal
D.   Britain
E.   France

d, hard, 154

#5-44 From the perspective of a domestic component producer, local content regulations work in a way that is most similar to a
A.   quota
B.   VER
C.   tariff
D.   subsidy

a, medium, 156

#5-45 What was the main impediment to the successful completion of the Uruguay round of GATT
A   Japanese intransigence on semiconductors and autos
B.   disputes over subsidies to government controlled firms
C.   disagreement over agricultural subsidies
D.   differences over tariff levels on manufactured goods
E.   failure to resolve intellectual property regulatory differences

c, hard, 165

#5-46 The primary role of the WTO is
A   act as a mediator in trade disputes
B.   set specific levels of tariffs that must be followed by all member countries
C.   provide export development assistance loans to developing countries
D.   monitor compliance with regulations and arbitrate trade disputes
E.   all of the above

d, medium, 165

#5-47 What is the difference between the WTO and GATT
A   trade dispute enforcement mechanisms
B.   coverage of intellectual property matters
C.   responsibility for trade in services as well as goods
D.   all of the above
E.   none of the above

d, easy, 165

#5-48 What is the main effect of the 1993 GATT agreement with respect to agricultural products
A   consumers will face higher prices
B.   farm subsidies will be reduced
C.   inefficient producers will be better off
D.   nothing, GATT failed to make progress on this issue because of French farmers and other
           narrow-minded groups that blocked the settlement
E.   developing countries will be able to buy North American wheat more cheaply

b, easy, 166

#5-49 Which firms or industries benefited the least from the 1993 GATT agreement
A   heavy construction equipment
B.   small exporters
C.   efficient agricultural producers
D.   pharmaceutical companies
E.   banks and financial services companies

e, medium, 167

#5-50 What nation is the largest exporter
A   Russia
B.   Japan
C.   US
D.   China
E.   France

c, easy, 170

#5-51Q: What is the aim of "strategic trade policy"?

#5-51A: Improving the competitiveness of a domestic industry or firm against its world wide competitors in the world market.

#5-52Q: What are the key limitations of "strategic trade policy"?

#5-52A: Intervention in trade policy can be self-defeating because it protects the inefficient and prevents resources from finding their most efficient use in an economy. It can also invite retaliation, and lead to an escalation of tariffs and a trade war. Finally, intervention is unlikely to be well executed, given the opportunity for such a policy to be captured by special interest groups or be managed for political interests rather than economic interests.

#5-53Q: What has been the main objective of GATT?

#5-53A: The main objective of GATT has been to liberalize trade by eliminating tariffs, subsidies, import quotas, and other restrictions to the free flow of trade among countries.

#5-54Q: What is the difference between a **specific tariff** and an **ad valorem tariff**? Is one better or more effective than the other?

#5-54A: Specific tariffs are levied as a fixed charge for each unit of a good imported (e.g. $3 per barrel olive oil). Ad valorem tariffs are taxes that are levied as a portion of the value of the imported good. Neither is more or less effective, or necessarily better. Since the amount collected on an ad valorem tariff will stay a fixed percentage of the value, ad valorem tariffs automatically correct for inflation or changes in the values of goods, while specific tariffs do not.

#5-55Q: With a tariff, who gains and who loses?

#5-55A: The government gains because a tariff increases government revenues. Domestic producers gain because the tariff affords them some protection against foreign competitors by increasing the cost of imported foreign goods. Consumers lose since they must now pay more for certain imports and certain domestic products that can now substitute for imports.

#5-56Q: What is the difference between a quota and a voluntary export restraint? Do they have different effects on domestic prices or consumer losses or gains?

#5-56A: A quota is imposed by the country into which the imports would be coming, while a voluntary export restraint is imposed by the country (or firms in the country) from which the goods are being exported. Both have the same effects on consumers and cause domestic prices to rise.

#5-57Q: Do administrative policies that limit the import of goods hurt consumers? Why, or why not?

#5-57A: Administrative policies that limit the importation of goods harm consumers by keeping out products that may be superior in quality and/or lower in cost than domestically produced goods. Consumers are forced to buy goods of inferior value to those available internationally. In some instances administrative barriers can provide for consumer protection from potentially dangerous goods.

#5-58Q: "There are political arguments for restricting trade, and several economic reasons for restricting trade, but the political arguments are not economically sound." Critically evaluate this statement.

#5-58A: Political arguments are generally not based on sound economic reasoning, yet in the cases of strategic trade policy and strategic bargaining to lower other countries' barriers, the political arguments are supported by economic principles.

#5-59Q: "The voluntary export restraints imposed by the Japanese on auto exports to the US helped consumers by helping the US auto industry become more competitive." Critically evaluate this statement.

#5-59A: The near term effect of the Japanese VERs on autos was devastating, costing US consumers billions of dollars in increased auto prices. It also protected US producers from having to compete fairly with the most competitive producers in the world. The long term effects are not as clear, as some would argue that the brief period of protection may have allowed the US producers to reinvest and become more competitive. Others point out that the VERs encouraged Japanese firms to invest in US manufacturing capacity, and now as members of the US auto industry have pushed the industry to become more competitive and helped in the development of a more responsive supplier network.

#5-60Q: If strategic trade policy is correct in its assumptions and arguments, what actions should governments take?

#5-60A: If the arguments for strategic trade policy are correct, they clearly suggest a rationale for governmental intervention in international trade. Specifically, governments should target industries and technologies that may be important in the future, and use subsidies to support development work aimed at commercializing those technologies. Furthermore, governments should provide export subsidies until domestic firms have established first mover advantages in the world market. Government support can also be justified if it can help domestic firms emerge as viable competitors in the world market..

#5-61Q: Given that the gains to protectionist policies usually accrue to the producers, why shouldn't an industry lobby its government for protection from imports?

#5-61A: Free trade has brought great advantages to the firms that have exploited it, and to consumers who benefit from the resulting lower prices. Given the danger of retaliatory action, business firms that lobby their governments to engage in protectionism must realize that by doing so they may be denying themselves the opportunity to build a competitive advantage by constructing a globally dispersed production system. Moreover, by encouraging their government to engage in protectionism, their own activities and sales overseas may be put in jeopardy if foreign governments retaliate.

CHAPTER 6

Students should be encouraged to choose the BEST answer, as more than one may be technically correct. Following each question is the answer, estimated difficulty, and page reference.

#6-1 Which statement best describes Honda's car production in the North America?
A   Honda began producing in the US to avoid US import quotas.
B.   Honda leadership position in the Japanese market allowed it the resources to undertake FDI.
C.   While successful in auto production, Honda's motorcycle production in the US was a failure.
D.   Nearly two thirds of US sales of autos were built by North American plants.
E.   The rise of the dollar relative to the Yen made US production more feasible.

d, medium, 196

#6-2 Which of the following is NOT an example of FDI?
A   US-based IBM deciding to build a new computer manufacturing in Scotland.
B.   US-based Hewlett-Packard buying a German software company from it's Swiss owner.
C.   US-based General Electric buying a 25% stake from Electrolux in Electrolux's US plant.
D.   Sony's purchase of CBS records and Columbia Pictures from US parents.

c, easy, 176

#6-3 Which of the following is an example of horizontal FDI?
A   An Austrian firm buying out one of its major German suppliers.
B.   A Norwegian fish processing plant buying an Icelandic fishing trawler.
C.   A Mexican salsa maker opening a new production plant in California.
D.   An English brewer starting a new brewery in Scotland.
E.   A Peruvian manufacturer buying its distributor in Bolivia.

c, hard, 176 (hint: while d looks correct, both England and Scotland are regions in the same country)

#6-4 Which statement best describes the relationship between world trade and FDI during the 1980s.
A   The flow of FDI accelerated, and accelerated faster than the growth of world trade.
B.   Both FDI and world trade grew, but world trade grew faster than FDI.
C.   Both FDI and world trade grew during the early part of the decade, but declined in the late 1980s.
D.   The growth of the flow of FDI was five times faster than the growth of international trade.
E.   Due to increasing protectionist pressures, FDI grew quickly while world trade remained flat.

a, hard, 178

#6-5 From 1990 to 1993, which country experienced a significant fall in the volume of its FDI outflows?
A   Sweden
B.   Germany
C.   Japan
D.   USA.
E.   Australia

c, medium, 179

#6-6 Which country dominated FDI outflow during the 1960s and 1970s.
A   Germany
B.   USA.
C.   Japan
D.   Britain
E.   Holland

b, easy, 179

#6-7 From 1986-1990, developing nations
A   were recipients of more FDI than developed nations
B.   were net investors rather than recipients of FDI
C.   had over 40% of the stock of FDI
D.   received just over 15% of all FDI flows
E.   saw a decrease in the receipt of FDI flows

d, hard, 180

#6-8 Which country had the highest stock of FDI in the US in 1994
A   Canada
B.   Britain
C.   Holland
D.   France
E.   Japan

b, medium, 182

#6-9 What factor may have been a key contributor to the growth of FDI into the US in the 1980s?
A   The rise of the dollar relative to other currencies.
B.   The rise in import tariffs.
C.   The attractiveness of the US market.
D.   Legal limits on licensing in the US
E.   Rising transportation costs made export less efficient.

c, medium, 182

#6-10 Which of the following statements is true
A   Since 1970 the stock of US FDI abroad has always been greater than the stock of foreign FDI in
         the US
B.   In 1988 the flow of US FDI abroad was greater than the stock of US FDI abroad
C.   By 1990 the stock of foreign FDI in the US exceeded the stock of US FDI abroad
D.   Between 1974 and 1994 the stock of US FDI abroad increased over ten times
E.   none of the above

a, hard, 182

#6-11 Which statement best describes the role of small, medium, and large companies in FDI.
A   Although large firms still account for the bulk of FDI, the importance of small and medium sized firms has been increasing.
B.   Small and medium sized firms looking to expand actually account for the lion's share of FDI.
C.   Almost all FDI is undertaken by large multinationals that have access to international capital markets.
D.   Small companies undertake the largest share of FDI, while large companies undertake the smallest share of FDI

a, easy, 185

#6-12 Which statement best describes the relationship between FDI and risk?
A   FDI is less risky than exporting.
B.   Licensing is always riskier than FDI, since know-how can be lost to the licensee.
C.   FDI is risky, since when doing business in unfamiliar countries and cultures, there is a greater probability that mistakes will be made.
D.   FDI is generally a low risk decision, since investments can be hedged in the international capital markets.
E.   FDI is riskier for large firms with established reputations than with small firms that have great new products.

c, medium, 185

#6-13 For which product is exporting likely to be the most feasible?
A   Cement
B.   Gatorade
C.   Bricks
D.   Diamonds
E.   Coal

d, easy, 185

#6-14 Impediments to the free flow of goods between nations
A   have increased dramatically in the 1980s.
B.   increases the viability exporting relative to FDI.
C.   are not considered in the market imperfections theory.
D.   makes FDI more attractive than licensing.
E.   decreases the profitability of exporting, relative to licensing and FDI.

e, hard, 186

#6-15 The main source of impediments to the free flow of goods between nations are
A   transportation costs
B.   governments
C.   competitors
D.   inefficient markets for the transfer of know-how.
E.   GATT regulations

b, medium, 186

#6-16 Which of the following is NOT a reason for why the market may not work well as a mechanism for selling know-how.
A   Loss of know-how to a potential competitor.
B.   Loss of tight control over manufacturing, marketing, and strategy in a foreign country.
C.   Know-how can be difficult to codify and hence license.
D.   Firms want to allow licensees autonomy to localize products for individual national markets.
E.   Know-how can be imbedded in an organization's culture.

d, medium, 186

#6-17 Which author is associated with the "follow the leader" or imitative explanation of horizontal FDI?
A   Vernon
B.   Krugman
C.   Knickerbocker
D.   Smith
E.   Hill

c, easy, 186

#6-18 What is the main flaw in the "follow the leader" or imitative explanation of horizontal FDI?
A   It is valid only in perfect competition, and not oligopolistic industries.
B.   It only explains the actions of large firms, and has no relevance for small or medium firms.
C.   It does not explain why exporting is superior to licensing in oligopolistic industries.
D.   It was only relevant for a limited period of time immediately after WWII.
E.   It does not explain why the first firm chose to undertake FDI.

e, easy, 188

#6-19 The product life cycle theory predicts that FDI
A   will only occur in mature industries.
B.   in other advanced countries will occur when local demand grows large enough to support local production.
C.   will occur in underdeveloped countries when their level of growth and local demand is sufficient to support local production.
D.   will occur in the US in certain circumstances, but says nothing about FDI in other countries.
E.   will be undertaken only to circumvent trade barriers and high transportation costs.

b, hard, 189

#6-20 The usefulness of the product life cycle theory to most businesses is
A   less than that of the follow the leader theory.
B.   limited since it does not explain why exporting or licensing would be inferior to FDI.
C.   significant, since it identifies with some precision the conditions under which FDI is appropriate.
D.   hard to know, since most business cannot judge the stage of the lifecycle of their products.
E.   is greater than that of the market imperfections theory.

b, medium, 189

#6-21 Volkswagen's acquisition of a number of US car dealers can be best classified as
A   forward vertical FDI
B.   FPI
C.   horizontal FDI
D.   backward vertical FDI
E.   really stupid, since there already were lots of car dealers in the US

a, medium, 191

#6-22 Alcoa and Alcan's controlling investment in bauxite mines in Jamaica can be best explained by which theory?
A   market imperfections
B.   follow the leader
C.   product life cycle
D.   market power
E.   comparative advantage

d, medium, 191

#6-23 Which of the following is NOT a condition that would lead a firm towards licensing?
A   High transportation costs
B.   Know-how is amenable to licensing
C.   Tight control over foreign operations is not required.
D.   Know-how cannot be protected by a contract.

d, medium, 193

#6-24 In which of the following industries is licensing most likely to be common as a form of international expansion?
A   medical diagnostic equipment
B.   automobiles
C.   photographic film
D.   bulk chemicals
E.   fast food

e, easy, 194

#6-25 Hanson PLC is headquartered in which country?
A   USA.
B.   Australia
C.   Britain
D.   Holland
E.   France

c, easy, 184

#6-26 Hanson grew in the US primarily through
A   setting up new manufacturing facilities
B.   licensing
C.   export
D.   acquisitions
E.   advertising

d, medium, 184

#6-27 The primary competitive advantage that Hanson has over many other firms is its
A   better products
B.   superior management skills
C.   creative advertising capabilities
D.   technological and R&D skills
E.   access to international capital markets

b, medium, 184

#6-28 Hewlett-Packard invested in manufacturing facilities in Germany after it had developed a strong customer base there for its high technology electronic test equipment. Based only on this information, which theory best explains Hewlett-Packard's FDI?
A   market power
B.   market imperfections
C.   follow the leader
D.   product life cycle
E.   transportation cost avoidance

d, medium, 189

#6-29 A Japanese operator of resorts and golf courses bought the Steamboat Springs Ski area. This is an example of
A   foreign portfolio investment
B.   backward vertical FDI
C.   horizontal FDI
D.   forward vertical FDI
E.   licensing

c, easy, 185

#6-30 Which of the following may be the most appropriate for licensing to a foreign firm?
A   a drug protected by a patent
B.   a new technique for searching for undersea oil
C.   a management skill used to motivate workers and encourage teamwork
D.   a methodology for increasing the yield of a common variety of corn
E.   the recipe for Coca-Cola

a, medium, 193

#6-31 Electrolux is one of the world's largest manufacturers of
A automobiles
B. consumer electronics
C. household appliances
D. telephones
E. all of the above

c, medium, 175

#6-32 The home market of Electrolux can best be described as
A a significant contributor to Electrolux's revenues
B. composed of relatively unsophisticated and undemanding customers
C. all of North America
D. small
E. customers that prefer disposable products with a short life cycle

d, medium, 175

#6-33 Electrolux's traditional markets
A were in severe recession
B. did not appreciate the product features of its goods
C. were expected to grow at 2-3% annually for the foreseeable future
D. were dominated by General Electric of the US
E. rejected the cheaply made products that it produced in its plant in China

c, medium, 175

#6-34 Knickerbocker's theory of FDI
A was the primary reason Electrolux undertook FDI in Eastern Europe and Asia
B. predicts that Electrolux should license its technology in most countries
C. was contradicted by Vernon's theory and empirically shown incorrect by Electrolux
D. provides a rationale that contributed to Electrolux's FDI decisions
E. is incapable in explaining foreign acquisitions, as it only addresses greenfield investments

d, hard, 175

#6-35 Electrolux's first move into Eastern Europe took place in
A the Czech Republic
B. Latvia
C. Russia
D. Poland
E. Hungary

e, medium, 175

#6-36 According to the US Department of Commerce, FDI occurs whenever a US citizen, organization of affiliated group takes an interest of what percentage or greater
A   1
B.   10
C.   25
D.   50
E.   80

b, medium, 176

#6-37 The inflow of FDI into developing countries is
A   over 5 times greater than the outflow of FDI from developing countries
B.   is greater than the inflow of FDI into developed countries
C.   is greater than the outflow of FDI from developed countries
D.   still only a very small percentage of the inflow of FDI into developed countries
E.   none of the above

a, hard, 177

#6-38 Which of the following is NOT a trend in FDI over the past 20 years
A   there has been a rapid increase in FDI
B.   the US has declined in relative importance as a source of FDI
C.   Japan has seen become a significant recipient of FDI inflows
D.   developing countries are becoming increasingly important as recipients of FDI
E.   small and medium sized enterprises have increased their share of FDI flows

c, medium, 177

#6-39 The flow of FDI
A   has increased steadily since 1980
B.   fell in 1991
C.   growth has been slower than the world trade growth since 1985
D.   peaked in 1988
E.   has never achieved the levels seen before the crash of 1979

b, hard, 178

#6-40 Lehel
A   was a state-owned enterprise prior to 1990
B.   authored a theory stating that licensing was preferable FDI when know-how was well codified
C.   controlled a controversial project in Malaysia
D.   is the site of Honda's first car plant in North America
E.   is a famous Japanese shrine

a, medium, 178

#6-41 In 1993 which country was the largest source of FDI outflows
A   US
B.   Britain
C.   Japan
D.   Germany
E.   France

a, medium, 179

#6-42 In 1993 which of the following countries had the lowest level of FDI outflow
A   France
B.   Britain
C.   Germany
D.   Japan
E.   US

d, hard, 179

#6-43 Which of the following countries has experienced a reduction in the percentage of the worldwide stock of FDI held by its citizens since 1960
A   France
B.   Germany
C.   Japan
D.   Britain
E.   none of the above

d, medium, 180

#6-44 Which of the following statements about Vietnam is NOT true
A   it has been shunned as potential investment location by auto manufacturers
B.   the domestic bicycle industry has outmoded equipment
C.   it is a member of ASEAN
D.   the GDP per capita is around $210
E.   it has a communist government

a, easy, 181

#6-45 The economic policy of Vietnam is similar to that of
A   Taiwan
B.   Hong Kong
C.   South Korea
D.   New Zealand
E.   China

e, easy, 181

#6-46 Dunning describes the nature of location specific advantages
A   as relating to endowments or assets that are tied to a specific location
B.   as being related to a firm's own unique assets
C.   as an extension of the market imperfections argument
D.   in his eclectic paradigm
E.   all of the above

e, hard, 189

#6-47 Which words best describe the Japanese auto industry
A   perfect competition
B.   intensely competitive
C.   dominated by Honda
D.   all of the above
E.   none of the above

b, medium, 197

#6-48 The location specific advantages argument
A   does not explain why firms prefer FDI to licensing or to exporting
B.   supports the argument of Knickerbocker
C.   contradicts the predictions of the life cycle theory
D.   explains licensing but not exporting
E.   has been largely discredited by the market imperfections perspective

a, hard, 193

#6-49 Which statement best describes Honda
A   It was a late entrant to the Japanese auto market
B.   although it failed in motorcycles, it succeeded in autos
C.   it collaborated with Nissan and Toyota in entering the US market
D.   all of the above
E.   none of the above

a, medium, 197

#6-50 Which is the dominant auto company Japan
A   Nissan
B.   Honda
C.   Suzuki
D.   Toyota
E.   Kawasaki

d, medium, 197

#6-51Q: Why did Honda decide to invest in North America?

#6-51A: A number of reasons seem to underlie Honda's decision to invest in North America. First, Honda may have invested in the US to circumvent the threat of protectionist trade legislation. A second reason may be the sharp rise in the value of the Japanese Yen against the US dollar, which dramatically increased the cost of exporting both finished automobiles and component parts from Japan. Thirdly, the establishment of North American assembly plants can be seen as part of a strategy designed to circumvent Toyota and Nissan and to make major inroads in the US market ahead of its Japanese rivals. Related to this is a belief that autos need to be customized to the requirements of the North American market, and that this customization could not be effectively undertaken from Japan.

#6-52Q: How does vertical FDI differ from horizontal FDI?

#6-52A: Horizontal FDI involves investing internationally in the same industry in which a firm operates domestically. Vertical FDI involves investing in an industry either upstream or downstream from the industry within which a firm operates domestically.

#6-53Q: What is foreign portfolio investment? How does it differ from foreign direct investment?

#6-53A: Foreign portfolio investment is investment by individuals, firms, or public bodies in foreign financial instruments. It does not involve taking a significant equity stake in a foreign business entity, nor entail any integration of business operations.

#6-54Q: Define the "flow of FDI". Define the "stock of FDI". How are these two concepts related?

#6-54A: The flow of FDI refers to the amount of FDI undertaken over a given period of time (usually one year). The stock of FDI refers to the total accumulated value of foreign owned assets at a given point in time. The yearly flows of FDI add or subtract from the stock of FDI.

#6-55Q: Why is the US now a major location for foreign direct investment?

#6-55A: A number of factors may be contributing to the rise of FDI in the US. Firstly, the US is a large and rich market for foreign producers. Secondly, the value of the dollar has been falling relative to other currencies, making investments in the US a good bargain. Thirdly, foreign firms may believe that they can manage US workers and assets more efficiently than they are currently being managed. Lastly, rising protectionist pressures may be encouraging firms to "become American" so that they are not locked out of the market.

#6-56Q: What types of goods are likely to have relatively high transportation costs, thus making export unfeasible or impractical?

#6-56A: Goods that have a low value to weight ration, like cement, asphalt, and bottled drinks may be impractical to export. For these goods the transportation costs may be much greater than the value of the goods, and even inefficient local production may be preferable to exporting.

#6-57Q: According to economic theory, why may licensing of know-how be an unattractive alternative for firms?

#6-57A: According to economic theory licensing may be unattractive under one or more of the following conditions: a) the firm has valuable know-how that cannot be adequately protected by a licensing contract, b) the firm needs tight control over a foreign entity to maximize its market share and earnings in that country, and c) a firm's skills and know-how are not amenable to licensing.

#6-58Q: According to Knickerbocker's theory, why do firms undertake horizontal FDI? What is the major deficiency with this theory?

#6-58A: According to Knickerbocker's "follow the leader" theory, firms undertake horizontal FDI when another firm in their industry has already done so. Hence they also invest overseas in order to keep from being locked out of other markets or to keep tabs on their international competitors. What this theory does not explain is why the first firm takes the action that the other firms subsequently imitate.

#6-59Q: According to Vernon's product life cycle theory, at what stages in a product's life is FDI likely to take place in what types of countries?

#6-59A: According to Vernon's product life cycle theory, firms will invest in industrialized countries when demand in those countries is sufficient to support local production, and invest in developing countries with low costs when products are mature and cost pressures are intense.

#6-60Q: During a late night get-together with a few classmates after a particularly difficult exam, you concocted a beverage that everyone thought was truly excellent. After developing a loyal following locally for your beverage, and beginning small scale manufacturing and bottling operations, a visitor from Finland stops by to see you. He tells you he thinks your drink will be a real hit in Finland, and wants to license the recipe from you and sell the beverage in Finland. Assuming he is correct and that the Finns will really enjoy your product, should you license your recipe to him and collect the royalties while studying for your next exam?

#6-60A: With know-how like a recipe, it could be very easy for someone to at first license this technology, and by only changing it slightly, be able to sell and compete against you in other markets. Hence since it could be very difficult to adequately protect this proprietary information in a licensing contract, if you choose to license you should either really trust this guy or be fairly uninterested in pursuing the idea any further yourself.

CHAPTER 7

Students should be encouraged to choose the BEST answer, as more than one may be technically correct. Following each question is the answer, estimated difficulty, and page reference.

#7-1 In recent years the Japanese government has pressured many Japanese firms to undertake FDI in order to
A　　　improve its trade balance
B.　　　reduce its balance of payments surplus
C.　　　find lower cost labor
D.　　　put pressure on Japanese bankers to provide funds internationally

b, medium, 200

#7-2 Which of the following countries most recently moved towards a freer market approach to FDI?
A　　　India
B.　　　Singapore
C.　　　Denmark
D.　　　Britain
E.　　　Hong Kong

a, hard, 205

#7-3 The primary motivation for the IBM in locating a plant in Guadalajara was
A　　　the expected growth and development of the Mexican market.
B.　　　access to Mexican technology.
C.　　　Mexico's lax FDI regulations.
D.　　　incentives provided by the Guadalajara government
E.　　　low labor costs

e, easy, 202

#7-4 The IBM plant in Guadalajara
A　　　was intended to produce computers primarily for the Mexican market
B.　　　had 51% ownership by IBM, with the remainder owned by the Mexican government
C.　　　required IBM to make few concessions, since the Mexican government was very interested in having the plant built
D.　　　involved an investment of $35 million in local R&D
E.　　　had no restrictions on local content, but was required to create nearly 900 jobs

d, medium, 203

#7-5 The radical view has its roots in the writings of
A　　　Smith
B.　　　Jones
C.　　　Ricardo
D.　　　Marx
E.　　　Vernon

d, easy, 200

#7-6 According to the radical view, FDI by MNEs
A   should be allowed only in high technology industries so technology can be transferred to the host government.
B.   should be encouraged to help developing countries grow economically.
C.   keeps the less developed countries of world relatively backward and dependent.
D.   should be limited to no more than a 25% stake.

c, medium, 200

#7-7 The US controls FDI in all of the following ways EXCEPT:
A   restricting outward investment in Cuba and Iran
B.   restricting inward investment in US airlines to no more the 25% without approval
C.   limiting ownership if it will lead to a monopolization of a domestic industry
D.   prohibiting foreign firms from buying defense firms and others critical to national security
E.   forbidding foreign ownership of semiconductor plants to protect US technology

e, medium, 203

#7-8 Most countries have adopted which policy towards FDI?
A   Radical
B.   Pragmatic Nationalism
C.   Dogmatic Realism
D.   Restrictive Protectionism
E.   Free Market

b, easy, 203

#7-9 "FDI should be allowed only if the benefits outweigh the costs" according to which policy?
A   Pragmatic Nationalism
B.   Free Market
C.   Radical view
D.   Restrictive Protectionism
E.   Dogmatic Realism

a, medium, 203

#7-10 Within the EU, which country has been most effective in attracting FDI from the Japanese auto industry?
A   Germany
B.   France
C.   Italy
D.   Spain
E.   Britain

e, medium, 204

#7-11 Which statement best describes the current trend among countries with respect their ideological position towards FDI?

A   Countries that have had a pragmatic nationalistic approach are becoming more free market oriented.

B.   Countries that have had the most pure free market views are now moving more towards a dogmatic realism approach.

C.   There is a overall movement away from the free market view, with more countries adopting the radical view.

D.   There is a movement away from the radical position and towards the free market view.

E.   Restrictive protectionism is replacing dogmatic nationalism as the dominant view.

d, hard, 204

#7-12 "FDI can make a positive contribution to a host country by supplying capital, technology, and management skills that would not otherwise be available." This statement best describes

A   employment effects
B.   balance of payments effects
C.   resource transfer effects
D.   market imperfections effects
E.   spurious effects

c, easy, 205

#7-13 According to economists that favor the free market view, in a perfect world the best policy for all governments would be to

A   maximize the benefits and minimize the costs of FDI in each country
B.   not interfere at all in the investment decisions of MNEs
C.   encourage and stimulate outward FDI
D.   provide inducements to MNEs considering FDI in their countries
E.   encourage and stimulate outward FDI while only rarely discouraging inward FDI

b, hard, 205

#7-14 In most high technology fields, the Japanese government

A   does not allow FDI, requiring that firms instead license technology to local firms.
B.   prohibits exports so that Japan does not lose its technological leadership.
C.   prefers imports over FDI, as this makes it easier for Japanese firms to reverse engineer products.
D.   prefers licensing over FDI, and has permitted FDI only when the firm has a strong bargaining position.
E.   prefers FDI over licensing.

d, medium, 207

#7-15 From the perspective of a host country, the

A   positive indirect employment effects are typically greater than positive direct employment effects.
B.   negative direct employment effects occur only in industries where there are no local competitors.
C.   positive direct employment effects are always greater than the negative indirect effects.
D.   negative indirect employment effects will occur only when the investing MNE has a monopoly

a, medium, 207

#7-16 The current account
A   records transactions that involve the purchase or sale of assets.
B.   and the capital account always sum to zero.
C.   records the stock of FDI.
D.   records the flow of FDI.
E.   records transactions that involve the export or import of goods, services, and investment income.

e, medium, 208

#7-17 When a Norwegian consumer purchases a Swedish chain saw, this is recorded as a
A   debit on the Norwegian current account.
B.   credit on the Norwegian current account.
C.   debit on the Norwegian capital account.
D.   credit on the Norwegian capital account.
E.   credit on the Norwegian current account and a debit on the US capital account.

a, easy, 209

#7-18 When a Swiss MNE purchases an Austrian company, it is recorded as a
A   credit on the Swiss current account
B.   debit on the Swiss capital account.
C.   debit on the Swiss current account
D.   credit on the Austrian current account.
E.   debit on the Austrian capital account.

b, medium, 209

#7-19 Which statement best describes the relationship between the capital and the current account.
A   A debit on the capital account is always offset by a credit on the current account.
B.   A debit on the current account is always offset by a credit on the capital account.
C.   These accounts rarely sum up to zero due to statistical discrepancies.
D.   A transaction on the current account will rarely have any effect on the capital account.
E.   A debit on the current account can be offset by a corresponding debit on the capital account.

c, hard, 209

#7-20 When a Swiss MNE exports products from its Italian subsidiary to Canada, this is recorded as a
credit on
A   Canada's capital account.
B.   Canada's current account.
C.   Switzerland's current account.
D.   Italy's current account.
E.   Switzerland's capital account

d, hard, 209

#7-21 The adverse effects on competition for the host country tend to
A   only be important when the domestic industry is dominated by MNEs.
B.   greatest in less developed countries.
C.   offset primarily by positive net direct employment effects
D.   be a major concern in advanced industrialized nations
E.   countered by the infant industry argument.

b, medium, 210

#7-22 If the Brazilian subsidiary of a Slovenian manufacturing firm requires a large number of component parts and equipment from Slovenia,
A   positive balance of payment effects for Brazil.
B.   a debit to Slovenia's capital account.
C.   positive resource transfer effects for Brazil.
D.   a reverse resource transfer effect for Brazil.
E.   this creates positive employment effects Slovenia.

e, medium, 212

#7-23 Which is NOT an adverse balance of payment effect on the home country.
A   Employment switches from the home country to the host country.
B.   When products produced offshore are imported into the home country.
C.   When exports decrease due to substitution effects from the FDI.
D.   The initial capital outflow.

a, medium, 212

#7-24 Performance requirements, as a condition for permitting inward FDI
A   rarely are adhered to.
B.   specify the maximum ownership allowed by the MNE.
C.   place controls over the operations of a local subsidiary.
D.   are less common in less developed countries than in industrialized countries.
E.   were not used by Mexico in the IBM case, since other requirements were deemed to be more important.

c, easy, 215

#7-25 Which of the following is NOT one of the four "Cs" of negotiation
A   concessions
B.   common interest
C.   conflicting interests
D.   compromise
E.   criteria

a, medium, 216

#7-26 The relative bargaining power of two parties is determined by all of the following EXCEPT:
A   value placed on what each has to offer
B.   the nationality of the parties
C.   number of comparable alternatives available
D.   each party's time horizon

b, medium, 216

#7-27 Which statement best describes the relative bargaining power of IBM and Mexico in the Guadalajara facility?
A   IBM's bargaining power was much greater than Mexico's.
B.   Mexico's bargaining power was much greater than IBM's.
C.   IBM was in a fairly strong position, since Mexico was eager to attract foreign investment.
D.   IBM had many comparable alternatives, putting it in a strong position relative to Mexico.
E.   Since IBM was in no great hurry to build additional manufacturing facilities, it could afford to wait until it got the deal it wanted from Mexico.

c, hard, 202

#7-28 What are the employment effects of Nissan in Britain
A   overall negative
B.   component suppliers created more jobs than Nissan
C.   the negative indirect effects are greater than the direct effect
D.   all of the above
E.   none of the above

e, medium, 199

#7-29 Which best describes the local content of Nissan vehicles produced in Britain
A   minimal
B.   around 40%
C.   just over half the value of the final product
D.   significant if the entire EU is considered "local", but minimal for Britain
E.   significant for Britain, and the EU as a whole

e, medium, 199

#7-30 How would you describe the bargaining power of a firm that had a short time horizon, few comparable alternatives, with a low value placed on its investment by the host country
A   very powerful
B.   strong
C.   moderate
D.   weak

d, easy, 217

#7-31 In recent years, what has been the policy of the Japanese government toward outward FDI?
A   It has installed strict exchange controls to reduce the high levels of outward FDI.
B.   It encourages outward FDI, as it sees FDI as a substitute for exporting and a way to potentially decrease its trade surplus.
C.   While acknowledging that it has a problem with excessive outward FDI, the Japanese government has taken no steps to formally stop outward FDI.
D.   It encourages FDI, believing that the current low level of FDI is unacceptable to many foreign governments.

b, hard, 200

#7-32 Which of the following was NOT a reason that likely affected Nissan's decision to invest in Britain
A   low wages
B.   significant tax breaks
C.   low worker productivity
D.   attractiveness of the location
E.   workforce capabilities

c, easy, 199

#7-33 Who characterized Britain as "a Japanese aircraft carrier sitting off the coast of Europe"
A   the queen of England
B.   the Japanese foreign minister
C.   the French president
D.   the British prime minister
E.   the US president

c, hard, 199

#7-34 Historically one of the most important determinants of a government's policy toward FDI has been
A   the success of its companies on the world market
B.   its political ideology
C.   economic strength
D.   GDP per capita
E.   its FPI as a ratio of GDP

b, easy, 200

#7-35 "No country under any circumstances should permit foreign corporations to undertake FDI, since they can never be instruments of economic development, only economic domination." This statement
A   is so ridiculous that it would have no support whatsoever, even among Marxists
B.   is generally accepted by most Marxist governments that still exist today
C.   reflects rather extreme radicalism
D.   expresses a mainstream pragmatic nationalist perspective

c, medium, 200

#7-36 Which statement best describes the current popularity of the radical view of FDI
A   The collapse of Eastern European communist states effectively eradicated any acceptance of this view
B.   The strong economic performance of countries embracing this perspective has led to a resurgence of interest
C.   Empirical evidence suggests that FDI is rarely a positive influence on countries that adhere to this view
D.   The generally abysmal economic performance of countries that adopted the radical approach has caused most all of them to abandon it
E.   China and Cuba are the only countries that still strongly support the radical view of FDI

d, hard, 201

#7-37 What was the Mexican government's response to IBM's request to invest $40 million in a PC factory in Guadalajara
A   It rejected the proposal due to insufficient local content
B.   It rejected the proposal due to IBM's insistence on 100% ownership
C.   It accepted the proposal on the condition that IBM invest more in local R&D
D.   It accepted the proposal on the condition that IBM create twice as many jobs
E.   It rejected it because the bribes offered to Mexican officials were too small

a, medium, 203

#7-38 Which words best describe the recent experiences of India and Vietnam with respect to inward FDI
A   there has been very little
B.   these country's tight controls on FDI effectively keep FDI out
C.   a dramatic increase has occurred
D.   India has seen a huge rise in FDI while Vietnam has not
E.   Vietnam has seen a huge rise in FDI while India has not

c, medium, 205

#7-39 Men's access to capital
A   provides them with some advantages over local host country firms
B.   has no effect on FDI given efficient international capital markets
C.   is the primary reason Mexico was interested in IBM's investment
D.   was not a factor in Venezuela's oil industry joint ventures
E.   all of the above

a, easy, 205

#7-40 For the past 20 years, Venezuela's oil industry has been
A   a leader in developing technology for cold deep water exploration
B.   dominated by foreign multinationals
C.   controlled by the influential Petogas family that has prevented most foreign exploration
D.   focused on natural gas while neglecting light crude reserves
E.   controlled by the government

e, medium, 206

#7-41 PDVSA is turning to foreign investors for all of the following reasons EXCEPT
A   access to capital
B.   access to technical resources
C.   opportunity to learn new management practices
D.   minimal success in attracting local investors

d, medium, 206

#7-42 In the case of technology intensive firms, Japan has historically
A   preferred licensing over inward FDI
B.   preferred licensing over outward FDI
C.   preferred exporting over inward FDI
D.   been ambivalent regarding MNE's entry strategies
E.   been a strong advocate of joint ventures in outward FDI

a, hard, 207

#7-43 Spin-off effects
A   arise when local personnel who are trained in a MNE subsequently leave and help indigenous
         firms to become competitive
B.   can be minimized by increasing the local or domestic content of goods produced
C.   only occur in technology intensive industries, thus causing little problem for much FDI
D.   all of the above
E.   none of the above

a, hard, 207

#7-44 Which of the following statements regarding the US balance of payments in 1993 is true
A   Imports of goods, services, and income exceeded exports of goods, services, and income
B.   Exports of services were of lesser value than exports of merchandise
C.   Imports of services were of lesser value than exports of services
D.   The balance on the capital account was positive
E.   All of the above

e, easy, 208

#7-45 The current account deficit is often referred to as
A   a statistical discrepancy
B.   the trade deficit
C.   the capital account
D.   a credit to the current account surplus
E.   none of the above

b, medium, 208

#7-46 Assume you (as a citizen and resident of Latvia) purchase a fine piece of British made stereo equipment. This would be reflected on the balance of payments as
A   credit on the capital account of the US
B.   credit on the capital account of Latvia
C.   debit on the current account of Latvia
D.   debit on the current account of Britain
E.   none of the above

c, medium, 209

#7-47 During the early 1990s, which statement best describes oil and gas production in Russia
A   it ceased
B.   it was reduced as factories closed, which lessened demand for oil and gas
C.   it declined dramatically as a result of poor maintenance and tensions with neighboring countries
D.   it remained constant, although demand grew as Russia sought to raise exports with rising oil prices
E.   it grew dramatically in order to finance the huge government deficits

c, easy, 219

#7-48 Conoco's experience in Russia
A   showed how foolish it was for Western firms to risk FDI in such a volatile country
B.   found that the technical skills of Russian workers was excellent
C.   underscored the efficiency of the transportation infrastructure in Russia
D.   gives significant cause for concern to any other oil firm interested in investing in Russia
E.   shows how far a few minor bribes can go towards getting a company into serious trouble

b, medium, 219

#7-49 Russia's tax code
A   often works at cross purposes with itself
B.   applies only to FDI and not licensing income
C.   encourages investment in natural resource industries over other industries
D.   all of the above
E.   none of the above

a, hard, 219

#7-50 Arkhangelskgeologia is a
A   Russian subsidiary of Conoco
B.   region in Venezuela with high potential oil reserves
C.   oil exploration joint venture partner of a DuPont subsidiary
D.   type of oil that requires a specialized refining process that required FDI
E.   world made up by a professor to fool you

c, hard, 219

#7-51Q: According to the radical view, what is the effect of FDI on developing countries?

#7-51A: According to the radical view, FDI by MNEs of advanced capitalist nations keeps the less developed countries of the world relatively backward and dependent upon advanced capitalist nations for investment, jobs, and technology. Taken to the extreme, this suggests that no country under any circumstance should ever permit foreign corporations to undertake FDI, since FDI is not an instrument of economic development, but instead of economic domination.

#7-52Q: As of the mid-1980s, characterize (describe or list) the countries that predominantly held the radical view towards FDI. Also characterize the countries that held a predominantly free market view. Describe the differences between these countries with respect to economic development.

#7-52A: Radical countries: most of Eastern Europe, China, Cuba, Cambodia, India, Iran, and socialist countries in Africa. Free market: Singapore, Hong Kong, South Korea, Taiwan, and many advanced nations like Britain, the US, Holland, and Denmark. The countries more aligned with the free market approach generally have higher levels of economic development and greater economic growth.

#7-53Q: What are the primary reasons why the radical view has become less common since the late 1980s?

#7-53A: Three reasons predominate for the retreat of the radical view: (1) The collapse of communism in Eastern Europe. (2) The generally abysmal economic performance of those countries that embraced the radical position, and a growing belief by many of these countries that, contrary to the radical position, FDI can be an important source of technology and jobs and can stimulate economic growth. (3) The strong economic performance of those developing countries that embraced capitalism rather than radical ideology.

#7-54Q: According to the free market view, what is the role of MNEs in FDI and the world economy?

#7-54A: The free market view argues that international production should be distributed among different countries according to the theory of comparative advantage - countries should specialize in the production of those goods and services that they can produce most efficiently. The MNE is thus an instrument for dispersing the production of goods and services to those locations around the globe where they can be produced most efficiently. Viewed this way, FDI by the MNE can be seen as a way of increasing the overall efficiency of the world economy.

#7-55Q: Countries adopting a pragmatic nationalistic approach to FDI try to adopt policies that will have what effect on FDI?

#7-55A: Countries that adopt a pragmatic nationalistic approach to FDI try to adopt policies that maximize the national benefits of FDI and minimize the national costs. Hence policies are intended to encourage FDI as long as the benefits to the country outweigh the costs. In reality, this is a tricky and hard to measure balance.

#7-56Q: Explain the employment effects of FDI on both the host and the home country.

#7-56A: From a host country's perspective, there are positive employment effects from both the direct hiring of people and the indirect job creation in firms that supply and service a new facility. More important than the number of new jobs, however, is the net effect on employment. If some domestic firms go out of business because of the more efficient MNE, then some or all of the job gains may be offset by the loss of other jobs. From a home country's perspective, there can be negative effects on employment if jobs are essentially exported overseas. But there can also be positive effects on the suppliers to the overseas plan, domestic users of the overseas plant's output, and on marketing and administrative staff that are responsible for coordinating worldwide sales and production.

#7-57Q: What is the current account? What is the capital account? In what way, if any, are these two accounts related?

#7-57A: The current account records transactions that involve the export or import of goods and services. The capital account records transactions that involve the purchase or sale of assets. In any given year the current account balance and the capital account balance should automatically add up to zero, but in actuality they rarely do because of statistical discrepancies.

#7-58Q: How could FDI affect the national sovereignty of a host nation?

#7-58A: Many host governments worry that FDI involves some loss of economic independence. The basic concern is that in the case of FDI, key decisions that can have an effect on the host economy may be taken by a foreign parent that has no real commitment to a host country - and over which the host government has no real control.

#7-59Q: Describe how a "reverse resource transfer effect" can benefit a home country and the parent MNE.

#7-59A: Reverse resource transfer benefits arise when the home country MNE learns valuable skills or technology from its exposure to foreign markets that can subsequently be transferred back to the home country. Through its exposure to a foreign market, a MNE can learn about superior management techniques or superior product and process technologies, and then transfer these back to the home country, with a commensurate beneficial effect on the parent company's success in the home market and the home country's economic growth.

#7-60Q: What are the main policy instruments available to countries interested in restricting outward FDI?

#7-60A: One of the most common policies to restrict outward FDI has been to simply limit capital outflows, primarily for balance of payments reasons. Countries can also manipulate tax rules to discourage foreign investment. Finally, countries can outright prohibit certain types of foreign investment, both inward and outward, for political or "security" reasons.

#7-61Q: Why might countries or regions seek to attract FDI? How do they most often do this?

#7-61A: It is increasingly common to find governments offering incentives to foreign firms to invest in their countries. Such incentives take many forms, but the most common are tax concessions, low interest rate loans, and outright grants or subsidies. Incentives are motivated by a desire to gain from the resource transfer and employment effects of FDI. They are also motivated by a desire to capture FDI away from other potential host countries.

CHAPTER 8

Students should be encouraged to choose the BEST answer, as more than one may be technically correct. Following each question is the answer, estimated difficulty, and page reference.

#8-1 The decision facing John Martin of Martin's Textiles
A   was about how he would tell his employees that half of them would be laid off.
B.   regarded whether he should relocate manufacturing to Mexico.
C.   was how he would pay the high union wages his employees were demanding.
D.   how to deal with the strengthening US dollar, which made foreign products less expensive.
E.   whether he should promote Mary Morgan, a 30 year employee, to head his new Mexican plant?

b, easy, 247

#8-2 According to the case, most of John Martin's competitors in the North Eastern US had
A   gone out of business.
B.   lobbied the government to protect their industry.
C.   moved production to the Southern US and Mexico.
D.   fired most of their union employees and hired illegal immigrants.
E.   been controlled by the Mafia and used for money laundering, making them less concerned about cost pressures.

c, medium, 247

#8-3 Which of the following is an example of political union?
A   EC
B.   EFTA
C.   NAFTA
D.   Switzerland
E.   COMECON

d, easy, 224, Switzerland is a country, and thus obviously an example of a political union, whereas all the others are examples of groups of countries.

#8-4 Which of the following is NOT a member of the EC?
A   Britain
B.   Germany
C.   Italy
D.   Luxembourg
E.   Norway

e, medium, 228

#8-5 Which of the following is a current member of EFTA?
A   Iceland
B.   Britain
C.   Poland
D.   Greece
E.   Denmark

a, medium, 224

#8-6 Which of the following forms of integration exhibits less integration than a customs union?
A   political union
B.   economic union
C.   free trade area
D.   common market

c, easy, 224

#8-7 In a free trade area
A   barriers to the trade of goods and services among members are removed.
B.   a common currency is adopted.
C.   a single parliament determines political and foreign policy.
D.   a common external trade policy is adopted.
E.   factors of production are free to move among member countries.

a, medium, 224

#8-8 EFTA
A   currently includes the Eastern European countries of Hungary and the Czech Republic.
B.   will be superseded by the EEA and thereafter be subsumed into the EC.
C.   countries have a common foreign policy, unlike the EC.
D.   was formed by countries that did not want to part of the EC.
E.   sets a common agricultural policy for all countries, but does not address trade in services.

d, hard, 224

#8-9 The EC originally began as a
A   common market
B.   customs union
C.   free trade area
D.   economic union
E.   military alliance

b, hard, 224

#8-10 The primary difference between a customs union and a common market is the
A   creation of a single currency.
B.   common external trade policy.
C.   free flow of goods and services among countries.
D.   common tariff policy for transit of goods between member countries.
E.   mobility of factors of production between member countries.

e, medium, 224

#8-11 Significant harmonization and cooperation on fiscal, monetary, and employment policies is required in

A   a free trade area
B.   a common market
C.   a customs union
D.   an economic union
E.   both a common market and an economic union

e, medium, 224

#8-12 Which statement best describes the relationship between a free trade area and GATT?

A   A free trade area is allowed under GATT, and allows neighboring countries to go beyond GATT.
B.   While establishing a free trade area is technically prohibited by GATT, there are no enforcement provisions to allow GATT to require that all countries be allowed the same access as the member countries of the free trade area.
C.   Free trade areas allow countries to establish stricter external trade policies than allowed under GATT.
D.   With a free trade area, countries can adopt a common currency, which is something that the members of GATT could never agree to do.

a, hard, 225

#8-13 Economic integration

A   can not be justified on political grounds.
B.   prevents neighboring states from going to war with each other, since they are dependent on each other for goods and services.
C.   decreases the political clout of a group of nations, since they then hold only one seat on the United Nations Security Council, rather than one seat for each country.
D.   creates incentives for political cooperation between nations.
E.   can not occur until true political union has been achieved.

d, medium, 225

#8-14 Which member of the EC has the right to opt out of the single currency?

A   France
B.   Germany
C.   Britain
D.   Italy
E.   Holland

c, medium, 235

#8-15 A regional free trade agreement

A   cannot benefit the countries involved unless trade creation exceed trade diversion.
B.   will only make the world better off if the amount of trade it creates exceeds the amount it diverts.
C.   cannot work if one of the neighboring nations does not agree to it.
D.   can be enforced under Article 3 of the GATT agreement.
E.   will always entail some degree of trade diversion.

b, hard, 226

#8-16 Which of the following has the highest population?

A   EU

B.   US

C.   Russia

D.   MERCOSUR

E.   India

e, easy, India has one quarter of the world's population, which in population terms dwarfs the others.

#8-17 Prior to the Single European Act, EU member countries

A   agreed to the mutual acceptance of product standards.

B.   had harmonized tax rates.

C.   simplified the paperwork and rules of sabotage.

D.   had not established common external trade policies for some products.

E.   had established common government procurement policies.

d, hard, 231

#8-18 What was the Delors Commission named after?

A   the Delors region of Luxembourg where the commission was headquartered

B.   Henrique Delors, CEO of Philips

C.   Jacques Delors, president of the EC

D.   the Delors region of France, which borders Germany, Luxembourg, and Belgium

E.   the Delors company, which sponsored its creation in the hope of improving the business
        environment in Europe

c, medium, 231

#8-19 What was the primary objective of the Roundtable of European Industrialists?

A   to push the EU to adopt a common currency, thus simplifying international transactions

B.   lobby the EU to adopt a common industrial policy

C.   encourage the EU to harmonize the rules of the game and remove trade barriers

D.   encourage the EU to prohibit state aid to nationally held firms, since this created unfair
        competition for the non-subsidized firms

E.   show that the Delors Commission had used flawed logic in its recommendations, which if
        implemented, would greatly harm businesses

c, hard, 231

#8-20 Which of the following was NOT an objective of the Single European Act?

A   removal of border controls

B.   increase competition

C.   create a single currency

D.   increase competition in the financial services industry

E.   decrease the number of standards that products produced for the European market would have to
        meet.

c, medium, 232

#8-21 Which EU country has the most product standards
A   Britain
B.   US
C.   France
D.   Norway
E.   Germany

e, medium, 232

#8-22 What affect will the Single European Act and the Maastricht Treaty likely have on the CAP?
A   the CAP will be eliminated
B.   the subsidies authorized under the CAP will be significantly reduced
C.   the CAP will be replaced by the BLAP
D.   the CAP will be continued without significant change
E.   since the CAP and the EC are governed by separate agreements, the Single European Act and the Maastricht treaty will not affect the CAP

d, hard, 236

#8-23 Brazil is a member of
A   CARICOM
B.   MERCOSUR
C.   Andean Pact
D.   both MERCOSUR and the Andean Pact
E.   none of the above

b, medium, 242

#8-24 Which of the following is NOT a member of the Andean Pact
A   Bolivia
B.   Peru
C.   Venezuela
D.   Argentina
E.   Columbia

d, medium, 241

#8-25 Which of the following is NOT a member of ASEAN?
A   Hong Kong
B.   Brunei
C.   Indonesia
D.   Philippines
E.   Singapore

a, medium, 243

#8-26 Which adjective best describes the progress of ASEAN towards its objectives?
A   phenomenal
B.   very successful
C.   moderate
D.   modest
E.   very limited

e, hard, 243

#8-27 What has been the response of many large non-EU firms to the single market?
A   they view it as having little effect on their operations
B.   they have greatly increased exports in advance of the expected higher tariffs
C.   they have rapidly increased FDI in the EU
D.   they have lobbied hard to be treated as insiders
E.   they view it as a political curiosity

c, easy, 244

#8-28 Which statement best describes the response of Minnesota Mining and Manufacturing to the EU?
A   It is decreasing its exposure to the European market.
B.   It has consolidated European manufacturing and distribution facilities.
C.   It fears the increased competition from European companies.
D.   It is greatly increased its investment in Europe and opened new plants in each country.
E.   It is locating R&D in one country, marketing in another, finance in a third, and dispersing
         manufacturing to the most efficient sites.

b, medium, 245

#8-29 Portugal
A   is not a member of the EU
B.   is a member of EFTA
C.   is not a member of any regional economic integration
D.   joined EU in 1986
E.   was refused membership in the EEA.

d, easy, 228

#8-30 Which of the following statements is NOT true about the treaty of Maastricht?
A   The EU is described as "an ever closer union in which political decisions have to be taken as near
         to the people as possible."
B.   The EU will move towards having a joint foreign policy, but with most decisions requiring
         unanimity.
C.   The Western European Union, a long dormant group of nine of the EC nations will be revived to
         act as the EU's defense body, but linked to NATO
D.   The EU will have jurisdiction in industrial affairs, health, education, trade, the environment, and
         tourism. Member states will vote to implement decisions.
E.   France was allowed to opt out of all regulations on culture, as it did not want to compromise its
         cultural identity to a Euro-norm.

e, medium, 232

#8-31 Which of the following statements is FALSE?

A   The population of the US is greater than that of Mexico and Canada combined.

B.   Mexico generally has more lax environmental regulations than the US or Canada.

C.   The NAFTA agreement was never ratified by the House of Representatives in the US, but the administration was able to implement the basics of the agreement regardless

D.   Wages in most industries are higher in Canada than Mexico.

E.   NAFTA will lead to the abolition within 10 years of tariffs on 99% of the goods traded

c, medium, 238

#8-32 A Canadian firm currently selling in Canada and exporting some goods to the US

A   may need to move production to the US as a result of NAFTA.

B.   may face increased competition from European firms in the future.

C.   will likely find it easier to now export to the EU than it was previously.

D.   will be forced to set up a manufacturing plant in Mexico if it is to remain competitive.

b, hard, 238

#8-33 The lowering of barriers to trade and investment between countries

A   will likely result in increased price competition.

B.   will increase the cost to consumers.

C.   in the EC will ultimately be reversed by political pressures from the poorer members.

D.   in NAFTA will lower the level of exports between the members.

E.   will likely lead to greater monopolization of many industries.

a, medium, 246

#8-34 Which of the following statements regarding the effect of the EU on Bernard Cornille is true.

A   Differences in taxes on alcohol between countries created a new business opportunity for him.

B.   His cash machine distribution business was hurt by cheap imports from Spain and Italy

C.   The establishment of the EU has provided him with the opportunity to expand his business across national borders since export tariffs are now zero

D.   All of the above

E.   A and B are true, but not C or D

e, medium, 221

#8-35 What is truck driver Barry Cotter's reaction to the EU

A   "the EU is run by a bunch of cloggies and kermits who just try to screw us limeys"

B.   "in this business time is money, and these days I've got a lot more of both"

C.   "in spite of the rules, the French border guards still stop me just to create hassles"

D.   "its great to be able to truck all the cheap wine from Italy and France to the Brits and sell it for a huge profit"

E.   "tell me why, in spite of the supposedly free flow of products, you still can't buy a good pint of beer in France"

b, hard, 221

#8-36 What is the primary business of Atag Holdings NV
A   kitchen appliances
B.   cash machines
C.   chemicals
D.   containers for consumer products
E.   insurance

a, medium, 221

#8-37 What has been the experience of Atag with the creation of the EU
A   It has been able to cater to both the "potato" and "spaghetti" belts with two product lines
B.   Foreign sales have increased from 4% to 25% of revenues
C.   It has been able to find a specific niche of "Euroconsumers" across the continent
D.   The French, famous for their cooking, prefer higher temperatures for boiling foods
E.   all of the above

b, hard, 221

#8-38 Britain, Denmark, Germany, and Norway
A   at one time have each been members of EFTA
B.   were all members of the EEC
C.   are current members of the EU
D.   all border the North Sea
E.   none of the above

d, easy, 228, obvious from any good map of Europe.

#8-39 Trade creation occurs
A   to the chagrin of most domestic consumers
B.   when domestic producers are able to build economies of scale as a result of trade barriers
C.   when the benefits of trade outweigh the loss of jobs in an industry
D.   when high-cost domestic producers are replaced by lower cost foreign producers
E.   only when trade barriers are reduced bilaterally

d, hard, 226

#8-40 This organization within the EU meets at least twice a year, resolves major policy issues, and sets policy directions
A   European Commission
B.   Council of Ministers
C.   European Parliament
D.   European Council
E.   none of the above

d, easy, 229

#8-41 This organization within the EU is responsible for proposing, implementing, and monitoring compliance with EU legislation

A   European Council
B.   Council of Ministers
C.   European Commission
D.   European Parliament
E.   European Court of Justice

c, easy, 229

#8-42 This organization within the EU is responsible for providing mediation services between individuals, corporations, and governments when there are different interpretations of EU regulations

A   European Court of Justice
B.   European Parliament
C.   European Council
D.   European Minister of Mediation
E.   none of the above

e, hard, 230

#8-43 Members of the European Parliament

A   are selected by the governments of member countries in proportion to population
B.   are to serve the interests of Europe as a whole, and not represent the people of their nation
C.   are elected by direct vote from each country
D.   all of the above
E.   none of the above

c, medium, 230

#8-44 Why do many observers expect that insurance rates within the EU will continue to differ greatly across countries for all of the following reasons EXCEPT

A   the frequency of claims varies widely
B.   the expected level of service varies widely
C.   variation in the tax treatment of insurance
D.   significant switching costs for consumers
E.   limitations built into the rules on prohibiting penetration of other countries markets

e, hard, 235

#8-45 One result of the Single European Act has been

A   elimination of agricultural subsidies to inefficient farmers
B.   a significant rise in the number of mergers and acquisitions in industries like insurance
C.   agreement on the mechanisms for setting up a common currency by 1999
D.   privatization of all government owned and controlled business enterprises
E.   all of the above

b, hard, 235

#8-46 In 1994 the EU voted to allow the following countries to join the existing 12 members
A   Austria and Norway
B.   Hungary and the Czech Republic
C.   Turkey and Greece
D.   Finland and Sweden
E.   A and D above

e, medium, 235

#8-47 The North American Free Trade Agreement
A   was opposed by President Clinton
B.   excludes Quebec, given its special political status
C.   did not address intellectual property rights, as these were already covered under the WTO
         agreement which all members of NAFTA had signed
D.   allows restrictions on FDI in the cases of US culture, Canadian airlines, and the Mexican oil
         industry
E.   none of the above

e, medium, 238

#8-48 Which of the following are NOT likely to benefit from NAFTA
A   Canadian consumers
B.   Mexican consumers
C.   US consumers
D.   US manufacturers
E.   All of the above will generally benefit from NAFTA

e, easy, 238

#8-49 What was one of the biggest problems Wal-Mart faced in opening its stores in Mexico
A   inability to find adequately trained employees
B.   Mexican governmental red tape
C.   the rise in the Peso made imported products too expensive for many consumers
D.   border guards decided to "inspect" most of the merchandise until it spoiled
E.   all of the above

b, easy, 241

#8-50 As a result of its problems in Mexico, Wal-Mart has decided
A   slow down its expansion plans
B.   close down Mexican operations
C.   lobby in Washington to put pressure on the Mexican government to improve the situation
D.   double its proposed investment in order to reach the economies of scale needed for efficient
         operations
E.   threaten the Mexican government with economic sanctions under GATT rules

a, medium, 241

#8-51Q: How are the New York employees of Martin's Textiles likely to be hurt by NAFTA? How are they likely to benefit? Overall, will they be better or worse off?

#8-51A: The New York employees of Martin's textiles may well lose their jobs in the next few years, whether a result of NAFTA or simply a result of the globalization of production in this industry in lower labor cost industries. As consumers, however, they are likely to have to pay lower prices for a number of products, and t hey may be able to get even better jobs in industries that export to Mexico and Canada. If in the end they are able to get another job that makes better use of their skills, they will certainly be better off. If, however, they are not able to find new jobs that pay as well or are as rewarding personally, the advantages of lower consumer prices will not likely offset the losses. What must be kept in mind, however, is that they may have in time lost their jobs anyway to more efficient foreign competitors.

#8-52Q: Describe the difference between a free trade area and a common market.

#8-52A: In a free trade area all barriers to the trade of goods and services among member countries are removed. In a common market, the factors of production are also allowed to move freely between member countries and a common external trade policy is adopted.

#8-53Q: Give an example of political union between independent states. What has been the result? What do you think is the most successful example?

#8-53A: The US, Switzerland, and the former Yugoslavian republic are all examples where separate autonomous states have been combined into a political union. The result in the US and Switzerland has been high economic growth while allowing some degree of autonomy at the state or canton level. In the case of Yugoslavia, the country collapsed with the death of General Tito and the fall of communism - with devastating results. As for success, in terms of longevity Switzerland has enjoyed prosperous economic and political union for over 700 years. The US clearly achieved phenomenal economic growth in the 200 years after the 13 independent colonies joined to create a more perfect union. The EU is clearly on this same path. (Students may also choose to cite other examples like the USSR or Hapsburg, Roman, or Ottoman empires, along with the successes and failures of each.)

#8-54Q: With an explicit goal of GATT being the removal of barriers to trade, why do countries establish free trade areas? Are not the essential requirements for a free trade area already included in the GATT agreements?

#8-54A: While GATT covers a broad range of issues and clearly moved the world towards freer trade, success has been less than total. A number of products and services are not covered under GATT, and we have seen how VERs and other administrative mechanisms that are outside the control of GATT can distort trade. It is much harder to get over 100 countries to agree to the further reduction of trade barriers (especially when they do not share many common interests), than it is to get a few neighboring countries to agree on matters that are clearly in their mutual interest.

#8-55Q: Describe the political case for integration? Did political considerations have any role in the formation of the EU? Why or why not?

#8-55A: The political case for integration has two main points: (1) by linking countries together, making them more dependent on each other, and forming a structure where they have to regularly interact, the likelihood of violent conflict and war will decrease, and (2) by linking countries together, they have greater clout and are politically much stronger in dealing with other nations. Coming right after the two world wars that were started by internal European conflicts, and wars in which other outside powers (USA and USSR) had gained significant power and influence, both of these political aspects were important considerations in the formation of the EU.

#8-56Q: In order to achieve full economic union the EU has reached agreement on the adoption of a common currency, controlled by a EU central bank. Britain, however, has decided it wants the option of not adopting the common currency. Other than wanting to preserve the right to have a picture of the queen on their currency, why is Britain holding out on this point?

#8-56A: A politically important segment of the public opinion in Britain is opposed to a common currency on the grounds that it would require giving up control of monetary policy to bureaucrats in the EU. They feel that British sovereignty would be compromised if monetary policy was decided by some group that did not have foremost in their minds the best interests of British citizens.

#8-57Q: Define trade creation and trade diversion with respect to regional economic integration. Given that integration can both create and divert trade, under what conditions will regional integration be in the best interest of the world economy?

#857A: Trade creation occurs when high cost domestic producers are replaced by low cost producers within the free trade area. Trade diversion occurs when lower cost external suppliers are replaced by higher cost suppliers within the free trade area. A regional free trade agreement will only make the world better off if the amount of trade it creates exceeds the amount it diverts.

#8-58Q: Describe or list the countries that are members of EFTA? What benefits do members of the EU have that EFTA members do not? What are the advantages of being in EFTA rather than the EU?

#8-58A: EFTA members include Norway, Iceland, and Switzerland. EU members have the added benefits of the free flow of factors of production, mutual recognition of standards, border-free transit, and a common external trade policy. These benefits, however, must be coordinated and enforced by a central bureaucracy. EFTA members advantage comes from the increased political and economic autonomy of having much more internal control over their own affairs. In the case of Norway, it chose not to join the EU primarily because it felt it would have little control over its important oil and aquaculture resources if it joined the EU.

#8-59Q: From the standpoint of businesses, what are the advantages of a single currency?

#8-59A: The gains to business from a single currency arise from decreased exchange costs and reduced risk of disruption from unexpected variations in the value of different currencies. A single currency would also reduce staffing requirements in accounting and finance departments.

#8-60Q: What are the similarities and differences between APEC and ASEAN?

#8-60A: The two major similarities between these two groups are that they relate to the Pacific area and that they haven't done much more than talk and agree that progress is important. ASEAN is much smaller and has the potential to make more significant progress, although to date has accomplished little. APEC is a much more visible organization and encompasses half of the world's GDP. But the differences among the countries are so great that not much of anything concrete has been agreed upon.

CHAPTER 9

Students should be encouraged to choose the BEST answer, as more than one may be technically correct. Following each question is the answer, estimated difficulty, and page reference.

#9-1 Allied-Lyons' primary business activity is
A   chemicals
B.   financial management
C.   currency trading
D.   food products

d, easy, 273

#9-2 The loss that Allied-Lyons incurred came as a result of
A   an unexpected fall in the value of the dollar
B.   risky speculation
C.   an exchange rate change between the time it submitted bids on a contract and when it was paid
D.   mismanagement of its foreign reserves by its bankers

b, medium, 273

#9-3 When the exchange rate is $1 = 120Yen, and a kimono costs 120,000Yen, what is the cost of the kimono in US$?
A   1000
B.   1,440,000
C.   120,000
D.   none of the above

a, easy, 271

#9-4 A tourist leaves New York with $10,000, and travels to Britain and exchanges his $ for British Pounds (BP). After spending 2 weeks in Britain he exchanges his remaining BP for 12,000 German Marks (DM), and travels to Germany. How much did he spend in Britain? Assume the exchange rates are $1 = .5BP = 2DM.
A   12,000DM
B. $10,000
C.   2000BP
D.   5000BP
E.   none of the above

c, hard, 271

#9-5 If someone believes that the US$ is overvalued relative to the Mexican Peso, they
A   should buy $ and sell pesos in advance.
B.   may believe that the Mexican inflation rate is greater than the US inflation rate.
C.   are expecting the peso to depreciate relative to the $.
D.   may have found that the money supply is growing faster in Mexico than the US
E.   are expecting the peso to appreciate relative to the $.

e, medium, 272

#9-6 When two parties agree to a currency exchange and execute the deal immediately the transaction is referred to as a
A   spot transaction
B.   forward transaction
C.   spot against forward swap
D.   arbitrage
E.   triage transaction

a, easy, 274

#9-7 If on January 10th a Canadian firm agrees to exchange 10,000C$ for 9,000US$ on April 10th, it
A   must expect the Canadian $ to appreciate
B.   is engaging in a forward exchange.
C.   must expect the US$ to appreciate
D.   expects the Canadian $ to be selling at a forward premium
E.   expects the US$ to be selling at a forward discount

b, medium, 274

#9-8 If the present exchange rate is 1DM = 4FF, and the 90 day forward rate is 1DM = 4.1FF,
A   the FF money supply is likely growing more slowly than the DM money supply.
B.   the DM is selling at a forward discount.
C.   the DM is expected to depreciate.
D.   the FF is selling at a forward discount.
E.   there is a good arbitrage opportunity.

d, medium, 275

#9-9 The world headquarters of the foreign exchange market is
A   Frankfurt
B.   New York
C.   London
D.   Tokyo
E.   none of the above

e, easy, 276

#9-10 The largest volume of foreign exchange transactions take place in
A   Frankfurt
B.   New York
C.   London
D.   Tokyo
E.   Paris

c, medium, 277

#9-11 If the exchange rate in Frankfurt is 1DM = 4FF and in Paris it is 1DM = 4.1FF
A   an arbitrage profit could be made by buying DM in Frankfurt and selling them in Paris
B.   the FF is selling at a forward discount in Paris
C.   the money supply in France is growing faster than the money supply in Germany
D.   an arbitrage profit could be made by buying FF in Paris and selling them in Frankfurt
E.   the FF is likely to depreciate against the DM.

a, hard, 277

#9-12 If the exchange rate in Toronto is $1 = 1.1C$ and in New York it is $1 = 1.2C$
A   an arbitrage profit could be made by buying C$ in Toronto and selling them in New York.
B.   the US$ is likely to appreciate in Canada relative to the C$
C.   the C$ is selling at a forward premium in New York
D.   the C$ is selling at a forward discount in New York

b, hard, 278

#9-13 Which of the following is often referred to as a vehicle currency?
A   Japanese Yen
B.   British Pound
C.   German Mark
D.   US Dollar
E.   French Franc

d, easy, 278

#9-14 The Law of One Price states that
A   it is illegal and discriminatory for a MNE to sell the same product for different prices in different countries
B.   a basket of goods bought in one country should cost the same in a different country, even after transportation costs are taken into consideration since they average out over the basket.
C.   in competitive markets free of transportation costs and barriers to trade, identical products sold in different countries must sell for the same price.
D.   purchasing power parity will not hold when differential inflation rates change relative prices

c, medium, 278

#9-15 What is a vehicle currency
A   the currency used to open daily trading on a currency exchange market
B.   a currency used as an intermediate currency when trading one relatively illiquid currency for another relatively illiquid currency
C.   the German mark was called this in the early 1980s since it was used for transporting goods and refugees out of eastern Europe
D.   the currency used by the automotive industry in Europe for pricing of all cars that are shipped to other European countries

b, hard, 278

#9-16 In a country where price inflation is very high relative to most other countries, it is likely that
A   its currency will depreciate relative to most other currencies
B.   it is being run under strict monetary growth constraints
C.   it will have an appreciation in its currency relative to most other currencies.
D.   PPP theory will not be a very good predictor of exchange rates

a, medium, 279

#9-17 What determines whether the rate of growth in a country's money supply is greater that the growth in output?
A   exchange rate differentials
B.   inflation rate
C.   forward exchange rates
D.   the level of currency swaps in and out of a country
E.   government policy

e, medium, 280

#9-18 Which statement best describes the empirical evidence on PPP theory?
A   Although PPP theory does appear be a reasonable predictor of short term exchange rates, it does not hold up well in the long run.
B.   The evidence supporting PPP theory is not as strong as that supporting the law of one price.
C.   While PPP theory makes sense in theory, in the real world of trade barriers and transportation costs, it not a good predictor of exchange rate changes in the short or the long run.
D.   While PPP theory does seem to yield relatively accurate predictions in the long run, it does not hold up in the short run.

d, easy, 283

#9-19 The Fisher Effect describes a relationship between
A   exchange rates and real interest rates
B.   nominal interest rates and exchange rates
C.   inflation rates and spot market exchange rates
D.   nominal interest rates and inflation rates

d, hard, 284

#9-20 The International Fisher Effect states that for any two countries,
A   the spot exchange rate should change in an equal amount and in the same direction as the difference in the nominal interest rates between the two countries
B.   the spot exchange rate should change in an equal amount but in the opposite direction to the difference in the real interest rates between the two countries
C.   the spot exchange rate should change in an equal amount but in the opposite direction to the difference in the nominal interest rates between the two countries
D.   the spot exchange rate should change in an equal amount and in the same direction as the difference in the real interest rates between the two countries
E.   the forward exchange rate should change to a greater degree but in the opposite direction to the difference in the nominal interest rates between the two countries

c, hard, 284

#9-21 If the current exchange rate is 4DM = 1BP, the 6 month forward rate is 4.1DM = 1BP, and the German nominal annual interest rate is 5%,
A   the British Pound is depreciating relative to the German Mark
B.   the British nominal annual interest rate is likely less than 5%.
C.   German nominal interest rates will most certainly rise
D.   the German Mark is selling at a forward premium relative to the British Pound
E.   none of the above

b, medium, 284

#9-22 If the current exchange rate is 4DM = 1BP, the 6 month forward rate is 4DM = 1.1BP, and the German nominal annual interest rate is 5%,
A   the British nominal rate interest rate should be about 18%
B.   the British nominal rate interest rate should be about 14%
C.   the British nominal rate interest rate should be about 5%
D.   the British nominal rate interest rate should be about 23%
E.   none of the above

d, hard, 284

#9-23 If Canadian nominal interest rates are 6%, US nominal interest rates are 9%, and the current exchange rate is 1C$ = .9US$, what will the exchange rate likely to be in one year according to the predictions of the international Fisher effect?
A   1C$ = .93US$
B.   1C$ = .9US$
C.   1C$ = .87US$
D.   1C$ = 1.03US$
E.   none of the above

a, medium, 284

#9-24 If the price of turnips is 33 Francs/kilo in Belgium and 11 Schillings/kilo in Austria, the law of one price would suggest that
A   people should buy turnips in Austria and ship them to Belgium
B.   the exchange rate should be 3Francs = 1 Schilling
C.   arbitrage possibilities would be available to people to export turnips from Belgium to Austria
D.   the exchange rate should be 1 Franc = 3 Schilling

b, easy, 279

#9-25 What is the primary difference between an efficient and an inefficient market?
A   only inefficient markets exist - no markets even approach efficiency in reality
B.   arbitrage profits are only possible in inefficient markets
C.   prices reflect all available information in efficient markets, but not in inefficient markets
D.   only efficient markets can produce unbiased predictors of future prices

c, hard, 286

#9-26 The fundamental analysis approach to forecasting
A   assumes currency exchange markets are efficient
B.   relies on economic theory to construct econometric models for prediction
C.   focuses on past trends to make future predictions
D.   explicitly excludes from consideration of balance of payments information
E.   has fallen out of favor due to the better track record of those using technical analysis

b, medium, 287

#9-27 When non-residents can convert their holdings of domestic currency into foreign currency, but
residents are limited in their ability to convert to foreign currencies, a currency is said to be
A   externally convertible
B.   internally convertible
C.   incontrovertible
D.   freely convertible
E.   untradeable

a, medium, 288

#9-28 What is the main reason governments typically impose convertibility restrictions on their currency?
A   encourage continued investment
B.   prevent hyper-inflation
C.   protect foreign exchange reserves
D.   to encourage countertrade

c, medium, 288

#9-29 An unbiased predictor of an exchange rate
A   is preferable to a biased predictor in all circumstances
B.   is also the most accurate
C.   does not typically either over or under estimate the future value
D.   is a countries inflation rate

c, medium, 286

#9-30 Most foreign exchange transactions
A   are undertaken by tourists traveling between countries
B.   occur on spot markets
C.   take place via swaps
D.   involve forward market purchases
E.   are cleared on the Zurich International Exchange

b, easy, 276

#9-31 Which statement best describes the relationship between growth in a country's money supply and the growth in its consumer prices?

A   The higher the growth in money supply, the lower the growth in consumer prices.

B.   For very low and very high levels of money supply growth, there is low growth in consumer prices.

C.   For very low and very high levels of consumer price increases, there are low levels of money supply growth.

D.   The higher the growth in consumer prices, the higher also is the likely level of the money supply.

d, medium, 280

#9-32 Countries with relatively high inflation tend to have

A   depreciating currencies

B.   low growth in their money supply

C.   their currencies selling at forward premiums relative to most other currencies

D.   low nominal interest rates

a, medium, 280

#9-33 Which of the following is LEAST likely to be a useful variable when trying to predict exchange rate changes?

A   Balance of Payments position

B.   Interest rate differentials

C.   inflation rate differentials

D.   real interest rates

E.   money supply differentials

d, easy, 284

#9-34 During the mid 1980s, Bolivia experienced all of the following EXCEPT

A   hyper-inflation

B.   money supply growth

C.   rapidly depreciating currency

D.   black market speculation

E.   restraint in monetary growth by the government

e, easy, 282

#9-35 Which of the following is the currency of Puerto Rico?

A   British Pound

B.   Puerto Peso

C.   Puerto Franc

D.   US $

E.   Cruzeiro

d, easy, Puerto Rico is a territory of the US, and thus uses the US $ as its currency.

#9-36 Why did Japan Air Lines enter into forward exchange contracts
A   so it wouldn't be hurt by an appreciating Yen
B.   to minimize the effect of an appreciating Yen
C.   to transfer the risk of exchange rate uncertainty from the airline to currency traders
D.   to minimize the effect of an appreciating dollar
E.   none of the above

c, hard, 269

#9-37 What was the effect on Japan Air Lines of changes in the exchange rates between 1985 and 1994 with respect to its purchase of Boeing aircraft in 1985
A   subsequent exchange rate changes had no effect on Japan Air Lines
B.   Japan Air Lines had to pay over $1.5 billion more than expected
C.   Japan Air Lines was fortunate to have locked in a favorable exchange rate by using a forward contract
D.   subsequent changes in the exchange rate made Japan Air Lines better off than expected
E.   none of the above

a, medium, 269

#9-38 What is a hedge fund
A   a fund that tries to prevent adverse effects from exchange rate changes
B.   an insurance fund for currency traders
C.   a fund that both buys financial assets and sells short on assets
D.   a fund that takes long positions in currencies
E.   a fund that buys and sells only forward exchange rate contracts

c, hard, 272

#9-39 A short seller
A   hopes a financial asset will decline in value
B.   typically sells dollars and buys other currencies
C.   uses foreign currencies to bet against a home currency
D.   typically buys dollars and sells other currencies
E.   none of the above

a, easy, 272

#9-40 The success of George Soros relies on
A   fundamental analysis
B.   bandwagon effects
C.   his ability to take very large positions
D.   all of the above
E.   none of the above

d, medium, 273

#9-41 The British Central Bank, in an attempt to prevent a fall in the value of the pound, spent over 20 billion buying Deutsche marks in 1992. What was the net effect on this for British tax payers
A   it had no effect on British tax payers
B.   British taxpayers benefited at the expense of George Soros
C.   they lost a great deal of money after the pound subsequently fell
D.   none of the above

c, medium, 273

#9-42 Which of the following countries had the slowest growth in money supply in the late 1980s
A   Turkey
B.   Poland
C.   Britain
D.   US
E.   Japan

e, medium, 280

#9-43 Which of the following countries had the smallest increase in consumer prices in the late 1980s
A   Ecuador
B.   Portugal
C.   Turkey
D.   Britain
E.   China

d, medium, 2880

#9-44 When the growth in a country's money supply is faster than the growth in output, its
A   currency is likely to depreciate
B.   likely to experience inflation
C.   nominal interest rates will be higher than its real interest rates
D.   all of the above
E.   none of the above

d, medium, 281

#9-45 Which of the following countries experienced lower inflation than Canada between 1973-93
A   Italy
B.   US
C.   Britain
D.   Germany
E.   all of the above

d, hard, 282

#9-46 Bolivia experienced hyperinflation in the mid-1980s
A   this completely contradicted what would be predicted by the law of one price
B.   this completely contradicted what would be predicted by the theory of purchasing power parity
C.   this completely contradicted what would be predicted by the international Fisher effect
D.   all of the above
E.   none of the above

e, medium, 282

#9-47 Which of the following may be best at explaining short term exchange rate changes
A   interest rate changes
B.   inflation rate changes
C.   bandwagon effects
D.   price levels
E.   Fischer effects

c, easy, 285

#9-48 Bandwagon effects
A   ease prediction of long run exchange rate changes
B.   are hard to predict
C.   rarely earn money for traders that "get on the bandwagon"
D.   all of the above
E.   none of the above

b, medium, 285

#9-49 Which of the following did NOT contribute to the collapse of the Russian ruble in the early 1990s
A   over supply of goods
B.   a high inflation rate
C.   liberalization of prices
D.   over supply of rubles
E.   budget deficits financed by printing rubles

a, medium, 291

#9-50 Prior to 1992, the Russian ruble was
A   overvalued relative to the US dollar
B.   freely traded on foreign exchange markets
C.   in short supply in Russia
D.   was pegged at 125 rubles to the US dollar by the US government
E.   none of the above

a, medium, 291

#9-51Q: Define what a foreign exchange risk is for a company.

#9-51A: A foreign exchange risk is a risk that the value of currencies will change in the future, making current business plans of company potentially inappropriate.

#9-52Q: An American tourist stops at a T-shirt shop on the Italian-French border, and finds one that she wants. The enterprising shopkeeper has the shirt priced in four different currencies. Given that $1 = 2DM = 1500Lira = 6 FFranc = .6BPounds, and that the T-shirt can be bought for 25DM, 17000 Lira, 70 FFrancs, or 6BPounds, show what the T-shirt would cost in US$ with all of these currencies. If the tourist had enough of any of the currencies in her pocket to buy the shirt, which currency should she use if she wants to pay the least.

#9-52A: The T-shirt would cost in US dollars:
$$25DM * (1\$/2DM) = \$12.50$$
$$17000Lira * (1\$/1500Lira) = \$11.33$$
$$70Franc * (1\$/6Franc) = \$11.67$$
$$6Pounds * (1\$/.6Pounds) = \$10.00$$
Hence the best deal would be to buy the shirt with British Pounds.

#9-53Q: Why do international businesses utilize foreign exchange markets?

#9-53A: There are four main reasons why international businesses utilize foreign exchange markets. First, the payments a company receives for its exports, the income it receives from foreign investments, or the income it receives from licensing agreements with foreign firms, may all be in a foreign currency. In order to use those funds in its home country, the company will have to convert them to its home currency. Second, international businesses use foreign exchange markets when they have to pay a foreign company in a foreign currency for its products or services. Third, international businesses use foreign exchange markets when they have spare cash that they wish to invest for the short term in foreign markets. The fourth reason for utilizing foreign exchange markets is currency speculation.

#9-54Q: Why might not the Law of One Price hold for a bottle of a particular brand of Scotch Whisky that can be bought in both the US and Scotland, assuming its readily available on store shelves in either place?

#9-54A: The law of one price assumes no transportation costs and efficient markets. Hence since it costs something to transport the whiskey from Scotland to the US, the price may be higher in the US. But taxes can also affect prices, and if the US taxes whiskey less than Scotland, then the same brand of whiskey might cost more in Scotland one mile from where it was made than it does all the way across the Atlantic Ocean.

#9-55Q: Why do forward exchange markets exist for many currencies? Why do they not exist for others?

#9-55A: Forward exchange markets allow firms to avoid the risks of currency fluctuations by locking in specific rates for future transactions. Between countries where firms transact a great deal of business, there is sufficient demand for forward exchange going both directions that markets for forward contracts can exist. For some other countries with lesser direct exchange (e.g. between Pakistan and France), there is unlikely to be sufficient demand for forward markets to exist.

#9-56Q: Why are there differences between the spot rate and the forward rate for a particular currency transaction?

#9-56A: Differences between the spot and the forward rate for a currency transaction reflect the market's expectation about future movements in the exchange rate. Hence if the market thinks a currency will depreciate, its value in the forward market will be less than its value on the spot market

#9-57Q: Why is the US dollar referred to as a vehicle currency?

#9-57A: Due to its central role in so many transactions, the dollar is sometimes referred to as a vehicle currency. While foreign exchange transactions can in theory involve any two currencies, many transactions involve dollars. Thus is true even when a dealer wants to sell one non-dollar currency and buy another. This is because the volume of transactions in dollars with other currencies is so high that it may be cheaper and more expedient for a trader to exchange French francs for dollars and then these dollars for Philippine pesos than it would be to try and execute a transaction directly between these relatively minor currencies. There will be plenty of other traders willing to trade dollars for pesos or francs, but few interested in trading pesos for francs.

#9-58Q: Under what conditions is inflation likely?

#9-58A: When the growth in a country's money supply is greater than the growth in its output, inflation is likely.

#9-59Q: What does the empirical testing of the purchasing power parity theory suggest? When does PPP tend to hold, and when doesn't it?

#9-59A: While PPP theory seems to yield relatively accurate predictions in the long run (i.e. several years), it does not hold up in the short run. Moreover, the theory seems to work best in predicting the exchange rate movements of countries with very high rates of inflation and underdeveloped capital markets. PPP theory is less useful in predicting exchange rate movements between advanced industrialized nations that have relatively small differentials in relative inflation rates.

#9-60Q: What is the international Fisher effect? What does it predict?

#9-60A: The international Fisher effect suggests a relation between exchange rate changes and differences in nominal exchange rates. More specifically, it states that for any two countries, the spot exchange rate should change in an equal amount but in the opposite direction to the difference in nominal interest rates between the two countries.

#9-61Q: Why does the efficient market school argue that forward rates are the best unbiased predictors of future spot rates? Is an unbiased predictor an accurate one? Why, or why not?

#9-61A: The efficient market school believes that all relevant factors go into the determination of forward rates. Hence, traders' best estimates of inflation, interest rates, monetary and fiscal policy, trends in exchange rates, and overall national economic health are taken into consideration when forward rates are determined by the market. The forward exchange rates reflect all available information about what could affect future exchange rates. Forward rates are not perfect predictors, however they are unbiased. Unbiased estimates still have inaccuracies, but the inaccuracies are random - the inaccuracies are not consistently above or below the future spot rate and are not predictable.

#9-62Q: "The technical analysis approach to forecasting exchange rates has no grounding in economic theory, and hence should not be used." Critically evaluate this statement.

#9-62A: The first part of this statement is true - the technical analysis approach to forecasting exchange rates has no grounding in economic theory. It simply looks at past trends and suggests that the future may be determined by the past, regardless of underlying economic fundamentals. Yet technical analysis still has a useful place if it makes accurate predictions. Most currency traders and firms would much rather have an accurate prediction of a future exchange rate (regardless of the method) than an inaccurate prediction that was based on sound economic reasoning and fundamentals that didn't hold in a given situation. Hence technical analysis should be used when there is a good reason to believe that it yields accurate predictions.

#9-63Q: Why do governments restrict the convertibility of their currencies?

#9-63A: The main reason governments limit convertibility is to protect foreign exchange reserves and prevent capital flight.

CHAPTER 10

Students should be encouraged to choose the BEST answer, as more than one may be technically correct. Following each question is the answer, estimated difficulty, and page reference.

#10-1 The Bretton Woods agreement called for
A   each exchange rate to be fixed to a gold standard
B.   fixed exchange rates
C.   freely floating exchange rates
D.   exchange rates within the EMS to move only within a small band
E.   a set "managed" floating exchange rates

b, medium, 294

#10-2 In 1980 Caterpillar
A   had a loss of over $1billion.
B.   was second only to Komatsu in market share outside Japan
C.   was the third largest exporter in the US
D.   had over 71% of the world market
E.   realized that it was in a difficult position due to the strength of the dollar

c, hard, 316

#10-3 A strong US dollar
A   helped Caterpillar make inroads into the Japanese market
B.   allowed Caterpillar to price its machines 40% below Komatsu's
C.   has long been advocated by Caterpillar in order to improve its international position.
D.   helped Caterpillar become the low bidder for many third world orders
E.   significantly hurt Caterpillar's cost structure vis-à-vis Komatsu's

e, easy, 316

#10-4 Which statement best describes the current relationship between the world's different currencies.
A   Most currencies are now free floating.
B.   Most third world currencies are pegged to gold, while most industrialized countries have free floating currencies.
C.   Less than one quarter of the world's currencies freely float, and many of those are better described as a "dirty float" (i.e. the US dollar).
D.   Most European countries and their former colonies peg their exchange rate directly to the ECU

c, medium, 294

#10-5 As of 1900, most of the major trading nations of the world
A   were on the gold standard
B.   had their currencies pegged to the dollar
C.   were using SDRs for international exchange
D.   had their currencies roughly pegged to the British Pound
E.   were still using gold and silver coins, so there were no problems with exchange rates

a, easy, 295

#10-6 A country is in a balance of trade equilibrium when

A   the outflow of its currency is equal to the inflow of currency from other countries.
B.   it has not had a revaluation in its currency for over one year.
C.   the income its residents earn from exports is equal to the money paid to foreigners to purchase imports.
D.   the capital account and the current account sum to zero.
E.   its products can be sold overseas for the same price as they are sold for domestically.

c, hard, 296

#10-7 Why did the gold standard collapse?

A   After the Germans were forced to devalue the mark, other Europeans and eventually the US, lost confidence it the future stability of the mark.
B.   World War I had wreaked havoc in the gold mines, causing a shortage of gold and limited convertibility.
C.   A large increase in the US money supply forced it to devalue the dollar, which due to the key role of the dollar in the system, forced other countries off the gold standard
D.   A series of competitive devaluations led to a demand for gold, forcing countries to suspend convertibility.
E.   After World War II and the devastation of the World Bank, no one had confidence that the security of nations gold reserves could be assured.

d, medium, 297

#10-8 The Bretton Woods conference established all of the following EXCEPT:

A   the IMF
B.   the IBRD
C.   the ERM
D.   the World Bank
E.   a fixed exchange rate system

c, easy, 297

#10-9 The original goal of the IMF was to

A   provide loans to help with the reconstruction of Europe
B.   provide funds on a short term basis to countries during balance of payments deficits
C.   monitor exchange rates and intervene in currency markets to support fixed exchange rates
D.   lend to developing countries to help improve their infrastructure

b, hard, 297

#10-10 Under the Bretton Woods system, which currency served as the base currency?

A   SDR
B.   German Mark
C.   British Pound
D.   ECU
E.   US dollar

e, easy, 299

#10-11 Which of the following was NOT part of the Jamaica accord?
A   floating exchange rates were declared acceptable
B.   gold was abandoned as a reserve asset
C.   the funding for the IMF was increased
D.   less developed countries were given less access and stricter guidelines for use of IMF funds
E.   countries were permitted to enter the foreign exchange market to even out unwarranted speculative fluctuations

d, medium, 301

#10-12 The rise in the value of the dollar between 1980 and 1985 occurred
A   in spite of a large US trade deficit
B.   as a result of the large US trade deficit
C.   due to strong growth in most other developed countries
D.   in spite of high nominal interest rates
E.   in spite of a large outflow of capital from the US

a, medium, 302

#10-13 The members of the "Group of Five" that signed the Plaza Accord included all of the following EXCEPT:
A   Japan
B.   France
C.   Germany
D.   USSR (as it was called at that time)
E.   US

d, medium, 303

#10-14 The key agreement in the Plaza Accord was a decision to
A   strengthen the value of the Yen relative to other currencies
B.   weaken the value of the dollar relative to other currencies
C.   return to the gold standard after currencies had stabilized
D.   rescind the agreement they had made in the earlier Louvre Accord
E.   restrict access to World Bank funds to those countries that pursued conservative economic practices

b, hard, 303

#10-15 The currency with the greatest weight in the ECU is the
A   British Pound
B.   French Franc
C.   German Mark
D.   US Dollar
E.   Italian Lira

c, medium, 308

#10-16 Which country is NOT a member of the ERM?
A   Germany
B.   France
C.   Luxembourg
D.   Greece
E.   Switzerland

e, medium, 308 (its not in the EU either)

#10-17 Britain and Italy left the ERM in 1992 because of
A   fundamental disequilibria in their economies that could not be corrected in the short term
B.   a disagreement with Germany over the role of the Bundesbank
C.   a argument with France over the location of the European central bank
D.   intense speculative pressure that was driving down their currency values
E.   their failure in meeting the fiscal policy requirements of the ERM

d, medium, 309

#10-18 Which statement best describes how industrialized countries have utilized the IMF funds over the past twenty years.
A   they have occasionally used the funds to temporarily prop up their weak currencies
B.   they have rarely borrowed funds from the IMF
C.   they frequently use IMF funds to help in the development of poorer regions of their countries
D.   they frequently use IMF funds to help blunt short term speculative pressures
E.   they use IMF funds only when funds are not available in the global capital markets

b, hard, 310

#10-19 Which statement best describes world wide interest rates during the early 1980s?
A   Rising short term interest rates increased the costs of debt.
B.   While short term interest rates remained low, long term rates skyrocketed, limiting long term investment.
C.   A dramatic fall in interest rates resulted in the funding of many ill-advised investments.
D.   High European interest rates, compared to low rates in the US, resulted in a huge outflow of funds from the US
E.   Although nominal short term interest rates fell, the real rate rose slightly in the US and Europe.

a, medium, 310

#10-20 Which third world country was the first to announce that it could not make its scheduled debt payments in the 1980s?
A   Brazil
B.   Turkey
C.   Mexico
D.   Liberia
E.   Pakistan

c, easy, 310

#10-21 Which statement best describes the current relationship between the IMF and the World Bank?
A   they are scheduled to merge in 1998
B.   the IMF is restricted to short term loans, while the World Bank is restricted to funding infrastructure and development projects
C.   the IMF is the financing arm of the World Bank
D.   the world bank is part of the IMF
E.   they are separate organizations, but the line delineating their current objectives is blurred

e, medium, 311

#10-22 When the World Bank examined a number of its less successful loans, it found
A   that most of the projects had never been completed, and the funds had ended up in the hands of crooked politicians
B.   many of the loans were ill-advised in the first place
C.   many projects were not carefully thought through (i.e. a mine was constructed without a railroad or port facilities to get the ore out for export
D.   that the broader macro-economic mismanagement of a country was limiting the effectiveness of projects
E.   that it had no records as to how the loan money was spent in most situations

d, medium, 312

#10-23 Given the evolution and development of world capital markets,
A   there is significant debate and questioning about whether the IMF and World Bank any longer serve a useful purpose.
B.   the level of speculation in the currency markets is likely to continue to decrease.
C.   industrialized countries have increasing autonomy over their own monetary policy, and are less impacted by IMF regulations
D.   it is increasingly difficult for firms to raise money in their domestic capital markets

a, hard, 312

#10-24 The present exchange rate system
A   decreases the cost of international business compared to the previous fixed rate system, as currency conversion is a much simpler process under floating exchange rates.
B.   makes it incumbent on firms to carefully limit their exposure to volatile speculative pressures.
C.   suggests that there are good opportunities for manufacturing firms like Allied-Lyons and Caterpillar to get into the currency trading business.
D.   decreases the need for strategic flexibility since exchange rates can move quite freely
E.   is the worst possible system from the perspective of business

b, medium, 312

#10-25 Dispersing production facilities to different locations around the world
A   is an example of the high costs floating exchange rates impose on business
B.   provides for greater strategic flexibility
C.   is an irrational response to exchange rate fluctuations
D.   should be done only for low value added manufacturing

b, easy, 313

#10-26 For the most part, international businesses
A   can ignore the actions of the IMF and World Bank, as these organizations' influence is rapidly
           waning.
B.   should be aware that the tight lending practices of the World Bank and the IMF limit growth
           opportunities in many countries.
C.   should avoid doing business in countries that have had strict controls placed on them by
           international lending agencies.
D.   should be aware that in the long run the current policies of the IMF and World Bank can promote
           economic growth and expand demand for products
E.   should not try to bid on contracts put out by the World Bank, but carefully consider those of the
           IMF.

d, medium, 314

#10-27 The Brady Plan
A   was implemented in the US congress by the Brady Bill
B.   resulted in a 12% devaluation of the US dollar
C.   was shot down by opponents that preferred the Plaza Accord
D.   focused on the reduction of third world countries' debt
E.   was named after James Brady, a speech writer and aide to US President Ronald Reagan

d, hard, 311

#10-28 Which of the following statements is true about US macro-economic data from 1964-72?
A   there was a slow and steady increase in the money supply growth rate
B.   there was a steady and rapid increase in the government purchases growth rate
C.   the current account was in surplus until the very end of this period
D.   the inflation rate was on average about 5%

c, hard, 300

#10-29 The US dollar reached its lowest level, as measured against most other major currencies,
A   in 1985
B.   just before the Plaza agreement
C.   shortly after the oil crisis ended in 1976
D.   at the time of the Jamaica agreement
E.   shortly after the Louve Accord

e, medium, 300

#10-30 Which statement best describes Cat's earnings and the foreign exchange market?
A   Cat made a great deal of money in the foreign exchange market in the early 1980s, enough to
           wipe out its losses from continuing operations.
B.   By taking a conservative policy and hedging, Cat was able to avoid significant losses in the
           foreign exchange market.
C.   Cat's earnings benefited greatly from the fall in the dollar following the Plaza agreement.
D.   Cat lost a great deal of money from unwise and uncovered speculation in the currency markets.

c, medium, 317

#10-31 The Plaza Accord was signed
A   after the failure of the Louvre Accord
B.   in Plaza, Brazil
C.   in order to stabilize the value of the US dollar
D.   when the dollar was put back on the gold standard
E.   in New York at a hotel

e, medium, 303

#10-32 What was the general reaction of the US auto industry to NAFTA
A   very favorable
B.   it opposed NAFTA out of fear of cheap Mexican imports
C.   it lobbied against it because the entire US market would then be opened to Canadian firms
D.   indifference
E.   it quickly closed a number of inefficient Mexican plants since it could now supply the growing
         Mexican market with duty free exports from the US

a, hard, 293

#10-33 What happened to sales of US autos in Mexico in 1994
A   they grew dramatically
B.   they fell back to the levels of 1990 following the peso crisis in 1993
C.   they held steady in spite of the difficult recession following the peso devaluation
D.   none of the above

a, medium, 293

#10-34 Why was the Mexican peso pegged to the US dollar from the early 1980s to the mid 1990s
A   IMF conditions on its loans that were intended to force Mexico to adopt tight financial policies
B.   after the US had bailed Mexico out in the early 1980s, Mexico graciously asked to peg the peso to
         the US dollar
C.   it was required under NAFTA rules
D.   to prevent speculative pressures for devaluation of the peso
E.   none of the above

a, medium, 294

#10-35 Why did the Mexican peso fall dramatically in value in 1994
A   Mexico had a huge trade deficit
B.   gradual exchange rate changes did not reflect ongoing inflation rates
C.   speculation and bandwagon effects
D.   all of the above
E.   none of the above

d, medium, 294

#10-36 The initial mission of the World Bank, as set out at the Bretton Woods conference
A   was to assist the IBRD in providing loans to developing countries in Asia and Africa
B.   was to serve as the depository agency for the IMF
C.   enabled it to overcome the subsequent disruption caused by German takeover in Austria
D.   was effectively taken over by the Marshall Plan
E.   none of the above

d, hard, 298

#10-37 The International Development Agency
A   is an arm of the World Bank
B.   provides lower interest rate loans than the IBRD scheme
C.   is funded directly by the governments of the richest nations
D.   all of the above
E.   none of the above

d, medium, 299

#10-38 The exchange rate of the US dollar over the past ten years has been
A   determined primarily by free market forces in foreign exchange market
B.   basically stable as a result of the Plaza Accord
C.   has moved only when forced by speculative pressures for devaluation
D.   affected by both market forces and governmental intervention
E.   pegged to a basket of currencies, including the German mark and the Canadian dollar

d, medium, 304

#10-39 The exchange rate between the US and Japan from 1971 to 1995
A   stayed relatively constant as a result of periodic governmental intervention
B.   changed as would be generally expected by differences in inflation rates
C.   did not reflect the large investments that the Japanese had made in the US
D.   suggested that the Japanese Yen was overvalued by the market
E.   none of the above

b, hard, 304

#10-40 Between 1993 and 1995
A   the Japanese Yen appreciated 50% relative to the US dollar
B.   Japanese financial institutions heavily invested in US assets
C.   the Beatles recorded their 37th album
D.   all of the above
E.   none of the above

a, medium, 305

#10-41 Which US president suspended the US dollar's gold convertibility
A   Lyndon Johnson
B.   John Kennedy
C.   Richard Nixon
D.   Jimmy Carter
E.   Ronald Reagan

c, medium, 300

#10-42 Which of the following is NOT an advantage of a floating exchange rate system
A   countries have greater monetary autonomy
B.   trade imbalances are adjusted through exchange rate changes
C.   less likelihood of speculative pressures forcing devaluations and large exchange rate changes
D.   greater uncertainty over future exchange rates

d, easy, 306

#10-43 Fixed exchange rates
A   encourage monetary discipline
B.   are not susceptible to speculative trading and bandwagon effects
C.   increase uncertainty over future exchange rates
D.   all of the above
E.   none of the above

a, easy, 306

#10-44 The EMS after 1992
A   provides much more rigid bands for currencies than it did in earlier years
B.   requires that countries with strong currencies also intervene to quell speculative pressures
C.   has worked much more effectively since Britain and Italy re-entered the system
D.   has worked effectively to eliminate any speculative pressures for devaluation of currencies
E.   none of the above

e, medium, 309

#10-45 Which of the following is NOT a recipient of IMF loans
A   Mexico
B.   Russia
C.   Ukraine
D.   Qatar
E.   Brazil

d, easy, 309-312 (Qatar is an oil rich country)

#10-46 Which agreement called for a devaluation of the US dollar
A   Plaza Accord
B.   Bretton Woods
C.   Brady Plan
D.   Louvre Accord
E.   Jamaica Agreement

a, medium, 303

#10-47 Which agreement was the first to declare that gold was not a reserve currency
A   Bretton Woods
B.   Louvre Accord
C.   Honda Accord
D.   Jamaica Agreement
E.   Brady Plan

d, medium, 301

#10-48 The Jamaica Agreement
A   established that the Jamaican dollar should be pegged to the US dollar
B.   accepted what had been de facto true for several years - exchange rates could float
C.   decreased the level of funding available to the IMF
D.   transferred more responsibility to the World Bank
E.   all of the above

b, hard, 301

#10-49 Between 1970 and 1994
A   the trade weighted value of the US dollar fluctuated considerably
B.   the world transformed from a generally fixed exchange rate system to a managed float system
C.   the Japanese Yen and German Mark both appreciated relative to the US dollar
D.   all of the above
E.   none of the above

d, easy, 299-303

#10-50 The Plaza Accord and the Louvre Accord demonstrate
A.   show how difficult it is to get any lasting commitment to stable exchange rates
B.   that governments when acting together can affect exchange rates
C.   the futility of governmental intervention
D.   that governments usually only can reach agreement after markets have forced a decision
E.   all of the above

b, medium, 312

#10-51Q: Why did Cat lose so much money and market share in the early 1980s? In retrospect, what could have it done to prevent these losses?

#10-51A: Cat's market share and financial losses were the result of an overall high cost structure (including low productivity), a large drop in the market in LDCs as a part of the third world debt crisis, and the strong dollar. After it realized the extent of its cost problems, Cat did close factories and significantly cut costs, but this could have been done sooner. It also could have shifted more of its production to its overseas sites, where the strong dollar would not have had as much effect. There is not much it could have done, however, about the fallout from the third world debt crisis.

#10-52Q: Explain how the automatic adjustment mechanism for balancing trade disequilibrium works under the gold standard.

#10-52A: The mechanism for trade balance disequilibrium adjustment can be most easily described with an example. Suppose that there are only two countries in the world - Japan and the US. Imagine that Japan's trade balance is in surplus because Japan exports more to the US than it imports from the US. Japanese exporters are paid in US$, which they exchange into Japanese Yen at a Japanese bank. In turn, the Japanese bank submits the $ to the US government for gold. It follows that under the gold standard when Japan has a trade surplus there will be a net flow of gold out of the US and into Japan. These gold flows automatically reduce the US money supply and increase Japan's. The increase in Japan's money supply will raise prices in Japan, while in the US prices will fall. The higher prices for Japanese goods will reduce their attractiveness in the US, while US goods will look more attractive in Japan. Thus Japan will start to buy more from the US and the US will buy less from Japan until the trade balance is again in equilibrium. This same logic can be extended to any number of countries.

#10-53Q: What were the primary points of the Bretton Woods agreement?

#10-53A: The Bretton Woods agreement established a system of fixed exchange rates, where the US$ was pegged to gold and other currencies were pegged to the US$. It also created the IMF, which was to help countries overcome short term monetary problems, and the World Bank, to help finance long term reconstruction and development.

#10-54Q: Historically, in what way were the funds of the World Bank used? How have the World Bank's lending practices changed, and why?

#10-54A: In the 1950s the World Bank concentrated its funds on public sector projects like power stations, road building, and other transportation and infrastructure investments. During the 1960s the World Bank also began lending to support farming, education, population control, and urban development. But by the 1970s the bank noticed that many of its specific loan projects were failing to produce the long term economic gains originally envisioned, not because the projects per se were defective, but because poor macro economic policies made even a good project in a bad economy a bad project. As a result, the World Bank now provides funds not just to support particular projects, but also for governments to use as they see fit in return for commitments on macro economic policy.

#10-55Q: Describe the special role of the US dollar in the fixed exchange rate system of the 1950s and 1960s.

#10-55A: The US dollar was pegged to and convertible into gold, while all other major currencies were pegged to the dollar.

#10-56Q: What explains the rise in the value of the US dollar between 1980-85? Why was the demand for dollars greater than the supply, even though the US was running a large trade deficit?

#10-56A: The US dollar rose in the early 1980s in spite of the trade deficit. Strong economic growth in the US attracted heavy inflows of capital from foreign investors seeking high returns on capital assets. Moreover, high real interest rates attracted foreign investors seeking high returns on financial assets. At the same time, political turmoil in other parts of the world, along with relatively slow economic growth in the developed countries of Europe, helped create the view that the US was a good place for investment. These inflows of capital increased the demand for dollars in the foreign exchange market, which pushed the value of the dollar upwards against other currencies.

#10-57Q: What is the difference between a free floating exchange rate and a "managed" or "dirty float system"?

#10-57A: In a free floating system there is no governmental intervention in the market, while in a dirty or managed float system governments intervene to influence the value of their currency.

#10-58Q: Under a system of freely floating exchange rates, how would trade balance disequilibria be adjusted?

#10-58A: Under a freely floating system if a country is running a trade deficit, the imbalance between the supply and demand of that country's currency in the foreign exchange markets (supply will exceed demand) will lead to a depreciation of its exchange rate. In turn, by making its exports cheaper, and its imports more expensive, an exchange rate depreciation should ultimately correct the trade deficit.

#10-59Q: "Under a fixed exchange rate system there will be no speculation, and hence no major changes in the value of currencies. This reduction in uncertainty will be good for business." Critically evaluate these statements.

#10-59A: To say that under fixed exchange rates there will be no uncertainty nor major changes in the value of currencies is to forget the lessons of history. If the economic fundamentals are such that an exchange rate change must be made, there is nothing that can be done to keep speculation from pushing a currency to the brink. Thus unless countries have entirely consistent economic policies and growth rates, the time will come when a fixed exchange rate will have to be changed. Given that this change will then likely come as a big adjustment (rather than the minor ones under a floating system) the effects on businesses may be more devastating and less insurable, than under a flexible system. Thus while fixed exchange rates many have good features for businesses, nothing can truly be fixed as long as separate countries, currencies, and economic policies persist.

#10-60Q: Given the current volatility in exchange rates, what actions can firms take to develop strategic flexibility?

#10-60A: Strategic flexibility can be gained by having production facilities in different locations world wide, and shifting production volumes to take advantage of favorable exchange rates. By contracting out low value added manufacturing, firms can also switch suppliers in order to adjust to changing exchange rates.

CHAPTER 11

Students should be encouraged to choose the BEST answer, as more than one may be technically correct. Following each question is the answer, estimated difficulty, and page reference.

#11-1 What was the reaction on the Belgium stock market to Biomedex's announcement that it was going to offer shares on the New York exchange.
A   Belgian officials were enraged the Biomedex was turning its back on its home market.
B.   Biomedex's stock price remained virtually unchanged.
C.   Investors were pleased by Biomedex's international acceptance, and share prices rose slightly.
D.   Other Belgian biotechnology stocks saw their share prices rise, as this indicated that increased funding may also be available for them.
E.   Biomedex's stock price fell 15%.

e, medium, 319

#11-2 Why did Biomedex look to international capital markets?
A   limited liquidity and a conservative mentality in its domestic capital market
B.   it anticipated that the Belgian currency would be appreciating in the near future, thus lowering the cost of capital
C.   the high integration between the Belgian and international markets made the transition easy.
D.   other biotechnology firms like Cetus and Genentech had recently floated Eurobond offerings

a, easy, 319

#11-3 Which of the following statistics is incorrect?
A   The stock of international bank lending rose from $324 billion to $7.5 trillion during 1980-91.
B.   While the Eurobond market grew at a compound annual rate of 22% between 1980 and 1988, the foreign bond market grew at an even greater 27% rate.
C.   In 1982 the total outstanding international bonds were $259million; by 1991 it was $1.65 trillion.
D.   In 1970 America's securities transactions with foreigners amounted to the equivalent of 3% of GDP. By 1990 was 93%.

b, hard, 320

#11-4 Which statement best describes the role of market makers?
A   Market makers arrange for the sale of new issues of stock.
B.   The liquidity of equities in the equity markets is insured by market makers.
C.   The electronic network of buyers and sellers is maintained by market makers.
D.   They are the financial service companies that connect investors to borrowers.

d, medium, 321

#11-5 Under which type of financial instrument do firms pay funds to investors in an amount determined by the board of directors, dependent upon the firm's profitability.
A   foreign bond
B.   Eurobond
C.   equity
D.   Eurocurrency

c, easy, 322

#11-6 The systematic risk faced by an investor

A   from holding 10 international stocks is lower than if an investor held 50 domestic stocks.

B.   is increased with increasing internationalization of a portfolio due to exchange rate risks.

C.   is about 27% for international stocks and 12% for US stocks.

D.   with international stocks is lower than that of an investor with only domestic stocks due to the lower correlation between stock returns in these portfolios

E.   is lower in equity investments than in bond investments

d, medium, 325

#11-7 International capital markets

A   are regulated by the IMF.

B.   are all outside the control of national governments.

C.   have grown partially as a result of de-regulation.

D.   require the disclosure of the international financial risks of firms.

E.   almost collapsed after the "Big Bang" of October 1986.

c, medium, 328

#11-8 Which international financial centers are in "tier one" according to a 1989 study of centers?

A   New York and London

B.   London, Frankfurt, New York, and Tokyo

C.   Tokyo and London

D.   New York, Zurich, Frankfurt, London, and Tokyo

E.   only London

a, hard, 329

#11-9 In 1990, seven of the world's top ten commercial banks when measured by asset value were Japanese banks. From this fact

A   it is incorrect to draw conclusions about their international presence since their value is biased upward by the unusually strong yen at this time.

B.   it can not be concluded that the Japanese banks are now the dominant market makers in the international market.

C.   it is clear that the Japanese banks have one of the most extensive foreign networks.

D.   one can conclude that their volume of international business must be greater than that of other countries banks.

E.   alone one can assume that there are high barriers to entry into the Japanese financial markets.

b, medium, 320-338

#11-10 A Eurocurrency

A   is typically denominated in ECU's.

B.   can be denominated in any European currency, but not in other currencies.

C.   will likely come into being by 1995, if the current trends in Europe continue.

D.   cannot be exchanged for a non-Eurocurrency.

E.   is any currency banked outside the country that issued it.

e, medium, 330

#11-11 The most common Eurocurrency is
A   Pound
B.   Dollar
C.   Mark
D.   Franc
E.   Yen

b, easy, 330

#11-12 What makes Eurocurrency loans attractive to borrowers?
A   The lack of regulation allows firms to disclose less information to their bankers.
B.   The spread is less on Eurocurrencies than domestic currencies.
C.   Borrower's reserve requirements are lower.
D.   Banks typically charge lower interest rates for Eurocurrency loans than for loans denominated in
         the domestic currency.
E.   They can earn higher interest rates on deposits.

d, medium, 332

#11-13 Foreign bonds are sold
A   inside the borrower's country and denominated in the currency of another country.
B.   inside the borrower's country and funded by foreign investors.
C.   outside the borrower's country and denominated in the currency of the country they are issued.
D.   outside the borrower's country and denominated in the currency of the borrower's country.

c, medium, 334

#11-14 A bond issued by a German corporation, denominated in Swiss francs, and sold to investors in the
US, Saudi Arabia, and Japan is
A   a Eurobond.
B.   a foreign bond
C.   a Eurocurrency transaction
D.   an example of equity financing
E.   illegal under US SEC regulations.

a, easy, 334

#11-15 Foreign bonds
A   are a type of Eurobond that are only sold in one country
B.   are denominated in the currency of the issuing company
C.   are much less common than Eurobonds
D.   are subject to less regulation than Eurobonds in most countries
E.   all of the above

c, hard, 334

#11-16 Which nation's stock exchange had the greatest number of foreign stocks listed?
A   Germany
B.   Britain
C.   US
D.   Japan

b, medium, 337

#11-17 The primary reason for a firm to list its stock on a foreign stock exchange is to
A   diversify its exchange rate risks.
B.   provide for the later issuance of additional securities in that market.
C.   improve its product market position through the visibility.
D.   appease governmental pressures in foreign subsidiaries.

b, hard, 336

#11-18 Which of the following exchanges has the greatest percentage of foreign firms among the stocks listed.
A   New York
B.   London
C.   Zurich
D.   Tokyo
E.   Amsterdam

c, hard, 337

#11-19 Jones Company wishes to raise $2 million in US dollars with debt financing. The funds, needed to finance working capital, will be repaid with interest in one year. If Jones borrows foreign currency it will remain uncovered. That is, it will simply change foreign currency for dollars at today's spot rate and buy foreign currency back one year later at the spot rate then in effect. Jones estimates that the rupee will depreciate 15 %, the pound will depreciate by 5% , the franc will appreciate 2%, and the yen will appreciate 3%, all relative to the dollar during the next year. Which of these options should Jones choose as long as it feels quite confident in its predictions about exchange rates?
A   Borrow US dollars from a US bank at 8%
B.   Borrow British pounds from a British bank at 14%
C.   Borrow Japanese yen from a Japanese bank at 5%
D.   Borrow Swiss francs from a Swiss bank at 5%
E.   Borrow Pakistani Rupees from a Pakistani bank at 28%

d, hard, 337

#11-20 The international capital market can typically provide funds to borrowers at
A   a higher rate than a domestic market
B.   the same rate as a domestic market
C.   a lower rate than the domestic market
D.   a lower rate than the domestic market for short term, but not long term lending.
E.   a higher rate than a domestic market for short term, but not long term lending

c, easy, 338

#11-21 The Fine Fly tackle company, a US based company with primarily domestic sales, is fishing around for a loan to help it expand production of its new flies. It could borrow money from a domestic bank at 10%, a Canadian bank at 12%, a British bank at 8%, a German bank at 6%, and a Finnish bank at 14%. It will not cover any exchange rate risk, and expects over the next year the Canadian dollar to depreciate by 1%, the pound to appreciate by 2%, the mark to appreciate by 4%, and the Finnish Markka to depreciate by 10%. From which country's bank should it choose to borrow if it plans to pay back the full interest and principal in one year.

A   British
B.   German
C.   Finnish
D.   Canadian
E.   US

c, medium, 337

#11-22 Which statement best describes the relationship between the forward market and the exchange rate risk of long term borrowings.

A   The forward market is a very good way to limit this type of exchange rate risk.
B.   The forward market can only be used to moderately cover this type of exchange rate risk.
C.   The forward market is not intended to cover this type of exchange rate risk.
D.   The forward market is not intended to cover any sort of exchange rate risk.
E.   The forward market can only be used to cover this sort of exchange rate risk if the investor also uses a simultaneous currency swap.

c, medium, 338

#11-23 The advantages of borrowing in the international capital market always have to be weighed against the increased

A   currency risk
B.   regulation
C.   spread of interest rates
D.   disclosure requirements

a, easy, 338

#11-24 Investors can best diversify their risks by

A   having a diversified domestic portfolio
B.   having a few foreign stocks included in their diversified domestic portfolio
C.   investing in European denominated Eurocurrencies
D.   having a diversified mix of domestic and foreign equities

d, easy, 338

#11-25 Which statement best describes the current state of Europe's capital markets?

A   They are highly integrated, with the exception of Britain.
B.   They are rather fragmented and introspective.
C.   The members of the EC have highly integrated markets, but non-EC members are excluded.
D.   They are quite open to foreign investors and equity issues from North America. and Japan

b, hard, 338

#11-26 By the time the New York Stock Exchange opens,

A   the Tokyo exchange has already closed.
B.   the London exchange has already closed
C.   both the London and Tokyo exchanges have closed.
D.   the London exchange has already been open for 6 hours
E.   the Bahrain exchange has closed.

a, easy, 327

#11-27 When the Tokyo exchange closes the

A   Singapore exchange has already closed
B.   Hong Kong exchange has already closed
C.   London exchange has not yet opened
D.   Bahrain exchange has not yet opened
E.   Toronto exchange opens

c, hard, 327

#11-28 Which of these financial centers is in the "second tier"?

A   Bombay
B.   Amsterdam
C.   Toronto
D.   San Francisco
E.   Sydney

b, medium, 332

#11-29 Which country has the earliest market opening most business days

A   Switzerland
B.   Britain
C.   Japan
D.   France
E.   US

c, easy, 327

#11-30 Which of the following is not a function of a commercial bank in the US

A.   holding financial deposits
B.   paying of interest to depositors
C.   issuing their own stock on capital markets
D.   floating new stock offerings for clients
E.   loaning funds to corporations

d, easy, 322

#11-31 For a Swiss corporation interested in raising money, it may be able to raise the money
A.   only in Switzerland because Switzerland is not a member of the European Union
B.   at a lower rate in foreign capital markets because of the larger pool of investors
C.   at a lower rate in foreign capital markets, but it must incur the added regulatory costs associated
          with international capital markets
D.   at a higher rate in foreign capital markets, thereby generating greater long term benefits
E.   only in Switzerland because of the risk of adverse exchange rate changes

b, medium, 322

#11-32 Daimler-Benz has issued stock in all of the following markets EXCEPT
A.   London
B.   Frankfurt
C.   Toronto
D.   New York
E.   Singapore

c, medium, 323

#11-33 Deutsche Telekom is headquartered in which country
A.   France
B.   Germany
C.   Austria
D.   Sweden
E.   Spain

b, easy, 324

#11-34 Deutsche Telekom's primary operations are in
A.   Eastern Europe
B.   the pharmaceutical industry
C.   need of additional funds that must be raised outside its home country as a result of regulatory
          limits
D.   desperate need of cash as a result of mismanagement by the German government and
          catastrophic losses
E.   managing a telephone system

e, medium, 324

#11-35 Why is Deutsche Telekom being privatized
A.   it has been losing money for decades
B.   EU regulations prohibiting state owned enterprises
C.   loss of market share in its home country
D.   all of the above
E.   none of the above

e, medium, 324

#11-36 Why doesn't Deutsche Telekom believe it will be able to raise all the necessary funds in its home market
A.   market is too small
B.   lack of interest by banks
C.   too many other privatizations are competing for investment funds
D.   all of the above
E.   none of the above

d, easy, 324

#11-37 Why is Deutsche Telekom looking to list equity on the London exchange
A.   to be able to attain investment in pounds, that can then be used for increasing its market share in Britain
B.   to raise visibility for the company in one of its most important markets
C.   to take advantage of the anticipated devaluation of the pound
D.   to have access to investors from around the world that buy stock in London
E.   to reap a first mover advantage over British Telecom

d, easy, 324

#11-38 The risk of exchange rate fluctuations
A.   negates the reduction in systematic risk implied by holding an internationally diverse portfolio
B.   contributes to the low correlation between stock price movements in different countries
C.   can only drive down the higher returns that might be available abroad for investors
D.   has essentially been eliminated as a factor when considering pan-European investments
E.   can drive up the systematic risk of an international investment portfolio

b, hard, 325

#11-39 The reaction of other markets around the world after notorious "Black Monday of October 19, 1987," shows
A.   how correlated many international markets have become, and thus suggests that the amount of systematic risk that is diversifiable internationally may be less than it previously was
B.   illustrates how information technology can rapidly disseminate information
C.   traders must keep abreast of what is happening in all markets, and must anticipate how events in one market can ripple into another
D.   all of the above
E.   none of the above

d, medium, 328

#11-40 When Britain allowed banks and stock brokers to enter each others businesses, this was widely referred to as
A.   Black Monday
B.   the Big Bang
C.   Wide-open Wednesday
D.   the Little Bang
E.   a catastrophe

b, easy, 328

#11-41 A study by Harvard economist Martin Feldstein found that
A.   although significant barriers to global capital flow still exist, savvy investors have the ability to invest just about anywhere by using careful planning
B.   most savings that are earned in a country remain in that country and are rarely invested in long term financial interests outside the home country
C.   the amount of systematic risk inherent in a purely domestic portfolio has decreased over the past decade
D.   the amount of regulation required by firms interested in issuing Eurobonds is severely limiting firms abilities to raise money internationally
E.   contrary to expectations, a well diversified domestic portfolio will frequently outperform an international portfolio once exchange rate risks are taken into consideration

b, hard, 328

#11-42 A country running a persistent current account deficit will
A.   tend to have an appreciating currency
B.   tend to also have a persistent capital account deficit
C.   experience fiscal governmental budget deficits roughly equivalent to the current account deficit
D.   not experience any significant problems as long as foreign investors reinvest money earned from exports into the local economy
E.   none of the above

d, hard, 330

#11-43 Which of the following was NOT a factor that increased the perceived risk of Mexican investments in the early 1990s
A.   an armed uprising in Chiapas
B.   an accelerating inflation rate
C.   an appreciating currency
D.   the assassination of the leading presidential candidate

c, medium, 331

#11-44 Why did London emerge as the leading center of Eurocurrency trading
A.   its pivotal role in financing European reconstruction after World War II
B.   British banks response to governmental regulation in the 1950s
C.   German financial institutions moved there in the 1960s to avoid German regulations
D.   Britain's strong support of European integration and leading role in the EU
E.   all of the above equally contributed to London's emergence

b, hard, 331

#11-45 Which of the following is NOT a second tier financial center
A.   Tokyo
B.   Amsterdam
C.   Frankfurt
D.   Paris
E.   Vienna

e, medium, 332

#11-46 Which of the following is not a name of a foreign bond
A.   bulldog
B.   Yankee bond
C.   Eurobond
D.   samurai bond
E.   all of the above are types of foreign bonds

c, medium, 334

#11-47 Negotiations between German firms and the US SEC regarding listing of German securities on American exchanges remained deadlocked for a long time over
A.   the SEC's insistence that German companies provide accounting information according to US accounting principles
B.   German concerns over US approaches that emphasize quick profits and short term thinking
C.   German use of hidden reserves to prop up profits in bad years
D.   all of the above
E.   none of the above

d, easy, 340

#11-48 Daimler-Benz broke ranks with other German firms over US reporting requirements
A.   because it needed the money
B.   it wanted to illustrate its interest in global cooperation
C.   it had been fighting with German authorities over its listing on the Frankfurt exchange
D.   all of the above
E.   none of the above

a, easy, 340

#11-49 Daimler-Benz is seeking funds from many different markets
A.   so that it can allude regulations regarding the amount of equity offered in any particular market
B.   in order to improve the company's tarnished image throughout the world
C.   so that it can use that money for investments primarily in the region where the money is raised
D.   because of disputes with German regulatory authorities
E.   none of the above

c, medium, 340

#11-50 Foreign firms listing on the US stock exchanges
A.   have been disappointed by the cool reception their offerings have received
B.   have rarely been able to raise additional funds
C.   generally have to pay a higher rate of interest than in their domestic markets
D.   usually encounter resistance from insular American investors
E.   were able to raise significant sums of money from the large market

e, easy, 337

#11-51Q: Why did Biomedex decide to list its shares on the New York Stock Exchange? What was the result? Was this Biomedex's first use of international capital markets?

#11-51A: By listing on the New York Stock Exchange and offering new shares, Biomedex was able to raise funds and increase its number of outstanding shares by about 20%. Given the strong appetite for biotechnology issues in the US by investors willing to take the risks, Biomedex was able to tap into an additional pool of funds. Biomedex had previously listed its shares on the NASDAQ and the London stock exchange, and floated Eurobonds.

#11-52Q: Why didn't Biomedex simply raise funds in its domestic market, rather than undertake the expense and hassle of dealing with international markets?

#11-52A: Because the Belgian market was small, lacked liquidity, and segmented from international markets, it would have been difficult for Biomedex to raise any additional funds in its home market. Even if it were able to raise the funds domestically, it would have likely been at a much higher rate than available internationally due to the market size and the appetite for risk.

#11-53Q: What is the difference between debt and equity? What obligations does each place on the issuer?

#11-53A: (refer to the section on page 322, "The distinction between debt and equity")

#11-54Q: Why are international capital markets needed? What functions do they provide beyond that available in most domestic markets - and especially domestic markets as big as the US or Japan?

#11-54A: There are two reasons why an international capital market offers an improvement over a purely domestic capital market: (1) From a borrower's perspective, it increases the supply of funds available for borrowing and lowers the cost of capital; and (2) from an investor's perspective it provides a wider range of investment opportunities, thereby allowing investors to build a portfolio of international investments that diversifies risk. In the case of small countries, these advantages for both borrowers and investors can be significant. In larger markets investors still benefit from the increased opportunities and risk diversification across less correlated securities, and borrowers also benefit if they are able to raise funds in the same region or country in which they wish to make foreign investments.

#11-55Q: What is a Eurocurrency? What are the advantages of borrowing Eurocurrencies?

#11-55A: A Eurocurrency is any currency that is banked outside of its country of origin. Due to the lack of regulation, the spread under which lenders operate is lower for Eurocurrencies than it is for domestic business. This allows borrowers to have access to money at a lower cost (interest rate) than they would have to pay for domestic funds.

#11-56Q: What is the difference between foreign bonds and Eurobonds? Which are more common?

#11-56A: Foreign bonds are bonds sold outside the borrower's country and denominated in the currency of the country in which they are issued. Eurobonds are typically underwritten by an international syndicate of banks and are placed in countries other than the one in whose currency the bond is denominated. Because of their wider coverage and lesser regulation, Eurobonds are much more common than foreign bonds.

#11-57Q: "Given the international capital markets firms use, it is senseless to any longer refer to firms as 'American' or 'British'. Firms are now truly stateless organizations without nationality." Critically evaluate this statement.

#11-57A: This statement perhaps overstates the current situation, but clearly identifies a trend. Firms are increasingly attracting shareholders from around the world, selling their stock on multiple international exchanges, and floating debt in a number of countries. But this is only true for a small percentage of companies world wide, and even then a majority of the shareholders and the management team are still typically from a single country.

#11-58Q: How do exchange rate changes influence the cost of capital?

#11-58A: (refer to the section on pages 337-8, "Foreign exchange risk and the cost of capital")

#11-59Q: What is the role of "market makers" in the international capital market?

#11-59A: Market makers are the financial service companies that connect investors and borrowers, including brokers, commercial banks, and investment banks.

#11-60Q: Explain how international investing can lower systematic risk for an investor below that which would be possible from a fully diversified domestic portfolio.

#11-60A: Because different economies can be in upswings or recessions at different times, the stock prices of firms that operate largely in one country or the other are likely to change in different directions at different times. Stated more formally, stock market price movements are more highly correlated within a country than stock price movements across different countries. Thus systematic risk can be reduced by holding stocks that have lower correlations in their movements.

CHAPTER 12

Students should be encouraged to choose the BEST answer, as more than one may be technically correct. Following each question is the answer, estimated difficulty, and page reference.

#12-1 Swan's first international expansion was
A   undertaken to lower costs over its previous suppliers
B.   in France to help it develop a designer series
C.   motivated by a need to improve its quality and delivery over that of its foreign suppliers
D.   in a mainland China plant that made inexpensive safety glasses

c, hard, 359

#12-2 Firms can make a profit if they
A   expand to low cost international manufacturing sites
B.   expand sales overseas in order to attain greater economies of scale
C.   have cultural sensitivity and are locally responsive
D.   can sell and charge a price for their output that is greater than the cost of producing it
E.   undertake a transnational strategy

d, easy, 357

#12-3 Why are customers prepared to pay more for a Mercedes Benz than a Hyundai?
A   German engineering and craftsmanship
B.   name brand recognition
C.   Hyundai cars fall apart too easily
D.   the strength of the German mark
E.   superior quality and value created by Mercedes

e, medium, 357

#12-4 A core competence
A   of McDonald's is its ability to create distinctly different menus for each country.
B.   can not serve as the basis of a competitive advantage
C.   is a skill that competitors cannot easily match or imitate.
D.   can be easily transferred between firms by licensing agreements
E.   of Toys "R" Us is its ability to find domestic suppliers for all its toys in each country in which it operates

c, medium, 360

#12-5 McDonald's success worldwide is based
A   on the unique recipe for the Big Mac
B.   its ability to find quality suppliers in each country
C.   achieving economies of scale in production
D.   realizing locational economies
E.   a competence in managing fast food operations

e, easy, 360

#12-6 If a firm bases different value creation activities in those countries where they can be most efficiently performed, it is focusing on realizing

A   locational economies
B.   the benefits of transnational management
C.   economies of scale
D.   the maximum value from its core competencies
E.   the benefits of a multidomestic strategy

a, hard, 361

#12-7 Even if New Zealand has a comparative advantage in the production of automobiles, auto production may not occur there due to

A   low trade barriers
B.   high transportation costs
C.   the need for a multidomestic strategy in New Zealand
D.   the high economies of scale in auto production
E.   other countries having an absolute advantage in automobiles production

b, medium, 362

#12-8 Which statement best describes the relationship between the experience curve and learning effects.

A   the experience curve can be only explained by considering the learning effects that take place
B.   learning effects are more important than experience curve effects in most instances
C.   experience curve effects and learning effects are two different explanations for scale economies
D.   learning effects may be part of the explanation for existence of the experience curve
E.   given the choice, most firms would choose learning effects over the experience curve

d, hard, 363

#12-9 Learning effects are

A   more important than economies of scale for mature products
B.   occur only in labor intensive industries
C.   really important only in the first few years of a new product or process
D.   less important for technologically complex tasks
E.   in spite of theory, rarely found in practice

c, medium, 363

#12-10 The most important factor contributing to economies of scale likely is

A   ability to spread fixed costs over a larger volume
B.   learning effects
C.   a reduction in variable costs
D.   the effectiveness of transnational management techniques
E.   national comparative advantages

a, medium, 363

#12-11 Matsushita utilized what strategy in getting its VHS format VCR accepted?
A   transnational
B.   global
C.   multidomestic
D.   international

b, medium, 364

#12-12 Firms in industries like pharmaceuticals and bulk chemicals typically utilize which strategy?
A   transnational
B.   global
C.   multidomestic
D.   international

b, easy, 365 & 370

#12-13 Firms that pursue a strategy that is based on reaping the cost reductions that come from experience curve and locational economies are said to be pursuing which strategy?
A   transnational
B.   global
C.   multidomestic
D.   international

b, easy, 366 & 370

#12-14 Firms that pursue a strategy that is based on creating value by transferring skills and products to markets where indigenous competitors lack those skills and products are said to be pursuing which strategy?
A   transnational
B.   global
C.   multidomestic
D.   international

d, easy, 368

#12-15 Procter and Gamble typically develops the product and marketing message for its products in the US, and then produces its products at facilities worldwide in or near local markets. This is an example of which strategy?
A   transnational
B.   global
C.   multidomestic
D.   international

d, medium, 369

#12-16 Firms that are oriented towards being locally responsive, and are not under intense cost pressures, typically pursue which strategy?
A   transnational
B.   global
C.   multidomestic
D.   international

c, easy, 369

#12-17 Firms pursuing which strategy are typically unable to realize value from experience curve and location economies, and tend to have a complete set of value creation activities in each major national market?
A   transnational
B.   global
C.   multidomestic
D.   international

c, medium, 369

#12-18 Firms pursuing this strategy frequently develop into decentralized federations in which each national subsidiary functions in a largely autonomous manner.
A   transnational
B.   global
C.   multidomestic
D.   international

c, medium, 369

#12-19 Philips is an example of a firm that pursues which has typically pursued this strategy.
A   transnational
B.   global
C.   multidomestic
D.   international

c, hard, 369

#12-20 In industries where major competitors are based in low cost locations, there is persistent excess capacity, and where consumers are powerful and face low switching costs,
A   a multidomestic strategy would probably be the best
B.   and customers are relatively homogeneous world wide, a transnational strategy would be preferred
C.   a international strategy would probably be the best
D.   the pressures for cost reduction are likely to be great
E.   is one where none of the basic strategies is likely to prove profitable for firms

d, medium, 369

#12-21 Most tire companies are now pursuing which strategy
A   transnational
B.   global
C.   multidomestic
D.   international

b, medium, 366 & 370

#12-22 During the 1970s, the worldwide television and consumer electronics industries switched from
A   a multidomestic to a global approach
B.   an international to a transnational approach
C.   a global to a international approach
D.   a transnational to a global approach
E.   a international to a multidomestic approach

a, medium, 369 & 370

#12-23 For Caterpillar to be successful, it most likely has to pursue which strategy?
A   transnational
B.   global
C.   multidomestic
D.   international

a, medium, 372

#12-24 When the flow of skills and product offerings are two way between the parent and subsidiaries, and between subsidiaries, a firm is trying to achieve global learning and undertaking which strategy?
A   transnational
B.   global
C.   multidomestic
D.   international

a, easy, 371

#12-25 Firms that suffer from an inability to transfer skills and products between countries, and from an inability to exploit experience curve and location economies
A   are unlikely succeed
B.   may find an international strategy favorable to a multidomestic strategy
C.   will not be able to pursue a multidomestic strategy
D.   are unlikely to be able to respond local needs
E.   can be successful if they pursue a multidomestic strategy

e, hard, 369

#12-26 McDonald's experience in Poland and Russia indicates

A   how by moving quickly it was able to achieve a first mover advantage over other firms that spent considerable time establishing contacts and undertaking studies

B.   the importance of maintaining a small full time staff of employees from other countries for the first five years so that training and headquarters control are assured

C.   supply arrangements with local firms experienced in the food industry are the key to a successful start up of a restaurant

D.   all of the above

E.   none of the above

e, hard, 355

#12-27 McDonald's biggest problem in its international expansion has been

A   finding well qualified local employees

B.   locating joint venture partners that are willing to work within McDonald's rigid system

C.   in finding suppliers that are willing to adapt to its specifications

D.   finding suitable locations for its restaurants in other countries

E.   an over reliance on Purchasing Power Parity rules for its setting of prices

c, hard, 355

#12-28 Which statement best describes the menu offerings at foreign McDonald's?

A   The menu in most foreign McDonald's is identical to that served in the US

B.   While US style fast food is mainly served, local products and flavors are added as appropriate.

C.   McDonald's, while adding sushi burgers in Japan, refused to sell beer in its German outlets even though many German customers would prefer beer to Coke.

D.   Each country sells food similar to that of the country, but utilizes the fast food preparation and serving techniques perfected by McDonald's.

b, medium, 355

#12-29 McDonald's international expansion

A   was stopped until it could get governmental approval for drive through style restaurants

B.   is still much slower than its domestic growth

C.   has been limited by its ability to raise funds in global markets for an American product

D.   means that revenues outside the US are almost half of its worldwide revenues

E.   has reached the point that market penetration is now higher outside the US than within the US

d, medium, 355

#12-30 Swan Optical's international strategy

A   has focused exclusively on finding the lowest cost suppliers and producers for its products

B.   can be best classified as multidomestic

C.   has relied on finding the best designers overseas in order to compete solely on differentiation

D.   involves both cost reducing and value creating actions

E.   is best classified as an example of a pure global strategy

d, medium, 358

#12-31 Swan Optical's initial international business experiences
A   involved sales of optical products into Western Europe, as suggested by the product life cycle
B.   were in importing low quality inexpensive products
C.   led it to conclude that joint ventures with local firms usually brought much greater benefits to the local firms than to Swan
D.   showed the importance of undertaking careful study before venturing overseas
E.   none of the above

b, hard, 359

#12-32 Expanding globally allows firms to increase their profitability in ways not available to purely domestic enterprises. This increased profitability can result from all of the following EXCEPT
A   they can participate in speculation regarding future exchange rate movements
B.   they can earn a greater return from their distinctive skills or core competencies
C.   they can realize locational economies by dispersing particular value creation activities to those locations where they can be performed most efficiently
D.   they can realize greater experience curve economies which reduce the costs of value creation

a, medium, 359

#12-33 Which of the following is NOT an example of a core competence facilitating international business expansion
A   McDonald's skills at managing restaurants
B.   Matsushita's skills at building small efficient VCR factories in most major markets
C.   Proctor and Gamble's adaptation of products and marketing over time to adjust to local needs
D.   Swan Optical's abilities to build a global web of inter-related business activities
E.   IKEA's skills at providing high value for the money home furnishings

b, hard, 364

#12-34 The potential for value creation from a strategy based on exploiting skills and competencies is greatest when
A   the skills and products are unique
B.   the value on them by consumers is great
C.   there are few capable competitors
D.   all of the above
E.   none of the above

d, easy, 360

#12-35 The strategy of Swan Optical
A   can be best described as multidomestic
B.   was based off realizing location economies
C.   failed as a result of its failure to adapt its products to local tastes
D.   exploited its core competencies by transferring its skills to its overseas operations
E.   was based off exploiting experience curve economies

b, medium, 361

#12-36 Experience curve effects
A   are most significant in firms with webs of activities across countries
B.   from learning become increasingly important after a plant has been operating for 3-5 years
C.   will be the greatest as production at a single plant increases
D.   apply in bulk chemicals and commodities, but not consumer products
E.   none of the above

c, medium, 364

#12-37 Differences in infrastructure and traditional practices
A   minimize the need for local responsiveness
B.   arise primarily from governmental attempts to create non-tariff barriers
C.   are greater in Europe than Asia
D.   all of the above
E.   none of the above

e, easy, 367

#12-38 When there are significant differences in distribution channels across countries
A   a global strategy tends to work the best
B.   multinational firms will clearly have a competitive disadvantage compared to local firms
C.   the best way to deal with this is to follow the approach advocated by Levitt
D.   it may be appropriate to delegate marketing to local subsidiaries
E.   none of the above

d, hard, 367 (while b may sound good, it neglects the fact that firms like P&G and Unilever have
          succeeded and beat many local competitors)

#12-39 Firms pursuing an international strategy
A   focus on maximizing experience curve effects
B.   generally have created value by transferring differentiated product offerings to new markets
C.   get more out of scale economies than learning effects
D.   usually switch to a transnational strategy after a few years
E.   earn lower returns than firms pursuing a global strategy

b, medium, 368

#12-40 An international strategy makes most sense
A   when cost pressures are high
B.   pressures for local responsiveness are low
C.   both a and b
D.   neither a nor b

d, easy, 369

#12-41 A multidomestic strategy makes most sense when there are
A   high pressures for local responsiveness
B.   high pressures for cost reduction
C.   high pressures for both cost reduction and local responsiveness
D.   low pressures for both cost reduction and local responsiveness
E.   none of the above

a, medium, 369

#12-42 Firms that have a global strategy
A   tend to pursue a low cost approach
B.   focus on product differentiation
C.   focus on localizing products to suit preferences in different countries
D.   almost always have higher profit margins than firms with international strategies
E.   none of the above

a, easy, 369

#12-43 Firms in the semiconductor industry tend to have which type of strategy
A   international
B.   multidomestic
C.   transnational
D.   global
E.   all of the above, different firms achieve competitive advantage by utilizing different strategies

d, medium, 370

#12-44 Proctor and Gamble's initial international expansion reflected the implementation of which
strategy
A   global
B.   multidomestic
C.   international
D.   transnational
E.   none of the above, it was a hybrid that does not easily fit any category

c, medium, 370

#12-45 Procter and Gamble
A   was not able to achieve a high market share in Japan until it introduced a trim fit diaper
B.   entered a joint venture with Kao in order to penetrate the Japanese market
C.   made few local adaptations in its marketing during its initial international experiences in
        Western Europe
D.   all of the above
E.   none of the above

e, medium, 370

#12-46 Procter and Gamble's Wash & Go shampoo
A   captured 30% of the market for shampoos in Poland after a heavy marketing blitz
B.   is a good example of a product developed and marketed using a transnational approach
C.   was developed considering specific local demands for each market in which it was introduced
D.   was improperly formulated for the needs of Japanese consumers
E.   all of the above

a, medium, 371

#12-47 Caterpillar utilizes which sort of strategy
A   international
B.   transnational
C.   global
D.   multidomestic

b, medium, 372

#12-48 IKEA was founded in which country
A   US
B.   Britain
C.   Germany
D.   Japan
E.   Sweden

e, easy, 375

#12-49 IKEA's initial experiences in overseas stores in the 1970s
A   were a dismal failure
B.   were successful only after product adaptations were made
C.   provided important new product ideas that it could use domestically
D.   showed the how easily transferable its basic strategy was to other countries
E.   all of the above

d, medium, 375

#12-50 IKEA's largest sales are in
A   Germany
B.   Sweden
C.   Japan
D.   US
E.   Switzerland

a, hard, 375

#12-51Q: Why did Swan Optical originally expand overseas?

#12-51A: Due to cost pressures from imports, Swan began importing products originally. Because the products it imported from independent manufacturers had often poor quality and delivery, Swan decided that the only way it could get control over its supplies was to set up its own manufacturing operation.

#12-52Q: Why did Swan Optical invest in factories in Japan, France, and Italy?

#12-52A: Swan wanted to launch a line of high quality "designer" eye wear, but did not have the design capability in house to support such a line. Thus it made minority investments in factories in Japan, France, and Italy to supply eye wear for its high end product line.

#12-53Q: Can firms increase their profitability beyond that available from purely domestic expansion by expanding internationally? Why or why not?

#12-53A: Expanding globally allows firms both large and small to increase their profitability in a number of ways not available to purely domestic enterprises. These arise from the ability of firms that operate internationally to (1) earn a greater return from their distinctive skills or core competencies, (2) realize location economies by dispersing individual value creation activities to those locations where they can be performed most efficiently, and (3) realize greater experience curve economies and thus lower the cost of value creation. The ability of a firm to increase profitability by pursuing these strategies is, however, constrained by the need to customize the product offering, marketing strategy, and business strategy to local conditions. While for many firms the benefits from internationalization are greater than the costs, in some situations it may not be possible for firms to increase their profitability by expanding internationally.

#12-54Q: What is a core competence?

#12-54A: The term core competence refers to firm skills that competitors cannot easily match or imitate. These skills may be found in any of the different value creation activities of a firm - production, marketing, R&D, management, etc. Core competencies provide the firm with competitive advantages with other firms that do not have the ability to compete on the same basis.

#12-55Q: If we assume that the world's best designers of brick buildings are in Germany, the world's most cost efficient source of brick is in Australia, the most skilled bricklayers are Greek, and the finest construction companies are American, why might there not be any vertically integrated international firms in the global brick building business to take advantage of these locational economies?

#12-55A: Firstly, bricks are a very heavy product for their value. Hence transportation costs may outweigh the benefits of lower production costs. Secondly, the skills required for most brick laying tasks are not so complex nor tacit that people in each country cannot be trained to perform adequately and less expensively than the cost of relocating personnel.

#12-56Q: What is the difference between learning effects and economies of scale?

#12-56A: Learning effects refer to cost savings that come from learning by doing - over time individuals and firms learn how to do things more efficiently. Scale economies are the unit cost reductions associated with producing a large volume of product, most typically from spreading high fixed costs over a large number of units of production.

#12-57Q: What is the difference between a global strategy and a multidomestic strategy.

#12-57A: While a multidomestic strategy focuses on local responsiveness and pays lesser attention to cost pressures, a firm with a global strategy focuses on minimizing costs and pays relatively little attention to the differences that may exist between countries.

#12-58Q: "Any firm currently pursuing a multidomestic strategy will not be able to survive much longer - going global or transnational is a competitive must." Critically evaluate this statement

#12-58A: While it may be true that the number of industries and firms that are truly multidomestic is decreasing, this can still be a viable strategy in some instances. With the removal of trade barriers and the movement towards more homogenous world wide consumer preferences, multidomestic firms will clearly be under cost pressures from firms that realize increased economies through integration and providing standardized products worldwide. But national idiosyncrasies will continue to exist, and multidomestic firms that can create greater value for the consumer will be able to charge more and cover the increased costs.

#12-59Q: In what types of industries are the pressures for cost reductions the greatest?

#12-59A: Pressures for cost reductions are greatest in industries producing commodity type products where price is the main competitive weapon. Expanding on this, pressures for cost reductions can be particularly intense in industries where meaningful differentiation on non-price factors is difficult. This tends to be the case for products that serve universal needs - when tastes and preferences of consumers in different nations are very similar if not identical. Pressures for cost reductions are also intense in industries where major competitors are based in low cost locations, where there is persistent excess capacity, and where consumers are powerful and face low switching costs.

#12-60Q: Under what conditions are the pressures for local responsiveness the greatest?

#12-60A: Pressures for local responsiveness arise from (1) differences in consumer tastes and preferences, (2) differences in infrastructure and traditional practices, (3) differences in distribution channels, and (4) host government demands.

#12-61Q: What is a transnational corporation?

#12-61A: A transnational corporation tries to simultaneously focus on reducing costs, transferring skills and products, and responding to local differences. It must be able to tap into t he capabilities of each of its subsidiaries and transfer knowledge and products efficiently between subsidiaries.

#12-62Q: Why is a transnational strategy so difficult? (After all, if it was easy and costless wouldn't all firms want to have low costs and high responsiveness?)

#12-62A: (see page 373)

#12-63Q: How would you characterize the strategy of _____ (a familiar MNE with local operations, or a firm that you discussed as a case study in a previous class).

#12-63A: (will depend upon the firm chosen and how much students know about the firm).

CHAPTER 13

Students should be encouraged to choose the BEST answer, as more than one may be technically correct. Following each question is the answer, estimated difficulty, and page reference.

#13-1 In the global chemical industry, the key competitive weapon for a firm is
A   brand recognition
B.   governmental relations
C.   product locations that circumvent trade barriers
D.   low cost structure
E.   superior R&D innovations

d, hard, 388

#13-2 Dow Chemical uses which type of organizational structure
A   world wide area divisions
B.   world wide product divisions
C.   an international division along side product divisions
D.   functional
E.   matrix

e, easy, 388

#13-3 Whether decision making should be centralized or decentralized in a hierarchy
A   has little effect performance ambiguity.
B.   does not depend upon the strategy chosen by a firm
C.   refers to the vertical differentiation approach taken by a firm
D.   is determined by the amount of responsibility top managers can handle
E.   is a function of the degree of horizontal differentiation of a firm

c, medium, 379

#13-4 Centralization of decision making
A   makes it more difficult to make major organizational changes
B.   facilitates coordination
C.   can lead to duplication of similar activities
D.   increases motivation at lower levels in an organization
E.   typically allows managers with better information to make decisions

b, easy, 379

#13-5 Decentralization of decision making
A   does not allow top management to focus on critical issues, as they get bogged down in details
B.   leads to greater individual freedom and control over work at lower levels
C.   decreases flexibility, making response to environmental change slower
D.   decreases control and accountability of lower units
E.   can be more reasonably done in global firms as opposed to multidomestic firms

b, medium, 380

#13-6 Firms with which type of strategy are most likely to have the most decentralized decision making?
A   global
B.   transnational
C.   international
D.   multidomestic

d, medium, 380

#13-7 As firms initially expand overseas they typically create an international division. A key problem with this structure is that
A   the heads of foreign subsidiaries are not given as much voice in the organization as the heads of domestic units
B.   firms usually then evolve into having international strategies without thinking of other options.
C.   the power of different country managers is much greater than the strategic significance of their positions would suggest is appropriate
D.   core competencies can be too easily transferred to overseas subsidiaries where they can then be lost to competitors

a, medium, 382

#13-8 A world wide product division structure tends to be
A   less efficient than a world wide area structure for most diversified firms
B.   chosen by firms that had a functional domestic structure
C.   adopted by diversified firms with domestic product divisions
D.   the second stage chosen by firms in Stopford and Wells "international structural stages model"
E.   preferred by country managers over a world wide area structure

c, hard, 386

#13-9 Firms that have a low degree of diversification and a functional domestic structure tend to over time favor
A   a matrix structure
B.   a world wide area structure
C.   a world wide functional product division structure
D.   an international division structure

b, medium, 383

#13-10 The greatest strength of the world wide area structure is that it facilitates
A   the transfer of competencies
B.   realization of location and experience curve economies
C.   coordination between different country managers strategic direction
D.   local responsiveness
E.   taking a low cost approach in strategy

d, easy, 385

#13-11 If a firm's international success is likely to be based on customizing products to local needs, including having all value creation activities in each country, the firm should adopt
A   a global matrix structure
B.   an international division structure
C.   a world wide area division structure
D.   a world wide product division structure

c, medium, 385

#13-12 Firms pursuing a transnational strategy often try to use which organizational structure
A   a global matrix structure
B.   an international division structure
C.   a world wide area division structure
D.   a world wide product division structure

a, medium, 387

#13-13 The need for coordination between sub-units tends to be
A   higher in multidomestic than international firms
B.   higher in global than multidomestic firms
C.   highest in international firms
D.   lowest for multidomestic, higher for global companies, and still higher for international companies
E.   unrelated to the international strategy of the firm

b, hard, 388

#13-14 Which of the following is NOT a formal integrating mechanism
A   direct managerial contact
B.   liaison positions
C.   management networks
D.   temporary teams
E.   matrix structure

c, medium, 390

#13-15 World wide information systems
A   may be of minimal use in creating a management network unless there are opportunities for making personal contacts
B.   are more important for world wide area structures than for world wide product division structures
C.   are unnecessary if there are firm wide management development policies
D.   are more important for firms pursuing international strategies than firms pursuing transnational strategies
E.   are preferable to organizational culture for improving coordination

a, hard, 392

#13-16 Informal integrating mechanisms
A   are less important than formal integrating mechanisms
B.   like matrix structures are difficult to implement
C.   are rarely effective unless there is direct managerial contact to force them to work
D.   include management networks and organizational culture
E.   are good in theory but rarely work in practice

d, medium, 391

#13-17 The use of electronic mail, teleconferencing, and high speed data systems
A   are of little importance as a coordinating mechanism
B.   facilitates the utilization of management networks
C.   are great in theory, but are usually not working and thus ineffectual
D.   are more important than management development programs for establishing managerial contacts
E.   are more important in multidomestic than transnational firms

b, easy, 392

#13-18 Most multinational firms tend to use
A   all types of control systems with varying degrees of emphasis
B.   bureaucratic controls more forcefully than all other control systems
C.   only two of the four types of control systems with any regularity
D.   capital budgeting as a form of personal control system
E.   all control systems other than cultural controls, since different countries have different cultures

a, hard, 394

#13-19 Which of the following is NOT one of the control systems we find within multinational firms?
A   personal
B.   bureaucratic
C.   mercurial
D.   output
E.   cultural

c, easy, 394

#13-20 Performance ambiguity
A   is rarely an issue in transnationals
B.   is most common when units of a firm are not interdependent
C.   can be controlled by rigorously checking out alibis
D.   is primarily a problem in Italy and France
E.   raises the costs of control

e, medium, 396

#13-21 The level of performance ambiguity is
A   unrelated to the strategy of a firm
B.   highest in transnational firms
C.   always higher in worldwide area structure firms than in world wide product division structures
D.   lower in global firms than it is multidomestic firms
E.   can be reduced to zero by making realistic budgets

b, hard, 396

#13-22 In firms pursuing either a global or transnational strategy
A   bureaucratic controls are more important than cultural controls
B.   the use of output controls is limited by performance ambiguities
C.   output controls are typically much more important than bureaucratic controls
D.   cultural controls tend to be relatively ineffective
E.   performance ambiguity is lower than for other strategy types

b, medium, 397

#13-23 A multinational firm with a world wide product division structure, a high need for coordination, and many integrating mechanisms is most likely to fit with which strategy?
A   multidomestic
B.   international
C.   transnational
D.   global

d, hard, 398

#13-24 A multinational firm with a moderate need for cultural controls, moderate performance ambiguity, and relatively few integrating mechanisms, is most likely to fit with which strategy?
A   international
B.   multidomestic
C.   global
D.   transnational

a, hard, 398

#13-25 A firm with a multidomestic strategy, if this strategy fits with its organization, will likely have
A   a world wide product division structure
B.   high need for coordination
C.   low performance ambiguity
D.   high need for cultural controls
E.   a fairly centralized decision making structure

c, medium, 398

#13-26 An informal matrix organization fits best when
A   there is a very high need for cultural controls and low need for coordination
B.   a global strategy is pursued
C.   there is a very high need for coordination and very high performance ambiguity
D.   core competencies and most decisions are centralized
E.   there is low performance ambiguity

c, medium, 398

#13-27 Unilever traditionally had which type of strategy?
A   international
B.   multidomestic
C.   transnational
D.   global

b, easy, 401

#13-28 Unilever changed its strategy because
A   its internal control systems did not fit with its strategy
B.   its core competencies were being lost to competitors
C.   Proctor and Gamble was effectively attacking it with a different strategy
D.   its country managers tended to introduce new products too quickly without consulting
           headquarters
E.   the Lever unit wanted more autonomy in order to better respond to the US market

c, medium, 401

#13-29 As a result of Unilever's changes
A   the size of packages of detergents and the motifs have been harmonized
B.   manufacturing will now take place at more plants closer to consumers
C.   country managers now have greater autonomy in responding to local demands
D.   new products now typically take only 4-5 years to introduce across Europe
E.   most national brands have been removed so that pan-European advertising can take place

a, hard, 401

#13-30 According to Stopford and Wells' international structural stages model, if foreign sales are low
percentage of foreign sales and foreign product diversity is low, a firm is most likely
A   have to move towards a global matrix structure
B.   high performance ambiguity
C.   still have a international division structure
D.   have a strategy consistent with a worldwide area division structure
E.   none of the above

c, hard, 385

#13-31 When there is a very high need for coordination
A   a multidomestic strategy will fit best
B.   a world wide product division structure will fit best
C.   many integrating mechanisms are required
D.   operating decisions should be decentralized

c, hard, 398

#13-32 According to Stopford and Wells' international structural stages model, if foreign sales are a high percentage of foreign sales and foreign product diversity is low, a firm is most likely to have
A   a global matrix organization
B.   a world wide product division structure
C.   an international division structure
D.   a world wide area structure
E.   low profitability

d, hard, 385

#13-33 For most of the past 40 years Shell has operated with a
A   multidomestic strategy
B.   a worldwide area division structure
C.   a global matrix structure
D.   growing net loss in operations
E.   low emphasis on personal interaction in managerial decision-making

c, medium, 377

#13-34 The oil industry is characterized by
A   having few scale economies
B.   having almost no firms with international operations
C.   few decisions with substantial capital expenditures and long term consequences
D.   all of the above
E.   none of the above

c, hard, 378

#13-35 Philips and Shell,
A   while facing different sorts of strategic challenges, find their industries converging into one
B.   both found that a global matrix structure was more appropriate than their previous structures
C.   each moved from other organizational structures towards worldwide product divisions
D.   have always based their success on achieving product differentiation rather than cost advantages
E.   only share a common Dutch heritage, but otherwise are in entirely different industries and face completely different strategic demands

c, hard, 379

#13-36 The most common organizational structure typically adopted by firms as they initially expand internationally is the

A   worldwide product division
B.   worldwide area structure
C.   international division
D.   global matrix
E.   none of the above

c, medium, 382

#13-37 In what industry is Abbott Laboratories
A   chemical
B.   oil
C.   health care
D.   computers
E.   none of the above

c, medium, 384

#13-38 Abbott Laboratories has been facing which of the following challenges
A   responding to needs for global product development
B.   rapid product introductions in many countries
C.   rise of powerful buyers
D.   all of the above
E.   none of the above

d, medium, 384

#13-39 As a response the challenges it is facing, Abbott Laboratories
A   it will change to a worldwide product division structure
B.   it will change to a worldwide area division structure
C.   it will switch to a transnational strategy with a global matrix structure
D.   it will refocus on only a few international markets where it can achieve economies of scale
E.   it doesn't plan to change its organizational structure

e, hard, 384

#13-40 The great strength of the worldwide product division structure is that it
A   provides an on organizational context in which it is easier to pursue the consolidation of value creation activities at key locations for location and experience curve economies
B.   absolves local managers from having to maintain responsibility and control over operations in each country
C.   facilitates the sharing of core competencies across different product divisions that share technologies
D.   gives country managers increased clout in dealing with local governments and suppliers
E.   none of the above

a, hard, 386

#13-41 Which of the following organizational structures often turns out to be clumsy and bureaucratic
A   worldwide area division
B.   worldwide product division
C.   matrix
D.   international
E.   functional

c, easy, 387

#13-42 Power struggles tend to be greatest under which type of organizational structure
A   worldwide area division
B.   worldwide product division
C.   matrix
D.   international
E.   functional

c, easy, 387

#13-43 Competition in the chemical industry
A   differs significantly from country to country
B.   has not been very intense, since demand has typically been greater than the supply
C.   can be best characterized as minimal, since the few firms that compete globally have such
           differentiated products that they do not compete directly with each other
D.   all of the above
E.   none of the above

e, medium, 388

#13-44 The primary basis of competition in the chemical industry is
A   price
B.   location
C.   size
D.   quality
E.   differentiation

a, easy, 388

#13-45 Dow Chemical's organizational structure is a
A   worldwide area division
B.   worldwide product division
C.   matrix
D.   international
E.   functional

c, easy, 388

#13-46 Although it had significant problems after introducing its matrix structure, Dow decision to keep the structure was prompted by

A   a strong belief that it would work if it were only adhered to more strictly
B.   its move into the pharmaceutical industry
C.   the huge losses it had experienced as a result of switching organizational structures
D.   studies by McKinsey that suggested that learning effects would eventually turn the situation around
E.   all of the above

b, hard, 389

#13-47 The simplest formal integrating mechanism is

A   direct contact
B.   liaisons
C.   culture
D.   networks
E.   teams

a, easy, 390

#13-48 Temporary teams work particularly well as a coordinating mechanism in

A   new product development
B.   cross-functional groups
C.   market introductions
D.   all of the above
E.   none of the above

d, medium, 391

#13-49 Firm-wide networks of managers

A   are one of the most effective formal coordinating mechanisms firms can institute
B.   work better in multidomestic firms than transnational firms
C.   are more effective in worldwide product division firms than worldwide area division firms
D.   can be best built through personal contacts

d, hard, 392

#13-50 The ability to establish a common vision for the company is

A   difficult for firms utilizing a global strategy
B.   critical for the development of an organizational culture
C.   facilitated by decentralizing decision making
D.   inhibited computerization and information systems
E.   none of the above

b, hard, 393

#13-51Q: Describe the dimensions or components of Dow's matrix organization.

#13-51A: Dow's matrix organization is based on three overlapping components: functions, businesses, and geography. Managers jobs are described by all three, and most managers report to at least two managers.

#13-52Q: Why has Philips been performing poorly for the past several years? Discuss its organization and strategy.

#13-52A: Philips markets have been under attack by Japanese competitors like Matsushita and Sony. These companies are pursuing a global strategy, using their resulting low costs to undercut Philips and its multidomestic strategy with relatively autonomous national organizations. To compete on an equal footing with Matsushita and Sony, Philips needed to be able to realize experience curve and location economies. It has made significant progress on this during the mid-1990s, but it is still not clear that it has completely turned the corner.

#13-53Q: What are the main arguments for the centralization of decision-making?

#13-53A: There are four main arguments for centralization: (1) facilitating coordination, (2) ensuring consistency between decisions and organizational objectives, (3) providing top management with the means to push through major changes, and (4) avoiding duplication of activities

#13-54Q: What are the problems associated with the use of "international divisions" in multinational firms?

#13-54A: (see pages 382-383)

#13-55Q: What are the advantages and disadvantages of the "world wide product division" structure?

#13-55A: The great strength of the world wide product division structure is that it provides an organizational context in which it is easier to pursue the consolidation of value creation activities at key locations necessary for realizing location and experience curve economies. It also facilitates the transfer of core competencies within a division's worldwide operations and the simultaneous worldwide introduction of new products. The main problem with the structure is the limited voice it gives to area or country managers, since they are seen as subservient to the product division managers. This can lead to a lack of local responsiveness.

#13-56Q: Under what conditions are world wide product division and world wide area structures most appropriate?

#13-56A: A worldwide area structure is more appropriate if the firm's strategy is a multidomestic one, whereas as world wide product division structure is more appropriate for firms pursuing global or international strategies. Elaborating, both the world wide area structure and the world wide product division structure have strengths and weaknesses. The world wide area structure facilitates local responsiveness, but can inhibit the realization of location and experience curve economies, and the transfer of core competencies between areas. The world wide product division structure provides a better framework within which to pursue location and experience curve economies, and for transferring core competencies internationally, but it is weak when it comes to local responsiveness.

#13-57Q: Why is it that experiences with the global matrix structure have generally been unfavorable?

#13-57A: In practice the matrix has turned out to be clumsy and bureaucratic. It can end up being so dominated by coordinating meetings that nothing gets done. All too often, the need to get both the area and product divisions to agree on a decision has slowed down decision making and produced an inflexible organization unable to respond quickly to market shifts. The dual hierarchical structure has led to conflict and a perpetual power struggle between the areas and the product divisions - with many managers being caught in the middle. Moreover, accountability in this structure is difficult to pinpoint.

#13-58Q: How does the need for coordination between units vary between different strategies of multinationals? Which strategies have the lowest and highest needs for coordination?

#13-58A: The need for coordination between sub-units varies systematically with the international strategy of the firm. The need for coordination is lowest in multidomestic companies, is higher in international companies, higher still in global companies, and highest in transnational firms.

#13-59Q: What are the four main types of control systems used by multinational firms? Why do different firms emphasized different systems.

#13-59A: There are four main types of control systems that we find within multinational firms - personal controls, bureaucratic controls, output controls, and cultural controls. Within most firms all four are in use, although the degree of emphasis upon different control systems does tend to vary with the strategy of the firm.

#13-60Q: What causes performance ambiguity?

#13-60A: Performance ambiguity arises when the causes of poor performance by a sub-unit are ambiguous. This is most likely to be the case when the performance of a sub-unit is in part dependent upon its relationship with other sub-units in the firm. The level of performance ambiguity is a function of the extent of interdependence between sub-units within an organization.

#13-61Q: What can a firm do to facilitate the development of intra-organizational networks?

#13-61A: (see page 392)

CHAPTER 14

Students should be encouraged to choose the BEST answer, as more than one may be technically correct. Following each question is the answer, estimated difficulty, and page reference.

#14-1 During the 1970s, Mazda
A   introduced a number of successful new cars in the US
B.   struggled with a sales slump and financial losses
C.   was quite successful in Japan, but did relatively poorly in the US
D.   introduced a new engine technology that Ford felt could help it in its smaller US cars
E.   was the fastest growing auto company in South East Asia, with sales growth throughout the region

b, hard, 423

#14-2 Ford
A   is now the best selling foreign nameplate in Japan
B.   entered into an alliance with Mazda initially to help it set up operations Mexico
C.   first made an equity investment in Mazda in 1971
D.   holds a 40% equity stake in Mazda

a, easy, 423

#14-3 The Ford/Mazda alliance
A   has mainly benefited Ford
B.   has mainly benefited Mazda
C.   has been generally unsuccessful in meeting its objectives
D.   is viewed as a success by both firms

d, medium, 423

#14-4 Which of the following statements is NOT true?
A   Mazda has refused to let Ford produce its own version of the Miata.
B.   Ford has refused to let Mazda have access to the design of the four door Ford Explorer.
C.   Ford wanted Mazda's rotary engine for use in a sports car, but Mazda refused.
D.   Ford and Mazda have jointly worked on the development of the Festiva, Tracer, 323, and Navajo.
E.   Mazda would not allow Ford access to its superefficient Hofu plant, which Ford wanted to model its Hermosilla plant after.

e, medium, 423

#14-5 Which of the following may be least important in determining the most appropriate mode of entry?
A   transport costs
B.   trade barriers
C.   cost of a particular acquisition
D.   firm strategy
E.   political and economic risks

c, medium, 404

#14-6 Most manufacturing firms first international expansion involves

A   licensing
B.   exporting
C.   turnkey projects
D.   wholly owned subsidiary
E.   joint venture

b, easy, 405

#14-7 Which of the following is NOT a disadvantage of exporting

A   home country may have high costs
B.   high transport costs
C.   ability to benefit from experience curve economics
D.   tariff barriers
E.   loss of control over marketing in foreign country

c, medium, 405

#14-8 Which of the following is an example of a turnkey project?

A   McDonald's allows a Indonesian firm to establish outlets on Bali
B.   Mazda designs an engine for use in Ford cars
C.   Toro buys a rototiller company in Slovenia
D.   Dow Chemical builds an ethanol plant for a Thai petroleum company
E.   A Chinese firm makes tail fins for Boeing airplanes

d, medium, 406

#14-9 The critical asset in a turnkey project is typically a

A   complex process technology
B.   patent
C.   management skill
D.   construction background
E.   source of raw materials

a, medium, 406

#14-10 Which of the following is one of the key advantages of licensing?

A   no tight control over the national operations
B.   ability to coordinate strategic moves across countries
C.   experience curve economies
D.   transfer of technological know-how
E.   lower costs of entering market

e, hard, 407

#14-11 Which of the following modes of entry is best at allowing firms to coordinate strategic moves in different countries?
A   franchising
B.   licensing
C.   wholly owned subsidiary
D.   joint venture
E.   turnkey project

c, easy, 412

#14-12 Which of the following modes of entry is best at allowing firms to maintain control over technology?
A   franchising
B.   licensing
C.   wholly owned subsidiary
D.   joint venture
E.   turnkey project

c, easy, 412

#14-13 Which of the following statements is NOT true?
A   Franchising usually involves service firms while licensing involves manufacturing firms.
B.   McDonald's is more likely to have franchisees than licensees.
C.   Franchising often involves the use of brand names
D.   Franchise contracts are usually for shorter duration than license contracts.
E.   Both licensing and franchising typically provide returns to the firm over a period of time, and not only as a one time lump sum.

d, medium, 409

#14-14 The most important advantage of franchising is that
A   development costs and risks are largely undertaken by a local firm.
B.   a firm can control the quality of the service delivered
C.   the costs of market failure are shared equally among the parties
D.   a parent firm has greater control over pricing than it does with other entry modes
E.   competitive cross-border strategic actions can be coordinated

a, medium, 409

#14-15 McDonald's, Kentucky Fried Chicken, and Hilton International have all tended to
A   work together to determine strategies for entering new markets
B.   set up subsidiaries in each country in which they have franchisees
C.   license rather than franchise, due to the added control this gives them
D.   expand primarily by having each outlet (restaurant or hotel) a wholly owned subsidiary
E.   locate in the same building in order to better attract consumers interested in US services

b, hard, 410

#14-16 Which of the following is an important advantage of joint ventures?

A   one firm bears all the risks while the other bears all the costs
B.   critical technology can be easily transferred to a partner
C.   ease of realizing experience curve and location economies
D.   learning skills and know-how from partners

d, medium, 410

#14-17 Which of the following is NOT an advantage of a wholly owned subsidiary?

A   control over technology
B.   ability to engage in global strategic coordination
C.   low cost relative to other modes of entry
D.   realization of experience curve and locational economies

c, easy, 413

#14-18 All other things being equal, if a high-tech firm is considering setting up operations in a foreign country in order to profit from a core competency in technological know-how, it should probably do so through a

A   wholly owned subsidiary
B.   joint venture
C.   licensee
D.   turnkey contract
E.   franchisee

a, easy, 412

#14-19 Brand names are

A   usually not important in international markets, since they lose meaning in translation
B.   best protected if markets are entered using joint ventures
C.   supposed to convey information about the quality and consistency of a product or service in any country
D.   rarely included in part of a franchise agreement
E.   more important in licensing than franchising agreements

c, medium, 409

#14-20 The greater the pressures for global cost reduction, the more likely a firm will enter a market with

A   franchising or licensing
B.   exporting or wholly owned subsidiaries
C.   joint ventures or strategic alliances
D.   turnkey projects

b, hard, 414

#14-21 Firms pursuing transnational strategies are most likely to use which mode of entry?
A   licensing
B.   joint ventures
C.   turnkey contracts
D.   franchising
E.   wholly owned subsidiaries

e, medium, 415

#14-22 Strategic alliances allow firms to do all of the following EXCEPT:
A   tightly control technology
B.   ease entry and access to foreign markets
C.   share fixed costs and risks
D.   bring together complementary skills
E.   establish technical standards

a, medium, 416

#14-23 The main point argued by Reich and Mankin is that
A   acquisitions of US firms by foreign firms gives away our technology to foreigners
B.   US firms are losing their competitive advantage and core competencies by entering strategic
        alliances with Japanese firms
C.   US firms should be more opportunistic in obtaining know-how from foreigners
D.   high Japanese trade barriers should be removed
E.   US firms should take a more proactive approach when entering foreign markets

b, hard, 416

#14-24 IBM's reputation as an alliance partner
A   was badly damaged as a result of its failed alliance with Toshiba and Siemens
B.   is generally quite poor
C.   is really not very important, since it provides other firms with access to such a huge market
D.   has benefited greatly from its close alliance with Microsoft in developing OS/2
E.   is important if it is to be able to work with new partners in the future

e, medium, 417

#14-25 Which of the following is NOT a good way for a firm to protect itself from opportunistic partners?
A   walling off sensitive technologies
B.   writing contractual safeguards into agreements
C.   agreeing to engage in reciprocal swaps of technological know-how
D.   threaten to end the alliance if it finds that the partner has learned all its critical know-how
E.   seeking credible commitments from partners

d, medium, 420

#14-26 In GM's joint venture with Toyota,

A   Toyota's majority ownership allowed it to make the radical process improvements needed

B.   the design work was done by GM in Detroit while the manufacturing was done by Toyota in Japan

C.   GM's personnel in the joint venture were later dispersed to a number of different GM subsidiaries

D.   Toyota used the joint venture's Kentucky plant to primarily make cars for its own sale

E.   GM achieved most of its objectives from the alliance while Toyota gained little

c, hard, 421

#14-27 In Schwinn's joint venture with Csepel,

A   Schwinn held a majority ownership

B.   Csepel held a majority ownership

C.   the government held a majority ownership

D.   each partner held an equal share in the venture

a, medium, 411

#14-28 Joint venture law in Hungary

A   prohibited Schwinn from having a majority ownership in the joint venture

B.   changed several times during the negotiations, and several times since, complicating the entire agreement

C.   required that the venture pay higher VAT taxes than domestic firms would have to pay

D.   would not allow Schwinn to import any component parts

E.   was not applicable in Schwinn's joint venture with Csepel, since Csepel is located in Slovakia

b, medium, 411

#14-29 Productivity at Schwinn-Csepel

A   is higher than that in the US

B.   is higher than that at Csepel's domestic plant

C.   is significantly lower than it is at most other Schwinn plants

D.   is quite low, but the quality is exceptionally high

c, easy, 411

#14-30 The primary market for Schwinn-Csepel's products was intended to be

A   USA.

B.   Western Europe

C.   Eastern Europe

D.   lesser developed countries in Africa and South America

E.   Japan

c, medium, 411

#14-31 The alliance Fuji-Xerox is based on firms from which countries
A   UK and Korea
B.   US and Korea
C.   US and Japan
D.   UAE and Hungary
E.   none of the above

c, easy, 403

#14-32 The prime motivation for the Fuji-Xerox joint venture from Xerox's perspective was
A   market access
B.   technology transfer
C.   locational economies in production
D.   franchise rights

a, hard, 403

#14-33 The Fuji-Xerox alliance
A   failed due to opportunistic behavior by Fuji
B.   never successfully introduced the product it was originally planning to develop, but succeeded
          anyway
C.   was successful in meeting initial objectives, but over time proved to be unnecessary for both firms
D.   has been one of the most successful and enduring corporate alliances
E.   was agreed to by the partners in spite of significant objections by their governments

d, medium, 404

#14-34 Xerox
A   has received only minimal benefits from its alliance with Fuji
B.   has received benefits from its alliance with Fuji primarily in the form of profit repatriation from
          the Japanese
C.   in recent years has reaped significant benefits from the product development and manufacturing
          capabilities of its alliance with Fuji
D.   learned from its alliance with Fuji that the long run interests of the firm would be better served
          via wholly owned subsidiaries than from alliance
E.   all of the above

c, medium, 404

#14-35 Strategic alliances
A   are the most common form of market entry for experienced multinationals
B.   were more popular in the 1970s and 1980s than in the 1990s
C.   are only one of the many ways firms may enter foreign markets
D.   have a higher success rate than most other modes of entry
E.   all of the above

c, hard, 404

#14-36 Which of the following is NOT a typical example of a strategic alliance
A   turnkey project
B.   cross-shareholding deals
C.   licensing agreements
D.   formal joint ventures
E.   informal cooperative arrangements

a, hard, 404

#14-37 Which of the following is a typical advantage of exporting
A   control over distribution in the market
B.   low risk on invested capital
C.   low transportation costs relative to local production
D.   avoids tariff and non-tariff trade barriers
E.   coordination of worldwide advertising message

b, hard, 405

#14-38 A turnkey entry strategy makes most sense for foreign firms when
A   the political and economic environment makes longer term investments risky
B.   governments encourage foreign investment in plants and equipment
C.   future growth rates and economic development in a country are expected to be high
D.   they need to protect technological capabilities and competences

a, medium, 406

#14-39 Which of the following is NOT a disadvantage of licensing
A   Lack of control over technology
B.   Inability to realize location and experience curve economies
C.   Inability to engage in global strategic coordination
D.   Low cost of entry

d, easy, 413

#14-40 A cross-licensing agreement
A   can reduce the risks of licensing technological know-how
B.   is generally much riskier than a normal licensing agreement, but if successful has a much higher return
C.   is common in franchising
D.   is usually a preliminary step to setting up a wholly-owned subsidiary
E.   all of the above

a, medium, 408

#14-41 Cross-licensing agreements are likely to most common in which industry
A   fast food
B.   lodging
C.   biotechnology
D.   beverages
E.   rubber

c, medium, 408

#14-42 Quality control of products is most commonly a problem associated with
A   exporting
B.   wholly owned subsidiaries
C.   joint ventures
D.   franchising
E.   none of the above

d, medium, 409

#14-43 Which mode of entry has significant risk of loss of technological know-how
A   licensing
B.   turnkey projects
C.   joint ventures
D.   all of the above
E.   none of the above

d, medium, 414

#14-44 Licensing technology to competitors
A   should be avoided at all times
B.   can help in having a firm's technology accepted as a standard
C.   should be done primarily when competitors have superior technology
D.   typically sabotages the competitors development efforts
E.   proved disastrous to Ford in its dealings with Mazda

b, easy, 414

#14-45 Trading of core competences between alliance partners
A   underlies many of the most successful strategic alliances
B.   is almost never done in the electronics industry in order to prevent competitors from gaining
C.   has been frequently cited by Japanese authorities as a threat to national security and should be avoided by Japanese firms in their dealings with foreign firms
D.   is common in the airline industry where air carriers from different countries typically have strong technological core competencies that firms from other countries lack
E.   all of the above

a, medium, 416

#14-46 Opel is
A   the name of a GM joint venture in Germany
B.   an Austrian licensee of a US auto company
C.   a wholly owned General Motors subsidiary in Europe
D.   the name of a failed US auto model
E.   the German manufacturer of a Korean designed car that is sold primarily in the US

c, medium, 418

#14-47 General Motors alliance in Korea was
A   successful from the standpoint Daewoo, but not GM
B.   part of a web of activities designed to take advantage of locational economies
C.   designed to provide GM with a market entry into a growing and dynamic economy
D.   an excellent example of cross-licensing

b, medium, 419

#14-48 The LeMans
A   turned out to have very poor quality
B.   had plummeting sales in the US in 1991
C.   was based off a German design of Opel
D.   all of the above
E.   none of the above

d, medium, 419

#14-49 How does Ford's experience with Mazda compare with GM's experience with Daewoo?
A   GM has been much more satisfied
B.   Ford has been much more satisfied
C.   Both have had severe problems and since abandoned the relationships
D.   Both have been very successful and lead to significant benefits for the firms

b, medium, 423

#14-50 The GM alliance with Toyota
A   was much more successful from Toyota's perspective than Daewoo's experience with GM was
         from its perspective
B.   has proved longer lasting for GM than its relationship with Opel
C.   has benefited GM much more than it has benefited Toyota
D.   ended after Toyota agreed to buy out GM's share in their plant

a, hard, 421

#14-51Q: What benefits has Ford had from its alliance with Mazda?

#14-51A: For Ford the benefits from the alliance have come partly in the form of sales from Japan. Ford is now the best selling foreign nameplate in Japan with a dealer network it owns jointly with Mazda. Ford also benefits from access to Mazda's manufacturing and engineering skills, and by being able to share the costs of developing new models with Mazda. Ford's top ranking Hermosilla plant was based on an adaptation of Mazda's Hofu plant. As for new product development, Ford and Mazda have worked together on the development of 10 new car models, usually with Ford doing most of the styling and Mazda making many of the key engineering contributions.

#14-52Q: What is the difference between licensing and franchising?

#14-52A: Conceptually there is really little difference between licensing and franchising. In both cases the firm gives up something it has to allow a foreign firm to be more successful in a foreign market. In the case of licensing, this usually involves the right to use some technological product or Porsches know-how that will be used by the licenser to help them create and sell products. In the case of franchising, the licenser usually gets access to a brand name and a set of managerial know-how that will allow it to set up a service cooperation in its home market. Franchising agreements tend to be for longer term commitments.

#14-53Q: What are the key advantages of exporting over all other modes of entry?

#14-53A: Exporting has two distinct advantages. First, exporting avoids the costs and risks of having to establish manufacturing operations in the host country; these are often substantial. Second, exporting may be consistent with realizing experience curve and locational economies.

#14-54Q: What is a turnkey project? Are there any long term advantages to a turnkey project?

#14-54A: In a turnkey project the contractor agrees to handle every detail of the building of a new production plant for a foreign client, including the training of personnel. At the completion of the contract the foreign client is handed the "key" to a completed plant that is ready for full operation. The primary advantages are really short term in nature. Some turnkey project agreement can be structured, however, so that a firm will receive payments into the future, perhaps have access to a portion of the goods produced by the plant, and/or have exclusive rights to supply certain inputs for the plants. Thus there is a potential for long term benefits.

#14-55Q: What are the advantages of licensing? How would you characterize the firms that are most likely to license their technology?

#14-55A: The advantage of licensing is that the firm does not have to bear the development costs and risks associated with the opening of foreign markets and operations. If firms believe that licensing a technology will increase its acceptance, or alternatively think that their competitive advantage would be lost before they could capitalize on it in another country, then licensing may also be optimal. These firms can be characterized as those that think they are unlikely to reap great benefits by keeping close control over their technology. In addition, licensing may be an attractive option for firms that are unwilling to commit substantial financial resources to an unfamiliar or politically volatile foreign market where political risks are particularly high, or lack the capital to do so.

#14-56Q: What is the most significant disadvantage of international franchising? What actions can a franchiser take to address this disadvantage?

#14-56A: The most significant disadvantage of franchising concerns quality control. The foundation of franchising arrangements is the notion that the firm's brand name conveys a message to consumers about the quality of the firm's product. The geographical distance of the firm from its foreign franchisees, however, makes poor quality control difficult to detect for the franchiser. In addition, the sheer number of individual franchisees can make it difficult to detect poor quality. One way around this disadvantage is to set up a subsidiary in each country or region in which the firm expands. The subsidiary might be a wholly owned company or a joint venture with local firm. The subsidiary then assumes the rights and obligations to establish franchisees throughout the region. The combination of close proximity and the limited number of franchisees that have to be monitored reduces the quality control problem.

#14-57Q: What are the main disadvantages of setting up a wholly owned subsidiary?

#14-57A: Establishing a wholly owned subsidiary is generally the most costly and risky method of serving a foreign market. While the risks associated with learning to do business in a new culture can be reduced if the firm acquires an established host country enterprise rather than starting its own, acquisitions raise a whole set of additional problems. Once a wholly owned subsidiary has been established, it is also much more difficult to switch to an alternative mode.

#14-58Q: When cost pressures are high in an industry characterized by firms utilizing a global strategy, are some modes of entry more likely than others? If so, what are they? If not, why?

#14-58A: In global industries with significant cost pressures, it is essential to locate various activities in the lowest cost locations for each and carefully coordinate activities. Firms in these situations are most likely to pursue a combination of wholly owned subsidiaries and exporting, by manufacturing in those locations where factor conditions are optimal and exporting to the rest of the world in order to achieve location and experience curve economies.

#14-59Q: What are the advantages of strategic alliances?

#14-59A: The advantages of alliances are that they facilitate entry into foreign markets, enable partners to share the fixed costs and risks associated with new products and processes, facilitate the transfer of complementary skills between companies, and help firms to establish technical standards.

#14-60Q: What are the primary characteristics of a good strategic alliance partner?

#14-60A: A good strategic alliance partner should be one that can help a firm to achieve its goals, has a similar vision with regard to the purpose and operation of the alliance, and is unlikely to act opportunistically.

CHAPTER 15

Students should be encouraged to choose the BEST answer, as more than one may be technically correct. Following each question is the answer, estimated difficulty, and page reference.

#15-1 Which country is generally the world's biggest exporter
A   US
B.   Japan
C.   China
D.   Britain
E.   Germany

e, medium, 446

#15-2 Small firms play a particularly large role in the exports of
A   US
B.   Japan
C.   China
D.   Britain
E.   Germany

e, medium, 446

#15-3 The textile firm Wilhelm Zuleeg is able to export products in an industry dominated by low cost Asian imports through the use of
A   large government subsidies
B.   state-of-the-art computerized manufacturing technology
C.   monopoly positions in the domestic market
D.   a strategy of matching the industrial technology of its Asian competitors

b, medium, 447

#15-4 A situation where payment for exports is received in goods and services rather than money is called
A   balanced trade
B.   weak currency trading
C.   countertrade
D.   deferred remuneration exporting
E.   counterexporting

c, easy, 442

#15-5 One of the biggest impediments to exporting is
A   lack of foreign exchange in the US
B.   an undervalued exchange rate
C.   ignorance of foreign opportunities
D.   analysis paralysis
E.   excess counter trade opportunities

c, medium, 444

#15-6 Trust is important to firms engaged in international trade because
A   international legal systems operate too efficiently
B.   it can be difficult to obtain payments from foreign firms if they default on an obligation
C.   letters of credit are an ineffective means of assuring payment
D.   sight drafts and time drafts are rarely honored across borders
E.   of the *sogo shosha* effect

b, easy, 449

#15-7 Evidence suggests that smaller US firms have begun to aggressively increase their export orientation in recent years due to
A   the gradual increase in trade barriers
B.   logistical problems associated with communication and transportation
C.   failure of regional economic arrangements
D.   services like international air express that reduce the hassles and costs of exporting

d, easy, 442-448

#15-8 The *Soga Shosha*
A   are Japan's large trading houses
B.   is a derogatory term for the planners in the Ministry of International Trade and Industry
C.   is a Japanese term for the large trade surpluses it has been running
D.   is another name for the kanban system
E.   are the equivalent of the Mafia in Japan

a, medium, 444

#15-9 Which two organizations located within the US Department of Commerce are dedicated to providing businesses with intelligence and assistance for exporting to foreign markets?
A   US Export Promotion Agency and the Foreign Service Desk
B.   International Trade Administration and the Inter-American Development Bank
C.   the Export-Import Bank and the US Export Promotion Agency
D.   International Trade Administration and the US & Foreign Commercial Service Agency
E.   U.S.F.I.A. and U.S.B.F.D.

d, hard, 445

#15-10 The matchmaker program organized by the Department of Commerce is a program where Department representatives
A   accompany groups of American business people abroad to meet with agents, distributors, and customers
B.   match small businesses with large multinationals or trading companies that can market their products
C.   match small US companies that can work together in order that they may be able to launch export initiatives that alone they could not
D.   try to match foreign investors with small US businesses

a, hard, 445

#15-11 Which of the following organizations in the US is NOT generally a source for firms looking for information about export opportunities?
A   US Department of Commerce
B.   trade commissions in states and large cities
C.   large consumer banks
D.   major accounting firms

c, hard, 445 (commercial, not consumer banks)

#15-12 A document used in international trade that states that a bank promises to pay a beneficiary (usually the exporter) is called a
A   bill of exchange
B.   exporter draft
C.   bank draft
D.   letter of credit
E.   bill of lading

d, easy, 450

#15-13 An order written by an exporter instructing an importer, or an importer's agent, to pay a specified amount of money at a specified time is called a
A   draft
B.   letter of credit
C.   trade acceptance
D.   bill of lading
E.   negotiable instrument

a, easy, 451

#15-14 A key document in international trade that is generally issued to the exporter by a common carrier and serves as a receipt, contract, and title is a
A   draft
B.   letter of credit
C.   trade acceptance
D.   bill of lading
E.   bill of exchange

d, easy, 452

#15-15 Exporters in the US can draw upon two different forms of government backed assistance to help finance their export programs. These two forms are
A   export credit insurance and the FCIA
B.   the Export-Import Bank and export credit insurance
C.   countertrade and the export promotion act
D.   the export promotion act and the Export-Import Bank
E.   export credit insurance and the export promotion act

b, hard, 453

#15-16 The mission of Eximbank is to

A	provide export credit assistance to US based firms

B.	supplement privately available export insurance and finance foreign receivables of US firms

C.	hold funds in escrow and provide letters of credit for exports, imports, and countertrade

D.	actively promote US exports and attempt to decrease imports into the US

E.	provide aid in financing and facilitating exports, imports, and commodity exchanges for the US

e, medium, 453

#15-17 Even when an exporter has to forego a letter of credit due to competitive pressures, they can still be assured of receiving payment if

A	the importer is located in a country with extradition and tax treaties with the US

B.	they engage in switch-trading in advance of shipment

C.	export credit insurance is obtained

D.	the importer is located in a low political and economic risk country

E.	the firm is a member of the United Nations Commercial Parties Assurance Association

c, medium, 454

#15-18 In the US, an association of private commercial institutions operating under the guidance of the Export-Import bank that provides insurance policies protecting US exporters is called the

A	Export Protection Bank

B.	Foreign Credit Insurance Association

C.	Foreign Service Account Assembly

D.	Export Discombobulation Administration

E.	World Bank

b, hard, 454

#15-19 Countertrade is one increasingly popular solution to the problems posed by

A	currency convertibility

B.	floating exchange rates

C.	excess foreign reserves being held by socialistic countries

D.	the growth of trading blocks

E.	the nonconvertibility of some currencies

e, easy, 454

#15-20 In 1992, it has been estimated that countertrade was involved in

A	around 5% of world trade

B.	around 20% of world trade

C.	around 50% of world trade

D.	around 75% of world trade

b, hard, 455

#15-21 Everything else being equal, a lack of hard currency and foreign exchange reserves in a developing country is likely to lead to
A   increased countertrade
B.   decreased countertrade
C.   increased barter only with no changes in other forms of countertrade
D.   decreased barter only with no changes in other forms of countertrade
E.   no difference in the level of countertrade compared to nations with greater reserves

a, easy, 455

#15-22 Which of the following is NOT one of the five distinct types of countertrade?
A   barter
B.   counterpurchase
C.   open purchase
D.   switch trading
E.   buy back

c, medium, 455

#15-23 The most restrictive type of countertrade is
A   barter
B.   counterpurchase
C.   switch trading
D.   offset
E.   open purchase

a, hard, 456

#15-24 A reciprocal buying agreement where a firm agrees to purchase a certain amount of materials from a country to which a sale is made is which type of countertrade?
A   buy back
B.   counterpurchase
C.   open purchase
D.   barter
E.   switch trading

b, medium, 456

#15-25 A countertrade agreement where a specialized third party trading house typically plays a role in matching traders is called
A   switch trading
B.   offset
C.   counterpurchase
D.   buyback
E.   barter

a, medium, 456

#15-26 Occidental Petroleum negotiated a deal with the USSR under which Occidental would build several ammonia plants in the USSR and as partial payment receive ammonia over a twenty year period. This type of agreement is called a

A   switch trading
B.   offset
C.   counterpurchase
D.   buyback
E.   open purchase

d, medium, 457

#15-27 One of the most common and serious drawbacks of countertrade is that countertrade contracts

A   are almost always unprofitable
B.   reduce the need for in-house trading departments
C.   reduce the need for in-house flexible manufacturing systems
D.   frequently reduce the opportunities a firm has to do business in developing countries
E.   may result in a firm receiving unusable or poor quality goods that cannot be easily disposed of profitably

e, easy, 457

#15-28 In general, countertrade is most attractive to

A   large firms that concentrate in one industry
B.   large firms that can use a worldwide network of contacts to dispose of goods received
C.   small firms that are adept at finding buyers and sellers
D.   firms other than the *Soga Shosha*
E.   high technology firms from third world countries

b, medium, 457

#15-29 The masters of countertrade are

A   the kanban firms
B.   Eastern European firms
C.   large domestic European firms
D.   Japanese trading firms
E.   Italian firms

d, medium, 457

#15-30 Unless there are no alternatives, small and medium sized exporters should probably try to avoid countertrade deals if possible since

A   countertrade deals are typically very complex and these firms lack the necessary expertise
B.   there is little contractual or fiduciary responsibility for their trading partners to live up to the deal
C.   the big multinationals already control the market
D.   they lack the network of operations required to make use of or dispose of goods received
E.   they will probably be taken advantage of

d, hard, 458

#15-31 Which country was the largest market for US exports in 1991?
A   France
B.   Britain
C.   Canada
D.   Germany
E.   Mexico

c, medium, common sense and obvious geography.

#15-32 Artais, a manufacturer of airport weather systems, has found that
A   it is actually easier to make sales in many foreign markets where there is less competition than in its home market
B.   overseas contracts tend to be more lucrative than its domestic sales
C.   the government subsidies it receives gives it a competitive advantage over foreign rivals
D.   all of the above
E.   none of the above

b, hard, 442

#15-33 The growth of exports is the result of all of the following EXCEPT
A   the reduction of trade barriers
B.   improved communication technologies
C.   the development of improved transportation systems
D.   increased economic development and prosperity in most countries
E.   the general acceptance of French as the language of international business, thus easing communication

e, easy, 442

#15-34 Large companies like Coca-Cola, IBM, and 3M
A   set up wholly owned subsidiaries and prefer not to export
B.   tend to be proactive in seeking out export opportunities
C.   prefer franchising of manufactured products over other market entry alternatives
D.   use a multidomestic strategy
E.   all of the above

b, medium, 443

#15-35 Many small firms choose to do little or no exporting for all of the following reasons EXCEPT
A   ignorance of opportunities
B.   unfamiliarity with languages, cultures, and currencies
C.   unwillingness to deal with all the legal and bureaucratic hassles involved in exporting
D.   there is little profit to be made for most exporters after considering transportation costs and import taxes
E.   bad initial experiences with exporting

d, hard, 443

#15-36 The "best prospects list" provided to firms by government agencies

A   are usually out-dated and contain many firms that have gone out of business

B.   contains the same information as in the "comparison shopping service", which is supplied by a different organization

C.   give the names and addresses of potential distributors in foreign markets

D.   describes the market characteristics of 14 different countries that may be of interest to a firm

c, medium, 445

#15-37 An EMC

A   is a Earnings Manipulation Conversion, which is used when translating currencies

B.   can help a firm identify foreign opportunities for its products

C.   usually adds significant costs to exports, thereby making exporting a low profit operation

D.   is a currency of the EU which is defined by a market basket of members' currencies

b, easy, 445

#15-38 Export management companies typically do all of the following EXCEPT

A   manage the ongoing export opportunities of a firm

B.   help a firm initially arrange for exports by introducing it to distributors in foreign markets

C.   provide manufacturing facilities in foreign markets where products can be customized for local markets

D.   provide consulting services to help firms with the bureaucratic hassles of exporting

E.   maintain a network of contacts in potential markets

c, medium, 445

#15-39 When beginning export operations, firms can improve their likelihood of success by

A   avoiding EMCs, as it prevents them from developing their own capabilities

B.   entering multiple markets simultaneously in order to achieve economies of scale

C.   starting on a large scale in a new market with high advertising in order to raise brand awareness

D.   avoiding local distributors, as they often take advantage of foreign neophyte exporters

E.   hiring additional people who can focus on managing the export business

F.   all of the above

e, easy, 442-448

#15-40 One of the most important factors in explaining Germany's export success is

A   central role in establishing the UN's EX-IM Bank

B.   the role of US banks in financing imports into the US

C.   its geographic location

D.   its strong relationship with the Soga Shosha

E.   none of the above

c, easy, 447

#15-41 Most of Minnesota Mining and Manufacturing's revenues come from
A   overseas manufacturing facilities
B.   exports
C.   imports
D.   domestic sales
E.   countertrade

d, hard, 448

#15-42 Minnesota Mining and Manufacturing establishes foreign manufacturing facilities
A   primarily in low labor cost countries to supply the North American market
B.   after exporting has convinced it that there is sufficient local demand to justify local production
C.   only in countries with convertible currencies so that it will not have to engage in countertrade
D.   according to its "FIDO" principles
E.   after obtaining approval from the Lake Wobegon Chatterbox Cafe Management Roundtable

b, medium, 448

#15-43 In introducing Post-it Notes in different countries, 3M
A   used a consistent distribution policy across all countries
B.   located factories only in each country's largest cities since that's where offices were located
C.   found poor acceptance of product samples in France (where they were considered "tacky"), and
         thus avoided the costs of building unnecessary manufacturing facilities
D.   all of the above
E.   none of the above

e, hard, 448

#15-44 In a typical international trade transaction
A   a letter of credit is sent only after goods are shipped
B.   drafts are presented prior to letters of credit
C.   an exporter agrees to fill an order only after it sells a draft to the its bank
D.   a foreign bank returns an accepted draft after goods have been shipped
E.   none of the above

d, hard, 452

#15-45 The FCIA
A   does not provide insurance against political risks
B.   is only available to foreign exporters
C.   has proved ineffectual as a facilitator of exports
D.   all of the above
E.   none of the above

e, medium, 454

#15-46 Which is type of countertrade is least commonly practiced
A   barter
B.   buyback
C.   counterpurchase
D.   offset
E.   switch trading

e, hard, 456

#15-47 Downey's Soup experience with exports to Japan
A   showed that perseverance can pay off in developing export markets
B.   illustrated how the Japanese government can help smooth over difficulties for foreign firms and get products through the difficult maze of regulations and customs inspections
C.   showed how important it is to adjust the flavor of products to local tastes
D.   all of the above
E.   none of the above

e, hard, 459

#15-48 Downey's international experiences
A   subsequently led to additional domestic opportunities
B.   showed how easy it can be for even small firms to develop export markets
C.   the importance of customizing products to local tastes
D.   shows how critical local testing can be for international success
E.   all of the above

a, medium, 459

#15-49 If a firm in one country agrees to trade a shipload of wheat for a container load of bicycles from a firm another firm in the same country, this is referred to as
A   offset
B.   barter
C.   buyback
D.   switch trading
E.   none of the above

b, easy, 455

#15-50 Compared to companies from Germany and Japan, US firms seeking out export opportunities
A   are informationally challenged
B.   receive relatively little governmental assistance
C.   often find that their banks are less familiar with international transactions
D.   have a less well developed business infrastructure to assist them
E.   all of the above

e, medium, 444

#15-51Q: What are the primary reasons why small German firms have been successful in exporting?

#15-51A: There are two factors which help explain the success of Germany's small firm sector in the export market - Germany's export infra-structure and the export orientation of small German firms. German embassies, banks, trade associations, and chambers of commerce in dozens of countries act as the foreign eyes and ears for small businesses. Perhaps more important than infrastructure in explaining German success, however, is the export orientation of German firms. Given its location in the middle of Europe, firms perspectives on international opportunities are much more open than in more insular countries.

#15-52Q: What trends can you identify that are making it easier for small firms to become exporters?

#15-52A: Several trends have made it easier for small firms to export. The gradual decline in trade barriers, modern communication and transportation technologies, information available from governmental agencies and independent organizations, and increasing homogenization of tastes and preferences all have made it easier for smaller firms to export.

#15-53Q: What are the primary sources of information for firms interested in gathering more information on export opportunities.

#15-53A: The primary sources of information for firms interested in gathering more information on export opportunities are governmental agencies, local trade commissions, banks, accounting firms, consulting firms, and industry trade associations. On top of these, a trip to the library (and hopefully a business school's library) can prove exceedingly valuable, as can some exploring on the world wide web. The usefulness and availability of all of these will depend, of course, on the country.

#15-54Q: What is a letter of credit? Who issues it? Why is a letter of credit often required in international trade?

#15-54A: A letter of credit is issued by a bank at the request of an importer and states that the bank promises to pay a beneficiary, normally the exporter, upon presentation of documents specified in the letter of credit. The letter of credit has evolved as an instrument for facilitating international trade between parties.

#15-55Q: What is a bill of lading? What purposes does it serve?

#15-55A: A bill of lading is issued to the exporter by a common carrier transporting the merchandise. It serves three purposes: a receipt, a contract, and a document of title.

#15-56Q: What is the Export-Import Bank? What are its objectives?

#15-56A: The Exim bank is an agency of the US federal government. Its mission is to provide aid in financing and facilitate exports and imports and the exchange of commodities between the US and other countries. Exim facilitates the financing of US exports through various loan guarantee programs.

#15-57Q: What types of risks does foreign credit insurance insure against?

#15-57A: Foreign credit insurance protects exporters against the risk of nonpayment by foreign debtors as a result of commercial and political risk.

#15-58Q: What are the primary problems with simple barter?

#15-58A: If goods are not traded simultaneously, one firm incurs the cost of financing until it receives its goods in barter. More important, however, is that it can be difficult to find goods that are of interest to both parties or which could be sold or bartered again for something of value. Lastly, the quality of goods bartered all to frequently is lower than that which is sold for currency.

#15-59Q: Explain how a buyback works.

#15-59A: In a buyback a firm builds a plant in a country, or supplies technology, equipment, training or other services to a facility. In return it agrees to take a specified amount of output from facility as partial payment for the initial investment.

#15-60Q: What are the advantages of using countertrade for a Canadian firm interested in selling its products into overseas markets?

#15-60A: The main advantage of countertrade is that it gives a firm a way to finance an export deal when other means are not available. Given the problems that many developing and third world nations have in raising the foreign exchange necessary to pay for imports, countertrade may be the only option available when doing business in these countries. At times countertrade may be only way a firm is able to make a potentially profitable deal.

#15-61Q: Why should small and medium firms shun countertrade unless it is the only way to make a potentially profitable deal?

#15-61A: Small and medium sized exporters should probably try to avoid countertrade deals if possible, since they lack the world wide network of operations that may be required to profitably utilize or dispose of goods acquired as a part of a countertrade agreement.

CHAPTER 16

Students should be encouraged to choose the BEST answer, as more than one may be technically correct. Following each question is the answer, estimated difficulty, and page reference.

#16-1 Which statement does NOT describe an aspect of the Bose's material management processes?
A   Bose uses a computer tracking system that tracks component parts as they move through the global supply chain.
B.   Bose's system allows shipments from component suppliers to actually clear customs before the product arrives in the US
C.   Bose's system allows managers to run simulations to examine such factors as the effect of duties on cost of goods sold.
D.   Bose has shifted component supply to US firms to reduce problems associated with just in time manufacturing and suppliers located overseas.

d, medium, 479

#16-2 Timberland's first international exporting success was to
A   Japan
B.   France
C.   Italy
D.   Indonesia

c, medium, 461

#16-3 The appreciation of the Yen against the US Dollar since early 1980's
A   has given Japan an advantage in world trade
B.   has not effected the advantage Japan had in the period 1950 through 1980 in world trade
C.   has not changed the relative attractiveness of Japan as a location for manufacturing
D.   has made Japan a less attractive place to locate manufacturing

d, easy, 465

#16-4 The minimum efficient scale of output is best defined as that which a plant must be operating at to
A   realize all major plant level scale economies
B.   achieve profitability in world markets
C.   achieve profitability in national markets
D.   have lower costs per unit than all competitors

a, medium, 466

#16-5 Everything else being equal, when the minimum efficient scale of production is relatively low it may be economical to manufacture a product
A   only in developing countries where wage levels are low
B.   at one central location and serve the entire world market from that location
C.   at several locations which may facilitate local responsiveness
D.   at several locations which may lead to a lower level of local responsiveness
E.   anywhere in the world without regard to minimum plant size considerations

c, medium, 467

#16-6 The type of manufacturing technology that is specifically designed to produce a wider variety of end products at a cost that at one time could only be achieved through the mass production of a standardized output has been called

A   computer based manufacturing
B.   the Deming method of manufacturing
C.   the Crosby method of quality control
D.   standardized cell based manufacturing technologies
E.   flexible manufacturing technologies

e, medium, 467

#16-7 A flexible machine cell is best defined as a grouping of

A   various types of machinery, a common material handler, and with multiskilled workers whose job it is to manually operate a variety of specialized machinery
B.   flexible machinery, multiskilled workers, and a material handler specialized to each separate machine
C.   various types of machinery, a centralized cell controller (computer), combined with unskilled tasks for low paid labor
D.   various types of machinery, a common material handler, and a centralized cell controller (computer)

d, hard, 468

#16-8 From an international business standpoint, the most important impact of flexible manufacturing systems is that it has enabled certain firms to

A   manufacture globally standardized products at several locations without cost penalties
B.   manufacture products that are customized to different national markets at a single factory sited at the optimal location
C.   manufacture standardized products at one central location
D.   reduce the cost penalties associated with global manufacturing

b, medium, 468

#16-9 Flexible machine cells can improve capacity utilization by

A   utilizing a single controller for a cell of identical machines
B.   evening out the flow rate of production lines
C.   having only the most skilled technicians serving as machine controllers
D.   decreasing the amount of time parts spend on any one machine
E.   reducing set up times

e, hard, 468

#16-10 Overall, technological factors seem to be creating pressures for multinationals to

A   locate manufacturing facilities in each country the firm does business in
B.   concentrate manufacturing facilities at the optimal location
C.   focus on flexible manufacturing technologies and decrease their responsiveness to local demands
D.   no longer consider trade barriers and transportation costs in their optimal location decisions
E.   return to traditional methods of manufacturing

b, medium, 469

#16-11 Which factor generally does NOT have an important impact on location decisions?
A   whether or not the product serves universal needs
B.   the product's value to weight ratio
C.   product utility
D.   minimum economies of scale in manufacturing

c, easy, 469

#16-12 Concentration of manufacturing makes most sense when
A   trade barriers are high
B.   important exchange rates are expected to remain relatively stable
C.   the product does not serve universal needs
D.   the product's value to weight ratio is low
E.   political risk is low

b, hard, 469

#16-13 Decentralization of manufacturing to multiple locations makes most sense when
A   differences between countries with regard to factor costs, political economy, and culture do not
           have a substantial impact on the costs of manufacturing in different countries
B.   the production technology has high fixed costs and a high minimum efficient scale
C.   flexible manufacturing technology exists
D.   the product serves universal needs
E.   trade barriers are low

a, medium, 469

#16-14 Which of the following is a decentralizing factor in the world automotive industry?
A   availability of flexible manufacturing technologies
B.   the world's current fixed exchange rate regime
C.   formal and informal trade barriers
D.   the relatively high value to weight ratio of autos

c, medium, 470

#16-15 The Ford Fiesta sold in Europe is assembled
A   in one factory in Spain due to low labor costs
B.   in one factory in Germany due to advanced manufacturing facilities
C.   in separate factories in the UK, Germany, and Spain
D.   in Korea and shipped to Europe
E.   in the US and shipped to Europe

c, hard, 471

#16-16 It has been argued that vertical integration may facilitate
A   investment in highly specialized assets and the diffusion of proprietary product technology to competitor firms
B.   investment in highly specialized assets and protect proprietary product technology
C.   protection of proprietary product technology, yet make the scheduling of processes more difficult
D.   investment in flexible assets and make the scheduling of adjacent processes more difficult
E.   investment in flexible assets and protect proprietary product technology

b, hard, 472

#16-17 In general, when substantial investments in specialized assets are required to manufacture a component part, the firm will
A   prefer to contract out the component rather than risk the dangers associated with investing in specialized equipment
B.   contract out the component to avoid a situation of mutual dependence
C.   have no clear preference to manufacture the part internally or contract it out
D.   have a wealth of suppliers willing to manufacture the component because of the desire of the suppliers to become mutually dependent
E.   prefer to make that component internally rather than contract it out to an independent supplier

e, medium, 473

#16-18 In general, firms which have a substantial amount of proprietary product technology will face pressures to
A   vertically integrate
B.   contract out component parts to independent firms
C.   increase the width of their value chain
D.   reduce their forward and backward integration
E.   reduce only their backward integration

a, easy, 473

#16-19 The argument that a firm should vertically integrate to improve scheduling
A   is supported by a great deal of empirical evidence
B.   was shown to be especially important to Bose Corporation
C.   is often made but not always supported by case examples
D.   is probably the strongest argument for vertical integration

c, hard, 474

#16-20 In general, sourcing component parts form independent suppliers might be a wise strategy when the optimal location for manufacturing a product is
A   located in a developing country
B.   located in a developed country
C.   located where possible local suppliers lack the necessary capital to invest in specialized machinery
D.   is in a country where the firm has had extensive previous experience
E.   beset by political risks

e, hard, 475

#16-21 Which of the following is an organizational advantage of making rather than buying?
A   increased scheduling flexibility
B.   increased organizational complexity
C.   inefficient internal suppliers shielded from the market
D.   the negotiation of transfer prices

a, easy, 476

#16-22 In order to build increased trust between a firm and a supplier and to encourage the supplier to invest in specialized assets, a firm may
A   increase horizontal integration
B.   enter into a strategic alliance with that supplier
C.   integrate forward in the supply chain
D.   integrate backward in the supply chain
E.   emphasize legal compliance with international suppliers

b, easy, 477

#16-23 In 1985 US manufacturers spent an average of $3,350 on parts, materials, and services for small cars, whereas the average Japanese company spent $2,750. This cost savings was achieved mainly through
A   more efficient labor relations at Japanese firms
B.   more efficient labor processes at Japanese firms
C.   the graft and corruption present in American firms
D.   more efficient vendor relations at Japanese firms
E.   less effective flexible manufacturing cells in US firms

d, medium, 477

#16-24 The spread of just-in-time systems, computer aided design and computer aided manufacturing seem to have
A   increased pressures for firms to enter into long term relations with suppliers
B.   decreased pressures for firms to enter into long term relations with suppliers
C.   decreased the need for credible commitments between a firm and its suppliers
D.   increased competitive pressures for internal customers to sell to both internal and external customers
E.   resulted in standardization of firm and supplier relations

a, easy, 477

#16-25 What is a major drawback of the just in time system
A   reduced inventory turnover
B.   no buffer stocks are held
C.   decreased product quality
D.   delayed response to defective inputs

b, easy, 480

#16-26 The major cost savings from JIT techniques comes from
A.   increasing cost of goods sold
B.   decreasing cost of goods sold
C.   increasing work in process inventory
D.   increasing inventory turnover
E.   decreasing inventory turnover

d, easy, 480

#16-27 It was suggested that to give the materials management function more legitimacy in the multinational firm it may be a good idea to
A.   incorporate it into the purchasing department
B.   incorporate it into the manufacturing department
C.   incorporate it into the marketing department
D.   separate it out by giving both the manufacturing and marketing departments separate materials control to foster integration with their other internal processes
E.   separate it out as a function within the firm and give it equal weight in comparison with other more traditional functional areas

e, easy, 480

#16-28 The great advantage of a decentralized materials management function in the multinational firm is that it allows plant level materials management groups to
A.   decrease coordination with headquarters and therefore find cheaper local suppliers
B.   develop the knowledge and skills needed to interact with foreign suppliers
C.   duplicate efforts and reduce the likelihood of downtime
D.   decrease their level of local sourcing
E.   reduce their time spent on administrative duties

b, hard, 482

#16-29 Probably the main disadvantage to decentralized materials management is that it can lead to
A.   a lack of knowledge on the part of centralized management to local plant needs
B.   an increase in the use of information systems to coordinate global sourcing
C.   the loss of power by central management
D.   a lack of coordination between plants and inefficient global sourcing
E.   the spread of authority to the local level

d, hard, 482

#16-30 Which of the following is NOT an advantage of EDI systems
A.   increasing intra-firm coordination
B.   paperless ordering
C.   real time communication with suppliers
D.   tracking of parts through the ordering process
E.   elimination of the need for decentralized materials management

e, medium, 483

#16-31 Which was one of the problems of mass production noted by Ohno Taiichi, one of the developers of Toyota's lean production system
A   short production runs lead to inefficient downtime
B.   too little inventory to buffer against defects
C.   too many defects and waste
D.   all of the above

c, hard, 467

#16-32 Timberland
A   has found out that foreign markets can be quite fickle, as its exports have fallen in recent years
B.   sells shoes in foreign markets for higher return than in its domestic market
C.   has found that while it can charge slightly higher prices in foreign markets, the transportation costs bring profit levels down to roughly domestic levels
D.   that it is most efficient to have one large plant with a central warehouse, and manage all shipping and logistics from a central location
E.   all of the above

b, hard, 462

#16-33 One can conclude from the Timberland case that
A   minimum efficient scale of manufacturing in this industry is quite low
B.   price competition is less important than efficient timing of arrival of goods for its dealers
C.   there are economies in shipping that actually improve cost performance if central warehouses are built and products are shipped there for warehousing rather than kept at factories and shipped directly to customers without the double shipping
D.   all of the above
E.   none of the above

d, medium, 462

#16-34 Improved quality control reduces costs in all of the following ways EXCEPT
A   lower scrap and rework costs
B.   lower warranty costs
C.   higher monitoring costs
D.   not wasting time manufacturing inferior goods

c, easy, 463

#16-35 The TQM concept was
A   developed primarily by US researchers
B.   popularized worldwide by its success in turning around France's bloated state owned firms
C.   the focus of Ohno Taiichi's studies in the auto industry
D.   found to be applicable to manufacturing, but not service firms
E.   found to work best if defect rates of 2% or less were set as the target

a, hard, 463

#16-36 ISO 9000

A   is a car model developed by Audi
B.   was the shoe model that launched Timberland's international expansion
C.   is a certification process in the EU focused on minimizing costs to the natural environment
D.   tends to focus management attention on business practices that can improve quality
E.   none of the above

d, hard, 464

#16-37 When the fixed costs associated with setting up a manufacturing plant are high

A   it makes sense to set up several plants in order to minimize political risk
B.   plants are usually more responsive to local consumer needs in their production processes
C.   minimum scale economies tend to be low
D.   it is very important to consider location economies in plant site selection
E.   all of the above

d, medium, 466

#16-38 Flexible manufacturing attempts to

A   reduce set up times for equipment
B.   increase equipment utilization
C.   improve quality control in all manufacturing stages
D.   allow plants to produce a wider range of products
E.   all of the above

e, easy, 467

#16-39 The major benefits of flexible machine cells include

A   improved capacity utilization
B.   increased set-up times
C.   decreased need for computers
D.   increased work in process inventories
E.   higher costs

a, easy, 468

#16-40 A product's value to weight ratio has the most effect on

A   the appropriateness of flexible manufacturing technologies
B.   transportation costs
C.   the applicability of flexible manufacturing cells
D.   minimum economies of scale
E.   profit margins in foreign markets

b, medium, 469

#16-41 Which of the following is least likely to be manufactured at plants with high minimum economies of scale
A   industrial electronics
B.   steel
C.   bulk chemicals
D.   handhold calculators
E.   shoes

e, easy, 469

#16-42 If a product has a low value to weight ratio and does not serve universal needs
A   manufacturing is likely to be decentralized
B.   manufacturing is likely to occur at plants with high minimum economies of scale
C.   firms are likely to have very complex international logistics systems for tracking shipments
D.   all of the above
E.   none of the above

a, medium, 470

#16-43 If fixed costs are high, the minimum efficient scale is high, and flexible manufacturing technologies are available
A   profits are almost always higher than otherwise
B.   there is little need for complex international logistics systems
C.   there are likely high trade barriers
D.   there are strong incentives for manufacturing to be centralized
E.   none of the above

d, medium, 470

#16-44 In Ford's production network in Europe for the Fiesta,
A   more plants are located in Britain than any other country
B.   final assembly is centralized in the geographic center of the web
C.   all plants are located within countries that are part of the EU's exchange rate mechanism in order to minimize the effect of exchange rate fluctuations
D.   most manufacturing is located in low labor cost countries in Eastern Europe

a, hard, 471

#16-45 Firms like Nike and Reebok
A   use highly centralized manufacturing plants, which is the opposite of Timberland's manufacturing strategy
B.   rarely invest in computerized logistics systems, as such systems become quickly obsolete
C.   outsource most or all of their manufacturing
D.   invest in specialized equipment in order to have a competitive advantage with radical new designs
E.   all of the above

c, medium, 472

#16-46 Why does Boeing produce aircraft wings itself rather than outsourcing them
A   it has low minimum economies of scale
B.   it is more efficient than potential suppliers
C.   the value to weight ratio is too low to make shipping economical
D.   all of the above
E.   none of the above

b, hard, 472

#16-47 Mutual dependency occurs when firms
A   invest in specialized assets
B.   invest in flexible machining cells
C.   decentralize manufacturing to many countries
D.   adopt lean production

a, hard, 472

#16-48 Which of the following criteria is least important in Boeing's make or buy decisions
A   basic economics
B.   strategic risk
C.   operational risk
D.   offsets
E.   current exchange rates

e, medium, 475

#16-49 Bose Corporation's
A   primary assembly plant is in a low labor cost country
B.   success in Japan is a result of its use of offsets
C.   logistics system is strictly under its own control so as to not lose this core competence
D.   all of the above
E.   none of the above

e, medium, 479

#16-50 Digital Equipment Corporation
A   moved to more centralized manufacturing to protect proprietary technology
B.   became less vertically integrated as technology became more standardized
C.   increased the number of plants producing finished goods in order to be more locally responsive
D.   chose to subcontract most all manufacturing when specialized assets became no longer critical to
           its success
E.   none of the above

b, medium, 484

#16-51Q: What types of services does W.N. Proctor provide to Bose to help it in its materials management?

#16-51A: (see page 479)

#16-52Q: In what ways can increased quality also reduce costs?

#16-52A: There are three ways in which improved quality control reduces costs. First, productivity increases because time is not wasted manufacturing poor quality products. Second, increased product quality means lower re-work and scrap costs. Third, greater product quality means lower warranty and after sales re-work costs.

#16-53Q: What is "time based competition"? Suggest some specific activities that can make firms better time based competitors.

#16-53A: When consumer demand is prone to large and unpredictable shifts, firms that can adapt most quickly to these shifts by introducing new products, adapting products, or changing the quantity and location where goods are shipped will be at a competitive advantage over their more lead-footed competitor.

#16-54Q: Under what conditions do technological factors suggest that firms centralize their manufacturing?

#16-54A: When fixed costs are substantial, the minimum efficient scale of production is high, and/or flexible manufacturing technologies are available, the arguments for concentrating production in a few locations are strong.

#16-55Q: What are the advantages of making components rather than buying them from independent suppliers?

#16-55A: The advantages of making components in house are that it facilitates investments in specialized assets, helps firms protect proprietary technology, and improves scheduling between adjacent stages in the value chain.

#16-56Q: When manufacturing specific components requires substantial investments in specialized assets, it can be difficult subcontract production to another firm due to mutual dependency. Describe how mutual dependency works.

#16-56A: When manufacturing specific components requires substantial investments in specialized assets, it can be difficult to subcontract out manufacturing if neither party completely trusts the other. The supplier becomes dependent upon the buyer to recover its investment in specialized assets, and the buyer is dependent upon the supplier for its components that it does not have available form other sources. This situation of mutual dependency makes the buyer hesitant to contract out production and makes suppliers hesitant to undertake investments in the specialized assets.

#16-57Q: In what ways does vertical integration increase organizational costs?

#16-57A: Vertical integration into the manufacture of component parts involves an increase in the scope of the organization. The resulting increase in organizational complexity can be costly. First, more organizational units and personnel necessarily lead to more units that need to be coordinated and controlled. Secondly, vertically integrated units that are not subjected to external price competition may not focus on and make available cost reductions. Thirdly, the complexity in determining internal transfer prices can reduce or miss-apply incentives within a vertically integrated unit.

#16-58Q: What are the advantages and disadvantages of a Just in Time system?

#16-58A: Just in Time systems generate major cost savings from reduced warehousing and inventory holding costs. In addition, JIT systems help the firm to spot defective parts and take them out of the manufacturing process - thereby boosting product quality - and catching quality problems quickly. The main disadvantage is that buffer inventories are minimized. Although buffer stocks incur holding costs, they also allow the firm to respond more quickly to changes in demand and can tide them over if an expected shipment of components is unexpectedly late.

#16-59Q: How can electronic data interchange systems help coordinate activities with suppliers.

#16-59A: EDI facilitates the ordering of parts, tracking of inputs, allows the firm to optimize is production schedule, allows the firm and its suppliers to communicate in real time and adapt to changing demands, and eliminates the flow of paperwork between a firm and its suppliers.

#16-60Q: What factors favor a concentrated manufacturing strategy? A decentralized manufacturing strategy?

#16-60A: (see page 470, especially Table 16.1)

CHAPTER 17

Students should be encouraged to choose the BEST answer, as more than one may be technically correct. Following each question is the answer, estimated difficulty, and page reference.

#17-1 Which statement best describes the new product development and marketing strategies used by Proctor and Gamble for the thirty years after World War II?
A   Products were carefully tailored to local markets to fit local tastes
B.   Substantial new product development activity occurred in many different countries
C.   Products were developed primarily in the US and were changed little for introduction overseas
D.   The strategies were success in Japan, but not Poland.
E.   Products were generally developed in low wage areas outside the US and exported globally

c, medium, 511

#17-2 Why was Wash & Go an apparent failure in Poland?
A   the high profile Western style advertising blitz apparently backfired
B.   the product caused dandruff and hair loss due to an unusual chemical reaction with Polish water
C.   the advertising was poorly targeted, as it showed someone taking a shower in the morning and going off to work, while most Poles prefer to take a bath in the evening before going to bed
D.   P&G used a push strategy and did not appeal directly to customers

a, easy, 512

#17-3 A global marketing strategy, which involves viewing customers worldwide as being similar in tastes and preferences, is consistent with which form of production?
A   a high level of adaptation of products in local markets
B.   a medium level of adaptation of products to regional, not local, markets
C.   batch processing of intermediate products
D.   flow production of capital goods
E.   mass production of standardized output

e, medium, 590

#17-4 In a famous Harvard Business Review article, Theodore Levitt state that the world is moving towards a "commonalty of preference". According to Levitt, the force causing this change is
A   democratization and free markets
B.   technology
C.   economic development
D.   multinational corporations

b, hard, 490

#17-5 A good general rule is that consumers in less developed countries want products
A   that are simple and reliable
B.   that are exactly the same as those sold in more developed countries
C.   with more product attributes, and particularly visual ones that convey greater status
D.   extra performance attributes

a, medium, 492

#17-6 Two of the main driving forces that result in the need to modify products to meet local tastes and preferences are
A   standardized marketing strategies and levels of economic development
B.   technology and economic development
C.   technology and culture
D.   culture and levels of economic development
E.   culture and mass production techniques

d, hard, 491

#17-7 Nestle has been able to successfully market its Lean Cuisine frozen dinners in essentially the same way in
A   North America and Japan
B.   North and South America
C.   North America and Europe
D.   Europe and Asia
E.   Scandinavia, England, and US

c, medium, 492

#17-8 McDonald's was cited by Theodore Levitt as one company that fits his description of the world well. Others have argued that McDonald's does not fit Levitt's view because
A   McDonald's produces the same products everywhere with little modification
B.   the menu in Mexico is identical to that in Moscow or Memphis
C.   McDonald's modifies the menu to meet local tastes
D.   McDonald's operates under a franchise structure
E.   McDonald's has to change the name of its products in different countries (i.e. a "quarter pounder" makes no sense in countries on the metric system)

c, medium, 490

#17-9 S.C. Johnson & Son had to adjust the smell of its furniture polish in Japan because
A   it smelled like a latrine disinfectant used in the 1940s
B.   it reminded them of an incense used during burials
C.   its scent was indistinguishable from a popular insecticide
D.   its scent was patented already by a aftershave manufacturer
E.   it smelled like "old grandmother's house" and was not popular with younger buyers

a, hard, 491

#17-10 Regional economic blocks, such as the EC, may make marketing standard products easier in these countries due to the fact that
A   advertising will be regulated by the same laws in all countries
B.   legislation will dictate uniform consumer preferences
C.   exchange rates will further stabilize
D.   product standards are being harmonized across countries
E.   a common language will simplify advertising and packaging

d, medium, 492

#17-11 Which country has the most concentrated retail channel for food products? (four chains control 65% of the market)
A   Spain
B.   US
C.   Italy
D.   Germany
E.   Japan

d, hard, 494

#17-12 Factors that are contributing most significantly to an increase in retail concentration in the developing countries are
A   increased product standardization, increased advertising expenses, and increased two income households
B.   increased number of households with refrigerators, increased advertising expenses, and increased urban concentration
C.   increased urban concentration, increased two income households, increased disposable income
D.   increased car ownership, increased number of households with refrigerators, increased urban concentration
E.   increased number of two income households, increased car ownership, and increased number of households with refrigerators

e, hard, 494

#17-13 An exclusive distribution channel can be defined as one
A   where the distribution channel is very concentrated
B.   in which outsiders find it difficult to gain access
C.   in which the product must go through a large number of intermediaries
D.   in which the desired product can only be found in specialty stores
E.   in which one wholesaler has the rights to distribute the product in a particular market

e, hard, 495

#17-14 Countries with fragmented retail systems tend to have
A   short channels of distribution
B.   medium length channels of distribution
C.   long channels of distribution
D.   few wholesalers
E.   intense retail concentration

c, easy, 494

#17-15 A classic example of a country with a fragmented retail system is
A   Britain
B.   Germany
C.   USA
D.   Japan
E.   Holland

d, easy, 494

#17-16 Apple Computer has been able to increase its market share in Japan by selling its products through
A   its own stores
B.   signing distribution agreements with major firms with strong reputations
C.   direct advertising and mail
D.   small retailers
E.   the *sogo shosha*

b, medium, 495

#17-17 REI, a manufacturer of outdoor clothing equipment, has been able to successfully sell its products in Japan through
A   its own stores
B.   signing distribution agreements with major firms with strong reputations
C.   direct advertising and mail
D.   small retailers
E.   the *sogo shosha*

c, medium, 494

#17-18 Which of the following is NOT one of the potentially critical variables that may inhibit international communication
A   cultural barriers
B.   source effects
C.   target mobility
D.   noise levels

c, medium, 496

#17-19 Generally, many international businesses try to counter negative source effects by
A   targeting lower income level consumers
B.   de-emphasizing their foreign origins
C.   increasing channel length
D.   changing distribution channels
E.   avoiding exclusive distribution channels

b, hard, 497

#17-20 A company which relied exclusively on radio advertising to target consumers in the US for the past 20 years would only be able to follow that same advertising strategy in which countries
A   Canada and Britain
B.   Japan and Canada
C.   Japan and Norway
D.   Norway and Sweden
E.   Sweden and Britain

b, hard, 498

#17-21 Which of the following arguments is NOT typically used as a reason for moving towards standardized worldwide advertising campaigns?
A   creative talent is scarce
B.   attractiveness of developing a global brand image
C.   standardization of media worldwide
D.   cost effectiveness

c, medium, 499

#17-22 In situations where consumers can practice arbitrage across international borders, it directly affects the likelihood that a firm will be able to practice
A   creative advertising
B.   pull strategies
C.   international pricing strategy
D.   experience curve pricing
E.   price discrimination

e, easy, 501

#17-23 In general, price elasticities tend to be greater in
A   countries with low income levels
B.   countries where consumers have low bargaining power
C.   profit maximizing countries
D.   high R&D countries
E.   countries with high GDP/capita

a, easy, 502

#17-24 Normally, for a firm to pursue a strategy calling for predatory pricing in a foreign market, it is helpful if
A   the foreign market has strict anti-dumping regulations
B.   the firm faces intense competition in all its markets
C.   the firm has a profitable position in a different market
D.   another multinational is also pursuing predatory pricing in the same market

c, medium, 504

#17-25 In 1988 the US placed a 25% duty on Japanese light trucks because the trucks were being sold in the US at a price lower than that in Japan. The Japanese manufacturers argued that they were not dumping their products and the price difference was due to
A   GATT regulations
B.   the intense competition in the US market
C.   low shipping costs
D.   Japanese government export subsidies
E.   predatory pricing

b, medium, 505

#17-26 Other things being equal, the rate of new product development is thought to be less in countries where

A   more is spent on basic R&D
B.   consumers are affluent
C.   competition is weak
D.   the culture supports individuality

c, hard, 508

#17-27 For most of the post World War II period, which country is regarded as being the leader in technological innovation?

A   USA
B.   Japan
C.   Germany
D.   Albania
E.   Britain

a, easy, 508

#17-28 Which country spends the greatest percentage of its GDP on non-defense R&D in 1990?

A   USA
B.   Japan
C.   Germany
D.   Albania
E.   Britain

b, medium, 509

#17-29 In a 1991 study conducted by the Japanese Economic Planning Agency, which firms appeared to be dominating the greatest number of leading edge technologies?

A   Japanese firms
B.   US firms
C.   European firms
D.   firms from Eastern Europe and the former USSR

b, hard, 509

#17-30 The need to adequately commercialize new technologies in product markets that may require some local adaptation appears to be creating forces requiring the need for technologically dependent multinationals to locate R&D

A   centers in several countries worldwide
B.   in only one location in order to achieve scale effects
C.   primarily in the US, as this is still the largest and most trend setting market
D.   primarily in Japan as it is on the forefront of technology today

a, medium, 510

#17-31 Polaroid originally marketed its instant camera the same in Europe as it had in the US because it felt

A   the additional expense of targeted European advertising would never pay off
B.   the market was more limited in Europe, but the target customers would be able to understand the ads
C.   the product served universal needs
D.   positive source effects would help the product sell
E.   the noise level in Europe was too high to justify expensive ads in 10 different languages

c, medium, 500

#17-32 To improve success in its European advertising, it

A   hired a British market research firm to better understand the European consumer
B.   used a strategy developed by its small Swiss subsidiary - the functional uses of instant photos
C.   imported a advertising strategy that had worked successfully in Australia
D.   used testimonials from famous personalities
E.   gave away cameras in schools. The children would take many pictures and their parents would have to pay for the film which had a high mark-up.

b, hard, 500

#17-33 The greater the difference in the elasticities of demand between different countries

A   the easier it will be to develop a global advertising theme
B.   the less likely that a firm will be able increase its profits through differential pricing
C.   the less attractive predatory pricing becomes
D.   the easier it is to use price discrimination

d, hard, 501

#17-34 MTV reaches the most households in

A   Europe
B.   US and Canada
C.   Asia
D.   Australia
E.   Africa

a, hard, 487

#17-35 MTV is owned by

A   a European firm
B.   an American firm
C.   an Asian firm
D.   a private reclusive former rock star
E.   Elvis

b, hard, 487

#17-36 MTV helped grunge rock become famous worldwide, although it developed primarily in
A   Singapore
B.   Sweden
C.   San Paulo
D.   Seattle
E.   Switzerland

d, medium, 487

#17-37 The advantage of advertising on MTV for firms like Pepsi is
A   global reach
B.   closely targeted market segment
C.   low cost
D.   all of the above
E.   a and b only

e, medium, 487

#17-38 Consumers' differing product preferences are often based on culture and tradition. These are particularly important in which industry
A   music
B.   food
C.   motor oil
D.   automobiles
E.   soft drinks

b, hard, 491

#17-39 There is a tendency for greater retail concentration in
A   countries with high GDP/capita
B.   Hispanic countries
C.   African countries
D.   personal care products
E.   none of the above

a, easy, 494

#17-40 Fragmented retail systems
A   are most common in Germany
B.   lead to greater levels of price competition
C.   are most common when there low price elasticities of demand
D.   promote short distribution channels
E.   tend to promote the development of wholesalers

e, hard, 494

#17-41 Longer distribution channels tend to
A   lead to higher retail price levels
B.   be disadvantageous when there is a high price elasticity
C.   be fairly common in Japan
D.   all of the above
E.   none of the above

d, medium, 495

#17-42 The best way to overcome cultural barriers to international communication is to
A   use only global advertising media like MTV
B.   develop cross cultural awareness
C.   hire multi-ethnic advertising agencies
D.   minimize negative source effects
E.   none of the above

b, easy, 496

#17-43 Multinational firms can minimize negative source effects by
A   de-emphasizing their national origins
B.   advertising only in local languages
C.   signing exclusive distribution agreements
D.   emphasizing the fact that their products are made in low cost countries
E.   employing foreign advertising agencies

a, hard, 497

#17-44 In its marketing of shampoo in Poland, Procter and Gamble
A   suffered from significant negative source effects
B.   may have been negatively impacted by the low noise levels in advertising
C.   utilized primarily a push strategy
D.   emphasized how the products were produced in local factories
E.   all of the above

b, hard, 497

#17-45 Pull strategies are most common in which industry
A   chemicals
B.   industrial machinery
C.   beverages
D.   transportation
E.   prescription drugs

c, easy, 497

#17-46 Pull strategies tend to be emphasized

A   for consumer goods

B.   when distribution channels are long

C.   if there are well developed advertising media channels

D.   all of the above

E.   none of the above

d, easy, 498

#17-47 Auto companies in Europe are able to relatively easily practice price discrimination between

A   Belgium and Germany

B.   France and Spain

C.   Britain and Italy

D.   Spain and Portugal

E.   Italy and Austria

c, medium, 501

#17-48 The price elasticity of stereo equipment is likely to be highest in

A   US

B.   Britain

C.   Iceland

D.   Lithuania

E.   Belgium

d, hard, 502

#17-49 Firms pursuing an experience curve pricing strategy internationally

A   will almost never use a pull advertising strategy

B.   tend to price their products low worldwide

C.   usually are not profit maximizers in the long run

D.   often face anti-dumping regulations

E.   all of the above

b, hard, 504

#17-50 Castrol Lubricants

A   attempts to use promote product differentiation in what is largely a commodity business

B.   is a British firm with extensive operations in developing countries

C.   has not used an experience curve pricing strategy

D.   modifies its communication strategy significantly across countries

E.   all of the above

e, medium, 507

#17-51Q: Based on experience with disposable diapers and laundry detergents in Japan, what has Procter and Gamble done to prevent similar problems in the future?

#17-51A: P&G's experience with disposable diapers and laundry detergents in Japan prompted the company to rethink its new product development and marketing philosophy. The company has now admitted that its US centered way of doing things will no longer work. Since the late 1980s P&G has been attempting to delegate far more responsibility for new product development and marketing strategy to its major subsidiary companies in Japan and Europe. The result has been the creation of a company that is more responsive to local differences in consumer tastes and preferences, and more willing to admit that good new products can be developed outside of the US.

#17-52Q: How do economic differences between countries affect the importance of different product attributes?

#17-52A: As a general rule, consumer behavior is influenced by the level of economic development of a country. Firms based in highly developed countries tend to build a lot of extra performance attributes into their products. These extra attributes are not usually demanded by consumers in less developed nations, where the preference is for more stripped down products. In fact, consumers in the most advanced countries often do not want globally standardized products that have been developed with the lowest common denominator in mind. The are prepared to pay more for products that have added features and whose attributes are customized to their own tastes and preferences.

#17-53Q: What are the major ways in which the distribution systems in countries differ?

#17-53A: The main differences that exist between countries with regard to distribution systems are threefold: the degree of retail concentration, the channel length, and the exclusivity of the distribution system.

#17-54Q: In countries with relatively fragmented retail systems, do there tend to short or long channels of distribution? Why?

#17-54A: Countries with fragmented retail systems tend to have long channels of distribution. While in countries where the retail systems are concentrated it makes sense for the firm to deal directly with retailers and cut out intermediaries, when the retail system is fragmented it is not economic for a manufacturer to have sales personnel call on every retailer. A wholesaler that carries a variety of related products is better able to serve these retailers with a family of products. In addition, there are often also other wholesalers that specialize in particular types of products that serve these wholesalers. Thus the distribution channels tend to be long when there are relatively fragmented retail channels.

#17-55Q: What are the primary barriers to international communication?

#17-55A: The primary barriers to international communication include cultural differences, source effects, and noise levels.

#17-56Q: Under what circumstances are pull strategies generally preferable to push strategies?

#17-56A: Pull strategies tend to be preferable to push strategies when: 1) consumer goods are involved, 2) distribution channels are long, and 3) sufficient print and electronic media are available to carry the marketing message.

#17-57Q: Describe the advantages of using a standardized world wide advertising campaign.

#17-57A: The advantages of a standardized worldwide advertising campaign are threefold. First, there are significant economic advantages in pursuing such a strategy. A standardized campaign helps lower the costs of ad creation by spreading the fixed development costs over a large number of outlets. Second, creative talent can be more readily and efficiently tapped. Third, a standardized campaign can help develop a global brand image.

#17-58Q: For a firm to practice price discrimination, what conditions must hold?

#17-58A: For price discrimination to work the firm must be able to keep national markets separate and different price elasticities of demand must exist in different countries.

#17-59Q: What is predatory pricing? Under what conditions is predatory pricing practical?

#17-59A: Predatory pricing involves using price as a competitive weapon to drive weaker competitors out of a national market. For such a strategy to work, a firm must be earning profits in another country that it can use to subsidize its predatory prices. There must also not be governmental restrictions to such a practice.

#17-60Q: What must a firm do if it is to build a competency in new product development?

#17-60A: In order to build up a competency in new product development an international business must disperse R&D to those countries where new products are being pioneered and integrate R&D with an understanding of market demands.

CHAPTER 18

Students should be encouraged to choose the BEST answer, as more than one may be technically correct. Following each question is the answer, estimated difficulty, and page reference.

#18-1 Colgate-Palmolive's training program, which is designed to develop an international cadre of executive managers, includes
A   programs designed to develop interpersonal skills
B.   executive MBA classwork
C.   language instruction
D.   training focusing specifically on HRM issues in global management
E.   development of product strategies on how to best "throw products over the wall" to subsidiaries

c, hard, 538

#18-2 An expatriate manager a
A   manager hired by a foreign subsidiary to work in the manager's home country
B.   manager who has worked in several different foreign subsidiaries
C.   manager hired by a transnational firm
D.   citizen of one country who has been transferred abroad to work in a different country

d, easy, 516

#18-3 The HRM function attempts to help a firm achieve its primary strategic goals through the efficient administration of activities such as
A   performance evaluation, management development, and compensation policy
B.   staffing, labor relations, and materials management
C.   strategic planning, staffing, and human resource strategy
D.   compensation, product development, and labor relations

a, easy, 517

#18-4 The HRM function can help build an informal management network by
A   administering compensation policies designed to equalize executive pay across countries
B.   developing a cadre of international managers who have worked in several different nations
C.   staffing foreign subsidiaries with skilled managers
D.   developing management development programs aimed at strengthening multidomestic strategies

b, medium, 520

#18-5 A firm pursuing a transnational strategy should emphasize selecting people who
A   are technically competent and who have value systems that support local subsidiary autonomy
B.   are technically competent and are comfortable with performance ambiguity
C.   are predisposed towards the value and belief systems of the host country
D.   are extremely technically competent. Attitudes and beliefs consistent with parent company goals can always be developed through management development programs.
E.   are technically competent and comfortable with a management philosophy that stresses the primacy of hierarchical control and planning

b, hard, 518

#18-6 A staffing policy where most key international jobs are still held by parent company nationals is a characteristic of
A   US firms
B.   Japanese firms
C.   European firms
D.   the geocentric approach
E.   the polycentric approach

b, medium, 518

#18-7 International firms may pursue an ethnocentric staffing policy because they believe it
A   is an effective way of avoiding cultural myopia
B.   creates promotional opportunities for host country nationals
C.   is cheaper to implement
D.   facilitates local responsiveness
E.   is an effective way of maintaining a unified corporate culture

e, medium, 519

#18-8 Tacit knowledge is knowledge that is
A   easily transferable
B.   gained through experience over time
C.   generally not important in the development of competencies
D.   codified in company handbooks
E.   most easily transferred by firms using a polycentric staffing policy

b, medium, 519

#18-9 Cultural myopia
A   can lead to a firm to fail to understand how cultural differences between nations require different approaches to marketing and management
B.   is most easily avoided by firms following an ethnocentric staffing policy
C.   is the belief that the culture of the host country is better than other cultures
D.   is the belief culture is irrelevant in business decisions
E.   is a common characteristic in truly transnational firms

a, hard, 519

#18-10 A third country national is more likely to gain a top management position in division of a multinational firm pursing a
A   polycentric approach to staffing
B.   ethnocentric approach to staffing
C.   geocentric approach to staffing
D.   holiocentric approach to staffing
E.   concentric approach to staffing

c, easy, 521

#18-11 The advantages to a firm pursuing a polycentric staffing policy include
A.   the fact that this policy is consistent with a multidomestic strategy
B.   the ability to easily shift to a geocentric approach
C.   the fact that this policy is consistent with a global strategy
D.   the ability of the parent firm to more easily control host country operations
E.   the ability of this policy to build a common culture across world wide subsidiaries

a, medium, 521

#18-12 A large cadre of international managers comfortable at working in different cultures is
characteristic of firms pursuing
A   an ethnocentric approach to staffing
B.   a polycentric approach to staffing
C.   a geocentric approach to staffing
D.   a heliocentric approach to staffing
E.   a concentric approach to staffing

c, easy, 520

#18-13 Multinational companies which typically have the highest rate of expatriate failure are firms from
A   Japan
B.   Britain
C.   Germany
D.   USA
E.   Sweden

d, hard, 522

#18-14 The most important factor leading to the premature return of expatriates for European and US
firms is the manager's
A   personal or emotional maturity
B.   inability to cope with larger overseas responsibilities
C.   lack of technical competence for the new job
D.   difficulty personally in the new environment
E.   spouse being unable to adjust to the new environment

e, medium, 522

#18-15 Perhaps the most striking difference between the reasons given for expatriate failure for Japanese
expatriates and US/European expatriates is that
A   language skills are much more a factor for Japanese expatriates
B.   adequate schooling for children is much more important for Japanese expatriates
C.   Japanese expatriates do not typically have a "expatriate enclave" that can help families adjust
          while allowing them to live in a familiar environment
D.   the inability of a spouse to adapt is much less a factor for Japanese expatriates
E.   the Japanese appear to suffer less trauma and emotional distress

d, hard, 523

#18-16 One of the main problems associated with the selection of expatriates for foreign assignments is that HRM managers assume

A   it is impossible to measure the performance dimensions important to international success
B.   that ability to perform in overseas assignments can not be predicted at the time of assignment
C.   host country managers should select the expatriates to assure cultural sensitivity and fit
D.   that if a person performs well in a domestic environment that they will likely perform well in a foreign environment
E.   "cultural toughness" is the most important characteristic for expatriate success

d, medium, 523

#18-17 Since a "willingness to communicate" can be critical to the success of an expatriate, it is

A   necessary that the expatriate be fluent in the host country language
B.   not necessary that the expatriate learn the host country language since "English is the language of business"
C.   not necessary for an expatriate to be fluent, but they should at least make an effort to use the host country language
D.   recommended that expatriates only use their own native language, since attempts to use another language can easily lead to miscommunication
E.   best if expatriates not attempt to use the local language, since they will likely make embarrassing mistakes, lose face, and appear incompetent when speaking in the host country language

c, hard, 524

#18-18 The use of formal procedures and psychological tests to assess the personality traits and relational abilities of potential expatriates

A   is very common in firms
B.   are commonly used only by large multinational firms due to the costs of developing these tests
C.   appear to be infrequently used by firms
D.   are not commonly used due to the fact that appropriate psychological tests are not available

c, medium, 524

#18-19 In designing the ideal training program for expatriates, which of the following types of training should an HRM manager include

A   cultural and language training
B.   language and practical training
C.   cultural, language, and practical training
D.   cultural and practical training

c, easy, 526

#18-20 Practical training involves helping expatriate managers and their families ease into day-to-day life in the host country. To facilitate this, multinationals typically

A   encourage managers to integrate into the local community and avoid "expatriate enclaves"
B.   encourage managers to locate in areas close to work
C.   discourage managers from placing their children in local schools
D.   encourage managers to integrate into the expatriate community

d, hard, 526

#18-21 One study of US multinationals that looked at the effect of foreign assignments on subsequent career success found that a majority of personnel managers surveyed believed
A   a foreign assignment is critical to career success in today's global economy
B.   a foreign assignment allows one to move up faster in corporations
C.   a foreign assignment is either detrimental or immaterial to career success
D.   that since expatriate managers typically have greater autonomy and responsibility in foreign assignments, they often lose valuable technical skills that will be needed on their return

c, medium, 529

#18-22 Many management development programs include initiation rites where personal culture is stripped, company uniforms are donned, and humiliation tactics are employed. The purpose of such tactics is to
A   reduce manager's inhibitions in embarrassing situations
B.   weaken manager's self concept to make them more adaptable to a foreign culture
C.   strengthen manager's identification with the company
D.   increase cultural toughness
E.   introduce humor so everyone realizes how silly most HRM functions are

c, hard, 527

#18-23 Expatriate managers may be evaluated by both their host country managers and home country managers. Which of the following is NOT one of the problems with home country manager's evaluations?
A   the accuracy of the appraisal is affected by the distance between the managers
B.   the home country manager may lack understanding of what it is like to work in the host country
C.   home country manager's often rely on hard quantitative data when making an evaluation
D.   home country manager's evaluations are rarely given any weight since the manager typically reports directly to a host country manager and only indirectly to the home country manager
E.   areas outside the control of the expatriate (e.g. exchange rate fluctuations) may affect subsidiary level performance information that is used when evaluating the expatriate

d, medium, 529

#18-24 The most common approach to expatriate pay attempts to equalize purchasing power so that employees can enjoy the same living standard in their foreign posting that they enjoyed at home. This approach is called the
A   balance sheet approach
B.   income statement approach
C.   equity theory approach
D.   cash flow approach

a, easy, 532

#18-25 In which country are pay rates for top executives the highest?
A   Germany
B.   USA
C.   Japan
D.   Sweden

b, easy, 530

#18-26 The belief that offering substantial performance related bonuses is a way of motivating managers to do a good job is most strongly reflected in which country's pay structure for top executives?
A   Germany
B.   USA
C.   Japan
D.   Sweden

b, medium, 531

#18-27 When all the different components of an expatriate's compensation package are added together, an average expatriate can end up costing a firm
A   double what it would cost in a home country posting
B.   three times what it would cost in a home country posting
C.   five times what it would cost in a home country posting
D.   actually less than a home country posting when the expatriate is assigned to live in a less developed country with a lower cost of living
E.   currently the same as a home country posting, since foreign service premiums are being reduced

b, medium, 533

#18-28 Organized labor has successfully been able to limit the bargaining power of multinationals by using which of the following strategies?
A   Lobbying groups like the UN to increase regulations that would limit the power of multinationals
B.   Setting up their own international organizations to coordinate bargaining with multinationals
C.   Lobbying for national legislation to restrict multinationals
D.   Increasing their level of cooperation with multinationals to facilitate power sharing
E.   Organized labor has been largely unsuccessful in using any strategies to limit the power of multinationals.

e, medium, 536

#18-29 Organized labor in countries that typically perform low skilled tasks may have low bargaining power with multinationals due to the fact that
A   unions are generally weak in low wage areas
B.   it is relatively easy for multinationals to switch production to a different location if no specialized skills are required
C.   unions in these areas typically have little negotiating experience
D.   unions are often corrupt in such countries and can be bought by the multinationals

b, hard, 535

#18-30 Which country's multinational firms are often non-union (even in industries with high union representation) or only make investments after negotiating radical changes in work rule practices with unions in foreign countries
A   USA
B.   Japanese
C.   German
D.   Swedish

b, medium, 535

#18-31 Which of the following statements describes the HRM perspective of Coca-Cola
A   "think globally, act locally"
B.   different national business are free to conduct business in a manner appropriate in each country
C.   the company tries to establish a common mindset that all employees worldwide share
D.   internationally minded midlevel executives are critical to the company's future
E.   all of the above

e, easy, 515

#18-32 What is Coca-Cola's view with respect to expatriate employees
A   expatriate assignments should be minimized to help control costs and improve profitability
B.   expatriate assignments should be minimized so that local personnel that know the market are
         placed in positions of authority
C.   expatriate assignments help ensure that a common corporate culture is developed globally
D.   expatriate assignments are appropriate for filling specific job requirements and assuring that
         future senior managers have international experience
E.   expatriate assignments are inconsistent with the overall corporate strategy, but occasionally are
         need to bring local operations under tight control

d, hard, 515

#18-33 The importance of a firm to have a strong unifying culture is the lowest in firms pursuing which
strategy?
A   international
B.   global
C.   polycentric
D.   multidomestic
E.   ethnocentric

d, medium, 518

#18-34 One significant advantage of an ethnocentric staffing policy is that it
A   is consistent with a global strategy
B.   facilitates the transferring of core competencies to subsidiaries
C.   minimizes the costs of expatriate salaries
D.   all of the above
E.   none of the above

b, medium, 519

#18-35 Ethnocentric staffing policies
A   may lead to an inability to attract and retain high quality personnel in local subsidiaries
B.   help minimize cultural myopia in local environments
C.   are most effective for postings in developed nations
D.   are consistent with a multidomestic corporate strategy
E.   all of the above

a, easy, 519

#18-36 A polycentric staffing policy
A   works best in firms pursuing international strategies
B.   can lead to the development of cultural myopia
C.   rarely works well in practice, as good local employees are very difficult to find
D.   may lead to poor integration between different subsidiaries' operations
E.   can be particularly expensive in terms of employees salaries and expenses

d, hard, 520

#18-37 A geocentric staffing policy
A   enables firms to make the best use of available human resources
B.   helps firms develop a group of internationally experienced managers
C.   may facilitate value creation from experience curve and location economies
D.   may reduce cultural myopia and enhance local responsiveness
E.   all of the above

e, easy, 520

#18-38 Immigration laws that discourage the use expatriate employees
A   are generally unacceptable under UN regulations
B.   severely limit inter-country transfers within the EU
C.   are not a significant problem for firms pursuing a polycentric staffing approach
D.   are uncommon in advanced countries, but quite common in developing nations
E.   all of the above

c, medium, 521

#18-39 According to a study by Tung, which was the most significant cause of an US expatriate employee's failure?
A   the employee's personal maturity
B.   inability to cope with the breadth of the new responsibilities
C.   inability to adjust to the differences of the new assignment and environment
D.   the employee's emotional maturity
E.   unhappiness on the part of school children

c, hard, 522

#18-40 According to a study by Tung, which was the most important factor contributing to the failure of a Japanese expatriate
A   difficulties with the new environment
B.   inability to cope with the larger overseas responsibilities
C.   personal or emotional problems
D.   lack of technical competence for the assignment
E.   inability of the spouse to adjust

b, hard, 523

#18-41 High self-orientation on the part of an expatriate employee
A   can hinder success, since these people typically lack sensitivity to local culture
B.   is a good indicator of future failure in an assignment
C.   helps individuals adapt interests to the new culture and environment
D.   a and b above
E.   all of the above

c, medium, 524

#18-42 For most US expatriates, an assignment in which country would likely be least challenging personally and culturally?
A   India
B.   Japan
C.   Germany
D.   Britain
E.   Saudi Arabia

d, easy, 524

#18-43 Research suggests that psychological tests and cultural comparisons are
A   standard in the evaluation of most employees for expatriate assignments
B.   common among most Fortune 500 firms, but rare among smaller companies
C.   given equal weight to technical competence in making expatriate selections
D.   rarely used in making expatriate selections
E.   none of the above

d, medium, 524

#18-44 Cultural training programs
A   typically take place once an expatriate and their family are in a new culture
B.   focus on social and business practices, and should not delve into controversial issues of politics and history
C.   typically can exclude the spouse, since the spouse has less need to deal with people
D.   are offered to most expatriate employees of Fortune 500 firms
E.   none of the above

e, medium, 526

#18-45 Monsanto's program for expatriates
A   has found that repatriation works best when sponsoring managers are not too explicit about future job opportunities, as this allows flexible adaptation of employee's new skills
B.   uses little cross-cultural training prior to departure, as it has found that this is best done in an intensive fashion once the employee is in the new environment
C.   includes debriefing sessions upon repatriation where the employee can showcase experiences gained to their peers
D.   all of the above
E.   none of the above

c, hard, 528

#18-46 Performance appraisal of expatriates
A   should be done only after the expatriate has been successfully repatriated
B.   may be particularly valid when an on-site manager with the same nationality as the expatriate is given primary responsibility for the evaluation
C.   should not include former expatriates, as they are often biased towards feeling sorry for an expatriate
D.   is best done by a manager from the home country that who can decide objectively based on other employees of the same nationality
E.   none of the above

b, hard, 530

#18-47 General managers from which country typically receive the lowest compensation?
A   Switzerland
B.   US
C.   Netherlands
D.   Britain
E.   France

b, hard, 530

#18-48 Salary policies for expatriates at firms like 3M, H-P, and Philips suggest that
A   the balance sheet approach is the best method for determining remuneration
B.   most any one policy cannot be entirely fair given the significant differences in traditional salaries and costs of living across countries
C.   expatriates should be paid at the prevailing level of peers in their host country
D.   expatriates should be paid at the prevailing level of peers in their home country
E.   expatriates should be paid at the prevailing level of peers in some third, or reference, country regardless of their nation of origin or location of employment

b, hard, 533

#18-49 As a component of remuneration, a "foreign service premium"
A   is tax exempt in both the host country and the home country
B.   can best be viewed as a inducement to accept a foreign posting and the attendant disruptions
C.   typically is over 50% of the total remuneration package
D.   all of the above
E.   none of the above

b, medium, 533

#18-50 The ILO and OECD have adopted codes of conduct for multinational firms to follow in labor relations. These codes
A   do not carry any enforcement mechanisms, however.
B.   severely restrict multinational's ability to undertake transnational and global strategies
C.   have been particularly effective in forcing Japanese manufacturers to adapt their personnel policies to local norms
D.   have been upheld by the International Court of Justice in the Hague

a, easy, 536

#18-51Q: What is an ethnocentric approach to staffing? With what type of strategy does it fit best?

#18-51A: An ethnocentric approach to staffing is a policy in which all key management positions in an international business are filled by parent country nationals. This policy makes most sense for firms pursuing an international strategy.

#18-52Q: Describe how staffing works in a polycentric organization. What are the advantages of this approach to staffing? With what type of strategy does it fit best?

#18-52A: A polycentric staffing policy is one in which host country nationals are recruited to manage subsidiaries in their own country, while parent country nationals occupy the key positions at corporate headquarters. While this approach may minimize the dangers of cultural myopia, it may also help create a gap between home and host country nationals. The policy is best suited to firms pursuing a multidomestic strategy.

#18-53Q: What are the major reasons why US managers fail in expatriate assignments? What are the major reasons why Japanese managers fail in expatriate assignments? What conclusions can you draw from the similarities or differences?

#18-53A: For US multinationals, the reasons for expatriate failure are: 1) inability of the spouse to adjust, 2) employee's inability to adjust, 3) other family problems, 4) the employee's personal or emotional maturity, and 5) inability to cope with the larger overseas responsibility. For the Japanese firms the reasons for expatriate failure are: 1) inability to cope with the larger overseas responsibilities, 2) difficulties in the new environment, 3) personal or emotional problems, 4) lack of technical competence, and 5) inability of the spouse to adjust. Perhaps the most striking difference between these two lists is that the importance of the spouse's was most important in the US and Europe, but ranked only fifth for Japanese. This difference reflects the traditional separation of work from home life in Japanese culture, and the relatively low status in society held by a spouse.

#18-54Q: "English is the language of international business. Hence there is little need for an expatriate who knows English well to learn the local language." Critically evaluate this statement.

#18-54A: For fairly short term assignments, this statement isn't too far off the mark - in many multinational firms business is typically conducted in English. Yet not speaking the local language will limit an expatriate's ability to be accepted by co-workers, and gather subtle information that can be lost when translated into English. And given that most of the week's hours are not spent at work, an expatriate can find it too intimidating to truly enjoy the surroundings if they cannot read signs, converse with shopkeepers, or chat with others at the local pub.

#18-55Q: What is the purpose of cultural training for an expatriate?

#18-55A: Cultural training seeks to foster an appreciation of the host country's culture so that the expatriate behaves accordingly. The belief is that through understanding a host country's culture, the employee can develop empathy with that culture. In turn, this will enhance effectiveness in dealing with host country nationals. Expatriates should receive training in the host country's culture, history, politics, economy, religion, and social and business practices. If possible, it is also advisable to arrange for an initial familiarization trip to the host country prior to the formal transfer, as this seems to ease culture shock. Given the problems related to spouse adaptation, it is also important that the spouse, and perhaps the whole family, be included in cultural training programs.

#18-56Q: Why do firms use a "balance sheet approach" to expatriate pay? What is the philosophy behind this approach? Why are expatriates often paid more than home country employees?

#18-56A: (See pages 532-534.)

#18-57Q: What types of allowances are often included in an expatriate's compensation package?

#18-57A: (See pages 533-534.)

#18-58Q: What concerns does organized labor often have about multinational firms?

#18-58A: One of the principal concerns domestic unions have about multinational firms is that the multinational can counter union bargaining power by threatening to move production to another country. Another concern of organized labor is that an international business will keep highly skilled tasks in its home country, while only farming out low skilled tasks to foreign plants. Unions tend to feel that if their members perform only low skilled tasks for which little training and experience is required, those tasks could just as well be performed by workers in another country, and their bargaining power is reduced. A final concern is that an international business will try to impose employment practices and contractual agreements that are imported from their home country. When these practices are alien to those common in the host country, organized labor might be concerned that the changes could reduce their influence and power.

#18-59Q: Given the increasing power of multinationals, what actions have labor unions taken? How effective have these actions been?

#18-59A: Organized labor has responded to the increased bargaining power of multinational corporations by taking three actions: 1) trying to set up their own international organizations, 2) lobbying for national legislation to restrict multinationals, and 3) trying to achieve regulations of multinationals through international organizations like the UN. None of these efforts has been particularly successful.

#18-60Q: Why is there a trend towards a centralized control over labor relations in multinationals?

#18-60A: The trend towards greater centralized control over labor relations in multinational firms reflects attempts to rationalize global operations. Since labor costs can be a significant factor in overall costs, firms must consider the feasibility of expanding in lower cost locations when negotiating agreements with labor unions. Such trade-offs require more centralized consideration of labor relations and work rules across multiple actual and potential locations. In addition, the organization of work and corporate culture can be important facilitators (and inhibitors) of knowledge transfer. Hence multinational firms may want to ensure their ability to transfer organizational and cultural attributes across national operations, and need to be certain that labor organizations will not resist such practices.

CHAPTER 19

Students should be encouraged to choose the BEST answer, as more than one may be technically correct. Following each question is the answer, estimated difficulty, and page reference.

#19-1 Which of the following correctly characterizes the consistency of international accounting standards?

A   Financial statements prepared in accordance with International Accounting Standards Committee (IASC) standards satisfy listing requirements of all major stock exchanges
B.   The EU and SEC accept each others' standards
C.   The EU and SEC require disclosure of the same information but require different formats
D.   The SEC has accepted a few IASC standards, but generally has held to its own standards.

d, medium, 550

#19-2 Which of the following is NOT a major determinant of the type of a country's accounting system?

A   the character of the primary external source of capital
B.   political and economic relationships with other countries
C.   levels of inflation
D.   linguistic relationships with other countries
E.   the overall level of economic development

d, easy, 543

#19-3 Accounting

A.   is evolutionary in nature, responding to the demands for accounting information
B.   is mechanistic, and once rules are set they are usually not changed
C.   influences the business environment, but is not itself influenced by the environment
D.   usually develops initial standards by international consensus

a, hard, 542

#19-4 Which of the following statements is true?

A   Individual investors demand accounting practices oriented toward protecting their investments
B.   In countries where banks are the major suppliers of capital, financial disclosures are extensive
C.   Compared to accounting systems oriented toward individual investors, those oriented toward bank investors tend to value assets conservatively and overvalue liabilities.
D.   Individual investors satisfy most of the financial information needs by direct management contact
E.   all of the above

c, hard, 544

#19-5 Extensive financial statement disclosures are made where individual investors provide capital because

A   as purchasers of large percentages of individual firms' outstanding stock, they have a lot at stake
B.   individual shareholders may generally get information on demand from management
C.   individual investors need information relevant to corporate stock and bond investment decisions
D.   individual investors obtain too much information from direct management involvement

c, hard, 544

#19-6 Economic and/or political ties between countries often lead to
A   uniform accounting systems
B.   similarities in accounting systems
C.   dissimilar accounting systems
D.   support for harmonized worldwide accounting systems

b, easy, 545

#19-7 The historic cost principle
A   relies on the assumption that the currency unit used is not losing value due to inflation
B.   is the basis of all accounting systems
C.   is most reasonable when inflation levels are high
D.   was developed in response to the problems created by current cost accounting
E.   results in total depreciation charges that are often in excess of the replacement cost of the asset

a, medium, 545

#19-8 The level of accounting sophistication
A   is inversely associated with the sophistication of capital markets
B.   is a function only of a country's level of development
C.   may decline as a country's education system improves and more efficient standards are developed
D.   can be influenced by the demands of providers of capital
E.   does not readily change as a country's level development changes

d, hard, 545

#19-9 Accounting clusters
A   are groups of countries with exactly the same accounting systems
B.   are geographically defined
C.   include the British-American-German Group and the Europe-Japan-Group
D.   are groups of accounting standards addressing similar issues
E.   may be defined by common accounting system features

e, medium, 546

#19-10 Accounting and auditing standards
A   are always the same
B.   define rules for auditing but not preparing financial statements
C.   help define what is reliable and useful accounting information
D.   are not subject to national differences
E.   result in comparability of financial reports from different countries

c, easy, 546

#19-11 Transnational financial reporting

A   is limited but has expanded much in recent years
B.   makes a lack of comparability of financial reports from different countries a significant problem
C.   is done so that a firm's financial position appears similar under any system of accounting
D.   simply involves the translation of financial reports from one language to another
E.   is primarily oriented at meeting the information needs of each firm's domestic investors

b, medium, 548

#19-12 The comparability of financial reports from different countries

A   is generally quite high due to the development of international standards by the IASC
B.   affects the ability of international businesses to assess the financial position of contracting parties
C.   matters more for internal management reporting issues than it does to international investors
D.   would be a major issue only if transnational financial reporting was limited
E.   All of the above

b, medium, 548

#19-13 Differences in national accounting standards can result in

A   higher net income and lower shareholder's equity under one countries standards versus another's
B.   a firm being required to prepare no more than two sets of financial statements
C.   only immaterial stock price effects on world stock exchanges at any given time
D.   income statement but not shareholder's equity differences
E.   financial reports that although different, can easily be compared by knowledgeable users

a, hard, 548

#19-14 The success of efforts to harmonize accounting standards across countries

A   has been extensive and harmonization is now almost completed
B.   has been unhindered by cultural and legal system differences
C.   has been enhanced by the mandatory compliance with IASC standards
D.   has been achieved by accommodating all current accounting practices in international standards
E.   has been limited by the IASC's lack of power to enforce its standards

e, hard, 549

#19-15 The International Accounting Standards Committee

A   is composed of representatives from only Western industrialized nations
B.   develops accounting, auditing, ethical, educational, and public sector standards
C.   has issued over 100 international accounting standards
D.   often allows for alternative acceptable treatments in its standards
E.   has only 14 voting members of its board, so it can easily reach consensus on proposed standards

d, hard, 549

#19-16 Consolidated financial statements combine parent and subsidiary company results in order to
A   be consistent with the separate legal entities of the various companies
B.   incorporate the many transactions that occur between companies with common ownership
C.   reflect the economic interdependence of companies within a corporate group
D.   exclude the effects of transactions with external third parties
E.   simply add together the sets of accounts of the companies in a corporate group

c, medium, 552

#19-17 Which of the following transactions between a parent company (P) and its foreign subsidiary (S) would be eliminated upon consolidation?
A   P purchases supplies on account from an unrelated company. The supplies will be sold to F
B.   S purchases supplies from P
C.   S incurs interest expenses on funds borrowed from a bank and used to purchase supplies from P
D.   P makes royalty payments to an unrelated entity
E.   The same unrelated company to whom P makes royalty payments purchases goods from S

b, easy, 552

#19-18 Preparation of consolidated financial statements of foreign subsidiaries of multinational firms
A   facilitates the concealment of subsidiary losses and thus the economic status of the group
B.   usually wipes out profits reported in the home country because of the high overseas losses typical in most multinational firms
C.   has been addressed in two IASC standards requiring preparation of consolidated financial statements, and are required by most industrialized nations
D.   is impossible since foreign subsidiaries of multinationals normally keep their accounting records in the currency of the country in which they are located rather than that of its home country
E.   is not currently required practice in most industrialized countries

c, medium, 553

#19-19 Which of the following is a major method of currency translation for financial statement preparation
A   the temporal method
B.   the geographic method
C.   the Lessard-Lorange method
D.   the contemporary method
E.   the Anglo-American method

a, easy, 553

#19-20 Regarding currency exchange translation methods,
A   the current rate uses the average exchange rate for the period of the financial statements
B.   the current rate method, unlike the temporal method, conforms to the historic cost principle
C.   balance sheets prepared using the current rate method often do not balance
D.   use of the current rate method can result in apparent fluctuations in the value of assets that are merely a function of changes in exchange rates
E.   the temporal method uses the exchange rate at the balance sheet date

d, medium, 553

#19-21 Under the US's FASB 52, "Foreign Currency Translation"

A   balance sheets are translated to the home currency using the exchange rate in effect at the balance sheet date

B.   an integral subsidiary is required to use US dollars as its functional currency

C.   a self-sustaining subsidiary will apply the temporal exchange method

D.   local currencies of foreign subsidiaries are never used as a functional currency

E.   a self sustaining subsidiary need not be incorporated into the parent company's financial statements

b, medium, 554

#19-22 The budgeting process

A   impacts the evaluation of the performance of foreign subsidiaries but not subsidiary managers

B.   develops goals that are often expressed in non-financial terms

C.   attempts to implement financial control of sub-units

D.   often does not involve negotiation of goals in an international business setting since most sub-units will be foreign subsidiaries and cultural differences may interfere with agreement on goals

E.   is unencumbered by additional complications in the international business context

c, medium, 557

#19-23 Which of the following is NOT an important function of accounting systems in the budget process?

A   monitoring of performance relative to goals throughout the year

B.   expression of goals and performance in financial terms

C.   collection of financial data

D.   evaluation of performance against goals

E.   determining the extent to which foreign subsidiary managers should participate in setting goals

e, medium, 555

#19-24 A "corporate currency" is

A   one that is not used in any country

B.   is unique to individual corporations

C.   normally the home currency of the parent company

D.   may make comparison between subsidiaries difficult

c, easy, 555

#19-25 International businesses which require that all internal budgets and performance data be expressed in one "corporate currency"

A   may complicate headquarters management's performance evaluation process

B.   eliminate the possibility of distortions in the control process arising from exchange rate changes

C.   will expect foreign subsidiaries to report results in terms of each subsidiary's local currency

D.   may result in the appearance that a foreign subsidiary's otherwise adequate performance is under budget due to a decline in its currency against the corporate currency

E.   requires management to fabricate a currency system for the corporation's internal use

d, hard, 555

#19-26 The Lessard-Lorange Model
A   develops a system for selecting exchange rates that eliminates exchange rate distortions
B.   suggests that apparently illogical and unreasonable combinations of exchange rates may be useful in practice
C.   recommends that the same exchange rate be used to translate both budget and performance figures
D.   recommends that all transfer prices be expressed in the "corporate currency"
E.   can be applied to develop optimal transfer prices

c, hard, 556

#19-27 Which of the following is NOT a possible exchange rate suggested under the Lessard-Lorange Model
A   the spot exchange rate prevailing at the time the budget is adopted
B.   the spot exchange rate that is forecasted for the end of the budget period
C.   the spot exchange rate that exists whenever a comparison between the budget and actual performance is being made
D.   the average of the spot exchange rates prevailing at the beginning and end of the budget period.

d, medium, 556

#19-28   According to the Lessard-Lorange Model, the combination of exchange rates used for the budget setting and subsequent performance tracking processes that most distorts the control process is
A   initial/initial
B.   initial/projected
C.   initial/ending
D.   projected/projected
E.   projected/ending

c, easy, 556

#19-29 The "transfer price" refers to
A   the external market price of a firm's final product
B.   the price at which intra-firm transactions take place
C.   the market price of a foreign subsidiary's final product expressed in the "corporate currency"
D.   the cost of transporting components between subsidiaries located in different countries
E.   transaction costs of transferring funds between countries

b, easy, 557

#19-30 The choice of transfer price
A   is rarely influenced by tax liability considerations
B.   may be manipulated to avoid government restrictions on capital flows
C.   is generally of little import since these transactions are eliminated upon consolidation of financial statements
D.   is generally a matter of indifference to managers of subsidiaries of multinational firms
E.   is often made in order to maximize import duties

b, medium, 557

#19-31 The increase in the transfer price of a component that is manufactured by a German subsidiary of a US multinational and transferred to a Mexican subsidiary of the same US parent for assembly into a final product will
A   have no effect on the German subsidiary's profitability
B.   increase the costs of the German subsidiary
C.   decrease the measured profit of the Mexican subsidiary
D.   increase the parent company's pretax per unit profit
E.   decrease the measured profit of the German subsidiary

c, medium, 557

#19-32 The manager of a foreign subsidiary
A   should be evaluated objectively despite temptations to subjectively consider how hostile or benign a country's environment is for that business
B.   may fairly have his performance compared to that of other managers based on an indicator of profitability such as return on investment
C.   that is unprofitable is performing below the level of the manager of a foreign subsidiary in a different country that is highly profitable
D.   will face costs of doing business that will be uniform across all other foreign subsidiaries
E.   may be performing at a superior level even though her subsidiary's performance is lower than that of any other subsidiary in the corporate group

e, medium, 558

#19-33 The Chinese government sees foreign direct investment as
A   something that should be avoided so that capitalist ideas are held in check
B.   appropriate as long as firms adhere to IASC standards
C.   a very important engine for economic growth
D.   acceptable only if a majority stake of any enterprise is held by Chinese and its currency is used as the functional currency of the subsidiary
E.   none of the above

c, medium, 559

#19-34 Accounting in China is
A   generally consistent with FASB regulations
B.   generally consistent with IASC regulations
C.   specifically focused on assessing profitability so that tax revenue can be maximized
D.   particularly effective in capturing the results of foreign operations
E.   none of the above

e, hard, 559

#19-35 Which accounting practice is common in China
A   allowances for bad debts
B.   lower of cost or market for valuing inventory
C.   accrual for unrealized losses
D.   not accounting for inventory aging or obsolescence

d, medium, 560

#19-36 Which of the following financial criteria is viewed as being most important in evaluating the performance of a foreign subsidiary?

A   Budgeted compared to actual profit
B.   Return on equity
C.   Return on assets
D.   Budget compared to actual return on equity
E.   all are viewed as being equally important, and should be weighted equally in an evaluation

a, hard, 555

#19-37 Which of the following financial criteria is viewed as being least important in evaluating the performance of a foreign subsidiary's manager?

A   return on sales
B.   residual income
C.   budget compared to actual sales
D.   return on assets
E.   budget compared to actual return on equity

b, medium, 555

#19-38 Ciba, one of the world's largest pharmaceutical and chemical firms, is headquartered in
A   US
B.   Britain
C.   Switzerland
D.   Sweden
E.   Japan

c, medium, 551

#19-39 Historically, Swiss accounting rules have been
A   in the forefront of adopting and encouraging IASC regulations
B.   fairly similar to those in The Netherlands
C.   very unusual and difficult for international investors understand
D.   been more focused on providing information to individual investors than banks
E.   none of the above

c, medium, 551

#19-40 Advantages of Ciba's new accounting and reporting system include all of the following except
A   increased value of inventories
B.   more efficient capital investment
C.   tighter cash management
D.   more useful information to international investors
E.   ability to benchmark its performance against global competitors

a, hard, 551

#19-41 Which of the following is NOT true about the financial situation of SmithKline Beecham at the time of merger.
A   its stock was listed in both the US and Britain
B.   British reported earnings were higher than those reported under US accounting standards
C.   Shareholder's equity was reported as positive in the US and negative in Britain
D.   Its stock traded at a higher price in London than in New York

d, hard, 549

#19-42 Which company was the first to simultaneously float a stock offering in multiple countries?
A   Ciba
B.   SmithKline Beecham
C.   Telefonica
D.   Daimler-Benz
E.   Toyota

c, hard, 549

#19-43 The US, Canada, Britain, Australia, and New Zealand are all in one accounting "cluster" - their accounting standards share many similarities. Which other country is also in this cluster?
A   India
B.   Sweden
C.   Brazil
D.   Spain
E.   Romania

a, easy, 547

#19-44 Egypt, Portugal, Greece, and Norway are all in one accounting "cluster" - their accounting standards share many similarities. Which other country is also in this cluster?
A   Libya
B.   Denmark
C.   Algeria
D.   Ukraine
E.   Argentina

b, medium, 547

#19-45 In 1995 a number of German firms indicated that they would soon adopt international accounting standards for reporting financial results. This decision was motivated by
A   IASC Ruling 2552
B.   deregulation of the German financial securities industry
C.   recognition that the German capital market was too small and illiquid to provide adequate funds at reasonable rates
D.   the privatization of Germany's previously state-owned enterprises
E.   all of the above

c, medium, 542

#19-46 The US SEC has objected to German firms interested in raising funds in the US reporting their financial information according to German standards because
A   German regulations do not require that firms disclose reserves
B.   German regulations do not require that firms disclose pension obligations
C.   German regulations liberal provisions for writing down goodwill
D.   all of the above
E.   none of the above

d, easy, 542

#19-47 When Daimler-Benz reported its 1994 financial results under both US and German standards
A   it showed a $100 million profit in Germany and a $1 billion loss in the US
B.   it showed a profit in both Germany and the US, but the German profit was much higher
C.   most analysts were surprised to see that the overall financial results did not differ significantly, as overvaluations on some items were generally offset by undervaluations on other items
D.   most US analysts viewed the results reported under US standards as irrelevant, since its operations in the US are considerably smaller than its operations in Germany

a, medium, 542

#19-48 In Germany, Switzerland, and Japan, accounting practices have traditionally been focused towards providing information
A   for banks
B.   to private investors
C.   to governmental authorities
D.   according to IASC regulations
E.   to independent auditing firms

a, easy, 544

#19-49 Financial accounting practices tend to be oriented towards the needs of governmental planners in
A   US
B.   The Netherlands
C.   France
D.   Norway
E.   Switzerland

c, medium, 544

#19-50 Current cost accounting
A   helps adjust financial reports for the effects of inflation
B.   has been particularly popular in the accounting systems of most South American countries
C.   is generally not used in Britain since inflation rates have been low
D.   all of the above
E.   none of the above

d, easy, 545

#19-51Q: What is the "historic cost principle"? Why do some countries feel this principle is important, while others do not?

#19-51A: The historic cost principal is based on the assumption that the currency unit used to report financial results is not losing its value due to inflation. The principle means that firms record sales, purchases, and the like at the original transaction price and make no adjustment to that price later. In countries where inflation is low, the historic cost principle makes sense. In countries suffering from high inflation, however, historic prices may not at all reflect current reality.

#19-52Q: Describe the likely relationship between a country's level development and its accounting system.

#19-52A: Accounting in developed nations tends to be far more sophisticated than accounting in less developed countries, where fairly primitive standards may prevail.

#19-53Q: How would you describe the success to date of the International Accounting Standards Committee?

#19-53A: The IASC has made some success, and has decreased the overall variation in accounting systems across countries. While compliance with the standards is voluntary, and more than one acceptable reporting approach is typically allowed in a standard, comparability of financial reporting is improving with the assistance of the IASC.

#19-54Q: "Since most multinationals are organized as separate legal entities in each country, it makes no sense for them to issue consolidated financial statements that combine the activities of all the separate firms." Critically evaluate this statement.

#19-54A: What makes legal sense doesn't necessarily make economic sense. As long as a firm is a single economic entity where all the separate legal units are economically interdependent, consolidated financial statements best represent the overall economic viability of the enterprise.

#19-55Q: Regarding currency translation, what is the difference between the current rate method and the temporal rate method.

#19-55A: While the current rate method uses the exchange rate at the date the financial statement is issued (i.e. year end), the temporal rate method uses the exchange rate at the time the transaction originally took place.

#19-56Q: What is the general relationship between the strategy of a firm and the functional currency used by its foreign subsidiaries?

#19-56A: Firms pursuing a multidomestic or international strategy are most likely to have self sustaining subsidiaries, and will tend to use the local currency as the functional currency in each country. Firms pursuing a global or transnational strategy will most likely have integral subsidiaries, and will tend to use the home country currency as their functional currency.

#19-57Q: "To keep matters simple, budgets should be set using the exchange rate at the time of the budget, and subsidiary performance should be based on the exchange rates at the end of the period. Its up to managers of subsidiaries to deal with any changes in the exchange rates. After all, they should be better at understanding and anticipating exchange rates for their country than some staff person at headquarters." Critically evaluate this quotation.

#19-57A: The quotation has two good points - this method is simple and country managers may be in the best position to understand what is going on with their country's exchange rate. The best counter to this statement, however, is to ask what the country manager is to focus upon - success in the domestic market over which he has some degree of control, or success in the domestic market as measured by the parent company's currency. Because of completely unanticipated changes in exchange rates, the performance of a subsidiary can be significantly distorted. Most human resource specialists would argue that performance should be evaluated only over those factors that the manager can control.

#19-58Q: Why should the evaluation of a subsidiary be any different than the evaluation of a subsidiary manager?

#19-58A: Foreign subsidiaries do not operate in uniform environments. Some environments are much tougher than others, some subsidiaries are more interdependent with the firm than others, some subsidiaries are exposed to greater risk than others, and some subsidiaries may be in different stages of development than others. All this more qualitative information may not be contained in the standardized reports prepared on the financial performance of individual subsidiaries (although some of it could be). Accordingly, the evaluation of a subsidiary should be separate from the subjective evaluation of the manager who must manage effectively given the particular situation.

#19-59Q: Why does Daimler-Benz prepare financial statements according to both US and German standards?

#19-59A: Daimler-Benz, like other German firms, has found the German capital market to be limited and expensive as a sole source of funds. In order to raise funds in the much larger and more open US capital market, the US SEC requires that firms issue financial statements according to US standards. Thus for it to be able to access these funds, it was necessary for Daimler-Benz to prepare financial statements according to US as well as German standards.

#19-60Q: What are the primary determinants of a country's accounting system?

#19-60A: Although many factors can influence the development of a country's accounting system, there appear to be five main variables: 1) the relationship between business and the providers of capital, 2) political and economic ties with other countries, 3) inflation levels, 4) levels of economic development, and 5) a country's culture.

CHAPTER 20

Students should be encouraged to choose the BEST answer, as more than one may be technically correct. Following each question is the answer, estimated difficulty, and page reference.

#20-1 The relationship between financial management and competitive advantage in the global market place is
A   less important for multinational firms than it is for domestic firms
B.   often a fundamental aspect in an international business
C.   one of the best researched and understood concepts in business
D.   of little economic significance

b, easy, 564

#20-2 FMC Corporation set up an in-house bank operation in order to
A   manage foreign exchange risk for its business units that make overseas sales
B.   provide short-term financing to its customers
C.   facilitate changing their prices rapidly in response to changes in exchange rates
D.   assist customers who are required to pay in dollars only
E.   to minimize FMC's hassles with foreign exchange rates

a, medium, 564

#20-3 FMC Corporation views its capacity to offer international customers stable long-term prices as
A   a creative use of its in-house bank that primarily exists for the convenience of FMC employees
B.   facilitating its customer's ability to plan
C.   detrimental to the maintenance and development of its customer base
D.   a traditional customer service that may be of declining utility
E.   a way to avoid the responsibility of managing foreign exchange risk for its business units

b, hard, 564

#20-4 Improvements in cash management procedures that result in conservation of a firm's cash
A   will rarely be substantial enough to compensate for the cost of identifying improvements
B.   might include changing the timing of cash flows through the international banking system
C.   can always be accomplished
D.   will typically affect customers and suppliers negatively
E.   will only be achievable in domestic forms since it its difficult to influence cash flows through different countries

b, hard, 590

#20-5 Procter and Gamble's centralization of its global treasury management functions
A   has led to an increase in intra-company loans
B.   was motivated in part by changes in its corporate global strategy
C.   has allowed it to save significant transaction costs of currency trades
D.   all of the above
E.   none of the above

d, easy, 563

#20-6 The scope of financial management
A   excludes decisions about how to finance activities
B.   includes decisions about how to manage the firm's financial resources efficiently
C.   is limited to financing decisions
D.   does not extend to investment decisions

b, easy, 564

#20-7 Which factor does NOT complicate financial management decisions in international business?
A   political risks
B.   currency differences
C.   tax regime differences
D.   global economic trends
E.   capital flow restrictions

d, medium, 565

#20-8 Good financial management in a firm will not affect its
A   cost of capital
B.   customer service
C.   ability to eliminate political risk
D.   competitive advantage
E.   foreign exchange losses

c, hard, 564

#20-9 Capital budgeting for a foreign project
A   need not facilitate intra-country investment alternative comparisons
B.   uses the same theoretical framework as domestic capital budgeting
C.   is a straight forward process in practice
D.   tries to quantify the costs and benefits of an investment without consideration of risk
E.   involves assumptions that limit its contribution to objective comparisons of investment alternatives across countries

b, medium, 565

#20-10 Factors complicating the capital budgeting process that are unique for an international business include
A   a distinction exists between cash flows to the project versus those to the parent company
B.   the estimation of cash flows associated with the project over time
C.   risk of changes in the value of an investment due to political circumstances
D.   selection of a discount rate that reflects the firm's cost of capital

a, medium, 566

#20-11 Restrictions on the remittance of cash flows from a foreign project to a parent company
A   affect the net present value of the project
B.   may result from requirements by the host government for reinvestment within the host nation
C.   will not affect the net present value of the project to the parent company
D.   may result from favorable tax rates
E.   are becoming increasingly likely in more countries due to opposition to free market economics

b, medium, 566

#20-12 Parent companies should consider the cash flows it will receive rather than those generated by a project when evaluating a foreign investment because
A   investments in other parts of the world will not be affected by blocked earnings
B.   blocked earnings are perceived by stockholders as contributing to the value of the firm
C.   dividends to stockholders may not be made from blocked earnings
D.   creditors will consider blocked earnings when calculating the ability of the parent to service debt
E.   blocked earnings can be used to repay worldwide corporate debt

c, easy, 566

#20-13 Political risk
A   can be easily quantified
B.   is concerned with potential adverse affects on profit
C.   is distinct from the concept of social unrest
D.   if incorporated into strategic plans will have little adverse impact of the attractiveness of a
         foreign investment project

b, medium, 567

#20-14 The most extreme outcome of political change is
A   increases in tax rates
B.   imposition of exchange controls
C.   expropriation of assets
D.   imposition of price controls
E.   government interference with existing assets

c, easy, 567

#20-15 Which of the following countries is rated most risky by the 1995 Euromoney Country Risk
Ratings
A   Philippines
B.   Poland
C.   Turkey
D.   Japan
E.   Oman

b, hard, 569

#20-16 In practice, the biggest problem arising form economic mismanagement seems to be
A   over investment in capital equipment
B.   too little money chasing too many goods
C.   expansion of the domestic money supply and inflation
D.   rapid price deflations
E.   appreciation of local currencies on the foreign exchange market

c, medium, 567

#20-17 Empirical studies of the relationship between a country's relative inflation rate and changes in its exchange rate show that
A   economic risk can consistently and reliably quantified
B.   in the long-run domestic inflation results currency depreciation
C.   the strength of the empirical relationship is inconsistent with that predicted by theory
D.   in the short currencies appreciate with inflation
E.   none of the above

b, medium, 567

#20-18 The depreciation of a country's currency on the foreign exchange market
A   may result from price deflation
B.   may cause a decline in the value of cash flows received by foreign investors from assets within the country
C.   is unlikely to be related to expansion of the domestic money supply
D.   will result in superior returns on the investments of foreign investors with assets in the country
E.   will have little impact on multinational firms that have access to multiple currencies

b, medium, 567

#20-19 Adjusting discount rates to reflect the riskiness of a foreign project
A   occurs in practice about as frequently as the revision of future cash flows downward
B.   may penalize distant cash flows too much and early cash flows too little
C.   may involve revising the discount rate downward to reflect higher risk
D.   adds a premium percentage for risk to the discount rate when evaluating investment projects in countries with economic and political stability
E.   is consistent with expectation of political or economic collapse in the distant rather than the immediate future

a, hard, 572

#20-20 The overriding factor in the selection of a source of financing is
A   transaction costs
B.   the cost
C.   the location of the source
D.   expectations of foreign exchange rates
E.   government restrictions on sources of financing available to foreign investors

b, easy, 572

#20-21 Host government policies adversely impact the cost of capital and financing decisions
A   only when the host country capital market is relatively illiquid
B.   by requiring foreign investors to use global capital markets to finance their investment
C.   only when the home country capital market is small and relatively liquid
D.   by requiring that foreign multinationals finance projects in their country by local debt financing or sales of equity if the cost of capital in the country is high
E.   by decreasing in the cost of capital used to finance a project

d, medium, 573

#20-22 The financial structure of firms
A   is known to differ across countries due primarily to differences in tax regimes
B.   in Japan relies less on debt financing than do most US firms
C.   reflects the mix of debt and equity used to finance a business and is similar for firms worldwide
D.   may reflect cultural norms

d, easy, 573

#20-23 In considering whether an international business should conform to local capital structure norms,
A   the most important consideration is the effects on the firm's image by its sensitivity to local monetary policy
B.   the capital structure of the parent company should be emulated in all affiliates
C.   a strong rationale for conforming to host country debt norms is the facilitation of comparisons of return on equity relative to local competitors
D.   the cost of capital should dominate all other considerations
E.   the adopted financial structure for all foreign affiliates should be the same to facilitate evaluation of relative affiliate performance

d, hard, 574

#20-24 A tax credit
A   is the offset on taxes a firm receives based on its credit rating
B.   is the offset on taxes a individual receives based on outstanding credit balances
C.   for US firms is not possible, although many other countries allow this deduction
D.   is invalid if a firm is operating under the deferral principle
E.   allows taxes in the home country to be reduced by the amount of taxes paid overseas

e, easy, 575

#20-25 Utilization of a firm's global cash resources in the most efficient manner is
A   best be accomplished by letting each affiliate manage its own cash reserves
B.   improved by increasing the number and speed of currency exchanges through international banks
C.   improved by maximizing cash balances
D.   facilitated by reducing the number of transactions between subsidiaries of firms
E.   all of the above

d, hard, 575

#20-26 Double taxation resulting from the worldwide principle of taxation as applied by many nations
A　　　　is an attempt to penalize firms locating in tax haven countries
B.　　　　involves the taxation of foreign subsidiary profits at the corporate level by the host country and the taxation at the individual level of the dividends distributed from this profit by the governments of shareholders
C.　　　　can be mitigated by the deferral principle
D.　　　　is completely eliminated for US firms by tax credit mechanisms inherent in global tax treaties
E.　　　　is an artifact of tax treaties

c, medium, 575

#20-27 Which of the following countries has the highest maximum corporate tax rate?
A　　　　Switzerland
B.　　　　USA
C.　　　　Bermuda
D.　　　　Britain
E.　　　　Japan

e, hard, 576

#20-28 Which of the following devices can NOT be used by US firms to minimize global tax liability
A　　　　tax haven subsidiaries
B.　　　　transfer pricing
C.　　　　fronting loans
D.　　　　lobbying for changes in tax credit policies

a, medium, 576

#20-29 Unbundling
A　　　　is the process of distributing dividends from foreign subsidiaries to the parent company
B.　　　　is unrelated to cash management objectives
C.　　　　involves mixing techniques to transfer liquid funds
D.　　　　maximizes dividend drains
E.　　　　can not by international law include fronting loans

c, medium, 577

#20-30 Advantages of manipulating transfer prices include all of the following EXCEPT:
A　　　　minimization of taxes
B.　　　　facilitation of funds transfers out of a country in anticipation of a significant currency devaluation
C.　　　　circumvention of government restrictions on capital flows
D.　　　　lack of regulation of transfer prices
E.　　　　reduction of import duties

d, medium, 578

#20-31 Fronting loans

A   are made between a parent and its subsidiary without the involvement of financial intermediaries
B.   are not often used when the level of political risk is high
C.   primarily benefit banks who make profits by paying the parent company a lower interest rate than it charges a foreign subsidiaries
D.   has no tax implications due to the worldwide principle
E.   are often effective since host governments are less likely to restrict funds transfers in repayment to international financial intermediaries than those to foreign parent companies

e, easy, 580

#20-32 Centralized depositories

A   limit the ability of firms to earn maximum interest on cash balances since under this system cash reserves are pooled and thus fewer investment options are available
B.   squander the investment skills and know-how of foreign subsidiary managers
C.   increases the size of the total cash pool held in liquid accounts
D.   may have limited ability to serve short term cash needs due to restrictions on cross-border capital flows
E.   all of the above

d, hard, 581

#20-33 Multilateral netting

A   is motivated by the reduction of transaction costs
B.   simplifies payment schedules between related entities at the cost of increased transfer fees
C.   may result in a net increase in the amount of funds transferred between subsidiaries
D.   may increase foreign exchange commissions

a, easy, 583

#20-34 Strategies to reduce foreign exchange risk

A   have been actively engaged in by Black & Decker to manage economic risk
B.   exist to reduce translation and transaction exposure, but are not as effective in reducing economic exposure
C.   include using leading and lagging to accelerate payments from strong currency countries to weak currency countries and delay inflows from weak currency to strong currency countries
D.   do not rely heavily on forecasting future exchange rate movements
E.   are best not controlled centrally since each subunit must adopt the correct mix of tactics in order for a firm's foreign exchange exposure to be minimized

a, medium, 587

#20-35 Transaction exposure in foreign exchange

A   is generally unavoidable
B.   is most easily reduced by the use of fronting loans
C.   has been eliminated across countries in the EU
D.   all of the above
E.   none of the above

e, easy, 585

#20-36 Translation exposure in foreign exchange
A   can be reduced by utilizing double or reverse translation techniques
B.   are of minor importance in all but the most underdeveloped countries
C.   cannot be reduced by using currency swaps
D.   is too long term in nature for forward purchases to be effective in reducing
E.   can be affected by the use of lag strategies

e, medium, 586

#20-37 Implementing lead and lag strategies
A   is relatively easy
B.   involve high transaction costs
C.   relies on the assumption that the other party to a transaction will not want to undertake the
         opposite strategy given the same economic expectations
D.   is always preferable to utilizing forward markets to reduce exposure
E.   all of the above

c, hard, 586

#20-38 Transaction and translation exposure can be reduced by all of the following except
A   manipulating transfer prices
B.   shifting location of debt financing
C.   currency swaps
D.   forward contracts
E.   implementing the Lessard-Lorange model

e, easy, 586

#20-39 Reducing economic exposure
A   is least expensively accomplished with forward contracts
B.   requires an ability to shift productive activities across locations
C.   is facilitated by having centralized cash management facilities
D.   is easiest through judicious use of lead and lag strategies
E.   all of the above

b, medium, 586

#20-40 Most firms have less sophisticated procedures for managing
A   translation exposure than other forms of exposure
B.   transaction exposure than other forms of exposure
C.   economic exposure than other forms of exposure

c, medium, 587

#20-41 Forecasting future exchange rate movements
A   is too complex and uncertain for most multinational firms to be concerned with
B.   can be essential for effective capital budgeting decisions
C.   is facilitated by analyzing a firm's lead and lag strategies
D.   can only be done with complex econometric models developed by central banks

b, easy, 588

#20-42 The experiences of Allied Lyons and Royal Dutch Shell
A   reveal that speculation on exchange rates can lead to significant losses
B.   show the extent of savings available from managing all foreign transactions through a central repository
C.   illustrate the difficulty of reducing a firm's economic exposure
D.   illustrate the difficulty of reducing a firm's translation exposure
E.   show how judicious use of forward contracts can help protect a firm from large exchange rate changes

a, medium, 588

#20-43 Motorola's global cash management system
A   was used by the firm to undertake ill-fated currency speculation
B.   is based on the concept of netting cash flows
C.   has been most effective in reducing the firm's economic exposure
D.   all of the above
E.   none of the above

b, medium, 590

#20-44 Firm's debt ratios are typically highest in
A   Norway
B.   Malaysia
C.   Canada
D.   Germany
E.   Mexico

a, hard, 574

#20-45 Firm's debt ratios are typically lowest in
A   Australia
B.   Germany
C.   Sweden
D.   France
E.   Finland

a, medium, 574

#20-46 Which of the following is most significant in determining Euromoney's country risk rating
A   debt indicators
B.   political risk
C.   credit ratings
D.   international bond and syndicated loan market access
E.   all of the above are equally weighted

b, medium, 571

#20-47 Which of the following is NOT directly measured in determining Euromoney's country risk
rating
A   balance of payments/GDP
B.   debt service/exports
C.   ease of debt rescheduling
D.   cumulative FDI
E.   credit ratings from Moody's, Standard & Poors, and IBCA

d, hard, 571

#20-48 Which of the following countries is the riskiest based on Euromoney's 1995 ratings?
A   Cuba
B.   Syria
C.   Malawi
D.   Myanmar
E.   Lebanon

a, hard, 570

#20-49 Manipulation of transfer prices
A   is extremely uncommon
B.   has undergone more intense scrutiny by the US and other governments
C.   can do little to affect tax liabilities, but can significantly improve dividend repatriation
D.   all of the above
E.   none of the above

b, easy, 579

#20-50 Political risk
A   tends to be greater in countries experiencing social unrest or disorder
B.   tends to be high in countries in the midst of a civil war
C.   is usually much more important than translation exposure for Western firms investing in
         countries of the former Soviet Union
D.   all of the above
E.   none of the above

d, easy, 567

#20-51Q: How do FMC's international financial management policies contribute its competitive advantage?

#20-51A: FMC will accept payment in different currencies, thus taking on the exchange rate risk itself and providing customers the option of paying in a currency of their preference. This gives FMC an advantage over most competitors. On a broader level, by having effective international financial management policies, FMC is able to have cost advantages over competitors with less efficient financial management.

#20-52Q: What can be done to minimize economic risk exposure?

#20-52A: The key to reducing economic exposure is to distribute productive assets to various locations around the world so that firms' long term financial well being is not severely impacted by exchange rates or economic conditions adversely impacting operations or profitability in one location. The Management Focus box on Black and Decker shows how this firm can shift production between locations as economic conditions make different locations more or less attractive.

#20-53Q: What is the purpose of capital budgeting? How is the process more complicated for international businesses?

#20-53A: The purpose of capital budgeting is to try and quantify the benefits, costs, and risks of an investment. Among factors complicating the process for an international business are: 1) a distinction must be made between cash flows to the project and cash flows to the parent company, 2) political and economic risks (including foreign exchange risk), 3) the connection between cash flows to the parent and the source of financing.

#20-54Q: "When evaluating a foreign investment opportunity, the parent should be interested in the cash flows that it will receive rather than the cash flows the project generates." Critically evaluate this statement.

#20-54A: The statement is basically correct. When evaluating a foreign investment opportunity, the parent should be interested in the cash flows that it will receive - as opposed to the cash flows the project generates - because the cash flows it receives are ultimately the basis of returns to shareholders. Shareholders will not perceive blocked earnings as contributing to the value of the firm, and creditors will not count on them when calculating a firm's ability to service its debt.

#20-55Q: Your firm is interested in building a hamburger processing plant in Russia. You estimate it will have a 10 year useful life, but that there is a 30% chance that political or economic turmoil during those 10 years will cause it to close or you to lose control of it. How would you include this risk in your capital budgeting analysis?

#20-55A: There are roughly two approaches for including this risk in an analysis - adjusting the discount rate or adjusting the cash flows. When adjusting the discount rate upwards, nearer term cash flows are affected more than later cash flows. By adjusting the cash flows down while maintaining the same discount rate, it is possible to more deeply cut later cash flows that are less certain. Either approach is reasonable. If the near term seems relatively certain, then it is perhaps best to instead adjust future cash flows or use a higher discount rate on future cash flows than on near term cash flows.

#20-56Q: Under what conditions is it preferable to use local debt over foreign debt to finance a project?

#20-56A: One obvious situation when it is preferable to use local debt over foreign debt is to finance a project is when the cost of capital is lower locally. This can be the case when the government is encouraging investment and will help fund new plants. The second situation is when the local currency is expected to depreciate relative to the currencies of the countries from which the funds would be obtained (and thus causing higher interest payments on the foreign debt than would be required on local debt, even if the nominal interest rate is higher locally).

#20-57Q: What reasons can you suggest for why there are such significant differences in the financial structure of firms across countries.

#20-57A: It is not altogether clear why the financial structure of firms should vary so much across countries. Governmental policies clearly can affect forms of economic organization. One example is that different tax regimes can determine the relative attractiveness of debt and equity in a country. Another possibility is that country differences in financial structure reflect deep seated cultural norms. It could also simply be the way things evolved, and "normal" practices are retained by cultures.

#20-58Q: What is a tax credit?

#20-58A: A tax credit allows an entity to reduce the taxes paid to the home government by the amount of taxes paid to the foreign government.

#20-59Q: What are the advantages to a multinational for charging subsidiaries royalties or fees rather than just earning dividends from foreign subsidiaries?

#20-59A: Royalties and fees are often tax deductible locally (they are viewed as an expense), so arranging for payment in royalties and fees will reduce the foreign subsidiary's tax liability. In contrast, if the foreign subsidiary compensates the parent company by dividends, local income taxes are paid on the dividend itself. Some host governments may also regulate the repatriation of dividends (because they would prefer reinvestment) more closely than royalties or fees.

#20-60Q: What are the potential benefits of manipulating transfer prices?

#20-60A: (see page 578)

#20-61Q: Describe the advantages of fronting loans.

#20-61A: There are two reasons why firms use fronting loans. First, fronting loans are a way of circumventing host government restrictions on the remittance of funds from a foreign subsidiary to the parent company; countries are unlikely to stop the repayment of loans as this can stifle future investments. The second reason for using fronting loans is that there may be tax advantages to having the subsidiary pay interest and the firm to earn interest.

#20-62Q: What must a firm do to effectively manage foreign exchange exposure?

#20-62A: In order to effectively manage foreign exchange exposure, the firm must exercise centralized oversight over its foreign exchange hedging activities, recognize the difference between transaction exposure and economic exposure, forecast future exchange rate movements, establish good reporting systems within the firm to monitor exposure positions, and produce regular foreign exchange exposure reports that can be used as a basis for action.

Notes

Notes

Notes

Notes

Notes